African Finance in the 21st Century

African Finance in the 21st Century

Edited by

Marc Quintyn

and

Geneviève Verdier

First published 2010 by
PALGRAVE MACMILLAN

Palgrave Macmillan in the UK is an imprint of Macmillan Publishers Limited, registered in England, company number 785998, of Houndmills, Basingstoke, Hampshire RG21 6XS.

Palgrave Macmillan in the US is a division of St Martin's Press LLC, 175 Fifth Avenue, New York, NY 10010.

Palgrave Macmillan is the global academic imprint of the above companies and has companies and representatives throughout the world.

Palgrave® and Macmillan® are registered trademarks in the United States, the United Kingdom, Europe and other countries

ISBN: 978–0–230–58050–3 hardback

This book is printed on paper suitable for recycling and made from fully managed and sustained forest sources. Logging, pulping and manufacturing processes are expected to conform to the environmental regulations of the country of origin.

A catalogue record for this book is available from the British Library.

A catalog record for this book is available from the Library of Congress.

10 9 8 7 6 5 4 3 2 1
19 18 17 16 15 14 13 12 11 10

Printed and bound in Great Britain by
CPI Antony Rowe, Chippenham and Eastbourne

Contents

Figures

Tables

Boxes

Foreword

Through its High-Level Seminars, the IMF Institute constantly aims at deepening the dialog among key policymakers and academia on topical issues in economic policy. In early 2006, such a High-Level Seminar focused on the conditions needed to realize the potential for profitable private investment in Africa. The seminar's objective was to go beyond prescribing macroeconomic stability, largely achieved at the time, and to focus on the continent's constant underlying challenge, achieving long-term private-sector-driven growth. What barriers needed to be removed to establish conditions conducive to investment and growth? Were these in the areas of governance, technology, infrastructure, finance, or human capital? The conclusion was "all of the above"—albeit to different degrees.

Two years later, in March 2008, a follow-up High-Level Seminar zoomed in on one specific component from the above list: the potential contribution of financial development to economic growth and development. Starting from the premise that financial development could make a decisive contribution to economic growth, the seminar brought African policymakers together with a select group of experts from all over the world. Together they diagnosed the challenges faced by financial systems in Africa and discussed a number of implementable and context-specific solutions to advance their development.

This volume is based not only on insights from the March 2008 seminar but also on some recent work on financial sector issues in Africa. It should be of great interest to any professional involved at the technical, academic, and policy level with macroeconomic and growth issues in general, but more particularly to those interested in financial sector issues in Africa. Its publication does follow in the steps of many other contributions on this topic in academic as well as policy circles. However, despite the consensus on the importance of financial development in lower-income countries, the literature has not produced an abundance of work focused on finance in Africa. In addition, the approach taken in this volume is to present both expert academic analyses and recent country-specific case studies and examples by field professionals.

In my view, the contribution of this volume to the current debate in Africa is twofold. First, it combines theoretical insights with empirical work that reinforces them. The overwhelming conclusion of the chapters in this volume is that pervasive weaknesses in the African institutional frameworks are a major barrier to financial development. The second contribution is the recognition that, while institutional change is slow and the creation of an environment conducive to financial development difficult, small-scale, incremental or sector-specific changes can be implemented relatively quickly by targeting specific populations or types of financial institutions, or by improving existing laws. The book presents and reviews a number of practical and country-specific solutions which indeed support the view that small steps can make a difference. These examples also indicate that initiatives in the financial system can have virtuous-circle-type positive effects on the institutional environment more generally.

I hope not only that this volume will be of practical use to African policymakers but also that it will inspire many readers and scholars in Africa and elsewhere to continue the exchange of ideas from which, over time, will come the best solutions.

LESLIE LIPSCHITZ
Director, IMF Institute

Contributors

Emma Andrianasolo is Director, Microfinance at the Commission for Banking and Financial Supervision and member of the Pilot Committee for the National Microfinance Strategy in Madagscar.

Ernest Aryeetey is Senior Fellow and Director of the Africa Growth Initiative in the Global Economy and Development program of The Brookings Institution in Washington, D.C. He is also Director of the Institute of Statistical, Social and Economic Research (ISSER) of the University of Ghana, Legon, where he has been on the research faculty since 1986.

Ama Pokuaa Fenny is a principal research assistant at ISSER, University of Ghana. Her primary focus in ISSER has been on developmental issues in health economics, regulatory governance, competition, and microfinance.

Dhaneshwar Ghura is a Division Chief in the African Department of the IMF. Before joining the IMF, Mr. Ghura taught at the State University of New York. He was also a consultant at the World Bank.

Stephen Haber is A.A. and Jeanne Welch Milligan Professor in the School of Humanities and Sciences, and the Peter and Helen Bing Senior Fellow at the Hoover Institution at Stanford University. He is also Professor of Political Science, Professor of History, Professor of Economics (by Courtesy), and a Senior Fellow of the Stanford Institute for Economic Policy Research.

Patrick Honohan is Governor of the Central Bank of Ireland. Previously he was Professor of International Financial Economics and Development at Trinity College Dublin and before then a Senior Advisor at the World Bank. His career has also included periods on the staffs of the IMF, and the Economic and Social Research Institute, Dublin and as Economic Advisor to the Taoiseach (Irish Prime Minister).

Jennifer Isern is the South Asia Business Line Leader for Financial Sector Advisory for the International Finance Corporation (IFC). From 1996 to 2009, she worked as Lead Microfinance Specialist at the Consultative Group to Assist the Poor (CGAP), a global resource center on access to finance issues, as member of the senior management team and managing CGAP's work in Africa and China. Prior to joining CGAP, Dr. Isern worked with CARE International in West and Central Africa, USAID in Costa Rica and Senegal, UNDP, AT&T, and other public and private sector consulting assignments. She received her master's degree from Princeton University and her doctorate in both finance and international business from Nova Southeastern University; she is a CFA charterholder.

Louis Kasekende is Chief Economist of the African Development Bank (ADB). Prior to joining the ADB, Louis Kasekende was Deputy Governor, Bank of Uganda. He has also served as an Executive Director on the Executive Board of the World Bank and as a lecturer in Economics in Makerere University, Uganda.

Kangni Kpodar is an Economist in the African Department of the International Monetary Fund. He holds a Ph.D. from the Centre for Studies and Research in International Development (CERDI).

Estelle Lahaye is Microfinance Analyst at the Consultative Group to Assist the Poor (CGAP), a global resource center on access to finance issues. Before joining CGAP, Ms. Lahaye worked in the banking sector with several organizations including Banco Itaú Europa and Merrill Lynch. She holds a master's degree in Business Administration from San Francisco State University.

Audrey Linthorst is the sub-Saharan Africa Analyst at the Microfinance Information eXchange, Inc. (MIX), the leading provider of comprehensive business information and data services for the microfinance industry. Ms. Linthorst has worked with a variety of organizations promoting African economic development including The Hunger Project and Réseau Africain pour le Développement Integré and has her B.A. in International Economic Development from Emory University.

Leslie Lipschitz has been Director of the IMF Institute since 2003. He joined the IMF in 1974 and has held increasingly senior positions in four area departments and the Policy Development and Review Department. He received his Ph.D. in economics from the University of London. Lipschitz has been a guest scholar at the Brookings Institution and has taught at Johns Hopkins University's School of Advanced International Studies. His publications are primarily in open economy macroeconomics and exchange rate policy.

Inutu Lukonga is a Senior Economist at the IMF in MCM/R1. Prior to joining the IMF in 1993, she was the Deputy Director of Research in Bank of Zambia where she worked for 12 years. She is trained as a macroeconomist and as a regulator for banks, securities, and pensions. She studied for a Ph.D. in Development Economics at the University of Sussex and also holds a master's degree in International Economics and Finance. She also worked at the FSA/UK as a supervisor.

Nataliya Mylenko is Financial Specialist at the IFC and is the Program Manager for the Global Credit Bureau Program and a Credit Bureau Advisor for Africa. Prior to joining the IFC, Ms. Mylenko worked as Economist at the International Monetary Fund and the World Bank.

Isaac Otchere is an Associate Professor of Finance at the Sprott School of Business, Carleton University in Canada. Prior to joining Carleton University, Isaac Otchere held similar positions at the University of New Brunswick (Canada) and the University of Melbourne (Australia).

Marc Quintyn is the Division Chief of the African Division at the IMF Institute. Before joining the IMF, Mr. Quintyn taught at the University of Ghent and the University of Limburg, Belgium. He also worked as an economist in the Research Department of the National Bank of Belgium.

Consolate Rusagara is the Director of the Financial Systems Department at the World Bank. Prior to joining the World Bank, she was the Deputy Governor of the National Bank of Rwanda.

Lemma Senbet is the William E. Mayer Chair Professor of Finance at the Smith School of the University of Maryland, College Park. He was also Chairperson of the Finance Department at the Smith School for eight years (1998–2006).

Raju Jan Singh is a Senior Economist in the African Department of the International Monetary Fund. Prior to joining the IMF, Mr. Singh held positions at the Swiss Ministry of Finance in Bern and at Lombard Odier & Cie (private banking) in Geneva. He was also a consultant for the Swiss Agency for Development and Cooperation, working with the central banks of Rwanda and Tanzania, and taught at the Graduate Institute of International Studies in Geneva.

Michael Taylor is currently Advisor to the governor of the Central Bank of Bahrain. He has extensive experience of central banking, financial stability, and regulatory issues gained senior positions with a number of central banks and at the International Monetary Fund. He has published widely on these issues, and his most recent book is *Towards a New Framework for Financial Stability* (London, 2009) edited jointly with Professor David Mayes and Robert Pringle.

Geneviève Verdier is an Economist in the African Department of the International Monetary Fund. Before joining the Fund, Ms. Verdier was an Assistant Professor at Texas A&M University. She has also worked as an economist at the Bank of Canada.

Smita Wagh works on issues of financial sector development in Africa at the World Bank, which she recently joined as a consultant. Prior to this, she spent over four years working at the International Monetary Fund in the Research and Africa Departments. She has also taught economics at the undergraduate level for several years, both in India and the United States.

Ms. Wagh received her Ph.D. in Economics from American University, Washington DC, and a M. A. in Economics from Bombay University.

John Wakeman-Linn is an Advisor in the African Department of the IMF. He has also worked for the Harvard Institute for International Development and has worked as a consultant advising the Zambian Ministry of Finance and Central Bank.

Introduction and Overview

Marc Quintyn and Geneviève Verdier

Despite achieving macroeconomic stability in recent years, many countries in sub-Saharan Africa (SSA) are still struggling to maintain a sustained economic growth path fostering economic development and poverty reduction. The consensus in academic as well as policy circles is that strong institutions are a necessary condition for sustainable growth. Many have argued that, among the wide array of institutions that foster growth, a well functioning financial system is a sine qua non. The financial sector facilitates market exchange and risk management, mobilizes and pools savings, and allocates capital efficiently.

The starting questions of this book are: to what extent does the financial sector in SSA fulfill the roles of saving allocation, risk management and diversification and growth promotion? And how can the efficiency of this institution be improved so that it can play a more prominent role in economic development? This volume brings together academic contributions, policy discussions as well as country case studies, thus spanning a wide horizon of viewpoints, experiences and insights that, in the end, provide a coherent picture of the direction policies for financial development should take. For example, the reader will find answers to questions as varied as: What is the theoretical link between finance and growth and what do we learn from it for SSA? Why do formal and informal financial intermediaries coexist? What role can regional integration play in fostering financial development? Should central banks be the main financial regulator? How can the experience in, for instance, Madagascar help in the design of policies to promote access to finance? How can credit bureaus contribute to improvements in the functioning of financial systems in Africa?

The volume is organized along two broad themes. The first part "Developments, Diagnosis and Determinants" is devoted to explaining the role of finance in development, the state of the financial sector in Africa and how it evolved to that point, with specific attention to key sectors. The second part "Policy issues and case studies", focuses on policies to ensure the proper functioning of financial markets in SSA. The first two chapters discuss the contribution of regulation and supervision to financial stability and deepening. The subsequent chapters explore from different angles initiatives to improve access to finance and financial deepening in typically weak institutional environments—the potential role of regional financial integration, the contribution of microfinance on the African continent, the potential contribution of credit and property registries, and finally two chapters which take the reader through country-specific initiatives to promote financial deepening, with case studies on Madagascar and Rwanda.

I.1 Developments, diagnosis and determinants

Is financial development important for growth? In the first chapter Stephen Haber reviews theory and evidence that links financial development and growth and argues that overall, the empirical literature supports the view that finance leads to economic growth. He then asks, if finance indeed matters for growth, what stands in the way of financial development. Why are not all countries actively fostering financial deepening? Haber argues forcefully that financial development, or the lack thereof, is ultimately the result of political forces. The chapter develops a simple model which shows that only in political systems with checks and balances the risks of expropriation by the government can be contained. Hence, it is the quality of political institutions which determines the level of financial development.

In Chapter 2, Patrick Honohan offers a more specific diagnosis of the financial sector in Africa. He identifies a number of important (interconnected) stylized facts which underscore the limited contribution of the financial sector in Africa to growth and development. He reviews two different agendas—the modernist and activist approach—in achieving "finance for growth" and "finance for all". The author warns against the excesses of modernism. For example, he underscores the importance of good regulation as part of the modernist agenda, but warns that Basel II bank regulations for instance could be counterproductive at this stage. Whereas, the modernist approach seeks to improve markets, the activist approach focuses on areas where the market has failed. Access to finance, or "finance for all" is usually the preserve of the activist agenda. The author does not reject an activist agenda given observed market failures. He does however, caution that the quality of governance of the sponsoring agencies is crucial to ensure that resources are not wasted.

Chapter 3, by Dhaneshwar Ghura, Raju Jan Singh and Roland Kpodar, presents evidence of the Haber's and Honohan's views with respect to the importance of institutions and governance for financial development. They investigate why financial development is lower in the CFA countries than it is in the rest of SSA despite similar reform efforts. The results suggest that the difference in financial depth between the CFA zone and the rest of SSA is determined by differences in institutional quality. In fact, this relationship becomes more negative over time. The authors argue that this suggests that time-variant factors have deteriorated in CFA countries, including the availability of credit information, the strength of property rights and their enforcement. The main policy implication is that the development of institutions which expand creditor information and strengthen creditor rights are important.

The next chapters turn to the main groups of financial institutions: banks, informal intermediaries and stock markets. In Chapter 4, Louis Kasekende focuses on banks—the dominant player in the SSA financial sector. An efficient banking sector should produce efficient intermediation, resolve agency problems, enable corporate monitoring, reduce uncertainty, facilitate information production, price discovery, and efficient payment, clearing and settlements. African banks however, do not perform these tasks very well, despite numerous reform efforts. Kasekende reviews the policy reforms undertaken since the mid-1990s to address these concerns and subsequently zooms in on Uganda and Nigeria. He lists a number of lessons which echo some of Honohan's arguments. For example, although the introduction of market-based mechanisms can be helpful, liberalization—which may encourage entry of small and fragile banks—does not always increase competition and reduce transactions costs, and at times, can increase instability. In addition, privatization of banks does not always lead to an improvement in bank governance as private bank owners often turn out to be a group of highly connected individuals. Implicitly, this chapter underlines the limits of liberalization efforts in weak institutional environments.

Despite the dominance of banks, a large share of African households remain "unbanked". This underscores the importance of informal financial intermediaries. In Chapter 5, Ernest Aryeetey and Ama Pokuaa Fenny focus on the role of these financial institutions and in particular on the optimality of linkages between the formal and informal sectors. The two sectors coexist because both bring advantages under specific circumstances (extensive infrastructure and opportunities for portfolio diversification in the case of the formal sector and informational advantage when it comes to poorer and rural populations for the informal sector). The authors argue that the integration of the two sectors and the creation of effective linkages can improve the effectiveness of the overall financial system. They review a number of models for these linkages which involve a collaboration in which each sector can specialize in different segments of the market. They conclude that the informal sector will exist as long as the social structure of African society—traditional, rural, sparsely populated, poor transportation networks—requires it.

In Chapter 6, Lemma Senbet and Isaac Otchere address the question: Why should stock markets matter for Africa? They argue that the value of stock markets for Africa is substantial and present empirical evidence that stock markets have promoted growth in Africa. They see stock markets as a conduit for the financial globalization of Africa and as a facilitator for further privatization of state-owned enterprises. However, their review of the state of African stock markets reveals a number of weaknesses broadly in line with Haber's and Honohan's views, finding their origin in operational inefficiencies, macroeconomic and political instability, and the perception by foreign investors of Africa as a homogenously troubled continent.

I.2   Policy issues and case studies

In Chapter 7, Inutu Lukonga uses the evaluations of the IMF-World Bank Financial Sector Assessments Programs (FSAP) to illustrate that the soundness and resilience of SSA financial systems has greatly improved in several countries. Subsequently the author zooms in on the regulatory and supervisory frameworks and shows that, despite improvements, important gaps continue to persist. These weaknesses are more pervasive in the frameworks for capital markets and the nonbanking sector. However, banking sector supervision also continues to exhibit important gaps. Due in part to limitations in capacity, including human resources and skills, technology and systems, regulatory and supervisory practices have not kept pace with developments in the financial sector, such as the increase in cross-sector and cross-border operations of financial institutions and financial innovations which require stronger systems and controls and management of operational risk. Further strengthening of financial surveillance is all the more important, in light of the weaknesses that surfaced during the global financial crisis.

Complementing the thoughts developed in the previous chapter, Quintyn and Taylor ask in Chapter 8: How should supervisory architecture and strategy be combined in SSA to arrive at the most effective outcomes? They start from the finding that financial developments in SSA—financial deepening and diversification—require an expansion of regulatory scope and intensity, but that these requirements are difficult to meet, mainly because of the continent's pervasive capacity constraints. To reconcile both, an analytical framework is presented to guide the decision making process about an appropriate regulatory strategy (a strategy to define scope and intensity of regulation in an environment of an expanding financial sector) and the appropriate institutional structure to support this strategy. By reviewing the pros and cons of a number of stylized institutional models in their relation to this framework, the authors conclude that under the current circumstances in SSA, those models that take advantage of the central bank's position should be preferred because they face fewer capacity constraints and are gaining credibility.

In Chapter 9, John Wakeman-Linn and Smita Wagh examine how regional financial integration can help foster financial development in SSA. Integration can complete markets, offers the possibility of scale economies, greater opportunities for the optimal allocation of capital and could raise the level of efficiency in regional markets by improving the ability to share risk. In addition, regional institutions can better withstand political pressure from national governments and other local constituencies. The authors review the attempts at regional integration in SSA and argue that the initiatives has not yet lived up to their promises, partly because of the haphazard nature of the arrangements. In addition, the lack of development in domestic markets has often been an obstacle to regional development. The authors conclude that regional integration can be successful if policymakers are committed to the process and allow regulation to be free of pressure from national governments.

In Chapter 10, in one of the most comprehensive studies yet about microfinance in SSA, Jennifer Isern, Estelle Lahaye and Audrey Linthorst analyze trends in microfinance, its contribution to access to finance and financial deepening on the African continent, as well as the challenges going forward. The authors show that relative macroeconomic stability in the past decade has made SSA a dynamic marketplace for microfinance growth. Yet, SSA is not a homogenous continent. Some regions record faster growth than others. Despite more attention to the legal and regulatory framework for microfinance and an increasing integration in the formal financial sector, going forward, the sector is facing a number of challenges: legal frameworks need to be strengthened further, and the best bet for improving profitability is a further integration into the formal sector accompanied by an increased focus on deposit mobilization.

Since the good outcome of financial transactions depends largely on trust between the parties involved, financial development is typically slow (or absent) in weak institutional environments. Yet, specific reforms can often have very positive results if they can count on a minimal degree of support from the government. In Chapter 11, Nataliya Mylenko takes the reader through a cross-country study in the development and role of public registries for credit and property. Credit information registries are essential for well functioning credit markets. They are crucial in achieving several objectives, including better assessment and management of risks, helping good borrowers to gain access to finance, and helping to reduce overindebtedness. Africa is the continent with the lowest level of credit penetration, and lending remains a challenge. Based on cross-country experience, the chapter shows that credit registries with appropriate legal backing supporting information exchange, preferably set up in a public-private partnership arrangements, and underpinned by a viable business model make a significant contribution to financial deepening.

The volume concludes with two extremely interesting country-specific case studies which offer food for thought for those involved in financial sector development and reform. In Chapter 12, Emma Andrianasolo reviews the experience of Madagascar since the late 1990s in reforming, supervising, training, and promoting microfinance institutions (MFI) as part of the

National Microfinance Strategy. Partly as a result of the reform measures, the microfinance sector has greatly expanded in Madagascar, improving access to finance for the unbanked. The chapter does, however, highlight a list of remaining challenges for the future of microfinance in Madagascar, including governance problems, growth crises, the balance between the social vocation and profitability, and the absence of competition. Nevertheless, the author argues that it is important to continue supporting microfinance as a way of improving access and to promote the overall development of the financial sector. She describes a number of initiatives aimed at confronting the remaining challenges but also leaves the reader with a number of questions: Can microfinance effectively contribute to poverty reduction? Can microfinance institutions serve the poor and be profitable? How can supervisory agencies promote the sector's integrity?

In Chapter 13 Consolate Rusagara provides an insider's account of Rwanda's Financial Sector Development Program (FSDP) which was established in the wake of the IMF-WB FSAP in 2005. Starting point was that, despite all the previous reforms, the Rwandan financial sector's ability to play its role of mobilization and effective intermediation of savings had remained limited. The financial sector was weak, undiversified and offered only basic financial products and services to a very limited section of the potentially bankable population. The FSDP therefore aimed at four objectives: increasing access to, and affordability of, financial services; enhancing savings mobilization; strengthening the policy and regulatory framework and strengthening the national payments system. While individual measures and their sequencing in such an all-encompassing plan are extremely important, the main message from this chapter is the crucial role of buy-in from all stakeholders to guarantee its success: the FSDP is embedded in a broader socioeconomic plan "Rwanda Vision 2020;" clear objectives were specified; responsibilities for implementation were clearly assigned; ownership by all stakeholders is being ensured at all times; and the program was endorsed by the highest political levels. Paying attention to these factors goes a long way in adopting the lessons learned from the first chapters in this volume.

I.3   Conclusion

The contributions to this volume on the future of finance in Africa provide the reader with a wealth of insights, lessons and policy recommendations. Yet, the main message from this book is fairly clear and is brought out most clearly in the first three chapters. Financial development crucially depends on the reform of political institutions. Political institutions need to be such that economic agents have the necessary guarantees that they can engage in financial transactions with no risks of expropriation. This political-institutions view of financial development is substantiated in several chapters in this book, but also increasingly elsewhere in the literature.[1]

This view also helps in understanding why earlier attempts through financial liberalization only succeeded to a degree in stimulating financial deepening.

However, the experience that reform of political institutions takes a long time, should not lead to immobilism in the short- and medium-run with respect to financial sector development. This volume discusses several initiatives that can be taken in institutionally weak environments and that, based on the evidence provided, can assist in financial deepening. Without being exhaustive, we refer to improving bank accounting standards to encourage the dissemination of accurate information about the banking sector's balance sheet and improve the quality of information; dissuading governments from engaging in ownership in the financial system, but rather encouraging them to actively create the appropriate infrastructure and regulatory framework for finance; promoting microfinance and bridging the gaps between microfinance—and other types of informal finance—and the formal sector; establishing registries for credit and property; promoting regional structures than can improve governance.

It is our sincere hope that the diagnoses and the remedies presented in this volume may help in deepening our understanding of the problems that have constrained financial development in Africa, and of the ways to address them, so that finance can contribute to the continent's growth and development in the twenty-first century.

Note

1. See for instance, Haber, North, and Weingast, eds. 2008. *Political Institutions and Financial Development*. Stanford, CA: Stanford University Press.

Part I

Finance in Africa—Developments, Diagnosis and Determinants

1
The Finance-Growth Nexus: Theory, Evidence, and Implications for Africa
Stephen Haber

1.1   Introduction

One of the challenges facing policy makers is to reignite African economic growth. Since the 1960s, when most Sub-Saharan African countries obtained independence, per capita GDP growth has averaged only 1 percent per year. The comparable rate for the OECD was 2.8 percent. Even Latin America, which "lost a decade" in the 1980s, grew almost twice as fast as Africa—1.9 percent per year. Even more stunning, per capita GDP actually decreased in 11 of the 46 African countries that reported data. The situation does not look better if we restrict the period of analysis. From 1990 to 2004, the average rate of per capita GDP growth has only been 0.9 percent in Sub-Saharan Africa, as compared to 2.1 percent in the OECD and 1.7 percent in Latin America.[1]

The causes of African economic stagnation are multifaceted, but one crucial piece of the puzzle is the region's inadequate financial system. In 2006, the average ratio of private credit to GDP (a standard metric by which to measure the development of banking systems) was 110 percent in the OECD, 31 percent in Latin America (notoriously under-banked), and only 20 percent in Sub-Saharan Africa. Worse, the average ratio for Africa is almost certainly biased upward because a large number of countries, presumably those with miniscule banking systems, do not report any data.[2] This outcome, we hasten to note, is not a product of a single cross-section. In fact, Kane and Rice (2001) document that Africa's banking systems were in a state of near-permanent crisis during the 1980s and 1990s: systemic crises were experienced in at least 50 of the region's 60 countries, with at least ten countries undergoing multiple crises.

The purpose of this chapter is threefold. First, I draw on the extant literature in financial economics to explain why the small size of African banking systems has negative implications for economic growth. Second, I explore why African financial systems are small by drawing on the extant literature on the political economy of financial development. Finally, I explore some ways in which African banking systems might be improved, short of the kinds of broad-institutional reforms to the region's fundamental political institutions that would be suggested by the political economy literature.

1.2 Finance as a crucial input to growth

The idea that financial development plays a leading role in economic growth traces its origins to Schumpeter (1983), and has subsequently been firmly established by a wide variety of scholarly literatures that employ long-run historical evidence, cross-country regressions, within-country studies that exploit variance across industries and regions, and combinations of all three approaches.

One body of literature has been written by economic historians, who have systematically explored the crucial role played by "financial revolutions" in the economic development of seventeenth-century Holland (Neal, 1990; de Vries and van der Woude, 1997), eighteenth century England (North and Weingast, 1989), and the nineteenth century United States (Rousseau and Sylla, 2004; Sylla, 2006, 2008). One of main points of this literature is that revolution in the way that financial markets and financial intermediaries operated not only allowed for the rapid growth of the real economy, they also were a crucial component in the rise to global economic and military hegemony of Holland, England, and the United States. There is also a sizable economic history literature on how the absence of financial revolution held back economic growth in a number of developing countries, including nineteenth century Russia (Anan'ich, 1999), nineteenth century Brazil (Summerhill, forthcoming), Argentina (Davis and Gallman, 2001), and early twentieth century Mexico (Haber, 1991, 1997; Maurer, 2002; Haber, Razo, and Maurer, 2003). Finally, there is a comparative historical literature that assesses the performance of countries against one another as a function of their level of financial development (Rousseau and Wachtel, 1998; Rousseau, 2003; Rousseau and Sylla, 2003). Indeed, the idea that successful economic development was typically preceded, or was accompanied, by a major episode of financial innovation is now taken by economic historians to be self-evident.

Financial economists, employing cross-country regression techniques, have come to broadly similar conclusions. The first work on the topic, by Goldsmith (1969) and McKinnon (1973) illustrated the ties between the financial sector and the real economy. King and Levine (1993) then formalized these insights by using cross-country regressions to demonstrate that higher levels of banking system development are positively associated with faster rates of physical capital accumulation and economic growth. Crucially, their study of more than 80 countries also found that the level of financial development predicts future rates of physical capital accumulation and long-run growth. Thus, finance does not follow economic activity; it leads it. Levine and Zervos (1998) then extended this work to include the independent impact of stock markets, as well as banks, on economic growth. They found that stock market liquidity and banking sector development are independently and positively correlated with both current and future rates of capital accumulation and economic growth.

One potential objection to the King and Levine (1993) and Levine and Zervos (1998) findings is that unobserved heterogeneity across countries—for example, differences in industrial composition—explains both the variance observed in financial development and the variance observed in growth. Another potential objection is that the regressions might induce researchers to draw spurious causal inferences: finance may not so much be a cause of growth as it a leading indicator of growth. Rajan and Zingales (1998) address these concerns by focusing on industries as well as countries. They show that industries that are relatively more in need of external finance grow disproportionately faster in countries with larger banking systems and stock markets. Their findings suggest that financial development has a substantial effect on economic growth by reducing the cost of external finance to financially dependent firms. Wurgler (2000), who also focuses on both industries and countries in order to mitigate problems of unobserved heterogeneity and spurious causal inferences, obtains roughly similar results. He finds that financially developed countries (as measured by the size of domestic stock and credit markets relative to GDP) increase investment more in their growing industries and decrease investment more in their declining industries. Thus, financially developed countries do not necessarily invest more than financially underdeveloped countries, but they allocate investments more efficiently. Fisman and Love (2004) extend the Rajan and Zingales (1998) methods in order to assess the implications of financial development for the growth of industries over the short- and the long-run. Their results indicate that in the short-run, financial development facilitates the reallocation of resources to any industry with a high growth potential. In the long-run, however, financially dependent industries will be more likely to grow in countries that have well-developed financial institutions. That is, countries with high levels of financial development will specialize in finance-dependent industries.

Beck, Levine, and Loayza (2000) also take on the questions of unobserved heterogeneity and spurious causality, but they do so not by considering industries as well as countries, but by applying novel econometric techniques: they use an instrumental variable estimator in order to extract the exogenous component of financial intermediary development; and they use a dynamic Generalized-Method-of-Moment (GMM) panel estimator that simultaneously allows for the exploitation of time-series variation in the data, accounts for unobserved country-specific effects, allows for the inclusion of lagged variables as regressors, and controls for endogeneity of all the explanatory variables. They also use an improved measure of financial intermediary development (financial intermediary credit to the private sector as a percentage of GDP). Their results indicate a robust, positive link between financial intermediary development and both total factor productivity growth and real GDP growth.

A third body of research, also designed to mitigate the problems of spurious causal inference and unobserved variable bias that may be present in cross-country studies, exploits variance across geographic units and across time within countries. Jayaratne and Strahan (1996) take advantage of the fact that prior to the 1970s U.S. states tended to restrict the ability of banks to open branches. They then exploit variance in the timing in which these laws were reformed in order to estimate the impact of the spread of branch banking on economic growth at the state level. They find that branch banking improved the quality of loans, but did not produce an increase in the volume of lending—implying that branching allowed banks to allocate credit more efficiently—and that branch banking produced a jump in the rate of growth of per capita income at the state level. Black and Strahan (2002) build upon these methods and findings to estimate the impact of changes in laws governing bank competition on entrepreneurial behavior. They find that states with more concentrated local banking markets have lower rates of incorporation, and when these states opened their banking markets to external competition (by allowing banks greater freedom to open branches) the rate of incorporation increased. In short, the removal of regulatory barriers increased bank competition, which, in turn, caused higher rates of business incorporation—suggesting that access to finance had been a constraint on entrepreneurship prior to the regulatory reforms. Dehejia and Lleras-Muney (2007), who exploit variance in branch banking laws over time within U.S. states during the period 1900–1940, take a somewhat similar approach. They find that regulations which lowered the cost of lending, such as allowing banks to open branches, had an unambiguously positive effect: it contributed to fewer, more intensively cultivated farms, and to the growth of the manufacturing sector. These results are consistent with those of Wang (2006), whose examination of loan books from early nineteenth century U.S. banks shows that as the density of banks increased, competition among them increased as well, so much so that they began to extend credit to an increasingly broad class of borrowers, including merchants, artisans, and farmers.

Economists have recently begun to focus on the specific mechanisms that link finance and growth. Guiso, Sapienza, and Zingales (2004) exploit variance across Italian regions in order to estimate the impact of differential financial development on entrepreneurship. They find that an individual's odds of starting a business increase by 5.6 percent if he moves from the least financially developed regions of Italy to the most financially developed. In addition, he is likely to start a business at a younger age than if he stayed in the financially underdeveloped region. As a consequence, the ratio of new firms to population is 25 percent higher in the most financially developed regions of Italy. They also find that Italy's most financially developed regions firms grow faster (by 6 percent) than would be possible if they had to finance all new investments out of retained earnings. Not surprisingly, they find that per capita GDP grows faster in those regions as well.

A related body of research has focused on how financial development affects the entry of new firms in nonfinancial industries. Haber (1991, 1997) and Maurer and Haber (2007) exploit the financial and industrial histories of Brazil and Mexico as natural laboratories. They find that restrictions on the growth of financial intermediaries gives rise to differential access to capital, which, in turn, gives rise to higher levels of industrial concentration than would be obtained otherwise. Haber (2003) then shows how the resulting low level of industry competition dampens the pace of productivity growth. In a related line of research, Cetorelli and Strahan (2006) find that more vigorous local banking competition across U.S. states is associated with more funding for new firms, more firm entry, and a smaller average firm size. Cetorelli and Gamberra (2001) develop this idea in a cross-country framework, and find that concentrated banking markets are associated with slower growth in downstream industries.

One implication of this research is that industries that have a larger share of small firms for technological reasons should grow faster in economies with well-developed financial systems. Beck, Demirgüç-Kunt, Laeven, and Levine (2007) pursue this question by estimating a variety of panel regressions on a sample of 44 countries and 36 industries. Their results not only indicate that financial development disproportionately accelerates the growth of industries that, for technological reasons, are characterized by small firms, but they also show that small-firm industries represent a greater proportion of total manufacturing value-added in countries that have higher levels of financial development.

Financial development has more than salutary effects on economic growth, generally speaking. It also appears to have positive effects on the distribution of income and the well-being of the poor. Beck, Demirgüç-Kunt, and Levine (2007b) pursue this issue using a variety of regression techniques on a panel data set. They find that financial development reduces income inequality, boosts the growth rate of the income share of the poorest quintile of the population, and is associated with poverty alleviation (where poverty is measured as the fraction of the population living on less than $1 per day).

In sum, the question of the relationship between financial development and growth is now a settled matter. There is a broad consensus that finance plays a crucial role in the process of growth, and that it does so through a variety of mechanisms: by reducing the cost of capital to firms, by allocating capital more efficiently to entrepreneurs, and by encouraging greater competition among nonfinancial firms.

1.3   The political economy of financial development

If it is common knowledge that finance is a binding constraint on growth, then why don't governments in poor countries simply create the conditions necessary for large banking systems and securities markets? This question has motivated a sizeable body of scholarship over the past decade.

One view, associated with La Porta, López-de-Silanes, Shleifer, and Vishny (1998), stresses that financial development is the outcome of the legal institutions that a country inherited during the process of colonization. In this view, whether a country inherited the British common law or French civil law determined the development of its institutions of corporate governance, and hence, the size of its equity markets. This view has come under considerable questioning and debate in recent years. Broadly speaking, there have been three lines of critique. First, the legal-origins view has tended to focus more on corporate governance and equities markets than it has banking systems—but banking systems are typically more important than equities markets in the early stages of economic growth (Haber, North, and Weingast, 2008). Second, some scholars have raised questions about coding and measurement in the legal-origins literature (Spamann, 2006). Third, Rajan and Zingales (2003a) have shown that there has been considerable variance over time within countries in their degree of financial development—and a theory based on a time-invariant factor, such as legal origin, cannot account for this within-country variance. Beck and Levine (2005) present an excellent summary of these debates.

An alternative view, which has gained considerable ground in recent years because it can account both for variance across countries and over time within countries, is that financial development is endogenous to a country's underlying political institutions. That is, financial development will be limited unless the authority and discretion of government are constrained by mechanisms that allow citizens to sanction public officials. At its core, this "political institutions view" of financial development is concerned with the government's inherent conflict of interest: the growth of banks and securities markets is not possible without a government that can enforce financial contracts; but the government relies on those same banks and markets to provide it with a source of finance. Unless there are political institutions that limit the government's authority and discretion, it will have strong incentives to govern the financial system to facilitate its own political survival, at the expense of the development of the securities markets and banking systems that finance the private economy. That is, the institutions of liberal democracy—broad suffrage, party competition, checks and balances—are causally linked to having a large financial sector that allocates capital broadly.

Space constraints prevent a full explication of the political institutions view of financial development.[3] Permit me, however, to briefly lay out a simple framework, focusing only on the impact of political institutions on the development of banking systems. Inasmuch as securities markets tend to develop only after there is a system of private banks, this focus on banking is the most reasonable place to start.[4]

1.3.1 A simple framework

The business of banking is the business of contracts. The emergence of banks, and the contracts they write, is not an automatic process. Without a series of institutions that align the incentives of government, bankers, and the firms and individuals who borrow from banks, the development of the banking system will be constrained or there will be no banking system at all.

As a first step, let us be clear what we mean by the term bank—a business whose purpose is to lend money at interest *that has a charter from the government*. A charter is not just a license to do business: it confers a number of very valuable concessions on its holders. These tend to include limited liability for shareholders, priority as a creditor in the event of debtor bankruptcy, insurance for depositors, and the right to create financial instruments (such as checks) that circulate as currency. In some economies, banks also serve as the government's financial agent, collecting taxes and holding government balances. Not surprisingly, potential bankers will pay handsomely for a charter—especially if they believe that they are receiving the only one.

As a second step, let us think about the incentives of the agents that have an interest in the development of the banking system. Imagine an economy in which there are three agents: (1) A group of incumbent financiers, who have accumulated wealth in commerce or industry and who have a comparative advantage in organizing markets and institutions; (2) A group of political entrepreneurs, who have a comparative advantage in organizing collective action and running the machinery of government; and (3) A group of entrepreneurs (farmers, manufacturers, and artisans) who need credit in order to run or expand their nascent enterprises. It will not take long to show that the incentives of these three groups are not perfectly aligned.

The goal of the financiers, first and foremost, is to maintain their control over the market that affords them considerable rents. This means that they prefer constraints on the number of banks—and that they receive whatever small number of bank charters are granted by the government. The lack of competitively structured credit markets not only affords them high rates of return in banking, but even more important, allows them to create financial barriers to entry in the rest of the economy because they can deny credit to rival entrepreneurs. These financial barriers to entry are particularly effective because they are stealthy: they do not require visible anticompetitive regulations, which might attract public protest, in order to persist: they may be justified on the basis that they serve the public interest by helping to maintain a stable banking system (Haber, Razo, and Maurer, 2003, chap. 4; Rajan and Zingales, 2003b; Perotti and Volpin, 2004).

The goal of the political entrepreneurs, first and foremost, is political survival—which is to say that they seek to maintain their control of the government (Bueno de Mesquita et. al., 2003). In order to do that, they need sources of public finance. This means that they have an obvious incentive to encourage the formation of banks, because those banks represent sources of tax income, fees for charters, or, most especially, loans.

The entrepreneurs have an obvious interest in obtaining low cost credit to finance their enterprises. Without credit, they can grow their enterprises only through retained earnings. Without credit, there may be industries (such as those with high minimum efficient scales) from which they are barred entry, because they cannot mobilize sufficient capital. They therefore favor competitive banking markets.

Aligning the incentives of these three groups regarding the banking system is not easily accomplished. There is an obvious mismatch between the interests of the financiers and the entrepreneurs: the financiers favor constraints on competition; the entrepreneurs favor competitive credit markets.

There is a less obvious, but no less consequential problem of interest alignment between the financiers and the political entrepreneurs. The financiers need a government strong enough to enforce debt contracts and structure markets; but any government strong enough to do that is also strong enough to seize the wealth of the banks. This problem is particularly difficult to solve because the government does not have to carry out a de jure expropriation in order to appropriate bank wealth: it can borrow from the banks and then default on the loans; it can require banks to hold part of their deposit base in government bonds so as to create a "deposit reserve" and then it can raise the deposit reserve rate to 100 percent; it can print money wildly, setting off an inflation that acts as a tax on the holders of cash; or it can raise taxes to the point that it expropriates all bank profits.

There is also a mismatch in incentives of the three groups regarding the property rights system. The entrepreneurs prefer a system that favors universal enforcement of property and contract rights, because such a system will allow them to collateralize their assets and reputations. The political entrepreneurs may not, however, favor the creation of strong property rights institutions, because that will prevent them from seizing assets in the event that they need to commandeer them to maintain their power. The incentives of the financiers are not clear-cut, but there are conditions under which their incentives will align with the political entrepreneurs. If they have been successful in making private deals with the political entrepreneurs to limit the number of banks, they may have strong incentives to prefer low levels of public investment in the institutions that protect universal property and contract rights. They can obtain all the protection they need through private deals with government officials, while the entrepreneurs face a barrier to entry imposed by an uncertain legal environment (Sonin, 2003).

The historical record suggests that there are a limited number of stable solutions to these problems of incentive alignment. Each of these solutions implies differences in the rules and regulations that govern the distribution of bank charters, differences in the size and competitive structure of the banking system, and differences in the institutions that limit the authority and discretion of government.

One quite common solution is that the financiers so fear government predation that they do not seek bank charters at all: they know that as soon as they deploy their wealth in a bank the government will expropriate it. The result is that there are no privately owned banks. To the degree that the society has any chartered banks at all, they will be government owned and will primarily exist to finance the government or government-owned firms— Iraq under Saddam Hussein being a classic case in point. In the African context, Idi Amin's forced merger of virtually all of Uganda's private banks into a single, government-owned bank (Uganda Commercial Bank) in 1972 stands as another stark case in point (Kasekende and Sebudde, 2002).

A second common solution is a coalition between the financiers and the political entrepreneurs that is based on the generation and sharing of economic rents. Such coalitions form when political entrepreneurs coax financiers to deploy their wealth in banks by granting them privileges that raise their rates of return high enough to compensate them for the risk of expropriation (Maurer and Gomberg, 2004). These privileges can include lucrative concessions, such as the right to collect taxes or hold government deposits, but they always come on top of tight restrictions on the number of chartered banks. The problem is that there is nothing that prevents the political entrepreneurs from reneging on the deal once the financiers have deployed their wealth. The financiers must therefore align the incentives of the political entrepreneurs, and they typically do this by sharing some of their rents with them, by putting the political entrepreneurs on their boards of directors, by making them loans with no expectation of repayment, or by bribing them (Haber, Razo, and Maurer, 2003, chap. 2). The Suharto regime in Indonesia, in which the dictator's family and friends populated the country's largest corporations, is a classic case in point (Fisman, 2001). These arrangements, however, come at a cost to the entrepreneurs, because their access to credit is constrained. In fact, in a political and economic system such as this, in which a set of privileged financiers has made a set of private deals with the government to constrain entry, the banks likely could not enforce arm's length loan contracts with entrepreneurs even if they wanted to: the institutions of universal contract enforcement are likely to be underdeveloped, because the financiers can get all the property rights protection they need privately.

A third solution is that the financers tie the hands of the political entrepreneurs by creating sets of institutions that limit their authority and discretion, thereby preventing expropriation. The exact configuration of
these institutions varies across societies, but one feature that they always
have is a legislature in which the financiers are represented. Putting the
financiers in the legislature in sufficient numbers to prevent expropriation
does, however, also give them the power to determine the rules about bank
chartering—which, as Summerhill (forthcoming) has pointed out, means
that they will constrain the number of chartered banks. The acts of parliament that made the Bank of England the only joint stock, limited liability
bank in the entire country from 1694 to 1825 is an obvious example of the
phenomenon (Cottrell and Newton, 1999; Broz and Grossman, 2004). The
limits on bank chartering in nineteenth century Brazil is another, somewhat less well-known example of the same mechanism at work (Summerhill,
forthcoming).

What would happen if the entrepreneurs elected the legislature, and they
had the ability to organize around the issue of the availability of credit?
They would be able to pressure the government into granting more bank
charters. This would be incentive compatible with the interest of the political entrepreneurs, because there is no reason why they could not use this
more competitive banking system as a source of government finance.
It would not, however, be incentive compatible with the interests of the
financiers, because they would only receive a competitive rate of return on
capital, and they would not be able to block entry into finance-dependent
lines of economic activity in which they had interests. The historical record suggests that if this solution is to be stable, there have to be institutions
that constrain the common people from voting in a legislature that will
expropriate the banks. These other institutions typically include executive
vetoes, judicial review, and super-majority voting rules in the legislature.
Not surprisingly, this particular solution is found in a very limited number
of countries—liberal democracies.

What it comes down to is this. Authoritarian governments may produce
no banks at all, government-owned banks, or concentrated banking systems
that allocate credit narrowly. Which of the three they wind up with depends
on the ability of political entrepreneurs and financiers to forge a coalition.
Democratic governments—which is to say governments in which the authority and discretion of political entrepreneurs is limited by political institutions,
such as elected legislatures, independent judiciaries, and the like—either
produce concentrated banking systems that allocate credit narrowly, or large
banking systems that allocate credit broadly. Which of the two they wind up
with depends on the degree to which the entrepreneurs can align the interest of political entrepreneurs with their own—and that depends crucially on
whether they have access to the suffrage and other institutions of democratic
governance that allow them to sanction government officials.

1.3.2   Evidence

The available quantitative evidence supports this political institutions view of banking development. Barth, Caprio, and Levine (2006) analyze a cross-section of 65 countries in 2003 and find that democratic political institutions are associated with greater ease in obtaining a bank charter and fewer restrictions on the operation of banks. They also find that the tight regulatory restrictions on banks created by autocratic political institutions are associated with lower credit market development and less bank stability, as well as with more corruption in lending. Regulatory frameworks in autocracies also tend to discourage the private monitoring necessary for the dissemination of independent financial information. Countries that are more autocratic also tend to use government-owned banks to direct credit toward the interests of the politically powerful. Importantly, their results are robust to controls for legal origin.

The relationship between political institutions and banking development also holds up when we look within countries over time. Bordo and Rousseau (2006) analyze a panel of 17 countries over the period 1880–1997, and find broadly similar results on the relationship between political institutions and financial development: there is a strong, independent effect of proportional representation, frequent elections, female suffrage, and political stability on the size of the financial sector. The result, while qualified because of the small cross-country sample, is impressive as it is robust to controlling for initial per capita income and legal origin.

One criticism of the Barth, Caprio, and Levine and Bordo and Rousseau results is that they are based on truncated samples: the former are truncated with respect to time, the latter are truncated with respect to the cases selected. The panel data analysis of the political institutions/financial development view is still in its infancy. As a first step, however, I offer some simple regressions below that draw on the Beck, Demirgüç-Kunt, and Levine (2007a) financial structure database and the Monty and Jaggers (2008). Polity IV database in order to estimate pooled, cross-sectional regressions on the relationship between the institutions that constrain the executive and the ratio of bank credit to GDP from 1960 to 2003. The results reported in specification 1 indicate that each step increase in constraints on the executive (the scale runs from 1 to 7) is associated with nearly a five-percentage point increase in bank credit. If we include country dummies, in order to control for unobserved heterogeneity (specification 2), as well as Driscoll Kraay standard errors to control for serial correlation, the relationship continues to hold: a one-step increase in executive constraints is associated with a 1.5 percentage point increase in private credit.

Scholars are also beginning to exploit variance over time within countries in order to test the political institutions/financial development hypothesis. The United States has proven to be particularly fertile ground for these studies because its political institutions vary over both time and across states.

Table 1.1   OLS regressions of private credit as a percent of GDP
(Robust T statistics in parentheses)

	Pooled OLS	OLS with country dummies
Constraints on executive	0.048	0.015
	[6.53]***	[5.39]***
Constant	0.073	–
	[3.35]***	
Observations	3,428	3,428
Number of countries	131	131
R-squared	0.18	0.73

Notes: *significant at 10%; **significant at 5%; ***significant at 1%
Driscoll-Kraay Standard Errors (Robust to AR1 serial correlation).

Source: Constraints on the executive from Jaggers and Gurr Polity IV
dataset; Private credit as percent of GDP from Beck, Demirgüç-Kunt, and
Levine 2007a.

In fact, at the time that the Constitution was signed, both the president and
the senate were indirectly elected, and all of the original 13 states restricted
the right to vote to male property owners (Keyssar, 2000). The original organization of the banking system was also dramatically different than it is
today: there was a single super-bank that was partially owned by the central government which acted as the treasury's financial agent and that had
the sole right to branch across state lines; and there was a system of segmented monopolies within each state which shared some of the resulting
rents with state governments (in the form of dividend payments) and with
state legislators (in the form of bribes). These banks, it should be pointed
out, did not lend to all comers: they discriminated on the basis of profession, social standing and political party affiliation (Wallis, Sylla, and Legler,
1994; Bodenhorn, 2003; Haber, 2008; Sylla, 2008).

As the American frontier expanded westward, however, the country's initial political institutions underwent considerable reform. States competed
against one another for capital and labor. They broadened the suffrage, in
large part to attract immigrants or hold on to the population they had.
Moreover, the states quickly came into conflict with the federal government
over its quasi-central bank (which state bankers saw as inimical to their
interests). The end result was that as political institutions changed, so, too
did the organization of American banking.

The history of banking in the state of New York perhaps gives some sense
of what occurred. From the 1810s to the late 1830s, bank chartering in
New York was controlled by the Albany Regency—a political machine run
by Martin van Buren. Bank charters were granted only to friends of the
Regency, in exchange for which the legislators received various bribes, such

as the ability to subscribe to initial public offerings of bank stock at par, even though the stock traded for a substantial premium. The Regency's hold on bank chartering came to an end when the state legislature was forced to change the state's voting laws in 1826, finally allowing universal manhood suffrage. Within a decade, the Regency lost its control of the state legislature, and in 1837 the now dominant Whig Party enacted America's first free banking law—a system in which the state legislature no longer gave charters at all, rather banks were allowed to operate so long as they deposited bonds backing their note issues with the state comptroller. By 1841, New Yorkers had established 43 free banks, with a total capital of $10.7 million. By 1849, the number of free banks mushroomed to 111 (with $16.8 million in paid capital). By 1859, there were 274 free banks with paid in capital of $100.6 million. Other states soon followed New York's lead. By the early 1860s, 21 states adopted some variant of the New York law, and as they did so, they encouraged bank entry and increased competition (Bodenhorn, 1990, 2003, 2004; Moss and Brennan, 2004).

The causal relationship between the extent of electoral suffrage and a variety of financial regulations that restricted entry in the nineteenth century is studied by Benmelech and Moskowitz (2005), who exploit variation across time and across U.S. states in the laws regarding suffrage, free banking, general incorporation, and interest-rate ceilings (usury). They find that usury laws were used by industrial incumbents to control entry and lower their own costs of capital. Suffrage laws and financial regulatory policies appear strongly correlated: voting laws that restricted the suffrage are associated both with tighter usury laws (which restrict the supply of credit, in particular to newer, riskier firms) and with the lack of general incorporation laws.

In sum, there is substantial evidence that there is a causal relationship between the degree to which citizens have access to the sanctioning mechanisms of democratic governance—particularly the ability to remove public officials who work against citizen interests—and the size and structure of banking systems. The implication for African economic development, I hope, is clear: the creation of liberal democratic orders is not just a good thing to do in and of itself; it will generate positive economic externalities, including more vibrant financial systems.

1.4   What if political institutions cannot be reformed?

Our discussions of the central role played by finance in economic growth, and the central role played by political institutions in financial development, imply that creating vibrant financial systems in Africa will not be easy. Indeed, authoritarian governments or democracies that are still in the process of consolidation rule most of Sub-Saharan Africa. Theory suggests, and the empirical evidence bears out, that such governments are not conducive to the creation of large and competitive credit markets. For somewhat similar reasons, they are also not conducive to the creation of active securities exchanges.

Given these constraints, are there any practical steps that policy makers might undertake to spur the development of financial systems? One must be careful here. There may be all kinds of steps that governments might take to improve the efficiency of the financial sector, but political economy considerations may mean that, as a practical matter, they are unavailable. For example, if concentrated banking systems dominated by an entrenched elite are an endogenous outcome of authoritarianism, then it does little good to say that authoritarian governments should encourage market entry. Similarly, if the authority and discretion of the government are not limited, then reforms designed to give bank supervisors greater powers may, as Barth, Caprio, and Levine (2006) point out, simply give the government a larger lever with which to expropriate bank assets. Finally, if the property rights environment is such that it is difficult to enforce arm's length contracts, then regulations designed to force banks to make arms' length loans (instead of making loans to firms related to the banks) may result in no credit being extended at all. There are, in point of fact, reasons to think that reforming the property rights or contracting environment under an authoritarian government will be difficult: an inefficient and corrupt legal system may be endogenous to a governance system in which a small group of entrenched economic incumbents gets all the property rights protection they want by making private deals with the political entrepreneurs who control the government (Sonin, 2003). We therefore offer a few ideas that have been tried in other contexts of authoritarian governments with low levels of financial development.

The first of these steps is the privatization of state-owned banks. There is no evidence that state banks have been good vehicles for diffusing access to finance in developing countries. The reason is not hard to divine: state-owned banks tend to get captured by specific interests. Indeed, state-owned banks that are putatively designed to help finance small and medium-sized producers are often quickly converted into sources of credit for large industrial conglomerates that already have access to credit from the financial firms that are affiliated with them. The state-owned bank becomes, in effect, a means by which the conglomerate can socialize risks. The end result is that the state-owned bank often becomes insolvent (Cull and Xu, 2000; Clarke and Cull, 2002; LaPorta, Lopez-de-Silanes, and Shleifer, 2002; Sapienza, 2004; Del Angel Mobarak, 2002, 2005; Clark, Cull, and Shirley, 2005). It is precisely for this reason that, in the privatization of state-owned banks, the auction process be designed so as to make sure that the sale of the bank is not reinforcing preexisting oligopolies. Past experience also suggests that governments should not make maximizing revenue from the sale their first priority, because this introduces problems of moral hazard (Haber,

2005). In the context of an authoritarian government achieving these goals may require outside technical assistance.

The process of privatizing state-owned banks may afford an opportunity for the reform of bank accounting standards. Typically, state-owned banks do not conform to generally accepted accounting principles, and that the same idiosyncratic standards apply to the private banking system as well. The reform of accounting standards will not only permit the purchasers of the state-owned banks the ability to more accurately gauge the value of the bank's assets, it will also force private banks to reveal a more accurate portrait of their financial health to their shareholders and depositors, as well as to bank supervisors. Both cross-country regression evidence (Levine, Loayza, and Beck, 2000; Barth, Caprio, and Levine, 2008) and country case studies indicate that there are large positive returns to improving the quality of information. Indeed, a large part of the collapse of Mexico's newly privatized banking system in the early 1990s can be tied to highly idiosyncratic accounting standards that allowed the government to hide nonperforming loans from potential bank purchasers, and that later allowed the directors of the newly privatized banks to hide losses from their shareholders (Haber, 2005; Del Angel, Haber, and Musacchio, 2006).

A recent study by Kane and Rice (2001) provides direct evidence about the importance of the information environment in the African context. They show that bank regulators often did not have strong incentives to monitor the banks because of incentive conflicts. In this situation, the ability of depositors to monitor the condition of their banks was crucial, but they were unable to do so because they could not obtain timely and accurate information. For example, they document that during 1995, 1996, and 1997, less than half of Kenya's 40 banks reported any nonperforming loans (NPLs) in any given year and that only seven banks actually reported any NPLs in all three years. The consequences of accounting sorcery of this type were that the stock of nonperforming loans in African banking systems tended to grow over time, and that the region's banks then followed increasingly aggressive and risky lending strategies to recoup past losses. In the end, the banks became completely insolvent, the government was forced to intervene, the intervention spurred a run on the banks, and the banking system had to be rescued at taxpayer expense.

The third of these reforms involves opening up the banking system to foreign competition. This may be difficult to do, because the same entrenched interests who resist the entry of new domestic competitors are also likely to resist the entry of foreign competitors. Nevertheless, there are occasions, such as the aftermath of a banking crisis, when governments have forced open the market to foreign banks. The effect of foreign bank entry is an area that has received considerable scholarly interest in recent years—in large part because of the rapidity with which developed countries lowered the barriers to foreign bank ownership in the 1990s. There is some evidence from studies of individual developing countries that suggests that foreign banks have a more difficult time lending to informationally opaque small firms: they are less willing to extend credit on the basis of "soft knowledge" about a firm and its owners. Foreign bank entry may therefore wind up giving larger firms even greater advantages (Clarke, Cull, D'Amato, and Molinari, 2000; Berger, Klapper, and Udell, 2001; Mian, 2006). Multi-country studies indicate, however, that this pattern may not be systematic. In a study of about 3,000 companies across 35 developing economies, Clark, Cull, and Martínez Peria (2006) find that enterprises in countries with high levels of foreign bank participation tend to rank interest rates and access to long-term loans as lesser constraints on their operations and growth than do enterprises in countries with low levels of foreign bank participation. They also find that while large firms seem to benefit disproportionately from foreign bank entry, small firms benefit as well.

Two recent studies, on the performance of foreign-owned banks, domestically owned banks, and one state-owned bank in Uganda, shed some light on the question of the impact of foreign entry in the African context. Kasekende and Sebudde (2002), using data aggregated by bank ownership type, find that foreign banks appear to base their lending decisions primarily on commercial viability, and hence have lower ratios of nonperforming loans than their domestically owned competitors. They suggest that domestically owned banks tend to make credit decisions based on political and social criteria, and thus their lending practices tend to be characterized by concentrated loans to insiders. Cull, Haber, and Imai (2007) build upon these findings using data on the loan portfolios and financial performance of individual banks. This allows them to explore the issue of insider lending, and its impact on bank financial performance directly. Their results indicate that banks with higher shares of lending to insiders (individuals or firms connected to the bank's directors) had lower profitability and higher shares of nonperforming loans than other banks. They also find that the problems with insider lending are mostly found in domestically owned banks. Domestically owned banks with high shares of insider loans tend to have higher shares of nonperforming loans and lower rates of return. However, foreign-owned banks with high shares of insider lending tend to have fewer nonperforming loans and rates of return no different from banks that have low levels of insider loans. In short, the results indicate that foreign banks appear to have better internal control mechanisms than domestic banks in terms of judging the quality of borrowers.

1.5   Conclusions and implications

There are three general implications that can be extracted from the three broad literatures that we have addressed in this chapter. The first is that finance is a driver of growth. Africa's economic problems are multifaceted, but one crucial piece of the puzzle to slow African growth are small financial systems that allocate capital inefficiently. The second is that it is difficult to bring about broad based financial development in the absence of political reforms that enhance democratic governance. This does not mean, however, that policymakers need to sit idly by and wait decades for the consolidation of liberal democracies. There are practical steps—the privatization of state-owned banks, improved accounting standards and greater financial transparency, and opening up markets to foreign bank competition—that have been undertaken elsewhere in the absence of democratization. Indeed, there are reasons to believe that these steps might help create constituencies that would favor further economic and political reforms.

Notes

Stanford University, Research assistance for this chapter was ably provided by Aaron Berg. The usual caveats apply.

1. Calculated from data on real chain weighted GDP per capita in PPP dollars in Heston, Summers, and Aten, 2006. Data covers first year of observation in the 1960s through 2004. Regional averages are unweighted.
2. Calculated from data in Beck, Demirgüç-Kunt, and Levine, 2007a. Regional averages are unweighted.
3. For a more complete discussion see Haber and Perotti (2007).
4. Banks tend to precede securities markets in the process of financial development for several reasons. First, most firms draw on bank credit for considerable periods of time before they are large enough to go public. Second, banks tend to play a major role as underwriters of securities. Third, banks, along with utilities, tend to be among the first securities listed on emerging exchanges.

References

Anan'ich, Boris. 1999. "State power and finance in Russia, 1802–1917: The credit office of the finance ministry and government control over credit institutions." In *The State, the Financial System, and Economic Modernization*, eds. Richard Sylla, Richard Tilly, and Gabriel Tortella, 210–23. Cambridge: Cambridge University Press.

Barth, James R., Gerard Caprio Jr., and Ross Levine. 2006. *Rethinking Bank Regulation: Till Angels Govern*. Cambridge: Cambridge University Press.

Barth, James R., Gerard Caprio, and Ross Levine. 2008. "The microeconomic effects of different approaches to bank supervision." In *Political Institutions and Financial Development*, eds. Stephen Haber, Douglass C. North, and Barry R. Weingast, 156–88. Stanford: Stanford University Press.

Beck, Thorsten, Asli Demirgüç-Kunt, Luc Laeven, and Ross Levine. 2007. "Finance, firm size, and growth." Mimeo. Brown University.

Beck, Thorsten, Asli Demirgüç-Kunt, and Ross Levine. 2007a. "A New database on financial development and structure," *World Bank Economic Review* 14 (597–605).

Beck, Thorsten, Asli Demirgüç-Kunt, and Ross Levine. 2007b. "Finance, inequality, and the poor." *Journal of Economic Growth*, 12(1): 27–49.

Beck, Thorsten and Ross Levine. 2005. "Legal institutions and financial development." In *Handbook for New Institutional Economics*, eds. Claude Menard and Mary Shirley, 251–80. Dortrecht, The Netherlands: Springer.

Beck, Thorsten, Ross Levine, and Norman Loayza. 2000. "Finance and the sources of growth." *Journal of Financial Economics*, 58(1–2): 261–300.

Benmelech, Efrain and Tobias J. Moskowitz. 2005. "The political economy of financial regulation: Evidence from U.S. state usury laws in the 18th and 19th century." AFA 2007 Chicago Meetings Paper.

Berger, Allen N., Leora Klapper, and Gregory F. Udell. 2001. "The ability of banks to lend to informationally opaque small businesses." *Journal of Banking and Finance*, 25: 2127–67.

Black, Sandra E. and Philip E. Strahan. 2002. "Entrepreneurship and bank credit availability." *The Journal of Finance*, 57(6): 2807–33.

Bodenhorn, Howard. 1990. "Entry, rivalry, and free banking in antebellum America." *Review of Economics and Statistics*, 72(4): 682–86.

Bodenhorn, Howard. 2003. *State Banking in Early America: A New Economic History.* New York: Oxford University Press.

Bodenhorn, Howard. 2004. "Bank chartering and political corruption in antebellum New York: Free Banking as Reform." NBER Working Paper No. 10479.

Bordo, Michael D. and Peter Rousseau. 2006. "Legal-political factors and the historical evolution of the finance-growth link." NBER Working Paper No. 12035.

Broz, Lawrence J. and Richard S. Grossman. 2004. "Paying for privilege: The political economy of Bank of England charters, 1694–1844." *Explorations in Economic History*, 41(1): 48–72.

Bueno de Mesquita, Bruce, Alastair Smith, Randolph M. Silverson, and James D. Morrow. 2003. *The Logic of Political Survival.* Cambridge: MIT Press.

Cetorelli, Nicola and Michele Gambera. 2001. "Banking market structure, financial dependence, and growth: International evidence from industry data." *Journal of Finance*, 56(2): 617–48.

Cetorelli, Nicola and Philip Strahan. 2006. "Finance as a barrier to entry: Bank competition and industry structure in US local markets." *Journal of Finance*, 61: 437–61.

Clarke, George and Robert Cull. 2002. "Political and economic determinants of the likelihood of privatizing Argentine public banks." *Journal of Law and Economics*, 45(1): 165–98.

Clarke, George, Robert Cull, Laura D'Amato, and Andrea Molinari. 2000. "The effect of foreign entry on Argentina's domestic banking sector." In *Internationalization of Financial Services: Issues and Lessons for Developing Countries*, eds. Stijn Claessens and Marion Jansen, 331–54. London: Kluwer Law.

Clarke, George, Robert Cull, and Mary Shirley. 2005. "Bank privatization in developing countries: A summary of lessons and findings." *Journal of Banking and Finance*, 29(8–9): 1905–30.

Clarke, George, Robert Cull, and Soledad Martínez Pería. 2006. "Foreign bank participation and access to credit across firms in developing countries." *Journal of Comparative Economics*, 34: 774–95.

Cottrell, P.L. and Lucy Newton. 1999. "Banking liberalization in England and Wales, 1826–1844." In *The State, the Financial System, and Economic Modernization*, eds. Richard Sylla, Richard Tilly, and Gabriel Tortella, 75–117. Cambridge: Cambridge University Press.

Cull, Robert, Stephen Haber, and Masami Imai. 2007. "Related lending and financial development." Stanford Center for International Development Working Paper.

Cull, Robert and L.C. Xu. 2000. "Bureaucrats, state banks, and the efficiency of credit allocation: The experience of Chinese state-owned enterprises." *Journal of Comparative Economics*, 28(1): 1–31.

Davis, Lance E. and Robert E. Gallman. 2001. *Evolving Financial Markets and International Capital Flows: Britain, the Americas, and Australia, 1865–1914.* Cambridge: Cambridge University Press.

Dehejia, Rajeev and Adriana Lleras-Muney. 2007. "Financial development and pathways of growth: State branching and deposit insurance laws in the United States, 1900–1940." *Journal of Law and Economics*, 50: 239–72.

Del ángel-Mobarak, Gustavo. 2002. "Paradoxes of financial development: The construction of the Mexican banking system, 1941–1982." Ph.D. diss., Stanford University.

Del ángel-Mobarak, Gustavo. 2005. "La banca mexicana antes de 1982." In *Cuando el estado se hizo banquero: consecuencias de la nacionalización bancaria en México*, eds. Gustavo del ángel-Mobarak, Carlos Bazdresch, and Francisco Suárez Dávila, 43–56. Mexico City: Fondo de Cultura Económica.

Del Angel, Gustavo, Stephen Haber, and Aldo Musacchio. 2006. "Normas contables bancarias en México. Una guía de los cambios para legos diez años después de la crisis bancaria de 1995." *El Trimestre Económico*, 73(4): 903–26.

de Vries, Jan and Ad van der Woude. 1997. *The First Modern Economy: Success, Failure, and Perseverance of the Dutch Economy, 1500–1815.* Cambridge: Cambridge University Press.

Fisman, Raymond. 2001. "Estimating the value of political connections." *The American Economic Review*, 91(4): 1095–102.

Fisman, Raymond and Inessa Love. 2004. "Financial development and growth in the short- and long-run." NBER Working Paper 10236.

Goldsmith, Raymond. 1969. *Financial Structure and Development.* New Haven: Yale University Press.

Guiso Luigi, Paola Sapienza, and Luigi Zingales. 2004. "Does local financial development matter?" *Quarterly Journal of Economics*, 119(3): 929–69.

Haber, Stephen. 1991. "Industrial concentration and the capital markets: A comparative study of Brazil, Mexico, and the United States, 1830–1930." *The Journal of Economic History*, 51(3): 559–80.

Haber, Stephen. 1997. "Financial markets and industrial development: A comparative study of government regulation, financial innovation, and industrial structure in Brazil and Mexico, 1840–1930." In *How Latin America Fell Behind: Essays on the Economic Histories of Brazil and Mexico, 1800–1914*, ed. Stephen Haber, 146–78. Pablo Alto: Stanford University Press.

Haber, Stephen. 2003. "Banks, financial markets, and industrial development: Lessons from the economic histories of Brazil and Mexico." In *Macroeconomic Reform in Latin America: The Second Stage*, eds. José Antonio Gonzalez, Vittorio Corbo, Anne O. Krueger, and Aaron Tornell, 259–93. Chicago: University of Chicago Press.

Haber, Stephen. 2005. "Mexico's experiments with bank privatization and liberalization, 1991–2003." *Journal of Banking and Finance*, 29(8–9): 2325–53.

Haber, Stephen. 2008. "Political institutions and financial development: Evidence from the political economy of banking regulation in the United States and Mexico." In *Political Institutions and Financial Development*, eds. Stephen Haber, Douglass C. North, and Barry R. Weingast, 10–59. Stanford: Stanford University Press.

Haber, Stephen, Armando Razo, and Noel Maurer. 2003. *The Politics of Property Rights: Political Instability, Credible Commitments, and Economic Growth in Mexico, 1876–1929.* New York: Cambridge University Press.

Haber, Stephen, Douglass C. North, and Barry R. Weingast. 2008. "Political institutions and financial development." In *Political Institutions and Financial Development*, eds. Stephen Haber, Douglass C. North, and Barry R. Weingast, 1–9. Stanford: Stanford University Press.

Haber, Stephen and Enrico Perotti. 2007. "The political economy of finance." Mimeo. Stanford University.

Heston, Alan, Robert Summers, and Bettina Aten. 2006. Penn World Table Version 6.2, Center for International Comparisons of Production, Income, and Prices at the University of Pennsylvania.

Jayartne, Jith and Philip Strahan. 1996. "The finance-growth nexus: Evidence from bank branch deregulation." *Quarterly Journal of Economics*, 111(3): 639–70.

Kane, Edward and Tara Rice. 2001. "Bank runs and banking policies: Lessons for African policymakers." *Journal of African Economies*, 10: 36–71.

Kasekende, Louis A. and Rachel Kaggwa Sebudde. 2002. *The Impact of Foreign Ownership and Financial Growth in Uganda's Financial Sector.* Bank of Uganda: Mimeo.

Keyssar, Alexander. 2000. *The Right to Vote: The Contested History of Democracy in the United States.* New York: Basic Books.

King, Robert G. and Ross Levine. 1993. "Finance and growth: Schumpeter might be right." *Quarterly Journal of Economics,* 108(3): 717–37.

La Porta, Rafael, Florencio Lopez-de-Silanes, and Andrei Shleifer. 2002. "Government ownership of banks." *Journal of Finance,* 57(1): 265–301.

La Porta, Rafael, Florencio Lopez-de-Silanes, Andrei Shleifer, and Robert W. Vishny. 1998. "Law and finance." *Journal of Political Economy,* 106(6): 1013–155.

Levine, Ross, Norman Loayza, and Thorsten Beck. 2000. "Financial intermediation and growth: Causality and causes." *Journal of Monetary Economics,* 46: 31–77.

Levine, Ross and Sarah Zervos. 1998. "Stock markets, banks, and economic growth." *American Economic Review,* 88(3): 537–58.

Marshall, Monty and Keith Jaggers. 2008. *Polity IV Project: Political Regime Characteristics and Transitions, 1800–2006.* University of Maryland.

Maurer, Noel. 2002. *The Power and the Money: The Mexican Financial System, 1876–1932.* Palo Alto: Stanford University Press.

Maurer, Noel and Andrei Gomberg. 2004. "When the state is untrustworthy: Public finance and private banking in porfirian Mexico." *Journal of Economic History,* 64: 1087–107.

Maurer, Noel and Stephen Haber. 2007. "Related lending, and economic performance: Evidence from Mexico." *The Journal of Economic History,* 67: 3.

McKinnon, Ronald. 1973. *Money and Capital in Economic Development.* Washington, DC: Brookings Institution.

Mian, Atif. 2006. "Distance constraints: The limits of foreign lending in poor economies." *Journal of Finance,* 61: 1465–505.

Moss, David and Sarah Brennan. 2004. "Regulation and reaction: The other side of free banking in antebellum New York." Harvard Business School Working Paper 04–038.

Neal, Larry. 1990. *The Rise of Financial Capitalism: International Capital Markets in the Age of Reason.* Cambridge: Cambridge University Press.

North, Douglass C. and Barry R. Weingast. 1989. "Constitutions and commitment: The evolution of institutions governing public choice in seventeenth-century England." *The Journal of Economic History,* 44(4): 803–32.

Perotti, Enrico and Paolo Volpin. 2004. "Lobbying on entry." Tinbergen Institute Discussion Paper No. 04–088/2.

Rajan, Raghuram and Luigi Zingales. 1998. "Financial dependence and growth." *American Economic Review*, 88(3): 559–86.

Rajan, Raghuram and Luigi Zingales. 2003a. "The great reversals: The politics of financial development in the 20th century." *Journal of Financial Economics*, 69(1): 5–50.

Rajan, Raghuram and Luigi Zingales. 2003b. *Saving Capitalism from the Capitalists: Unleashing the Power of Financial Markets to Create Wealth and Spread Opportunity.* New York: Crown Business.

Rousseau, Peter. 2003. "Historical perspectives on financial development and economic growth." *Review of the Federal Reserve Bank of St. Louis*, 84(4): 81–105.

Rousseau, Peter and Paul Wachtel. 1998. "Financial intermediation and economic performance: Historical evidence from five industrialized countries." *Journal of Money, Credit, and Banking*, 30(4): 657–78.

Rousseau, Peter and Richard Sylla. 2003. "Financial systems, economic growth, and globalization." In *Globalization in Historical Perspective*, eds. Michael Bordo, Alan Taylor, and Jeffrey Williamson, 373–413. Chicago: The University of Chicago Press.

Rousseau, Peter and Richard Sylla. 2004. "Emerging financial markets and early U.S. growth." *Explorations in Economic History*, 42(1): 1–26.

Sapienza, Paola. 2004. "The effects of government ownership on bank lending." *Journal of Financial Economics*, 72(2): 357–84.

Schumpeter, Joseph. 1983. *The Theory of Economic Development: An Inquiry into Profits, Capital, Credit, Interest, and the Business Cycle.* New Brunswick, NJ: Transaction Books.

Sonin, Constantine. 2003. "Why the rich may favor poor protection of property rights." *Journal of Development Economics*, 31(4): 715–31.

Spamann, Holger. 2006. "On the insignificance and/or endogeneity of La Porta et al.'s anti-director's rights index under consistent coding." European Corporate Governance Institute Working Paper No. 67/2006.

Summerhill, William R. Forthcoming. *Inglorious Revolution: Political Institutions, Public Debt, and Financial Underdevelopment in Imperial Brazil.* New Haven: Yale University Press.

Sylla, Richard. 2006. "The political economy of financial development: Canada and the United States in the mirror of the other, 1790–1840." *Enterprise & Society*, 7(4): 653–65.

Sylla, Richard. 2008. "The political economy of early U.S. financial development." In *The Politics of Financial Development*, eds. Stephen Haber, Douglass C. North, and Barry R. Weingast, 60–91. Palo Alto: Stanford University Press.

Wallis, John, Richard Sylla, and John B. Legler. 1994. "The interaction of taxation and regulation in nineteenth century U.S. banking." In *The Regulated Economy: A Historical Approach to Political Economy*, eds. Claudia Goldin and Gary D. Libecap, 122–44. Chicago: The University of Chicago Press.

Wang, Ta-Chen. 2006. "Courts, banks, and credit market in early American development." Ph.D. diss., Stanford University.

Wurgler, Jeffrey. 2000. "Financial markets and the allocation of capital." *Journal of Financial Economics*, 58(1–2): 187–214.

2
Finance in Africa: A Diagnosis

Patrick Honohan

2.1 Introduction

After a decade of reform, African financial systems are diversifying their activities, deepening their lending, and increasing their reach with new products and new technologies. Financial repression and the practice of directed credit are both much diminished, and there has been extensive privatization of state-owned banks—often to foreign-owned banks, the reentry of which represents only one aspect of a growing potential in internationalization and regionalization.

Yet financial development in Africa is still constrained by four pervasive challenges: a lack of scale, the informality of so much of African business activities, difficulties of governance, and the frequency and scale of shocks to the system. Although these are certainly present difficulties, they also represent opportunities in that much of the machinery of finance is specifically designed to repair, circumvent or cushion against problems of scale informality, governance and shocks.

Until recently there was a large gulf between the interests and views of financial policy specialists focusing on mainstream, formal sector, finance and those with an interest in informal and microfinance. But a growing awareness has emerged in the financial policy community worldwide that good development policy needs to pay attention to both aspects: "finance for growth" and "finance for all", that there is no significant conflict between policy designed to develop each of these aspects, and indeed that there can be a degree of convergence between the two (Caprio and Honohan, 2001; Demirgüç-Kunt et al., 2008).

In Africa, neither dimension is working well at present. Finance at the micro level is needed to get the bulk of the population (median income is still about a dollar a day in Africa) to the "bottom rung of the ladder", to use the image popularized by Jeffrey Sachs. Large-scale finance—banking, securities markets, and regional cooperation—is needed to make sure the ladder exists and is worth climbing.

Some of what is needed corresponds to what are by now highly conventional recommendations consistent with the essentially *modernist* approach of the Washington-based International Financial Institutions (IFIs). However, not all that is conventional is good. African policymakers should, for example, beware of those who over-enthusiastically apply the modernist agenda by unthinkingly transplanting advanced economy regulatory models such as Basel II into an African environment where they could be not merely ineffective, but actually counterproductive and damaging. Likewise, regional cooperation in finance will only progress if a realistic prioritization is adopted—and in most cases, the list likely should not start with a common currency.

In contrast to some fundamentalists, I do not reject an *activist* perspective on financial sector policy, recognizing that Africa can present a somewhat unpromising prospect to some market participants and may need the push of committed people of good will. For example, I believe there is room and need for many more providers of financial services to small and microenterprises and poor and near-poor households. Microfinance is currently provided in Africa by a myriad of different types of institution and I believe that this diversity should be encouraged, given that nobody has the monopoly of wisdom on what can work in the difficult environment that is Africa, hampered by small scale, informality, inadequate governance and repeated major shocks.

We begin (Section 2.2) by documenting the key facts about African financial systems, before looking in turn at the policies needed to ensure that the financial services needed to lubricate and accelerate African growth are provided at sufficient scale and with sufficient efficiency (Section 2.3). We then turn to finance at the small scale, asking how policy can help ensure that financial systems have sufficient outreach (Section 2.4). Concluding remarks are in Section 2.5.

2.2   Facts

For money doctors, Africa is, or should be, a priority. Mapping the responses of surveyed entrepreneurs around the world to questions about what they see as the main obstacles to their firm's business operation and growth, we find[1] that African entrepreneurs identify the cost of finance as an obstacle more frequently than those of any other regions. The same is true for access to finance. In both cases—cost and access—the next closest region is unsurprisingly Latin America, a region notorious for its history of financial crises and crippling nominal interest rates. Most outsiders express surprise at the fact that Africa tops the list here. After all, given the low level of infrastructure, the weaknesses in health and education and the troubled political and security history of Africa, one might well suppose that other considerations would loom larger as obstacles to African business people. Yet, of 18 different types of problem, cost of finance is the most frequently mentioned obstacle mentioned by African entrepreneurs. So, not only is

Africa the region in which finance looms largest, but also, the number one barrier in Africa is finance.

Turning from perceptions to objective indicators of financial sector development, it is not hard to find evidence that Africa's financial systems are indeed an area of weakness. Using the size of the banking system, whether measured by total monetary liabilities or by the volume of bank credit outstanding, Africa's systems are small in a global comparison. That is especially evident if we simply look at absolute size: only South Africa and Nigeria are above the world median. Absolute size does matter for achieving economies of scale,[2] though it is evident that the small absolute size of the typical African financial system is largely a reflection of the small size of the economies. Still, scaling these measures by GDP reveals that the banking systems in African countries are not only small, but also shallow. Indeed, although four African countries make it above the global median of monetary depth, three of them do so because they are offshore centers— Mauritius, Seychelles and Cape Verde (Figure 2.1). So it's not just because the economies are small that they have small financial systems. The shallowness is correlated with *per capita income*, yet even after taking account of this (and also of the cross-country variation attributable to persistent inflation lowering money demand) more African countries fall below the line than above it (Figure 2.2—though the wide cross-country variation means that this may not be a statistically significant difference).

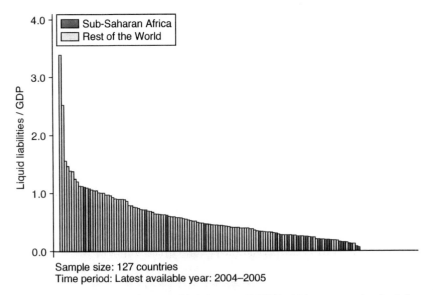

Figure 2.1   Financial depth (Liquid liabilities as % GDP): African countries shaded
Source: Financial Structure Database, rev. 2006 (The World Bank).

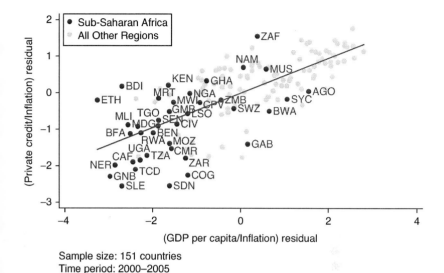

Sample size: 151 countries
Time period: 2000–2005

Figure 2.2 Financial depth (Private credit as % GDP) versus GDP per capita
Source: Financial Structure Database, 2006; World Development Indicators, 2005
(The World Bank).

One important reason why there is less money held "onshore" in African banks is that so much is held "offshore". Data collected by the Bank for International Settlements (BIS) on the nationality of deposit-holders at banks in advanced economies reveals that African offshore deposits represent a high proportion of the onshore deposits in their countries—over 100 percent in one case and typically in the region of 25–60 percent. These are much higher percentages that reported for any other region (Figure 2.3), and point to an exceptional lack of confidence among African liquid asset holders, corporate and individual.

But there is a deepening in progress and it is not just a question of the last few years or of the oil-producing countries. Median banking depth, whether measured by deposits or credit as a percentage of GDP, bottomed out in 1996, and has been rising steadily ever since. Four out of every five countries has seen deepening since 2000. An important point to which we will return is the fact that the deepening has been more pronounced for deposits than for private credit. This reflects the growing pattern whereby African banks place a much lower proportion of their resources with private sector borrowers than do banks in other regions (Figure 2.4); instead their claims on government and on state-owned enterprises are much higher than in any other region, and only the Middle-East and North Africa banking systems place a higher proportion in foreign assets. While crowding-out by government is part of the story, bankers' risk aversion is here also a factor to which we will return.

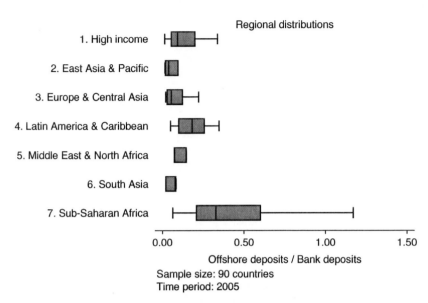

Figure 2.3   Offshore bank deposits divided by domestic bank deposits in different regions

Source: Financial Structure Database, 2006; BIS, 2006.

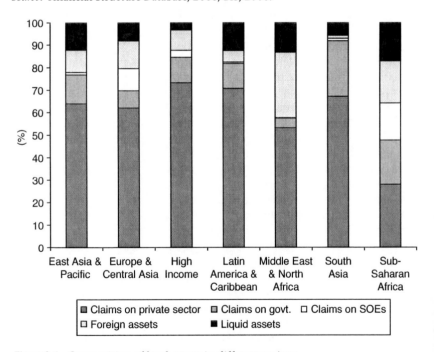

Figure 2.4   Composition of bank assets in different regions

While banking depth is a convenient general-purpose indicator of financial development, it doesn't capture all of the relevant components. It's
important in particular not to neglect issues of efficiency and of the nonbank financial sector. Interest rate levels and spreads can throw light on
the efficiency of banking, and the story they tell is broadly in line with
the message from data on depth. It's not just a question of overall interest
rate levels; these are largely determined by macroeconomic considerations
including inflation expectations, as well as by the degree of financial repression. The liberalizations of the late 1980s and 1990s largely removed the
repression that had kept real interest rates negative, and rates bounced-up
to heights that compensated financiers for the perceived risks in holding
assets denominated in local currencies. There was probably an overshoot,
especially on bank lending rates, with median real lending rates soaring to
above 20 percent by 2001, and the subsequent decline may have been associated with some more increase in competition associated with liberalized
bank entry. The competitive situation in African banking cannot, however
be considered vigorous. Net interest margins in African financial systems are
higher than in any other region of the world—albeit not much worse than
Latin America. Part of this can be attributed to the insecurity of property
rights, part to insufficient scale, part to higher historic inflation, but after
adjusting for these and other bank-specific factors, we still find an unex-
plained average 60 basis point excess in African bank margins. Insufficient
competition is a likely culprit. Banks in Africa returned an average of 2.1
percent on assets during 2000–2004, compared with a world average of 0.6
percent. Of course, banks are a heterogeneous collection of diverse entities,
but even more tellingly, taking the subsample of international banks with
operations in Africa and in other parts of the world, an even larger difference emerges: 2.8 percent in Africa compared with 0.9 percent elsewhere.

Not that foreign entry has been systematically blocked. Far from it. The
foreign banks are back to a greater extent than elsewhere. Characterizing the
ownership of banking systems around by whether they are dominated by
banks owned by foreigners, by the state, or by non-state nationals, we find
that about half of African banking systems are mainly foreign-owned, with
just a handful mainly government-owned. The degree of foreign ownership
is much higher—and of government ownership much lower—in Africa than
in other regions of the world. The foreign banks are a diverse lot. They vary
from the traditional European-owned banks—some of the biggest of which
trace their African business back more than a century—to a new breed of
multi-country banks headquartered in Africa. Though there have been false
starts before, this emergence of truly African-based regional banks, which is
being accelerated by the huge regulated increase in bank capital in Nigeria,
is to me a most promising development.

The ability of the Nigerian equity market to raise almost USD 3 billion
in new bank capital during 2003–2005 also points to a somewhat unexpected resilience of African equity markets. Of course most of them are very

38 *Patrick Honohan*

small and many cannot cover their operating costs or the costs of regulating them, but a quantitative assessment (based on data collected in World Bank, 2006) along dimensions of efficiency, stability, access as well as size show African stockmarkets—even excluding Johannesburg—to be not far behind the average of developing countries except on the dimension of pricing efficiency (see Yartey and Adjasi for a discussion of the role of African stock exchanges in contributing to growth). Even if the vast majority of the listed firms has raised little new money on these markets, their presence on the exchange and even modest local holdings can provide a degree of political protection for enterprise and involve African elites in the development of the private sector more widely.

2.3 Finance for growth

What cross-country studies have shown rather consistently is a causal impact of deep financial systems on national growth. Finance seems to represent one of the crucial institutions needed to underpin sustained growth. (And there is no compromise here with inequality: contrary to what one might suppose from the degree to which the direct dealings of mainstream finance are mainly with higher income groups and formal sector enterprises, a

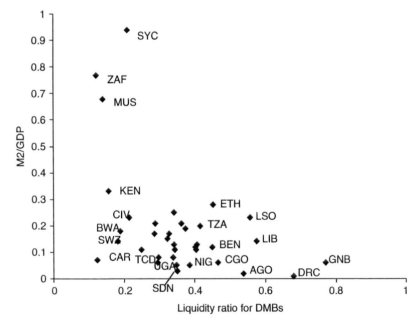

Figure 2.5 African banks: Financial depth and liquidity

finance-intensive growth pattern is associated across countries with *less* inequality, not more.) The key dimension here seems to be credit to the private sector and as we have just seen, it is in this dimension that African banking systems are weakest in terms of both cost and volume.

The unwillingness of African banks to lend even the limited resources they are able to mobilize likely reflects their perception of risk. Evidence in support of this comes from the clear cross-country negative correlation between (1) the share of banks' resources held in liquid form (and thus not lent out) and (2) the ratio of bank deposits to GDP (Figure 2.5). In other words, it is in the countries where depositors are most reluctant to entrust their savings to the banks that banks are most reluctant to entrust their resources to local borrowers. Building the confidence of both is a clear priority for improving the functioning of financial systems.

There is a well-defined modernist agenda for making progress here. For the most part, it involves adopting and importing mechanisms that work in advance economies. Yet the modernists sometimes go too far and attempt inappropriate and unwise transplantation.

For instance, the modernist agenda seeks to make bank lending easier and safer for banks by

1. working on information infrastructures as well as legal and judicial ones. This includes for example the creation or improvement of credit registries allowing (and indeed obliging) lenders to pool information about their borrowing customers' credit history. It includes refinements to the law on secured lending for example where additional protections are needed for leasing or lending warehouse receipts. It can require improvements in the administration of the courts.
2. pruning unnecessary regulations. As much as an adequate and incentive-compatible regime of prudential regulation and supervision is essential if the banking system of any country is to be protected against damaging systemic collapses into insolvency, it does not follow that all and any prudential regulations are productive or needed. There are still a number of outdated and regulations in place that unduly constrain African lenders, though probably fewer than the banks themselves believe.

But modernists are also pushing for the introduction of the Basel II regulatory system in African countries. While the bank risk management systems that are promoted by Basel II have much to recommend them, it is quite a different matter to base one's regulatory system on premature adoption of what will, for the foreseeable future in the African context, inevitably be unproved and largely unverifiable systems. Supervisors will be put on the defensive if they try to restrain risky practices adopted by a bank which has calibrated its internal ratings systems (based on purchased software) is such a way as to make the practices seem safe. As for the alternative "standardized" version of Basel II, which bases required capital on independent borrower ratings, this is a wholly incredible approach for low-income economies with no existing rating industry and no credible incentive mechanism for ensuring reliable ratings (Quintyn and Taylor, 2007, discusses regulatory structures for banking in Africa).

The modernist agenda also seeks to improve the environment for long-term and risk finance by

1. building on the growing investable funds of pension and social security funds, including by removing unduly constraining portfolio allocation restrictions, and replacing with enhanced mechanisms of governance and transparency (for instance putting the reporting mechanisms of the stock market to good effect).
2. putting in place administrative, tax and other arrangements that are needed to underpin the emergence of a sizable mortgage finance market and new risk-sharing mechanisms of infrastructure financing.

But again, the modernists can over-reach. The tendency, in particular, to adopt the full panoply of investor protections in securities markets may have resulted in entry costs that deterred many would-be issuers. A lighter and more pragmatic form of capital market regulation, for example using the AIM approach of the London market, which relies to a somewhat greater extent on *caveat emptor* which retaining considerable disclosure, could open the door to more listings and more capital being raised from the institutional and wealthy investors that already predominate in African markets.

When it comes to macroeconomic and fiscal stability (including predictable government debt management), there can be no disagreement with the main thrust of the modernist agenda, which seeks to build a firm overall macro platform on which financial intermediation can be built. Yet even here, the modernists can get carried away. As recent IMF studies have suggested (cf. Adam et al., 2007) monetary management in an environment of growing inflows, fairly common across the continent in recent years, whether due to oil price rises or increasing aid, becomes quite tricky. The growing inflows swell the money supply, prompting a contractionary reflex by mechanical monetarists; but this may prove to be the wrong reaction if demand for money is also growing as a result of the favorable external conditions. After all, avoiding overvalued exchange rates is one of the key requirements for sustained growth in Africa as has been pointed out by Johnson et al. (2007).

Finally, there is a modernist agenda on regional arrangements. Indeed, regional cooperation has been advocated for African states by external advisors for a century and a half. But a pragmatic approach to sequencing of regional cooperation in finance is needed to avoid the risks and disappointments inherent in a no-holds-barred modernist attempt to leap to a single currency in the image of Europe. Instead, regional cooperation should concentrate on high yield, feasible dimensions. These could include deeper cooperation in banking supervision, including cross-country sharing of supervisory responsibility as has already been put in place in the two francophone zones. Attempts to gain economies of scale from one or other of the possible hub-and-spoke models of securities market organization could be another example of a worthwhile and low-risk form of regional cooperation.

2.4 Finance for all

Fewer than one in five African adults have access to a formal or semiformal financial intermediary. This striking if not very surprising statistic is again partly a reflection of the low-income levels and infrastructure weaknesses across the continent—indeed, while lower than other regions, these household access percentages are not as far below the rest of the world as are the financial depth measures described above.

Aspects of the four underlying challenges mentioned above make direct access to financial services particularly problematic in large parts of Africa. This is evident where population is sparse, incomes low, infrastructure weak. There are some things that can be done by modern technology, both physical and financial. Mobile phones and the internet are already overcoming isolation and costly teller services in several parts of Africa. Weather and price insurance programs for farmers have been piloted with some success. And there are a few age-old techniques that mainstream banks have not until recently bothered to introduce in Africa and which could improve credit availability especially for the farm sector.

While the employment of new technology has thus been shown to offer considerable potential for improving outreach in Africa, it is not going to be enough. Certainly, the mainstream banks have not delivered long-term or risk finance; or any services for the majority.

Therefore, if it is the modernists that mainly set the agenda when it comes to improving "finance for growth", the many evident shortcomings of mainstream financial systems even in advanced countries for delivering services directly to the poor or marginalized means that anybody concerned with improvements here is likely to be an activist.

If there is to be the needed progress in outreach, there will have to be new (or reengineered) entrants with a dedicated mission. They will need to be patient, to take risks, and to experiment with new technology. In particular, they have to make better use of soft information and relationship lending, which have been rather neglected in the modernization of modern banking.

There must also be a policy response, for which an interesting model is found in the South African financial sector charter of 2003 and subsequent developments.

However, effective activism in finance presupposes good governance. Activists are not restrained by immediate market pressures; they have chosen to plough money and effort into endeavors that the market has turned down. Hidden among the patient and motivated idealists can be rogues and opportunists who are difficult to detect. To be even reasonably confident that these efforts and resources will not be wasted or subverted, the sponsoring agency of financial activism must have good governance.

The disappointing experience of state-owned Development Financial Institutions (DFIs) across much of Africa is testimony to the importance of these cautionary remarks about activism. Indeed, because of this experience, it seems clear that government-run DFIs will rarely be the optimal solution. If state-owned financial firms are present, at the very least it is essential that they should be operating with as level a playing field as possible, and under good governance procedures. The mandate and business of state-owned firms should be designed to limit their exposure to downside risk. This argues for service provision rather than risk assumption. In the case of state-owned guarantee funds—seemingly the intervention of choice today for numerous financial activists—it argues great attention to incentive structures built into the risk-sharing element of the guarantee programs (cf. Demirgüç-Kunt et al., 2008, pp. 168–75).

So if there are to be activists, one has to be careful about who does what. Numerous different players will need to be involved in the effort to make finance work for Africa. There are messages here for all the players. Regulators should be flexible in admitting a wide range of institutions, building on what is already a very diverse population of financial service providers across the continent.[3] Mainstream banks will need to play a role, though this is likely to be mainly as wholesalers until and unless they can get costs down and improve relationship lending.

Donors and development partners can contribute a lot in helping promote greater access in the form of resources, of innovation, of independence (where they might partly compensate for local governance gaps). Finally, the message for governments is that, while they should probably try to stay as far away from ownership of financial firms as they can, nevertheless they should be actively creating infrastructures and ensuring that they are not choking innovation with over-regulation.[4]

2.5   Concluding remarks

Better financial systems with a wider reach represent a key ingredient in getting African economies onto a sustainable growth path. By providing an alternative to government patronage as the basis for entry into business, a strong, independent financial system can transform the business environment for enterprise.

There are echoes here of the recent paper by Nobel prize winner Douglas North and his co-authors (2006) who claim that the key difference in history between economies that have achieved rapid and sustained growth and those which have languished is the difference between open access and closed access societies. This is a political as well as an economic concept, and access to finance is only one ingredient in transforming your society into an open access society, but it is a necessary ingredient. Besides, if the elite truly set about creating the conditions for financial access, then the rest will fall into place.

African elites, responding rationally to the recurrent cycle of national social, political and economic meltdowns, have looked to extracting their slice of a transitory pie instead of looking toward what would be a smaller slice of a bigger pie if they were prepared to build for the long term. A financial system that allows elites to participate more effectively in the fruits of a broad-based sustained economic growth could help shift their incentives, opening up a new vista for the continent.

Notes

Trinity College, Dublin. This chapter draws heavily on my 2007 book with Thorsten Beck.

1. The data underlying the assertions in this section are presented more fully in Honohan and Beck (2007), from which the figures are also drawn. The Fund's Regional Economic Outlook series, 2006 and 2007 contain additional analytical data.
2. For example, the fact that mean operating (administrative) costs of African banks is almost 2 percentage points above the world mean may owe much to lack of scale economies (Honohan and Beck, 2007, p. 36; see also Bossone et al., 2002).
3. For example, the unproven and constraining idea that only cooperative entities, or alternatively only corporate entities, can work well in delivering microfinance should not be embodied in legislation.
4. Not least in overzealous and poorly designed Anti Money Laundering (AML) regulation and its potential strangling effect on microfinance (Isern et al., 2006).

References

Adam, Christopher, Stephen A. O'Connell, Edward F. Buffie, Edward F., and Catherine A. Pattillo. 2007. "Monetary policy rules for managing aid surges in Africa." IMF Working Paper No. 07/180.

Bossone, Biagio, Patrick Honohan, and Millard Long. 2002. "Policy for small financial systems." In *Financial Sector Policy in Developing Countries*, eds. Gerard Caprio, Patrick Honohan, and Dimitri Vittas. Washington, DC: The World Bank.

Caprio, Gerard and Patrick Honohan. 2001. *Finance for Growth: Policy Choices for a Volatile World.* New York: Oxford University Press.

Demirgüç-Kunt, Asli, Thorsten Beck, and Patrick Honohan. 2008. *Finance for All: Policies and Pitfalls in Expanding Access*. Washington, DC: The World Bank.

Honohan, Patrick and Thorsten Beck. 2007. *Making Finance Work for Africa*. Washington, DC: The World Bank.

IMF. 2006, 2007. *Regional Economic Outlook: Africa*. Washington, DC: International Monetary Fund.

Isern, Jennifer, David Porteous, Raul Hernandez-Coss, and Chinyere Egwuagu. 2006. "AML-CFT regulation: Implications for financial service providers that serve low-income people." CGAP Focus Note 29. Washington, DC: World Bank.

Johnson, Simon, Jonathan Ostry, and Arvind Subramanian. 2007. "The prospects for sustained growth in Africa: Benchmarking the constraints." IMF Working Paper No. 07/52.

North, Douglass C. John Joseph Wallis, and Barry R. Weingast. 2006. "A conceptual framework for interpreting recorded human history." NBER Working Paper 12795.

Quintyn, Marc and Michael W. Taylor. 2007. " Building supervisory structures in Sub-Saharan Africa—An analytical framework." IMF Working Paper No. 07/18.

World Bank. 2006. "Equity market indicators: A primer." Financial Sector Indicators Note 3. Washington, DC: The World Bank.

3
Financial Deepening in the CFA Franc Zone: The Role of Institutions

Raju Jan Singh, Kangni Kpodar and Dhaneshwar Ghura

3.1 Introduction

During the 1980s and early 1990s, many Sub-Saharan African (SSA) countries undertook reforms to deepen their financial sectors. They liberalized interest rates, phased out direct credit, moved to indirect monetary policy instruments, restructured and privatized banks, and reinforced banking sector supervision and microfinance.[1] However, these reforms had mixed results. Financial sectors in SSA countries remain among the shallowest in the world and, within sub-Saharan Africa, they are even shallower in the CFA franc zone.

This chapter sets out to empirically investigate factors that may explain why financial sectors in the CFA franc zone are less deep even than in the rest of SSA. Recent studies have emphasized the linkage between legal institutions and financial development. Empirical work has shown that countries whose legal systems are based on the English tradition tend to have deeper financial markets, while the French legal traditions seem to hinder financial development. Although these studies have not focused explicitly on Africa, the implication would be that financial deepening in CFA franc countries could be hampered by their cultural heritage.

This chapter contributes to the literature in two ways. First, it explores the possible influence of legal traditions explicitly in SSA using panel data for a sample of 40 countries for 1992–2006. Second, the chapter challenges the view that legal heritage is time-invariant and policy-independent. The results indicate that the gap in financial development between the countries of the CFA franc zone and the rest of SSA can be explained by differences in institutional quality (e.g., availability of credit information, and strength and enforcement of property rights), variables that policy makers can influence.

The chapter is structured as follows: Section 3.2 presents some stylized facts about recent developments in the financial sector in SSA; Section 3.3 provides a brief review of the literature; Section 3.4 discusses the data, methodology, and main empirical results; and Section 3.5 concludes the chapter.

3.2   Recent developments

Financial sectors in SSA countries (measured as credit to the private sector in terms of GDP) are among the shallowest in the world. On average, in 2006, credit to the private sector represented the equivalent of 16 percent of GDP in SSA countries, while the same ratio was above 35 percent in the rest of the developing world (low-income and middle-income countries). Focusing on sub-Saharan Africa more closely, financial sectors in CFA franc countries are even shallower. On average, in 2006, credit to the private sector in terms of GDP amounted to about 14 percent in the Western African Economic and Monetary Union (WAEMU) and 7 percent in the Central African Economic and Monetary Community (CEMAC), compared with 19 percent for the rest of sub-Saharan Africa.

CFA franc countries seem, however, to have undertaken similar efforts to liberalize and reform their financial sectors. As elsewhere in the continent, bank restructuring took place in the late 1980s and was followed by a strengthening of bank supervision with the creation in 1991 of a single supervisory institution in each of the two CFA franc sub-zones (Gulde et al., 2006).[2] So what could explain the relative shallowness of financial sectors in the CFA franc countries?

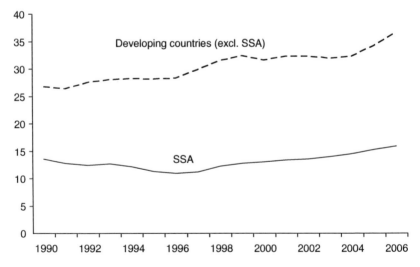

Figure 3.1   Private sector credit in SSA and other developing countries, 1990–2006 (in percent of GDP)

Source: World Bank.

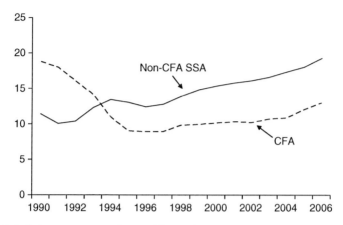

Figure 3.2 Private sector credit in CFA and non-CFA countries, 1990–2006 (in percent of GDP)
Source: World Bank.

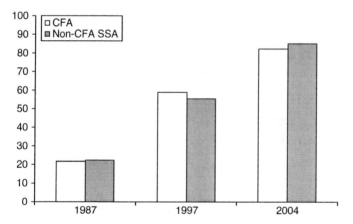

Figure 3.3 Financial liberalization index, 1987–2004
Source: Gelbard and Leite (1999) and McDonald and Schumacher (2007).

There is a growing body of literature arguing that macroeconomic stability and financial liberalization, while necessary, are not sufficient conditions for enhancing financial sector deepening and should be accompanied by other institutional reforms. In particular, recent research suggests that insufficient legal protection of creditor rights and information asymmetries about borrowers' ability and willingness to repay debts could explain why some financial markets remain shallow. How do the CFA franc countries compare in this regard?

According to these studies, the ability of borrowers to provide adequate financial statements is essential to encourage the expansion of credit. Better accounting and auditing would therefore be a key requirement. In many SSA countries, however, the accounting profession is not well regulated, and the quality of accounts varies widely, hampering transparency (Sacerdoti, 2005). OHADA (the Organisation for the Harmonization of Business Law in Africa) and the WAEMU Council of Ministers adopted a uniform accounting system in 2001, but have had trouble implementing it.[3] Furthermore, lack of a standard for auditing practices raises serious concerns about the quality of financial statement audits.

The dissemination of the information available seems also problematic. In advanced countries, databases centralizing information on borrowers are often established by the private sector or maintained by central banks. These credit information registries collect information on the standing of borrowers in the financial system and make it available to lenders. This system improves transparency, rewarding good borrowers and increasing the cost of defaulting. Despite efforts to set up public credit information registries in CFA franc countries, however, their coverage is still minimal.

Property rights in the CFA franc zone have also weakened over the past decade. The regional OHADA legal framework has led to a number of improvements, but there are significant deficiencies in its implementation. Debt collection and foreclosure on collateral are inefficient because of uncertainties in each country's civil procedures, and inadequate capacity and problems of governance in the judicial systems. Court proceedings are lengthy and unpredictable. These problems are common to many SSA countries,

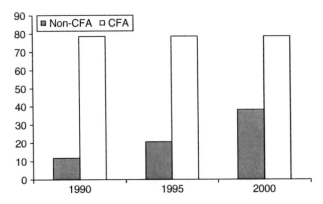

Figure 3.4   Credit registries, 1990–2000 (percentage of countries with credit registries)
Source: Djankov, McLiesh, and Schleifer (2005).

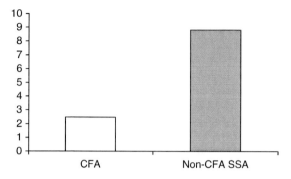

Figure 3.5 Credit information, 2008 (Number of individuals and firms in percent of adults)

Source: World Bank.

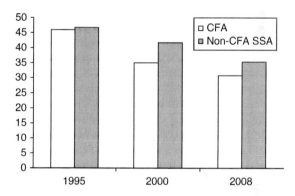

Figure 3.6 Property rights index, 1995–2008

Source: Heritage Foundation and Fund Staff calculations.

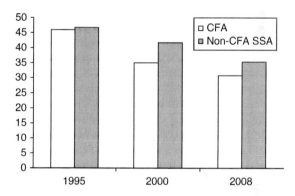

Figure 3.7 Bureaucratic quality index, 1990–2005

Source: Political Risk Services and Fund Staff calculations.

but seem more acute in the CFA franc zone. According to the World Bank, enforcement costs there represented on average more than 45 percent of a loan in 2008 compared with 30 percent in the rest of SSA. In Burkina Faso the costs amounted to 95 percent and in the Central African Republic to 72 percent, in striking contrast to less than 9 percent in Mauritius or 12 percent in South Africa.

Therefore, as McDonald and Schumacher (2007) and Tressel and Detragiache (2008) have pointed out, while the financial liberalization of the late 1980s and early 1990s was necessary, it may not have been sufficient. Efforts to establish the conditions for the financial market to function may have fallen short, particularly with respect to the system's ability to gather information and use collateral. Improvements in information collection and dissemination, as well as in the legal and judicial framework, would be essential to creating an environment more conducive to credit expansion.

3.3   Theoretical background and review of the literature

Financial institutions operate in settings where complete information is often not available. Entrepreneurs seeking financing normally have more information about their projects than their banks. In such a setting, projects that may differ with respect to their probability of success are indistinguishable from the viewpoint of a financial institution. This information asymmetry requires a screening effort in order for banks to grant loans only to the most promising projects (Singh, 1992).

The lender cannot rely simply on increasing the interest rate, however. As Stiglitz and Weiss (1981) demonstrated, increases in the interest rate charged on loans may adversely affect the pool composition of borrowers. For a given expected return, an increase in interest rates will induce low-risk projects to drop out first, keeping only the riskier ones in the pool.

Lenders could require collateral instead. By requiring collateral, the lender imposes a cost on the entrepreneur in case of default. As the probability of failure is greater for high-risk projects, the same amount of collateral will reduce the expected profit of these projects by more than that of less risky ones. Bester (1985, 1987) demonstrated that lenders could design attractive contracts for the various qualities of borrowers, leading to perfect sorting. Alternatively, fund providers could invest in gathering additional information on projects. This information will lead to a better perception of the probability of success attached to a given project (Devinney, 1986; Singh, 1994, 1997).

Against this backdrop, the empirical literature has examined factors beyond the level of economic development to explain the extent of a country's financial deepening, looking at variables that influence the degree of information asymmetries. In this regard, macroeconomic variables like inflation as well as legal aspects have attracted particular attention.

Huybens and Smith (1998, 1999) suggest that inflation may aggravate asymmetries of information in credit markets, reducing the real rate of return and the volume of credit. Consistent with these views, Boyd, Levine, and Smith (2001), Detragiache, Gupta, and Tressel (2005), and Dehesa, Druck, and Pleckhanov (2007) find inflation to be negatively associated with measures of financial depth.

The law and finance literature focuses on the role of legal institutions (especially the protection of private property rights) in explaining international differences in financial development. In countries where legal systems enforce private property rights, support private contracts, and protect the legal rights of investors, lenders would be more willing to finance firms. Acemoglu and Johnson (2005), Cottarelli, Dell'Ariccia, and Vladkova-Hollar (2003), Dehesa, Druck, and Plekhanov (2007), McDonald and Schumacher (2007), and Tressel and Detragiache (2008) find that stronger creditor rights tend to promote financial development.

In this regard, a country's legal origin has been shown to be an important determinant of both creditor rights and private credit (La Porta et al., 1998). This literature distinguishes four main legal origins: English, French, German, and Nordic. The English legal origin includes the common law of England, and its former colonies, such as the United States, Australia, and Canada. The French legal origin covers the civil law of France, countries Napoleon conquered (including Portugal and Spain), and their former colonies. The German legal origin includes not only the laws of the Germanic countries in Central Europe, but also countries in East Asia where German law was adopted.[4] The Nordic legal origin refers to the laws of the four Scandinavian countries. La Porta and others (1998) find countries with an English legal origin to have deeper financial markets than others: the French legal tradition appears to hinder financial development.

Enforcement of rules and rights also matters to financial development. Speedier enforcement of contracts is associated with deeper credit markets (Detragiache, Gupta, and Tressel, 2005; McDonald and Schumacher, 2007). Similarly, poor governance may increase the cost of doing business and create uncertainty about property rights. Detragiache, Gupta, and Tressel (2005) and McDonald and Schumacher (2007) find that countries with governance issues have shallower financial sectors.

Finally, efficient exchange of information can reduce the cost of screening borrowers. Credit agencies, for instance, could collect and disseminate information on credit histories. Djankov, McLiesh, and Shleifer (2005), as well as McDonald and Schumacher (2007) show that information sharing is associated with greater financial development. Furthermore, among the many business environment indicators, the availability of credit information and coverage of credit registries are associated with deeper credit markets (Detragiache, Gupta, and Tressel, 2005).

3.4 Empirical analysis

3.4.1 Data

Financial development is a complex process involving a number of intermediaries and could be captured by a variety of indicators. The empirical literature has typically used a banking indicator, such as the level of credit to the private sector in terms of GDP. This chapter adopts this approach. The econometric analysis uses panel data for 40 SSA countries, of which 14 belong to the CFA franc zone. The data are averaged over five-year periods from 1992 to 2006.[5]

Regarding the right-side variables, the *financial liberalization index* is constructed for SSA countries by McDonald and Schumacher (2007) building on an earlier study by Gelbard and Leite (1999). This aggregate index is between 0 and 100, and captures whether or not interest rates are liberalized, the number of years real lending and deposit rates have been positive, the existence of a significant informal financial sector and directed credit allocation mechanisms.

The legal variables come from various sources. The *Heritage Foundation* compiles the property rights index bounded between 0 and 100 yearly. It measures the ability of individuals to accumulate private property, secured by clear laws that the state fully enforces.

The *information-sharing* index, a dummy variable recording the presence of either public or private credit registries, is taken from Djankov, McLiesh, and Shleifer (2005). The authors defined credit registries as databases managed by a government agency or a private organization that collect information on the standing of borrowers in the financial system with a view to making it available to actual and potential lenders.

Both *rule of law* and *government effectiveness* are taken from Kaufmann, Kraay, and Mastruzzi (2007). The former measures the extent to which agents have confidence in and abide by the rules of society, especially the quality of contract enforcement, the police, and the courts, as well as the likelihood of crime and violence. The latter assesses the quality of public services, the quality of policy formulation and implementation, and the credibility of the government's commitment to such policies. The two governance indicators range from −2.5 to 2.5, with higher values corresponding to better governance.

Bureaucratic quality, an index calculated by the Political Risk Services Group, measures the ability of the bureaucracy to minimize revisions of policy when governments change. It ranges from 1 (low) to 4 (high). Because *government effectiveness* and *bureaucratic quality* are highly correlated with the *rule of law*, these variables are used alternatively in the regressions as a robustness check.

Table 3.1 Test of mean differences between CFA and non-CFA Franc countries, 1992–2006

	CFA	Non-CFA	Difference	
Credit to private sector over GDP	0.10	0.15	−0.05	**
GDP per capita ($US)	851.2	913.4	−62.2	–
Inflation (log)	0.1	0.3	−0.2	**
Property rights Information sharing (percent)	36	44.9	−8.9	***
Countries with credit bureaus	57.6	21.6	36.0	***
Coverage (2008)[a]	2.5	8.8	−3.8	–
Financial liberalization	58.5	58.1	0.4	–
Rule of law	−0.9	−0.7	−0.2	*
Government effectiveness	−0.8	−0.6	−0.2	*
Bureaucracy	1.1	1.4	−0.3	–

Notes: [a]Number of individuals and firms in percent of adults. Differences in the information coverage ratio is only significant at 12 percent, reflecting a larger disparity among non-CFA countries.
*significant at 10 percent; **significant at 5 percent; ***significant at 1 percent.

Table 3.1 presents the difference of the averages of the data between CFA and non-CFA franc countries. CFA franc countries on average are not statistically different from the rest of SSA in terms of economic development (GDP per capita) or efforts to liberalize their financial sector. However, they have experienced lower inflation than other SSA countries. Despite this more favorable macroeconomic environment, credit to the private sector remains significantly lower. Consistent with our hypothesis, the indicators capturing the availability of information, property rights, and their enforcement are generally lower for the CFA zone.

3.4.2 Methodology and main results

To explain the level of financial development, a standard model where financial development depends on the level of economic development, macroeconomic conditions, and financial reform is extended to include variables capturing the availability of credit information and the quality of the legal environment. The model specification is as follows:

$$F_{i,t} = \alpha_0 + \alpha_1 * log(y_{i,t}) + \alpha_2 * log(1 + Infl_{i,t}) + \alpha_3 * CFA$$
$$+ \alpha_4 * Fl_{i,t} + \alpha_5 * X_{i,t} + u_i + v_t + \epsilon_{i,t}$$

where $F_{i,t}$ is the credit to the private sector-over-GDP ratio in country i at time t; y stands for the per capita GDP; *Infl* represents the inflation rate; *CFA* is a dummy variable for CFA franc countries; $Fl_{i,t}$ is the financial liberalization index; X is a set of institutional variables; u_i is an unobserved country-specific effect; v_t is a time dummy; and $\varepsilon_{i,t}$ is the error term.

A two-step feasible generalized least squares (FGLS) is used to estimate the model and address the problem of heteroscedasticity. This econometric approach makes it possible to estimate the impact of time-invariant variables while controlling for country-specific effects. This feature is particularly relevant for empirical models like the one used here, where the statistical significance of the coefficient of a CFA dummy variable is estimated and analyzed while additional variables capturing the institutional framework are introduced into the model.[6]

Several model specifications are estimated (Table 3.2). As expected, the level of development, captured by per capita GDP, is positively associated with financial development across all the specifications. Higher income stimulates demand for financial services, and could also translate into higher savings, thus improving the ability of the financial system to extend credit to the private sector.

The results suggest that financial liberalization is positively associated with deeper financial markets. In line with McDonald and Schumacher (2007), one would expect that easing interest rate ceilings, lowering reserve requirements and entry barriers, and reducing government involvement in credit allocation decisions would promote financial development. Also consistent with the literature, inflation has a negative effect on financial development, though this effect is significant only in some specifications.

Several specifications related to the legal environment were examined. The model was first estimated by including a dummy variable for CFA franc countries to capture their French legal heritage (column 1). The coefficient on this variable is negative and significant. A gap in financial depth between CFA and non-CFA areas cannot be explained even after controlling for the level of economic development, macroeconomic stability, and financial liberalization. This result is consistent with previous findings that countries whose legal systems are inspired by French institutions have been on average less successful in promoting financial development.

The stability of this result was tested by estimating the model over a five-year rolling window for 1992–2006 using annual observations. The finding was that the coefficient of the CFA variable was not constant over time but deteriorated. This observation would suggest that legal origin cannot be the only factor accounting for the financial development gap between CFA franc and other SSA countries. Time-variant factors have probably deteriorated, hampering the development of the financial sector in CFA countries.

To examine this hypothesis, variables capturing the availability of credit information, the strength of property rights, and their enforcement were

Table 3.2 Institutions and financial development in SSA countries, 1992–2006

	Feasible generalized least squares							
	(1)	(2)	(3)	(4)	(5)	(6)	(7)	(8)
GDP per capita (log)	0.037	0.030	0.035	0.032	0.027	0.024	0.026	0.017
	(5.03)***	(4.02)***	(4.64)***	(3.71)***	(3.20)***	(2.84)***	(4.16)***	(1.66)*
Inflation (log)	−0.037	−0.022	−0.013	−0.018	−0.002	0.005	0.008	−0.010
	(2.08)**	(2.29)**	(2.02)**	(1.61)	(0.29)	(0.49)	(0.96)	(1.12)
CFA	−0.027	−0.022	0.000	−0.032	0.010	0.010	0.008	−0.004
	(3.15)***	(2.54)**	(0.01)	(2.42)**	(0.99)	(0.59)	(0.58)	(0.25)
Financial liberalization	–	0.002	0.002	0.002	0.002	0.002	0.002	0.001
		(6.50)***	(6.70)***	(5.33)***	(5.61)***	(3.81)***	(4.50)***	(2.31)**
Property rights	–	–	0.002	–	–	0.002	0.001	0.001
			(3.74)***			(2.25)**	(2.04)**	(1.97)**
Information sharing	–	–	–	0.041	–	0.038	0.030	0.064
				(2.22)**		(1.75)*	(1.67)*	(3.33)***
Rule of law	–	–	–	–	0.039	0.030	–	–
					(3.93)***	(2.01)**		
Government effectiveness	–	–	–	–	–	–	0.066	–
							(4.72)***	
Bureaucracy quality	–	–	–	–	–	–	–	0.001
								(0.14)
Constant	−0.100	−0.226	−0.268	−0.234	−0.193	−0.182	−0.141	−0.142
	(2.27)**	(3.55)***	(4.57)***	(3.56)***	(2.94)***	(2.72)***	(2.72)***	(2.00)**
Observations	117	93	86	93	93	86	86	70
Number of countries	40	33	33	33	33	33	33	26
Chi square (Wald test)	48.3	67.7	117.8	57.1	102.5	79.4	137.7	48.3

Notes: Data are averaged over five years. Absolute value of robust t statistics in brackets; *significant at 10 percent; ** significant at 5 percent; *** significant at 1 percent.

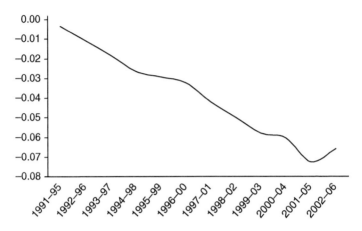

Figure 3.8 Coefficient on CFA variable (5 year rolling regression)
Source: Fund Staff calculations.

added to the model (Table 3.2, columns 3, 4, and 5). The coefficients on these variables show the expected signs and are significantly associated with the level of financial development. With a similar level of financial liberalization and similar macroeconomic conditions, countries that better protect property rights, encourage information sharing, and promote the rule of law are likely to have deeper financial systems.

Interestingly, the coefficient related to the CFA variable is no longer significant when controlling for property rights or rule of law, two institutional aspects in which CFA countries underperformed.[7] This result is confirmed when the three institutional variables are jointly included in the regression (column 6).

Alternative measures for legal enforcement were used to test for the robustness of the results. Replacing rule of law with government effectiveness and the bureaucratic quality index left the results broadly unchanged (columns 7 and 8). To address the endogeneity issue, regressions were run using the lagged values of GDP per capita and inflation. The results (see Table 3.3) confirm the positive correlation between legal institutions and financial development. Finally, given the 50 percent devaluation in the CFA franc in 1994, GDP per capita in purchasing power parity terms is used to capture differences in level of development. The results are not qualitatively different.

3.5 Summary and Conclusions

Deepening the financial sector is a complex process that goes beyond mere economic factors. This chapter has examined the reasons why financial

Table 3.3 Institutions and financial development in SSA countries: Instrumental variable approach, 1992–2006

	Feasible generalized least squares (Instrumental variable)							
	(1)	(2)	(3)	(4)	(5)	(6)	(7)	(8)
Lagged GDP per capita (log)	0.041 (5.15)***	0.034 (4.43)***	0.041 (5.92)***	0.041 (4.57)***	0.037 (4.43)***	0.031 (3.52)***	0.032 (4.91)***	0.023 (2.25)**
Lagged Inflation (log)	-0.060 (4.13)***	-0.050 (7.83)***	-0.037 (4.89)***	-0.039 (3.78)***	-0.004 (0.30)	0.001 (0.05)	0.007 (0.60)	-0.027 (2.27)**
CFA	-0.034 (3.72)***	-0.029 (3.04)***	-0.016 (1.55)	-0.042 (3.25)***	0.009 (0.84)	0.006 (0.35)	0.011 (0.70)	-0.014 (0.81)
Financial libéralization	–	0.002 (5.77)***	0.002 (6.38)***	0.002 (5.12)***	0.002 (5.40)***	0.001 (3.35)***	0.002 (4.55)***	0.001 (1.89)*
Property rights	–	–	0.001 (2.69)***	–	–	0.001 (1.74)*	0.001 (1.59)	0.001 (1.84)*
Information sharing	–	–	–	0.048 (2.73)***	–	0.038 (1.93)*	0.025 (1.43)	0.069 (3.64)***
Rule of law	–	–	–	–	0.041 (4.21)***	0.037 (2.55)**	–	–
Government effectiveness	–	–	–	–	–	–	0.071 (5.40)***	–
Bureaucracy quality	–	–	–	–	–	–	–	-0.002 (0.19)
Corruption	–	–	–	–	–	–	–	-0.156 (1.87)*
Constant	-0.107 (2.36)**	-0.159 (3.06)***	-0.363 (6.16)***	-0.214 (3.82)***	-0.165 (3.09)***	-0.222 (3.20)***	-0.209 (3.66)***	
Observations	116	92	85	92	92	85	85	70
Number of countries	40	33	33	33	33	33	33	26
Chi square (Wald test)	63.9	385.0	327.1	113.8	102.4	72.6	131.4	73.5

Notes: Data are averaged over five years. Absolute value of robust t statistics in brackets; * significant at 10 percent; ** significant at 5 percent; *** significant at 1 percent.

sectors in the CFA franc countries are shallow and traced them back to a lack of progress in improving the availability of creditor information and protecting investors. While financial liberalization and macroeconomic stability are necessary conditions for financial deepening, they are not sufficient. In this regard, the results of this chapter are consistent with a growing body of literature underscoring the role of legal factors in financial development.

The main policy implications are that expanding creditor information and strengthening creditor rights in CFA franc countries deserve more attention. These, however, are equally complex processes. The coverage of existing credit bureaus should be extended and include as much information as possible on the repayment profile of customers. This must be achieved while preserving an appropriate degree of privacy and safeguarding sensitive information. Strengthening creditor rights would require changes in legislation governing debt collection and collateral. Some reforms may have regional as well as national dimensions. Legislation on debt recovery would depend in turn on efficient property registration and land surveying in both cities and countryside. Finally, reform of the courts is vital for improving enforcement.

Further work to refine the analysis in this chapter could thus include the study of country cases where such improvements have been achieved. Although this chapter has indicated that the legal heritage is not time-invariant and policy-independent, legal origin nevertheless sets boundaries on the extent of possible institutional reforms.

Appendix 3.1   Summary statistics

Table 3A.1   Descriptive statistics, 1992–2006

Variable	Observations	Mean	Standard deviation	Minimum	Maximum
Private credit over GDP	117	0.13	0.13	0.00	0.70
GDP per capita (log)	135	6.07	1.07	4.31	8.89
Inflation (log)	121	0.19	0.49	−0.02	4.14
Property rights	115	42.14	16.03	10.00	70.00
Information sharing	144	0.32	0.43	0.00	1.00
Financial libéralization	109	58.22	25.64	1.50	100.00
Rule of law	138	−0.75	0.71	−2.27	0.87
Government effectiveness	141	−0.70	0.62	−2.17	0.77
Bureaucracy	96	1.28	0.89	0.00	3.67

Table 3A.2 Correlation matrix

Variables		1	2	3	4	5	6	7	8	9
Private credit over GDP	1	1.00	–	–	–	–	–	–	–	–
GDP per capita (log)	2	0.47	1.00	–	–	–	–	–	–	–
Inflation (log)	3	−0.19	−0.14	1.00	–	–	–	–	–	–
Property rights	4	0.38	0.31	−0.13	1.00	–	–	–	–	–
Information sharing	5	0.08	−0.05	−0.16	−0.04	1.00	–	–	–	–
Financial liberalization	6	0.41	0.34	−0.32	0.01	−0.06	1.00	–	–	–
Rule of law	7	0.56	0.51	−0.34	0.74	0.05	0.32	1.00	–	–
Government effectiveness	8	0.62	0.51	−0.30	0.63	0.18	0.33	0.87	1.00	–
Bureaucracy	9	0.32	0.55	−0.03	0.46	0.19	−0.04	0.50	0.59	1.00

Table 3A.3 Variable definitions and sources

Variable	Definition	Source
Private credit over GDP	Private credit by deposit money banks to GDP.	Financial Structure Database (2007) and International Financial Statistics (2007)
GDP per capita	Nominal gross domestic product divided by the size of the population.	International Financial Statistics (2007)
Inflation	Change in consumer price index (CPI).	International Financial Statistics (2007)
Property rights	An index measuring the ability of individuals to accumulate private property, secured by clear laws that are fully enforced by the state.	Heritage Foundation database (2007)
Information sharing	A dummy variable recording the presence of either public or private credit registries.	Djankov, McLiesh, and Shleifer (2005)
Financial liberalization	An aggregate index capturing whether interest rates are liberalized or not, the number of years real lending and deposit rates have been positive, the existence of significant informal financial sectors and presence of directed credit allocation mechanisms.	McDonald and Schumacher (2007)

Table 3A.3   Continued

Variable	Definition	Source
Rule of law	A score measuring the extent to which agents have confidence in and abide by the rules of society, and in particular the quality of contract enforcement, the police, and the courts, as well as the likelihood of crime and violence.	Kaufmann, Kraay, and Mastruzzi (2007)
Government effectiveness	A score measuring the quality of public services, the quality of the civil service and the degree of its independence from political pressures, the quality of policy formulation and implementation, and the credibility of the government's commitment to such policies.	Kaufmann, Kraay, and Mastruzzi (2007)
Bureaucracy	An index capturing the ability of the bureaucracy to minimize revisions of policy when governments change.	Top of Form Political Risk Services database (2008) Bottom of Form
Credit registry coverage	The number of individuals and firms listed by credit bureaus with current information on repayment history, unpaid debts or credit outstanding. The number is expressed as a percentage of the adult population.	Doing Business database (2008)

Notes

This paper was presented at the conference on Financial Sector Development in the CEMAC, Yaoundé, June 3–4, 2008. We wish to thank Anne Grant and Thierry Tressel, as well as seminar participants at the African Department, for useful comments.

1. See, for example, Mehran and others (1998) for a description of the reforms.
2. Large bank restructurings took place in Senegal (1988–1989), Côte d'Ivoire (1988–1989), Benin (1988–1989), Mali (1989), Niger (1989–1990), and Cameroon (1990–1997).
3. The accounting framework includes accounting standards, and a standardization and updating of procedures to be implemented with the assistance of the West African Accounting Council. The Council, however, only met once in 2004 and the technical committees have never met.

4. This group includes China, Japan, Korea, and Taiwan (Djankov, McLiesh, and Shleifer, 2005).
5. The choice of period (1992–2006) is dictated by the availability of data on the institutional variables.
6. Right-hand-side (institutional) variables exhibit relatively little variation across time. A random effects estimation may therefore be preferable because fixed effects methods can lead to imprecise estimates (Wooldridge, 2002), if the right-hand-side variables are not correlated with the error term: an assumption that the Hausman test statistic could not reject.
7. The coefficient on the CFA variable is, nevertheless, negative and significant after controlling for information sharing. This variable captures the presence of credit bureaus, but does not take into account the coverage, because time series data on the coverage of credit registries was not being available throughout the period under study.

References

Acemoglu, Daron and Johnson, Simon 2005. "Unbundling institutions." *Journal of Political Economy*, 113: 949–95.

Beck, Thorsten and Levine, Ross 2003. "Legal institutions and financial development." World Bank Policy Research Working Paper No. 3136. Washington: World Bank.

Bester, H. 1985. "Screening versus rationing in credit markets with imperfect information." *American Economic Review*, 75 (September): 850–55.

Bester, H. 1987. "The role of collateral in credit markets with imperfect information." *European Economic Review*, 31 (June): 887–99.

Boyd, John, Levine, Ross, and Bruce, D. Smith 2001. "The impact of inflation on financial sector performance." *Journal of Monetary Economics*, 47: 221–48.

Cottarelli, Carlo, Dell'Ariccia, Giovanni, and Vladkova-Hollar, Ivanna 2003. "Early birds, late risers, and sleeping beauties: Bank credit growth to the private sector in central and eastern Europe and the Balkans." IMF Working Paper WP/03/213. Washington: International Monetary Fund.

Dehesa, Mario, Druck, Pablo, and Plekhanov, Alexander 2007. "Relative price stability, creditor rights, and financial deepening." IMF Working Paper WP/07/139. Washington: International Monetary Fund.

Detragiache, Enrica, Gupta, Poonam, and Tressel, Thierry 2005. "Finance in lower-income countries: An empirical exploration." IMF Working Paper WP/05/167. Washington: International Monetary Fund.

Devinney, T.M. 1986. *Rationing in a Theory of the Banking Firm*. Berlin, Springer-Verlag.

Djankov, Simeone, McLiesh, Carales, and Shleifer, Andrei 2005. "Private credit in 129 countries." National Bureau of Economic Research Working Paper No. 11078. Cambridge, MA: NBER.

Gelbard, Enrique and Leite, Sergio 1999. "Measuring financial development in sub-Saharan Africa." IMF Working Paper WP/99/105. Washington: International Monetary Fund.

Gulde, Anne-Marie, Patillo, Catherine, and Christensen, Jakob 2006. *Sub-Saharan Africa: Financial Sector Challenges*. Washington: International Monetary Fund.

Huybens, E. and Smith, Bruce 1998. "Financial markets frictions, monetary policy, and capital accumulation in a small open economy." *Journal of Economic Theory,* 81, 353–400.

Huybens, E. and Smith, Bruce 1999. "Inflation, financial markets, and long run real activity." *Journal of Monetary Economics,* 43, 283–315.

Kaufmann, Daniel, Kraay, Aart, and Mastruzzi, Massimo 2007. "Governance Matters VI: Aggregate and individual governance indicators, 1996–2006." Policy Research Working Paper Series 4280. Washington: World Bank.

La Porta, Rafael, Lopez-de-Silanes, Florencio, Shleifer, Andrei, and Vishny, Robert 1998. "Law and finance." *Journal of Political Economy,* 106(6): 1113–55.

McDonald, Calvin and Schumacher, Liliana 2007. "Financial deepening in sub-Saharan Africa: Empirical evidence on the role of creditor rights protection and information sharing." IMF Working Paper, WP/07/203.

Mehran, Hassanali, Ugolini, Piero, Briffaus, Jean Philippe, Iden, George, Lybek, Tonny, Swaray, Stephen, and Hayward, Peter 1998. "Financial sector development in sub-Saharan African countries." IMF Occasional Paper 169. Washington: International Monetary Fund.

Sacerdoti, Emilio 2005. "Access to bank credit in sub-Saharan Africa: Key issues and reform strategies." IMF Working Paper, WP/05/166. Washington: International Monetary Fund.

Singh, Raju, J. 1992. "An imperfect information approach to the structure of the financial system." UNCTAD Discussion Paper No. 46. Geneva: UNCTAD.

Singh, Raju, J. 1994. "Bank credit, small firms, and the design of a financial system for eastern Europe." UNCTAD Discussion Paper No. 86. Geneva: UNCTAD.

Singh, Raju, J. 1997. "Banks, growth, and geography." UNCTAD Discussion Paper No 127. Geneva: UNCTAD.

Stiglitz, Joseph, E. and Weiss, Andrew 1981. "Credit rationing in markets with imperfect information." *American Economic Review,* 71, 393–410.

Tressel, Thierry and Detragiache, Enrica 2008. "Do financial sector reforms lead to financial development? Evidence from a new dataset." IMF Working Paper WP/08/265. Washington: International Monetary Fund.

Wooldridge, Jeffrey 2002. *Econometric Analysis of Cross Section and Panel Data.* Cambridge, MA: MIT Press.

4
Developing a Sound Banking System in Sub-Saharan African Countries

Louis Kasekende

4.1 Introduction

Many African countries including Ghana, Nigeria, Cameroon, Kenya, Tanzania and Uganda, experienced a banking crisis in the 80s and 90s, mainly due to weak legal and regulatory systems to support banking laws, contract enforcement, accounting and disclosure standards as well as transparency and supervision. At the same time, the weaknesses in the financial sector made it extremely difficult for the sector to support the growth process in these countries.

Academic literature and experience have shown that, a sound, developed and well functioning banking and financial system is critical for macroeconomic stability and long run economic growth (see for example, King and Levine (1993), Levine and Zervos (1998) and Ncube (2007). There is a correlation between financial sector development with broad economic growth and development, but this depends on having a sound and safe financial sector, and its ability to adequately play its role in supporting the real sector and efficiently allocate resources within the economy. An efficient financial sector mobilizes savings that are channeled into productive investments which in turn, improves the efficiency and productivity of investments. In addition, such a sound financial environment acts as a signal for a healthy economic environment, which in turn supports resource mobilization and attracts foreign capital.

The correlation of financial sector development with broad economic growth and development revolves around the ability of the financial sector to adequately play a critical role in supporting the real sector, and in the efficient allocation of resources within the economy. Regrettably, the financial sector in many African countries today ineffectively plays such a role. Indeed, given the dominance of commercial banks in the financial systems of most African countries, there is a heavy concentration of financial assets in the short term end of the market, leading to a significant unavailability of long-term financial resources to the real sector—something which, as we know, is necessary for productive investments. Credit, when available, is very costly to the average firm, as has been indicated by numerous studies detailing the inadequacy and high cost of credit as one of the main constraints to the growth of firms in Africa.

The objectives of this chapter are twofold: first, to reiterate the importance of sound finance and banking systems as a condition for economic growth, and second; to provide the reader with a general overview on the respective developments in this area in African economies. In particular, the experiences in banking and financial sectors in Uganda and Nigeria will be highlighted so as to demonstrate the positive impact of reforms.

The rest of the chapter is structured as follows. The second section provides a brief overview of the recent empirical literature on the "finance-led growth hypothesis"—which purports that the financial sector plays a more vital role in economic growth than has traditionally been ascribed to it. The third section on the "Criteria for sound financial systems" describes the characteristics of a sound banking and financial system. The fourth section on "Sound banking system and costs of Bank Failure" highlights the risks and inefficiencies of the African Banking system. The fifth section on "Status of the Banking and Finance in Africa" expounds on the general status of banking and finance in Africa while the sixth section reviews the progress made with regard to banking and financial liberalization. Section seven distills some of the key lessons from financial sector reforms in Sub Saharan Africa. This also includes a brief summary of banking and financial sector reforms in two countries: Uganda and Nigeria as illustrative case studies. The seventh section "Strengthening sub-Saharan Africa's Banking Sector: Agenda for the future" discusses the future reform agenda. Finally, the conclusion emphasizes the most important issues raised in this chapter.

4.2   Recent trends in the literature: Finance-led growth

In contrast to traditional growth theories that tend to underplay the role of the financial sector within the growth process, many new growth theories highlight the financial sector as critical driver of economic growth. In particular, the latter theories underscore the sector's role in engendering greater efficiency of the intermediation process as well as in increasing both the productivity of capital and the savings rate.

Although space considerations preclude a comprehensive examination of work in support of this "finance-led growth hypothesis", a sampling of some recent empirical work in this area is worthwhile. Beck, Levine and Loayza (2000) examined the influence of financial intermediaries and cross-country differences in legal and accounting systems on economic growth and the level of financial development respectively. On the basis of a traditional cross-section, instrumental variable procedure and recent dynamic panel techniques, they concluded that financial intermediation was positively associated with economic growth. Furthermore, their results showed that interregional differences with respect to the level of financial development can be explained by the state of the countries' legal and accounting systems. Together, these results strongly suggested that reforms toward sound banking and accounting practices can be a motor for financial development and economic growth.

In a slightly earlier study based on a sample of 49 countries, some of them from Africa, Levine (1998) focused on the relationship between the legal system, banking development, and economic growth, in the form of long-run rates of per capita GDP, capital stock, and productivity growth. The results indicated that in countries where the legal system emphasizes creditor rights and the rigorous enforcement of contracts, banks are better developed. Furthermore, the exogenous component of banking development—the component defined by the legal environment—was positively and robustly associated with per capita growth, physical capital accumulation, and productivity growth. Levine and Zervos' (1998) results supported Levine's results showing that the level of stock market liquidity and bank development were positively related with economic growth, capital accumulation and productivity improvements.

The role of the banking system was further emphasized in a work by King and Levine (1993a). In a cross-country analysis comprising 80 countries, they examined the influence of four indicators of the level of financial sector development on economic growth. These indicators represent certain characteristics of a country's banking system, reflecting the level of its development. Their results showed that the size of the financial intermediary sector to GDP, the importance of banks relative to central bank, percentage of credit allocation to private firms and the ratio of credit issued to private firms to GDP were strongly and robustly correlated with economic growth, physical capital accumulation and efficiency of capital allocation.

Several other more recent studies focusing on the influence of the banking system, including La Porta, Lopez-De-Silanes and Shleifer's (2002) have found that the efficient functioning of the banking system is negatively influenced by government ownership of banks. Likewise, Levine (2002) found that regulatory restrictions on foreign bank entry hurt the efficiency of bank operations.

Freedman et al. (2006) show that better-functioning financial systems ease the external financing constraints that impede firm and industrial expansion. It is now established that when enterprises are able to obtain credit rather than rely on internally generated funds the economy is able to growth faster. Financial development is particularly beneficial for the growth of small firms, which in developing countries provide most jobs. Moreover, Beck et al. (2004), argue that a well-developed financial system reduces income inequality, because it benefits the poor, who would otherwise remain unbanked, lack access to credit and remain outside the formal banking system, thus further supporting the notion that an efficient financial system may of itself be a source of growth.

In sum, recent banking and finance literature strongly suggests that countries with better-developed financial systems tend to grow faster; with the levels of banking development and stock market liquidity exerting a positive influence on economic growth. Furthermore, the literature supports the view that better-functioning financial systems ease the external financing constraints that commonly impede firm and industrial expansion. Accordingly, inefficient financial systems bear the risk of bank failure, which represents a major public policy concern and implies potential for economic contraction.

4.3 Criteria for a sound financial system

This section provides an overview of the characteristics and framework related to a sound finance and banking environment. As already pointed out, the proper functioning of a country's financial and banking system are critical ingredients for economic development. Figure 4.1 presents a simplified representation of the flow and transformation of the money from depositors through the banking sector into credit and investments.

A sound financial system fulfils four main functions. *First*, an efficient financing system mobilizes financial resources and collects savings (1) for investments while diversifying and controlling for risks at the same time. The financial system pools together savings from different individuals and makes them available for investment purposes. These investments can be considered as safe if financial intermediaries (particularly banks) are not only managed professionally, but are also supervised by an effective regulator, for example, a central bank. Sound financial systems entail strict corporate monitoring regimes so that efficient governance is imposed and administrative discipline is maintained. Likewise, sound financial systems entails sophisticated risk reduction safeguards (for example, bank credit

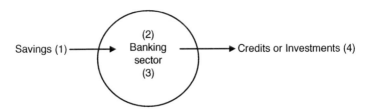

Figure 4.1 Flow and transformation of money

Note: The numbers refer to the functions of the banking system as described in the following explanation.

Source: Own illustration.

reference bureau), the portfolio diversification by financial intermediaries through hedging and leveraging, adequate insurance, and so on.

Second, the financial system has to transform savings (2) into an adequate credit supply. It is important that banks allocate money from savings to investments prudently, that is, carefully vetting borrowers and by having an asset allocation mix that ensures asset quality and preservation/adequacy of capital, while having the ability to react to changes in savings or investments without any risk to incur debts or not being able to serve depositors or investors.

Third, financial intermediaries help ensure a cost-effective and efficient system for handling financial transactions in an economy by, among other things, providing efficient payment, clearing and settlement arrangements via speedy and secure completion of transactions (3). In sound financing systems, agency problems are resolved through managing issues associated with asymmetric information, incentive conflicts among shareholders, designing well-defined contracts and procedures, to mention a few.

Finally, a sound financial system—through various financial intermediaries—plays an indispensable role in credit allocation throughout an economy (4). This is done most efficiently if projects that are implemented both economically and financially viable. An efficient financial system should provide for the possibility of exit on short notice (liquidity) so that the transaction costs of converting credit to liquid assets are generally kept low. Since most developing countries enterprises and households are too small to provide the necessary collateral, it is important to develop adequate credit technologies matching the respective situation.

4.4 Sound banking system and costs of bank failure

Whereas financial systems comprise various institutions, including, among others, credit unions, building societies, financial advisers or brokers, insurance companies, collective investment schemes, pension funds, etc., banks represent the most important intermediaries in most countries. This is certainly the case in most of sub-Saharan Africa where the banking sector is the predominant source of financing. For this reason, it is important that banks operate within not only a robust legal and regulatory framework, but one that is characterized by a high level of transparency in monetary and supervisory policies—requirements that collectively imply the existence not just of strong central banks, but also sound banking laws together with contract enforcement.

Not surprisingly, major weaknesses and short-comings in the financial system often lead to banking crises, which, in turn, invariably affect the macroeconomic environment. In particular, weak internal governance of financial intermediaries as well as supervisory inadequacies usually engender unstable banking environments.

In a study of banking crises in Africa, Daumont et al. (2004) found that heavy government intervention in the banking system, coupled with poor banking supervision and regulation were significant explanatory variables for the occurrence of such crises on the continent. The authors also highlighted a general lack of strong legal and institutional environment to support the banking system as well as the fact that unlike in other regions with relatively more sophisticated financial systems, contagion did not play an important role in propagating banking crises in Africa.

A malfunctioning banking system imposes various financial and economic costs on both depositors and other creditors. For example, depositors are hurt by declines or even losses in deposits or delays in access to savings caused bank measures imposed by the bank to recoup loan losses or delays in a bank liquidation following intervention by a regulator. What follows from there can be a downward spiral: a loss of confidence among ordinary consumers can lead to unwillingness to place savings in banks which, in turn, can wreck severe damage to a country's payments system, and thereby severely impacting economic activity.

Likewise, borrowers might find it difficult to obtain credit from other (nonbank) sources due to asymmetric information on say, their creditworthiness. Indeed, bank failures or bank capital constraints often cause rationing of credit by price and/or quantity—something that, in turn, tends to weaken consumers' and enterprises' expenditure behaviors and thereby causing economic contraction.

Elsewhere, severe problems in the banking environment almost invariably entail adverse fiscal impacts, as taxpayers are burdened with additional cleanup costs. Among other things, this can in turn lead to a loss of confidence in key institutions in a country's financial system causing bank runs and capital outflows. Recent work by Caprio and Klingebiel (2002), as well as earlier studies by Lindgren, Garcia and Saal (1996) on the overall costs of bank runs to an economy estimated output losses in the ranges of 10 percent of annual GDP on average. The costs to African economies of resolving banking crises have been significant. For example, it cost the Ugandan government the equivalent of 2 percent of GDP in 1998 to clean and prepare Uganda Commercial Bank for privatization.

4.5   Status of banking systems in Africa

Financial sectors in low-income sub-Saharan Africa are among the world's least developed. In fact, assets in most low-income African countries are smaller than those held by a single medium-sized bank in an industrial country (see, Gulde, Pattillo et al., 2006). For example, only five countries in the region can be classified as having achieved a high to medium development level in terms of the depth of the investor base and the maximum maturity of the yield curve (see Figure 4.2). Indeed, the financial sector in

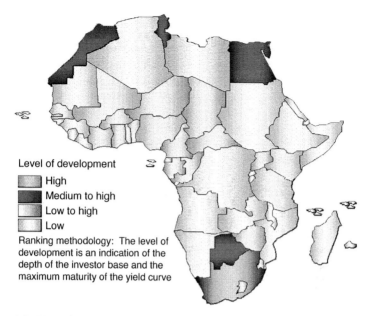

Figure 4.2   Map of the level of financial development

the majority of these countries is characterized by, among other things, low rates of private credit, which collectively accounts for only 18 percent of GDP in Africa. The poor performance of financial intermediaries can partly be explained by difficulties related to operation in a high risk environment, shocks in countries' terms-of-trade and the generally volatile climate that all financial intermediaries in Africa are facing.

A key challenge is the lack of access to financial services in most low-income sub-Saharan African. The formal financial sector does little to address the needs of the poor, whose financial services needs remain largely unmet. Furthermore, banks are disinclined to service low-income businesses or households. It is estimated that fewer than 20 percent of African adults have an account, either with a bank or with a semi-formal financial intermediary. Even in South Africa, where the financial sector is far more sophisticated, almost half of adults do not have bank accounts, while opening an account in Cameroon requires a minimum of US$700 (more than many Cameroonians earn in a year). Microfinance Institutions (MFIS) and Savings and Credit Cooperatives (SACCOs) are gradually providing some of the financial services that the formal financial sector has failed to deliver to the poor and to rural areas. However, the MFIS and SACCOs have limited outreach; capitalization and skills and in most countries such as Uganda, are not regulated or supervised by the authorities.

Another key feature of the financial sector, particularly the banking sector, in most African countries is that it tends to be oligopolistic—something that severely limits competition. In most countries, the banking sector is dominated by a few institutions, and the resulting concentration of market power leads to an inefficient pricing of financial intermediation. In turn, that translates into adverse consequences for consumers, notably costlier financial services than would otherwise be the case. Other adverse effects due to the oligopolistic nature of financial services include, generally high interest rate spreads, usually more than 10 percent (as against 3–5 percent seen in efficient markets). Likewise, credit to the economy as a ratio of total bank assets averages less than 40 percent while the ratio of private sector credit to GDP averages only about 20 percent in most countries. And apart from such unfavorable terms for consumers in terms of high prices, all the inefficiencies in financial intermediation have broader economic consequences as they reduce the overall effectiveness of monetary policy on macroeconomic aggregates.

In a nutshell, the financial system in Africa remains extremely inefficient. Banks maintain high levels of liquid assets in short-term government securities, central bank paper and cash and only a modest amount of funds are channeled to the private sector as credit.

Figure 4.3 below shows that the ratio of liquid assets to total deposits exceeds 60 percent in Uganda and Nigeria compared to 6.5 percent in the United States. Several studies suggest that banks may have valid reasons for such behavior. For example, high reserve requirements on banks remain prevalent across sub-Saharan Africa. Further, banks in sub-Saharan Africa

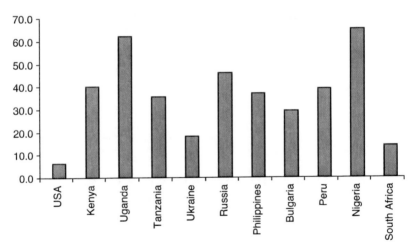

Figure 4.3   Liquidity ratios (liquid assets as a percentage of total deposits)
Source: International Financial Statistics and Freedman and Click (2006).

operate in an environment subject to higher levels of macroeconomic volatility than in the developed countries. Larger swings in real exchange and interest rates, private capital flows and terms of trade changes relative to GDP expose countries to greater risks. The higher levels of liquidity in banks may be an optimal response to generally volatile economic and financial climate.

Furthermore, credit extension is limited by the legal and regulatory bottlenecks, which make contract enforcement difficult. In addition, the widespread availability of government bonds helps to crowd out private investment and attracts banks to maintain excess liquidity rather than participate in the credit market. Low credit extension is also explained by the existence of substantial asymmetric information, which implies that lenders often know little about prospective borrowers. In addition, inadequate skills for assessing and managing risk in African banks also helps to curtail credit delivery (Freedman and Click, 2006). This is one of the reasons why sustained growth in African economies has been elusive, because such financing constraints make it very difficult for small businesses to launch, grow and expand.

4.6 Experiences with financial sector reforms in Africa

Since the mid-1990s, a number of African countries have implemented wide-ranging policy reforms with a view to making the financial system more efficient. Measures have included the elimination of directed credit lending practices, a shift to market based pricing in the sector, and a reduction of entry barriers for foreign institutions. These reforms have not only contributed to additional inflows to the continent, but have resulted in a greater diversification of risk sharing with foreign investors, financial portfolio diversification, consumption smoothening, the development of more sophisticated insurance institution to mitigate against risk, the liberalization of interest rates, as well as the removal of various quantitative restrictions. Lastly, the reform process also pushed forward both the privatization of state institutions and the increased independence of central banks which, in turn, enacted provisions for more prudential regulations of the continent's financial intermediaries.

Indeed, the financial sector in Africa has been strengthened since the 1990s, captured in part by the increase in bank deposits relative to GDP in both low and middle-income Africa countries (see Table 4.1). Similarly, M2 and liquid liabilities have risen amounting to more than 50 percent of GDP in the middle-income countries in the 2000–2004 period. With regard to private sector credit, small positive trends can be observed in the low-income region while middle-income countries have experienced a significant increase in private sector credits.

Table 4.1 Indicators of financial development by income group in sub-Saharan Africa

	Sub-Saharan Africa				Other			
	Low-income countries		Middle-income countries		Middle-income countries without South Africa		Middle-income Countries	
	1990–1999	2000–2004	1990–1999	2000–2004	1990–1999	2000–2004	1990–1999	2000–2004
Bank deposit to GDP	13.6	18.0	44.5	50.7	29.7	29.2	31.7	39.4
Private sector credit to GDP	12.3	13.3	52.1	64.0	21.5	21.0	39.4	40.3
M2 to GDP	21.9	26.9	49.8	55.6	35.0	32.1	77.3	94.2
Liquid Liabilities to GDP	19.1	23.8	47.9	53.4	34.5	32.5	36.6	41.2

Note: The Average Weight of South Africa among middle-income countries over the 2000–2004 periods is 84.5 percent.

Source: IMF, International Financial Statistics (2005).

It should be noted, however, that the positive developments in the middle-income countries have largely been driven by the changes in South Africa, with the evolution in the rest of middle-income sub-Saharan Africa actually being negative particularly with regard to quasi-money relative to GDP, which declined by almost 3 percent.

Other notable improvements with respect to the financial sector in many low-income sub-Saharan countries include general increases in the capitalization and profitability of institutions, general reductions in the risk potential due largely to enhanced risk management strategies, a general reduction of systemic problems in an increasing number of countries, and a general improvement in the conduct of monetary policies.

The implementation of far-reaching reforms in the financial sector accompanied by strengthened supervision has increased the soundness of the financial sector. However, this is yet to lead to the policy objective of a diversified efficient sector that effectively supports real sector activities. The sector has remained highly liquid and private sector credit levels relative to GDP remain very low especially in the low income sub-Saharan Africa. The experiences with regard to the timing, nature and success of banking sector reforms in Africa countries have varied across countries. In the next section, I briefly highlight the experiences of two countries, Nigeria and Uganda, with regard to financial sector reforms in recent years.

4.6.1 Banking sector reforms in Uganda

The economic reforms in Uganda, which started in 1987, placed a lot of emphasis on reestablishing macroeconomic stability. A premium was placed on controlling inflationary pressures in the economy and a shift to market based pricing thus deferring most of the structural reforms to the 1990s. Early in the 1990s, Uganda experienced a banking crisis with half of the banking sector facing insolvency. The government decided to embark on a financial sector reform with a primary objective of improving the efficiency of financial intermediation in the country. A key element of the reforms was to limit state intervention in the financial sector. Substantial legal, structural and institutional reforms were undertaken during the 1990s. One of the initial reforms involved a shift to a market based mechanism of interest rate determination. The setting of interest rates was initially linked to monthly inflation rates. In April 1992, the sale of treasury bills through periodic auctions for monetary policy purposes commenced. This provided an anchor for linking interest rates to market determined discount rates. The liberalization of interest rates was in parallel to measures that led to market based determination of the external value of the shilling in 1993. Some of the other changes in the foreign exchange market included the granting of permission to residents and nonresidents to hold foreign exchange deposits. Allowing new types of financial institutions into the financial market while at the same time weeding out insolvent banks expanded the financial sector and a premium was placed on the promotion of new types of financial products. To give impetus to market forces, new regulations in the operation of the interbank foreign exchange market were adopted.

As early as 1992, some of the direct credit programs that operated at preferential interest rates were eliminated and in 1993, the interbank money market was established in order to improve the financial system's liquidity. For monetary policy purposes, emphasis increasingly shifted to the use of open market operations. Open market operations helped improve banks portfolios. In particular, trading in repo transactions, government bills and bonds enriched portfolios. Furthermore, the introduction of the Uganda Securities Exchange (USE) in 1997 helped strengthen capital market activity and provided more investment avenues for banks. In the area of bank supervision, unified accounting principles and standard reporting systems were adopted. The Uganda Commercial Bank (UCB) which played a dominant role in the sector was successfully privatized in 2002 to Standard Chartered Bank of South Africa. This followed a botched privatization in 1998 to a Malaysian firm. Other key interventions that the Ugandan Government undertook in the financial sector include strengthening monetary policy management and efficient allocation of resources; establishment of Bank of Uganda's independence legally; establishment of a credit reference bureau; licensing of new foreign banks to spur competition; and strengthening financial regulation and supervision. In a nutshell, the late 1990s can be characterized as a period in which Uganda's reform programme moved to full ownership of market-based reforms (Holmgren, Kasekende, Atingi-Ego and Ddamulira, 1999). In the particular regard to the financial sector, the reforms resulted in a significant improvement in the soundness of the banking sector, which has had positive implications for the economy (Bank of Uganda, 2006).

To date, there are several indicators that demonstrate the degree of improvement in Uganda's financial sector, notably in banking. For example, the ratio of money and quasi-money to gross domestic product improved from 16.9 percent in 2000 to 20.7 percent in 2005 (Table 4.2). Indeed, the monetary indicators in Uganda have kept pace with other stronger economies in East Africa such as Kenya and Tanzania. These improvements in monetary indicators reflect a high and increasing degree of confidence in the economy as a result of the reform process.

The level of private credit in Uganda has remained around the average in sub-Saharan Africa, amounting to 7.3 percent of GDP in 2007 (Table 4.3). Though higher than the level recorded for Tanzania, the level of private sector credit to GDP is much lower than that in Kenya or the average for SSA. The level of monetization has improved from 16.93 percent (2000) to over 20 percent (2005); the equivalent level in 1998 was 10.3 per cent. This again compares unfavorably with the level of monetization in Kenya and Tanzania (refer to Table 4.2). The ration of overheads to total earnings is slightly higher than in case of Kenya and Tanzania, meaning that the banking sector in Uganda has higher costs which may affect the sector's profit levels (refer to Table 4.3).

In spite of the apparent low intermediation in the banking system, Ugandan commercial bank financial indicators suggest a general improvement in bank soundness and performance. The earnings of the sector at an aggregate level as depicted by the ratio of returns on assets (ROA) and returns on equity (ROE) have remained high at above 3 percent and 20 percent respectively despite the fall in real interest rate margins which are an indication of improving industry turnover. The shares of Tier 1 and Tier 2 capital to risk-weighted assets also indicate sufficient capitalization of banks at about 7 percent and 1.5 percent respectively between 2000 and 2007. In addition, bank liquidity indicators continue to depict a decline in liquidity in banks with the share of liquid assets to total deposits falling from 84.2 percent in 2000 to 46.7 percent in 2007 while the share of liquid assets to total assets dropped from 62.2 percent to 30.2 percent in the same period. The reduction in liquidity seems to confirm the view that more active resources are now being channelled by banks to private sector lending as opposed to the skewed investment in short-term government securities that was the practice in the period 2000 to 2004. In addition, the decline in liquidity did not occur at the expense

Table 4.2 Financial deepening in Uganda

Indicators	2000	2001	2002	2003	2004	2005
Uganda						
GDP (US$m)	5,775.8	5,865.2	5,763.6	6,261.3	6,990.6	8,446.5
Monetary Growth (M2)	18.1	9.2	25.0	17.9	11.1	16.5
Money and Quasi-Money as % of GDP	16.9	16.5	20.1	20.7	20.5	20.7
Kenya						
GDP(US$m)	12,604.1	12,983	13,147	14,987	16,249	19,132
Monetary Growth (M2)	4.9	2.8	11.7	11.9	13.7	10.0
Money and Quasi-Money as % of GDP	35.2	34.1	37.6	38.3	38.7	37.9
Tanzania						
GDP (US$m)	1,387.6	1,259.8	1,191.6	1,906.5	2,382.5	2,612.8
Monetary Growth (M2)	14.8	17.1	25.1	16.6	19.2	38.2
Money and Quasi Money as % of GDP	19.2	19.8	21.7	22.4	23.0	27.7

Source: ADB Statistics Department; IMF: World Economic Outlook and International Financial Statistics.

of asset quality. Banks have generally maintained their level of asset quality as indicated by the share of earning assets to total assets lying at about 80 percent during the period 2000 to 2007. The second indicator of asset quality (share of nonperforming assets to total advances) shows an improvement in asset quality as it fell from 9.8 percent in 2000 to 4.1 percent in 2007 attesting to gains that the sector has recorded via the adoption of a risk-based portfolio management. The challenge that remains is for banks to expand credit further without undermining the recent improvements in asset quality. Table 4.4 shows some of the key commercial bank financial indicators.

Other areas where Uganda has made tremendous progress are in capitalization of commercial banks and capital requirements. New capital requirements implemented in 200 raised the minimum unimpaired capital to Shs 2 billion and Shs 1 billion for banks and credit institutions respectively. In 2004, after enactment of the Financial Institutions Act 2004, the minimum unimpaired capital was raised to Shs 4 billion for banks. thus increasing confidence in the financial system.

Table 4.3   Uganda's financial system

Country	Liquid liabilities/GDP	Private credit/GDP	Loan/ Deposit ratio	Overheads/ Total earning assets	Net interest margin/Total earning assets
Uganda	19.0	7.3	50.0	9.1	13.4
Kenya	37.8	25.7	78.9	5.7	7.6
Tanzania	20.2	5.7	38.1	6.9	7.3
SSA	27.7	17.0	72.3	6.3	8.0
Low income	26.4	13.6	70.7	5.8	7.5

Source: ADB Statistics Department; IMF: World Economic Outlook and International Financial Statistics.

In terms of access, the banking system in Uganda is comparable with other countries such as Kenya, Tanzania and Namibia (see Table 4.5). To date, Uganda has relatively higher numbers of ATMS per 1,000 sq km than all the three countries. However, there is need to increase the number of branches per 100,000 persons and the number of deposit account per 1,000 people. To improve the efficiency and security of the banking system, in 2003 the Government of Uganda launched an electronic cheque clearing system, in which the processing and clearing of cheques is automated.

The Government of Uganda also used micro-finance as a vehicle for providing market-responsive financial services to the population, as part of the objective to reduce poverty. In addition, it has encouraged the establishment of SACCOs in each unit of local government. There are currently SACCOs in 381 out of 970 sub countries, many of which are located in rural areas where there are no other formal banking services (MFEP, 2008). However, the concern remains that the financial system is not meeting the needs of vital areas in the private sector for poverty reduction. Trade and other sectors catering mainly importers continue to be major recipients of credit within the private sector, while lending to agriculture, where the bulk of the population earn a living, remains rather low. Banks view agriculture as highly risky and a number of players in the agricultural sector do not meet the collateral requirements set by banks. On the whole, the picture from Uganda reveals an example of low-income sub-Saharan country that has discernible progress in some key areas of its financial sector. Nonetheless, key challenges remain, requiring additional initiatives and reforms. Not only is the support by commercial banks (i.e., the country's principal financial intermediaries) to the real sector still weak, but corporate lending is concentrated in short term lending, and bank balance sheets are dominated by short-term deposits. Likewise, Uganda's banking sector

Table 4.4 Key commercial bank financial ratios and indicators, 2000–2007

	Dec-00	Dec-01	Dec-02	Dec-03	Dec-04	Dec-05	Dec-06	Dec-07
Profitability indicators (Annualized)								
1. Return on Ave. equity	59.18	45.56	30.58	43.16	37.81	29.63	28.32	31.41
2. Return on Ave. Assets	4.77	4.48	2.99	4.51	4.25	3.55	3.37	3.86
Capital adequacy indicators								
1.Tier I/RWAs	17.35	20.51	19.37	14.45	18.71	16.75	16.53	17.77
2.Tier II/RWAs	3.16	2.55	2.69	2.50	1.78	1.55	1.49	1.69
Asset quality								
1. NPAs/Total Advances	9.82	6.52	2.97	7.25	2.19	2.32	2.95	4.11
2. Earning assets/Tot. Assets	80.91	79.96	83.57	83.44	80.94	77.58	78.55	79.24
3. Acc loan loss Prov/ NPAs	61.71	70.00	81.46	76.52	97.76	103.83	74.44	71.78
4. Spec Prov/NPAs	50.50	61.19	53.17	62.90	45.10	66.79	41.44	52.47
Liquidity indicators								
1. Liquid Assets/Tot. Dep.	84.15	87.59	86.08	59.46	63.08	60.03	50.66	46.72
2. Liquid Assets/Tot. Assets	62.23	65.30	64.98	45.38	46.39	42.23	33.64	30.09
3. Advances/Deposits	39.94	35.33	36.39	38.35	37.40	48.46	57.50	60.17

Notes: Figures are reported as at end December of each year. The figures from closed banks are excluded from the data. Capital excludes end of year profits and does not consider end of reporting period for individual banks. RWA: Risk Weighted Assets; NPA: Non Performing Assets; Tot Dep: Total Deposits; Tot Assets: Total Assets; Spec Prov: Special Provisions for bad debts, Tier 1 Core capital, Tier II Supplementary capital, Acc loan loss Prov Provisions for accumulated loan losses, Ave average.

Source: Bank of Uganda.

is not only very oligopolistic, but deposit transformation rates remain low, and intermediation inefficiency reduces the effectiveness of monetary policy.

4.6.2 Banking sector reforms in Nigeria

Reforms in Nigeria's financial sector began in 2004 and are more recent compared to Uganda, which makes an interesting contrast. Prior to the reforms, Nigeria's financial sector, and in particular, its banking sector was plagued with numerous ills: weak corporate governance (reflected by high turnovers in Board and management staff), inaccurate reporting and other noncompliance with regulatory requirements, as well as frequent ethical

Table 4.5   Outreach of the banking system

Country	Branches per 1,000 sq km	Branches per 100,000 persons	ATM per 1,000 sq km	ATMs per 100,000 persons
Uganda	0.7	0.5	0.9	0.7
Kenya	0.9	1.6	0.6	1.0
Tanzania	0.2	0.6	0.1	17.0
Namibia	0.1	4.5	0.3	12.1
	Loan accounts per 1,000 people	Deposit accounts per 1,000 people	Average loan size/Income per capita	Average deposit size/Income per capita
Kenya	6.0	47.0	10.7	3.9
Tanzania	–	70.0	–	6.3
Namibia	81	423.0	5.16	1.3

Source: ADB Statistics Department; IMF: World Economic Outlook and International Financial Statistics.

breaches (see, Elumelu, 2005). This all led to gross insider abuses, resulting in huge nonperforming insider related credits; fraud, and even relatively frequent insolvency, as shown by the negative capital adequacy ratios and shareholders' funds that had been completely eroded by operating losses; weak capital base; and over-dependency on public sector deposits, and neglect of small and medium class savers.

Earlier, in 2003, the Nigerian government had initiated a banking industry deregulation exercise which had reduced the number of commercial banks to 89. However, even the regulatory framework that had covered that exercise had been weak and the new entrants were poorly managed and capitalized. These factors led to an overhaul of the banking sector in 2004.

The major reforms, which started in July 2004, had far-reaching effects. First, major consolidation of the banking sector—largely through various incentives for mergers and acquisitions—resulted in the number of commercial banks declining to 25 by 2006 (see Table 4.5). More significantly, the reforms resulted in an increase of the minimum Shareholders' Fund for banks to over US$200 million (up from only US$15 million in the pre-reform period). Elsewhere, other reforms sought to encourage banks to play a more active and concerted developmental role in the Nigerian economy, while also being competent and competitive players in the wider regional and global financial systems. Lastly, the reforms required most of Nigeria's banks to recapitalize to meet new minimum shareholders' fund requirements, largely through private placements, right issues and public offers; and sound macroeconomic environment.

Overall, the 2004 bank restructuring went a long way toward helping Nigeria's banking sector evolve into a sounder one with more sophisticated financial products than during the period before the reforms. Not only did Nigerian banks develop new products for consumer finance to serve the country's growing middle class, but they also developed new products for corporate and project finance which, in turn, allowed them to finance large infrastructure projects in the oil and gas, telecommunications, and other capital-intensive sectors.

In its 2007 bank Supervision Annual report, the Central bank of Nigeria noted that asset quality and efficiency have improved since the restructuring of the banking sector. The ratio of nonperforming credits to total credit has declined from 18.1 percent in 2005 to 8.8 percent in 2006 and 8.4 percent in 2007. The ratio of bad debt provision to total credit has also declined from 19.1 percent in 2005 to 6.3 percent in 2006, though it went up in 2007 to 8.1 percent. In terms of efficiency in the banking sector, the return on assets increased from 1.6 percent in 2006 to 3.3 percent in 2007.

Yet, whereas Nigeria has made tremendous progress in its financial sector reforms, many challenges remain if the country is to maximize opportunities in the sector. In particular, the Nigerian banks still have a long way in reducing their costs of operation; in increasing their market power; in reducing their earnings volatility and; and in harnessing economies of scale.

In the section that follows, I will return to a broader discussion of some general lessons from sub-Saharan experience with banking and financial sector reforms in recent years.

Table 4.6   Pre and post reform era in Nigeria

	2004 (Pre-reform)	2006 (Post-reform)
Number of banks	89	25
Regulatory capital to risk-weighted assets (%)	14.6	25.8
Return to Equity (%)	27.4	1.9
Liquid Assets to total assets (%)	47.5	60.8

Source: Nigerian Authorities.

4.7   Lessons from banking and financial sector reforms in sub-Saharan Africa

The experience of sub-Saharan Africa with financial sector reforms has a number of important lessons for the sustainability of the reforms and the attainment of the policy objective of support to real sector activities. These lessons are mainly supported by the analysis of the impact of reforms in Uganda and Nigeria. *First,* removing barriers to entry in the financial sector does not necessarily increase competition. Across Africa, in countries that have deregulated the financial sector, one finds that the new (mostly indigenous) banks remain small and fragile, and their entry into the system did not introduce any competition. Moreover, despite years of financial liberalization policies in many African countries, government ownership of banks in a number of countries has actually changed very little, which may explain why there has been little financial development, or in some cases, increased financial instability. In addition, the increase in the number of banks also drastically increased the supervision costs to the central banks, both financial and human resource wise.

Second, with liberalization, intermediation margins increased or stabilized at high levels, making it difficult to support the growth and development of the private sector. Liberalization did not eliminate costs imposed on banks by an inefficient institutional system in most of Africa. *Third,* it is important to balance outreach and profitability when reforming the financial sector. In much of Africa where the financial sector has been liberalized, there remain significant gaps in the provision of services by the formal financial system. Many micro enterprises and other small producers still have tremendous difficulty accessing formal finance.

Fourth, government exit from ownership and management of financial intermediaries did not necessarily get rid of the sort of destructive patronage that characterized many state-owned institutions. Indeed, liberalization often times simply meant that there was a substitution of state banks with highly connected private banks, some of which were only involved in "round-tripping" activities.

Fifth, the cleanup of a country's financial system after years of overregulation is a costly exercise. Here, a case from Uganda is illustrative. Preparing the Uganda Commercial Bank for privatization—a formerly state-owned institution, which was the country's largest commercial bank—cost a massive 2 percent of the country's GDP in 1998, while the recapitalization of the country's Central Bank cost 1 percent of GDP. There are several other similar examples from elsewhere in Africa.

Sixth, when privatizing state-owned banks, it is not only advisable to get strategic partners with substantial financial, technical and management resources at their disposal, but also, partners with long established international banking reputations to protect. Similarly, it is advisable to leave as much of the restructuring to the new owners than for a government or a central bank to undertake the exercise.

Finally, the success of the reforms heavily depends on a government's willingness to take hard decisions. In Nigeria for example, the success of Central Bank-led reform effort to consolidate the country's banking system heavily depended on the support of the Federal Government, which saw financial restructuring as part of a wider economic reform program. Yet, selling the reforms to the country's politicians was never a foregone conclusion. Not only did reformers have to deal with politicians who stood to lose control of the financial sector, but must also carefully manage tensions between strict prudential requirements and politically motivated goals and objectives, and, even the ever-present danger of the entire process being hijacked by politicians.

4.7.1 Remaining challenges

While African countries have had reasonable successes in their first and second generation financial sector reforms, as discussed above, much work remains, particularly if those reforms are to be deepened enough to effectively deal with lingering inefficiencies and more challenging problems in the financial systems of many African countries. It is against that backdrop that differences of opinions have developed as to the best options with regard to both deepening the earlier reforms as well as to addressing the remaining challenges.

To be sure, differences in opinion at this stage would be both expected and understandable, especially given the fact that the first and second generation reforms dealt with the more obvious issues, such as macroeconomic stability, liberalization of interest rates, abolition of credit allocation and controls, and so on. In general, these are issues that most policy makers and development experts can agree on (even though their implementation was never very easy, given the political nature of these reforms in most African countries). However, there was a general consensus on what needed to be done, and each country had to chart the most appropriate political course to get them done.

In order to discuss the differences of opinion that exist in Africa today regarding the third generation financial sector reform measures, it might be useful to quickly review the main areas in which the financial sector has not been able to fully play the role expected of it in the continent's economic development. This is what I briefly do in the next section.

4.8 Strengthening sub-Saharan Africa's banking sector: Agenda for the future policies

Significant obstacles remain in national and regional efforts to strengthen banking systems in African countries. In many countries, many of the fundamental causes of unsound banking systems persist including poor internal governance, inadequate supervision, lack of transparency about the operation and financial condition of banks. Thus, to spur growth and poverty reduction, governments in Africa should take measures to strengthen and enhance the soundness, functioning, development and deepening of the banking and financial sector.

Reform measures are required in Africa to address some of the problems that underpin the root causes for the lack of credit to the private sector. There are numerous legal and regulatory reforms that could help to expand the flow of credit to the private sector. Contract enforcement can be improved through a variety of measures including easier debt collection procedures, simplified judicial procedures and establishment of special commercial courts to ensure speedier contract enforcement. A good start would be to make more robust the debt recovery processes and to simplify the myriad bankruptcy laws in many countries. Making it possible for creditors to foreclose on collateral and obtain faster repayment would provide a boost to credit support to the private sector. In addition, there is need for supportive fiscal policies. In a number of countries, financing requirements for the government deficit have diverted resources from credit delivery to the private sector. Reductions in domestic borrowing can help to drive down local interest rates and spur more lending to the private sector for new investment projects (Freedman and Click, 2006).

There are problems related to asymmetric information in the credit markets which must be tackled by governments to support credit assessments of potential borrowers. Governments can enact laws and regulations that promote sharing of credit information among lenders and credit bureaux. The increased sharing of information will create competition among banks, will reduce the likelihood of defaults, help to lower interest rates and increase the levels of credit delivered by banks to the private sector (Jappelli and Pagano, 1999).

Improving the banking infrastructure necessitates strengthening economic and prudential regulations and the supervisory capacity of a country's banking system. Prudential guidelines are needed to specify the terms and conditions of loans to insiders clearly and explicitly. Likewise, prudential regulations for screening owners and managers of new banks are just as important. Experience has shown that most small banks fail as a result of poor management or so called crony lending. More sophisticated systems for screening of owners and managers of these financial institutions can go a long way in precluding potentially disastrous bank failures, among other benefits.

Banks must also be encouraged to be transparent in their operations, through strengthening the banking information system, along with the accounting and auditing and reporting framework. The development of a strong accounting profession in particular, can ensure the establishment of uniform accounting standards that accurately and properly reflect each bank's true financial condition. Likewise, a good auditing infrastructure provides a system of checks and balances which helps to not only improve accounting and administrative controls, check compliance with laws and regulations, but also, to detect and prevent fraud. Similarly, additional reforms to promote more reliable financial information can help improve financial disclosures by African banks and other financial intermediaries, and in turn make investors more willing to risk their funds.

Credit extension to the private sector is also impacted negatively by the limited technical skills of banks and their capacity not only to evaluate but also to manage risk. Recent efforts to remove barriers to the entry of foreign-owned banks are likely to help improve the technical skill component of banks. Entry of foreign banks with skills in credit delivery will increase competition with domestic banks in credit delivery. Typically, the presence of foreign firms prompts domestic banks to more aggressively pursue lending opportunities with traditionally marginalized sectors or with small and medium scale enterprises. Other innovative schemes like initial loan guarantees to underserved sectors by government might also help to overcome the high-risk aversion that banks associate with these sectors.

The banking system in many African countries is still highly concentrated, with a few institutions dominating the sector. Excessive concentration of deposits within a few institutions constitutes a potential problem for the economy in case of failure. It can also result in cartelization, reducing efficiency, while amplifying moral hazard and transaction costs. There is, in this regard, a need to restructure the system and promote competition among Africa's financial sector, for both banks and nonbank institutions. In restructuring the banking system in particular, there is need to encourage greater diversification of operations across banks than is currently the case. Likewise, rural financial institutions directed at small farmers (such as community banks) should also be developed and deepened, as they constitute another approach for promoting competition among the financial sector.

Another important area that needs much attention across almost all financial intermediaries in Africa, is the need to upgrade services, particularly in relation to the efficiency improvements in payments systems. Speedy and efficient payment systems are pre-requisites for the development of a market economy. Indeed, in the absence of efficient and disciplined payments system based on trust and efficient service, economic agents are reluctant to accept promissory notes (e.g., cheques) as substitutes for cash.

Lastly, few African financial intermediaries have given much attention to following international "best practices" such as the Basel Accords. Only in isolated cases such as South Africa, which adopted Basel I capital ratio of 8 percent in the 1980s as an instrument to convert building societies to Banks, are reigning international "best practices" implemented. South African exceptionalism is also notable in that it may be the only sub-Saharan African country that has implemented Basel II. Basel II hinges on three pillars (minimum capital requirements, supervision and market discipline), all which support the financial stability objectives. At regional level, joint supervision initiatives/efforts would enable countries to make improvements in domestic regulation, particularly as cross border listing and trading by African banks has increased in recent years. It would also assist countries in the region to leverage the scarce human resources. Central banks in the East African Community (EAC), for example, have stepped up cooperation, with joint supervision efforts and harmonization of standards, further strengthening the banking sector in the region. There is need for replication of these efforts in other regions.

Indeed, to support the additional requisite financial sector reforms in Africa, countries need to strengthen existing instruments for monitoring various indicators and progress in the sector—something that will entail making substantial financial and human resources investments in data collection systems and improving data quality.

4.9   Conclusions

This chapter sought to briefly highlight some of the key changes made in the financial sector in much of low-income, sub-Saharan Africa. The chapter also drew attention to illustrative case studies from the recent reforms in both Uganda's and Nigeria's banking sectors, where reforms have given some impetus to the private sector while in turn boosting economic confidence. For the most part, these reforms have engendered real improvements in the financial sectors of both countries.

Nonetheless, most African countries still face daunting challenges underlying weaknesses across the continent. Beyond the first- (and for some countries, second-generation) of reforms, much work still needs to be done to complement financial liberalization and ensure banking stability. The critical challenge is to find mechanisms through which savings in the financial systems are channeled to investment in productive enterprises rather than maintained in high levels of liquid assets. In addition, there is need for enhancing depth in the sector to improve the access of the poor and small-scale producers to financial services plus boosting medium and long-term credit delivery.

For many countries in Africa, this means improving the financial sector's infrastructure through strengthening prudential regulations and the legal frameworks, restructuring the breadth of the sector, deepening capital markets and improving the access of the poor and small-scale producers to financial services.

Note

Chief Economist, African Development Bank, The views expressed in this chapter are those of the author only, and the presence of them, or of links to them, on the IMF and African Development Bank Group websites does not imply that the IMF or the African Development Bank Group, their Executive Boards, or their managements endorses or shares the views expressed in the chapter.

References

Bank of Uganda 2006. *Bank Uganda Achievements and Contributions 1987–2005*. Bank of Ugan Kampala, Uganda: Mimeo.

Beck, T., Demirguc-Kunt, A., and Levine, R. 2004. "Stock markets, banks, and growth: Panel evidence." *Journal of Banking & Finance*, 28(3): 423–42.

Beck, T., Levine, R., and Loayza, N. 2000. "Financial intermediation and growth: Causality and causes." *Journal of Monetary Economics*, 46: 31–77.

Caprio, G., Jr., and Klingebiel, D. 2002. "Episodes of systemic and borderline banking crises. In *Managing the Real and Fiscal Effects of Banking Crises*, eds., D. Klingebiel and L. Laeven. World Bank Discussion Paper No. 428, 31–49.

Daumont. R., Gall, F., and Leroux, F. 2004. "Banking in sub-Sarahan Africa: What went wrong?" IMF Working Paper WP/04/55.

Elumelu, O. 2005. "Investment, finance, and banking in Nigeria: Evolution and new opportunities." Paper Presented at the 2005 U.S.—Africa Summit of the Corporate Council on Africa, Baltimore, USA.

Freedman, P.L. and Click, R.W. 2006. "Banks that don't lend? Unlocking credit to spur growth in developing countries." *Development Policy Review*, 24(3): 279–302.

Gulde, A.M., Pattillo, C.A., Christensen, J., Carey, K.J., and Wagh, S. 2006. *Sub-Saharan Africa: Financial Sector Challenges*. Washington, DC: International Monetary Fund.

Holmgren, T., Kasekende, L., Atingi-Ego, M., and Ddamulira, D. 1999. "Aid and reform in Africa: The Case of Uganda." In *Aid and Reform in Africa: Lessons from Ten Case Studies*, eds. Devarajan, Shantayanana, David Dollar and Torgny Holmgren. The World Bank (2001).

International Financial Statistics 2006. IMF Publication. Washington, DC.

Jappelli, T. and Pagano, M. 1999. "Information sharing, lending and defaults: Cross-country evidence." CSEF Working Paper No. 22. University of Salerno.

King, R.G. and Levine, R. 1993a. "Finance and growth: Schumpeter might be right." *The Quarterly Journal of Economics*, 108 (3), August: 717–37.

King, R.G. and Levine, R. 1993b. "Finance, entrepreneurship, and growth: Theory and evidence." *Journal of Monetary Economics*, 32: 513–42.

La Porta, R., Lopez-de-Silanes, F., and Shleifer, A. 2002. "Government ownership of banks." *Journal of Finance*, February, 57(1): 265–301.

Levine, R. 1998. "The legal environment, banks, and long-run economic growth." *Journal of Money, Credit, and Banking*, August, 30(3, part 2): 596–613.

Levine, R. 2002c. "Denying foreign bank entry: Implication for bank interest margins." Unpublished manuscript, University of Minnesota.

Levine, R. and Zervos, S. 1998. "Stock markets, banks, and economic growth." *American Economic Review*, June, 88(3): 537–58.

Lindgren, Carl-Johan, Garcia, Gillian and Saal, Matthew, I. 1996. *Bank Soundness and Macroeconomic Policy.* Washington: IMF. Part I (Worldwide experience with bank fragility), 3–35.

Ministry of Finance, Planning and Economic Development 2008. Budget Statement 2007/8 MFEP, Kampala Uganda.

Ncube, Mthuli 2007. 'Financial services and economic development in Africa.' *Journal of African Economies,* 16(Supplement 1): 13–57.

5

From Informal Finance to Formal Finance—Lessons from Linkage Efforts

Ernest Aryeetey and Ama Pokuaa Fenny

5.1 Introduction

Most African economies are characterized by a financial system that has both formal and informal segments. The informal financial sector is often involved with financial transactions that are not regulated by central bank supervisory authorities. Unlike formal institutions, such transactions rarely use legal documentation or the legal system to enforce contracts. However, within these two broad segments are several different types of operators that usually have very little contact with one another and whose clients often do not overlap. Even when the clients overlap, the clients are able to sort out clearly which aspects of their financial business will be handled by which financial arrangement. It is generally difficult to determine how the allocation of financial assets among different operators is made since this is not determined solely on the basis of the intrinsic return on the asset (Aryeetey, 1997). The same low level of interaction among the operators is also observable, except in a few cases. The fact that interaction among the operators is minimal ensures that the flow of funds among the operators is very limited and does not allow the financial system to act as an effective and efficient intermediary at most times (Nissanke and Aryeetey, 1998).

Many analysts who see informal finance as a consequence of inadequate formal financial systems expected that financial sector reforms will lead to a decline of informal finance. There is no sign of that happening in any country yet. On the contrary, there are signs of formal institutions borrowing from the informal sector. It is the expectation of that this relationship will increase that often leads to calls for properly regulated linkages to be developed between formal and informal finance. It is argued that integrating these two segments of financial markets and ensuring effective linkages between them can improve the efficiency of the financial system by enabling different agents to specialize for different market niches and by facilitating the flow of savings and credit up and down the system. Whatever transformation the informal sector will undergo then will be driven the desire to access the resources of the formal sector. It will not diminish or disappear so long as the socioeconomic structures of African countries require informality.

But not all analysts believe in the need to develop strong linkages between formal and informal finance at all cost. This position is often driven by the notion that the informal sector cannot really change in view of social structures. Floro and Ray (1997) considered evidence from the Philippines and suggested that in the absence of a competitive informal market a vertical linkage that allows banks or formal financial institutions to provide credit through informal lenders was unlikely to lead to an expansion of the supply of credit significantly. This was because credit availability was driven by a whole range of complex arrangements between lenders and borrowers that led to strategic cooperation or collusive behavior among informal lenders.

While the debate about how best to reach small or marginal borrowers has been going on, there have emerged several other financing arrangements that seek in part to address the same issues confronting the financial systems. There are organizations that are registered under nonfinancial legislation, for example as cooperatives, businesses or non-governmental organizations (NGOs) and micro financial institutions (MFIs) are sometimes referred to as "semiformal", acting as a link between what is considered formal and informal. For instance, in the past two decades, the emphasis has been on establishing microfinance schemes as the best alternative to ensuring access to financial services for small borrowers. This has been based on the success of institutions such as the Grameen Bank. In spite of these efforts, many potential clients are still not reached and a number of (MFIs struggle to operate, remaining very dependent on donor support. The proliferation of microfinance institutions in many countries has not necessarily benefited clients since only a few of these institutions have reached the scale necessary for the provision of efficient financial services. This situation has led to new calls for the adoption of methods that will help bridge the gap between those who can provide financial services and those who require those services. Thus, in general, complementarity in service provision is often touted as the way forward. Lately, there have been quite a number of studies into the development of new strategies that will encourage linkage between the informal and formal financial markets as a possible solution to this problem, with microfinance seen as a step in the progression of the informal sector.

Despite the existence of both informal and formal financial arrangements in sub-Saharan Africa and the fact that they appear to be both growing in many countries, the problem still remains how to ensure that small borrowers have significantly improved access to credit. The problem has always been that credit from informal sources was often not seen to have the attributes essential for investment in small growing businesses. It was often too little, interest rates were too high or the maturity periods were too short. That does not seem to have changed much in the last decade.

The potential for transforming the informal sector and for developing financial linkages depends on how developed a country's financial system is. In countries where both formal and less formal institutions are weak, the potential for transformation and linkage is extremely low. In contrast, in countries where formal and less formal institutions are both strong the potential for linking up is quite high (Conning and Kevane, 2002). There is the obvious need for national policy frameworks that have appropriate levels of incentive and regulatory policies as a context for achieving these desired linkages. It is also necessary for this framework to draw on broader economic relationships by ensuring that the approach is truly driven by demand from the real sector. It has been argued that as countries grow the potential for financial linkages grow but it seems best to implement policies that provide the platform for these linkages to come about.

The main argument of this chapter is that the "transformation" of the informal financial sector can take place if driven by a need to increase access to the resources of the formal financial sector. But that will first have to come from increased and expanded linkages in the two sectors. The growth of the formal sector is not necessarily going to reduce the size of the informal sector. In this chapter, we explore the existing literature on financial linkages for proven examples of financial linkages in some developing countries. In doing this, the chapter assesses what role still remains for the informal sector with the gradual growth of formal financial sectors in SSA. In providing a summary of the state of both formal and informal financial arrangements in Africa, the chapter notes the changes in the environment for their operations, including the transformation of some operations into microfinance activity. The chapter also examines the extent to which informal financial arrangements are still useful despite the presence of growing and diversifying formal institutions. It discusses whether microfinance institutions are sustainable in both the short-run and the long-run. Some thought is also given to the current phenomenon of microfinance institutions transforming themselves into more formal intermediaries such as banks and banks engaging in microfinance activities. The role that governments may have in bringing about a greater complementary relationship between informal and formal finance is discussed, bearing in mind the several past failures of government support through state-owned banks. The chapter finally explores the mechanisms that could be used to facilitate the transition for individual institutions from the informal to the formal sector by developing effective linkages and adopting the necessary policies.

5.2 Transforming the informal sector: A framework for linking informal and formal finance

The literature on financial linkage is based on modern economic theory which explains that, due to information asymmetry in financial markets and the lack of regulation of credit markets, there is a relevant mismatch of resources and abilities between formal and informal lenders (Armendáriz de Aghion and Morduch, 2005; Bell, 1990 and Varghese, 2005). This creates a dualistic system with formal financial institutions on one hand and informal financial markets on the other. Formal financial institutions have to their advantage extensive infrastructure and systems, funds and opportunities for portfolio diversification which allows them to present a wide range of services to their clients. However, they are mostly accessible to populations in the upper and middle income strata and very often inaccessible to rural and the urban low income populations.

As seen earlier, in contrast, informal financial institutions operate close to rural populations and have information on their clients which enables them to conduct their operations productively. However, given their mode of operation they are unable to offer services beyond a small geographic area, resulting in highly concentrated loan portfolios. We have argued that it is possible to link the advantages of both formal and informal segments to overcome the gaps in financial markets (Aryeetey, 1994). For example, commercial banks may provide on-lending facilities to informal lenders. Or banks may link up with informal groups which will distribute or collect funds, or act as a guarantor for credit security through collective responsibility or peer monitoring (Seibel, 1989 and 2006).

Attempts to integrate informal financial institutions into formal ones have been wide and varied. Although the institutionalization of informal activities into the operations OF formal establishments may not be desirable in practice (Ghate, 1990; Seibel, 1989), many policy-makers today recognize that integration is possible through other ways. Ghate and Seibel suggest three ways:

- infusing into the formal institutions some of the flexibility of informal operations;
- strengthening the structure and performance of informal market operations;
- developing linkages between the formal and informal financial sectors.

The first two options are considered appropriate when the two sectors can potentially compete in providing finance, but the formal sector lacks the technology to deal with small-scale borrowers and savers while informal agents are not subject to the competitive pressure to improve their performance.

However, the third option seems to be the most practical, given the high risk factors and high cost of transactions that characterize the informal financial sector in many developing countries as well as the limited capital-base and excessive cost of funds which prohibits further expansion of informal agents/institutions. The development of better linkages could be seen as leading to a financial system where the formal and informal markets could specialize and function complementarily, reinforcing each others' strengths.

In spite of the advantages of such a system, there is also the view that the different financial markets exist as a result of the different conditions and requirements of the population, which may lead to either complementary or competitive situations. Changing these institutions may therefore not achieve the intended results, as the circumstances may not be ready for such a change. Rather, informal institutions should be strengthened so that the many small-scale borrowers can still have access to the small-scale credit they need for their businesses (Schrader, 1994).

However, advocates of financial integration emphasize that they do not seek to do away entirely with informal financial institutions, since they have a lasting comparative advantage in serving certain segments of the financial market especially in Africa. Measures to link and integrate formal and informal finance are necessary to take advantage of specialization, not simply to extend the formal sector's frontier (Seibel, 1989). What this means is that informal finance will continue to be relevant and significant no matter how extensive formal finance becomes so long as the socioeconomic circumstances of people do not change drastically.

5.2.1   Possible approaches to financial linkages

A number of strategies have been proposed for the development of linkages between informal finance and formal finance. In each case, it is a matter of a formal institution deciding what form of relationship it would like to have with an existing informal arrangement, or what supporting role it would like an informal unit to play. In the case of a relationship with microfinance institutions it is possible for the formal institution to modify its own structures in order to collaborate with the MFI or even allow the MFI to run specific aspects of the bank's operations.

A number of Asian practices have followed what has been described in the literature as two models. These involve (1) banks working with self-help groups directly to reach clients and (2) using the self-help groups as facilitators.

5.2.1.1   *The self-help group (SHG) model*

In this model, there is an attempt to mainstream informal finance by enhancing management skills and operational practices. It involves transforming small-scale deposit collectors into financial intermediaries with permanent loan funds. This is very much like the on-lending proposals made earlier (Seibel and Marx, 1987). The main aim of this model is to provide cost-effective financial services to the poor. It involves three partners: (1) the SHGs, (2) the Banks as wholesale suppliers of credit, and (3) NGOs, government agencies and individuals as agencies to organize the poor, build capacities and facilitate empowerment. The SHGs are quite similar to credit unions (CUs), though unlike CUs, they are not bound by any legal requirements (Christen, 2006).

5.2.1.2   Business facilitator/business correspondent models

The other approach suggests linking banks to self-help groups by building on the existing formal and informal financial infrastructure. In January 2006, the Reserve Bank of India permitted banks to use a variety of organizations as intermediaries under two models: the business facilitator model and the business correspondent model with the intention of achieving greater outreach of the banking sector (Jones, et al., 2007). The main difference between the business facilitator model and business correspondent model is primarily in the mode of operation and range of people/organizations who could act as intermediaries. In the business facilitator model, the services of an intermediary include the identification of borrowers and activities, collection and preliminary processing of loan applications, financial education, submission of applications to banks, promotion and nurturing of joint liability groups, monitoring and recovery of loans. This role could be played by a wide variety of locally based organizations that are identified as suitable for such an intermediary function as well as one type of individual: insurance agents.

In the case of the business correspondent model, a narrower range of organizations (NGOs/MFIs, cooperatives, registered nonbank financial companies) was identified as suitable intermediaries. In addition to the functions listed above for the Facilitator Model, intermediaries in this model were expected to offer services such as the disbursement of small value credit, collection of principal/interest, sale of other microfinance services (e.g., insurance) and receipt of small value remittances and other payments (Jones et al., 2007).

In Aryeetey and Fenny (2006), there is considerable discussion of how banks in Asia have dealt with the issue of reaching out by employing the ways of microfinance institutions. There is emphasis on the decentralization of banking operations to include outsourcing and networking with existing MFIs. Several examples are provided of how banks have developed partnerships with informal groups and MFIs. One good example of this the interest that Barclays Bank has developed in savings collectors, which we highlight later (Box 5.1).

Whichever model for linkage development is followed, capacity building will play a major role in fostering the relationship between different institutional actors. The need for capacity building can be looked at from two levels. At one level, there continues to be a significant need to build the capacity of informal actors, to enable them effectively to manage the traditional business of savings and credit, if they are to engage with commercial banks, apex institutions and insurers. At another deeper and more interesting level, there is a huge need to strengthen SHGs in the mechanics of building and maintaining the new linkages or partnerships.

5.2.2 Potential benefits of integration

5.2.2.1 Deposit mobilization

In the increasingly competitive environment that African formal institutions are beginning to find themselves, the mobilization of deposits at reduced cost is essential. A closer relationship with savings collectors and savings and credit associations, as well as NGOs, is likely to enhance the capacity of formal institutions. The informal units have the prospect of becoming effective mechanisms to mobilize deposits from the household and micro-business sector. The agents can bulk up small savings at relatively low cost.

5.2.2.2 Credit allocation

The main advantage of informal agents is that they have much better information about small borrowers than do formal institutions. Informal lenders are often able to build a personal relationship with their borrowers that can ensure an extremely low loan default rate. So long as informal agents are made to operate within the particular groups that they are well-informed about and to which they have access, they are likely to extend the outreach of formal lenders at a low marginal cost.

5.3 Evidence of growing financial linkages

The emergence of commercial banks and apex organizations that are linked to less formal institutions, such as MFIs, savings and credit cooperatives and in some cases NGOs in order to increase their supply of funds is evident in many developing countries. There is evidence especially in Asia of how successful these linkages have been. The most notable case in this region is in India, where the National Bank for Agriculture and Rural Development (NABARD) since 1996 has reached 1.6 million SHGs, representing 21 million members, through its extensive network of 41,082 branches (Christen, 2006).

Over the past five years, many private banks and insurers have entered the microfinance market by establishing direct financial and facilitating linkages with less formal actors. Indeed several banks in Africa have also shown keen interest in acquiring more information about the informal sector and making inroads into strengthening group schemes which have led to the successful turnaround of micro-credit programs. An example is the recent merger of the Nigerian Agricultural and Cooperative Bank (NACB), Peoples Bank of Nigeria and Family Economic Advancement Program (FEAP) to form Nigerian Agricultural Cooperative and Rural Development Bank (NACRDB).

In Tanzania, CRDB Bank Limited, a private bank has established financial links with the informal sector by offering MFIs a range of financial services from long and short term loans and credit lines to various payment and transfer instruments (Piprek, 2005). State-owned development banks continue to engage in partnerships, mainly through direct financial linkages with less formal institutions. In Mali, the *Banque Nationale de Développement Agricole (BNDA)* has a long history of serving less formal institutions through bulk loans and lines of credit, as well as savings accounts to help institutions like *Kafo Jiginew,* the largest network of savings and credit cooperatives. It also works with CVECA-ON, a large village bank network, dealing with their cash flow variability and/or portfolio expansion.

Privatized microfinance banks, incorporated firms and financial NGOs have established linkages with various actors in an effort to expand the scope and scale of their businesses, enabling them to survive in competitive, maturing microfinance markets. In Kenya, the famous microfinance bank, K-Rep Bank, links up with various MFIs and SACCOs as a way to minimize costs and further its business (Sabana, 2005).

In Ghana, for a long time, individual savings collectors saved with commercial banks without receiving any acknowledgement for their role in deposit mobilization (Aryeetey and Gockel, 1991). The 1990s saw several proposals for formal links to be developed between banks and *susu collectors* but with little interest from the banks, since the banks made more money lending to the government and had easier access to low-cost public funds. The situation has changed today with greater fiscal discipline leading to reduced public borrowing and lower inflation in turn leading to lower interest rates. Coupled with the significant reduction in reserve requirements, banks are under pressure to find good quality clients in the private sector. The search for that client in a more competitive environment is forcing banks to increasingly move toward marginal clients. It is this new environment that has led to more and more banks developing products that are increasingly informal and require the involvement of the informal financial operators. The result is an increase in the proportion of *susu* depositors that gain access to credit facilities from their *susu collectors.* For *susu collectors* in a working relationship with the largest commercial bank in Ghana, their loans to deposits ratio is reported to have risen from 9 per cent to 60 per cent after two years of an improved relationship with the bank. The scheme was based on the observation that increased lending by collectors often led to larger numbers of depositors.

Apart from the largely spontaneous linkages described above, in recent years there have also been an increasing number of financial institutions in Ghana seeking to establish more formal, purposive linkages with informal financial agents. To date, attention has concentrated on formalizing linkages with individual financial agents such as *susu collectors* and traders, and with *susu groups'* (SCA) agents and organizations that have the potential to channel substantial informal savings into the formal financial sector.

Examples are the links an Accra-based nonbank financial institution (Citi Savings and Loans Company) developed with *susu collectors*; the links established between an Accra-based Commercial Bank (The Metropolitan and Allied Bank) with ROSCAs, and the links another Rural Bank (Ahantaman Rural Bank) had established with ROSCAs and the ways in which this bank had incorporated susu-like operations into its own banking practices.

Beyond increasing access to finance, these financial linkages have the potential to positively impact on education, empowerment of women, child mortality and decreased dependency on moneylenders (Thorat, 2006), although there is currently no clear evidence of this.

In spite of these milestones, the linkages between self-help groups and banks face a number of challenges. In India for example, there are noticeable disparities in geographical coverage, with the majority of SHGs concentrated in the southern part of the country. Sadly, some northern states with a high incidence of poverty, for example, Bihar and Uttar Pradesh, have lagged behind in the formation of SHGs linked to banks (Pagura and Kirsten, 2006). Other problems identified are the capture of SHGs by local elites, inadequate risk management, and lack of administrative capacity (Christen, 2006). In addition, the total disbursement of credit through the SHGs is limited. For 2005/06 the average loan per member was less than Rs 4,000 (approximately $94). There is also a question of sustainability of the SHG infrastructure. The SHGs often lack the capacity and resources to deal with nonperforming clients. It is necessary for the SHG to factor all these operational costs into the price of their financial services in order to ensure their sustainability.

5.3.1   Do financial linkages really work in Africa?

Despite the growing links among informal finance, microfinance and formal finance, there is still room to ask about the effectiveness of these arrangements in terms of filling the financial gap earlier identified. Although microfinance has been successful in enabling small businesses and individual entrepreneurs to get started, access to capital is still one of the key obstacles hindering the development of micro-businesses. Currently, the need to "formalize microfinance" is on top of the agenda in many countries as a way for the MFIs to access more capital for their operations, even though many analysts do not see a need for it.

The main problem with current linkage arrangements is with the unit costs of offering these services. Even though many aid-agencies are encouraging the move toward increased financial linkages, catering for the small transaction costs involved in dealing with the poor can be prohibitively expensive for banks if not properly constructed. To rise above these challenges, technological innovations in finance are often proffered as the solution. There are ongoing efforts to incorporate these innovations into the financial sector and some have been piloted in a number of African countries. It is expected technology can significantly reduce transactions costs significantly especially in areas where there are fewer people dispersed over wide areas.

5.3.2   Technological innovations in the financial market

There are many sources of technological innovation applicable to the financial services industry, such as broadband internet and mobile devices. During the last decade, the banking industry has pursued all sorts of innovative ways that could be less expensive than the traditional branch operations and as secure and friendly to nonexpert customers. Currently, there are millions of households worldwide using internet banking. A CGAP survey conducted in 2006 indicated that 62 financial institutions in 32 countries reported using technology channels to handle transactions for poor people. With technology channels, such as POS devices and mobile phones, banks in South Africa and Brazil are quickly opening basic accounts for customers who were previously excluded from the formal financial system (CGAP, 2006).

5.3.2.1   *Mobile phone banking*

A number of major international banks have been reported to be considering various approaches for the industry to reach what they generally refer to as "the unbanked" segments of the market without the expense of opening branches (Imboden et al., 2006). Customers can add savings via SIM (scratch and load) and send SMS with PIN to deposit to account. They can also repay loans with SIM and follow-up work by loan officers is made easier as they can also send SMS, or call their clients directly.

The Citigroup's Mexican unit, *Grupo Financiero Banamex*, is known to provide simple bank services over the counters of gas stations and small businesses. In South Africa, Standard Bank Group Ltd., First National Bank of South Africa and *Wizzit* (a unit of the South African Bank of Athens Ltd.) have teamed up with mobile-phone operators to offer phone-based money transfers. In the Philippines, customers of cellphone companies, Globe Telecom, Inc. and Smart Communications, Inc., can use their phones to make money transfers.

5.3.2.2   *Other innovative applications*

Apart from mobile phones, there are other branchless banking applications gaining footing as well. For instance, Brazil's use of local merchants and post offices equipped with card-swipe and barcode-reading point-of-sale (POS) terminals have increased access to finance. Other countries such as Russia and the Philippines have made inroads in branchless banking (CGAP, 2006). In South Africa, there is also the use of biometric mobile ATMs to issue pension payments to rural clients.

The financial environment is rapidly changing, and to remain competitive, many financial institutions need to tackle issues relating to technology and innovation as they create opportunities and pose threats. Banks continue to explore opportunities to ensure broader access to financial services in emerging and developing countries and also to devise better service packages. Yet fraud and security risks often hamper such efforts.

5.3.3 Mainstreaming banks to reach the "unbanked"

Many commercial banks in developing countries are beginning to examine the micro-finance market. During the past few years, their exploration of this new market has been facilitated by donor-funded loan guarantees, central bank rediscount lines, and specialized technical assistance. Presently, commercial banks are beginning to draw on their own deposit sources for a growing share of their total funds for micro-loans (CGAP, 2005).

Institutions such as Centenary Rural Development Bank (CERUDEB) in Uganda, Equity Bank and K-Rep in Kenya, CRDB and Akiba Bank in Tanzania, BNDA in Mali, MFRC in Malawi, Afriland Bank, BICEC, and Union Bank in Cameroon, and CNCA in Senegal are reported to have shown in different ways that licensed commercial banks in Africa can be effective in microfinance on a substantial scale. Other banks, rather than linking up with the MFIs, have established microfinance subsidiaries. Notable examples are in Benin (CGAP, 2005).

Indeed, many traditional banks which have intentions of introducing microfinance operations as an integral part of their operations have been held back by some challenges. Microfinance divisions within corporate banks experience recurrent tension with other divisions, because they need to allow for differences in operating, remuneration, and reporting procedures. They also recruit a different type of staff member, and train them in different ways. To be successful, the commercial bank must have branches or mobile services where microentrepreneurs are concentrated. Second, the role of computer technology to lower operational costs must be coupled with a well-designed management information system.

Staff training is key to the success of microfinance operations. Staff members must be properly recruited, well-trained, highly motivated and given appropriate incentives. They should be knowledgeable about small and micro-business owners and their environment. Some banks, such us Cooperative Bank of Kenya (CBK) and the Commercial Bank of Zimbabwe (CBZ) which started microfinance operations in the 1990s, faced challenges in integrating the human resource requirements of microfinance operations with those of a mainstream commercial bank (Bell et al., 2002). Microfinance operations thrive on the personal relationship between credit officers and clients—a relationshipwhich is often missing in traditional bank settings. Most importantly, the bank should provide attractive bonuses or commissions for high productivity and maintenance of portfolio quality. This will offset the tendency of loan officers to disburse loans without regard to loan collection.

Above all, commitment at the highest levels of the bank is necessary to make a microfinance program work successfully. Without this support, microfinance programs will not receive the human and financial resources they require to consolidate and expand. A study of banks in microfinance by CGAP in 2005 identified at least six key related issues banks need to resolve to enter the microfinance market successfully (CGAP, 2005):

- **Commitment** from board and management and alignment with the bank's core commercial strategy
- **Knowledge** of microfinance best practices and how to serve micro-clientele
- **Infrastructure** located conveniently close to clients
- **Products** especially adapted for the low income and informal markets
- **Systems and procedures** that are adapted to microfinance operations
- **Appropriate staff training** and incentives on new clients, products, and delivery systems

The experience of private commercial banks in microfinance is still relatively limited. Inarguably, the success rate of these developments in the African financial sectors is yet to be properly assessed. Commitment to microfinance among commercial banks appears to be more likely in small, specialized institutions with few shareholders, or in large institutions that have created an independent unit or subsidiary dedicated exclusively to microfinance. A pilot scheme being carried out by Barclays Bank Ghana

Figure 5.1   Conditions for banks to enter the microfinance market successfully
Source: CGAP, 2005.

Box 5.1   Barclays Bank "Aba Pa Account" in Ghana

Barclays Bank Ghana Limited outdoored another innovative product onto the Ghanaian market with the aim of extending its banking services to the largely "unbanked" population. The new product named: *"Aba Pa Account,"* (meaning good seed) had been specifically designed and tailored for traders, carpenters, household workers, taxi drivers, farmers, hawkers, wayside mechanics, and farmers among others. The bank would operate *"Aba Pa Current Account"* and *"Aba Pa Savings Account".* The two products were the result of an extensive research conducted by Barclays into the needs, preferences, unique profile and requirements of the mass market. With only ¢40,000, one could open any of the two accounts and enjoy a free bank statement, higher interest rates, free ATM card, and many more services.

Barclays, which launched the project in 2007 started with 100 *susu collectors* and plans to increase the number in subsequent months. At about 500 clients each, Ghana's estimated 5,000 *susu collectors* represent a customer base of 2.5 million. Barclays Ghana has adopted plans to aggressively increase the size of its business, with the mass market being its strategic focus. The bank has so far advanced ¢3.6 billion to them to lend to their clients with about 30,000 pounds sterling (¢510 million) provided to the Ghana Cooperative Credit Union Association to set up 20 pilot credit unions across the country and procure special savings boxes to help the association in its work.

Source: The Ghanaian Daily Guide, March 2007.

Ltd. with 100 *susu collectors* is reported to have the potential to reach a client base of almost 2.5 million (see details in Box 5.1). Barclays is currently considering entering informal banking systems in Zambia, Zimbabwe, Kenya, Botswana, South Africa and Tanzania.

5.4   Policies to enhance financial linkage development

Linking informal and formal finance seems to be the more realistic way to reach the unbanked. Indeed, the microfinance market is typically the largest under-exploited market segment available for banks seeking to grow market share and strengthen the bottom line. Some banks that have been able to manage the risks associated with such operations have made some profit. However, many banks are deterred from moving into microfinance due to the high risk, and uncertainty of realizing any profits. The initial investment to adapt products, systems and people may not pay off immediately, if at all. Hence, there should be policy designed to overcome this.

There are two possible ways for policy to be used to enhance the development of linkages between the various segments, including the informal sector and such semiformal lenders as MFIs including NGOs. That is, the use of the fiscal system and the regulatory and supervisory systems to provide incentives for formal institutions who desire to offer wholesale credit through informal agents. Tax relief on profits granted to banks that allocated credit through informal and semiformal agents could be recovered by imposing higher taxes on banks that do not channel credit through the informal sector. Some banks, such as merchant banks, will have no need to use informal agents for allocating credit and will therefore be the actual financiers of the subsidy. Since the higher tax is on the profits of the bank, it should not be transferred to users of those banks.

The regulatory and supervisory systems could be of considerable importance in providing incentives to banks. If banks perceived that risk was considerably reduced by dealing with credible semiformal and informal agents, they would be encouraged to use them. Effective regulation and supervision of semiformal and informal institutions would tend to be problematic, in some cases, however. Governments would require a proactive approach. This would embrace a legal, regulatory and prudential framework that fosters, and when possible, accelerates financial market development. This framework supports the setting up of mechanisms, institutions and instruments that promote and facilitate this development as the economy grows and market functions expand.

Regulation should steer away from restrictive laws and focus on removing the obstacles to financial market development. Restrictions on what assets banks may hold could be modified to encourage them to invest in semiformal financial institutions. Banks must communicate with banking authorities to ensure that reporting and regulatory requirements take into account the specialized nature of microfinance programs.

It is not clear whether the use of technological innovation is encouraging more banks to reach out to the unbanked. There is not enough evidence to prove that poor people are using formal financial services just because a technology channel is available to them. In spite of this, what is clearly needed is supportive government policies that encourage banks to use the available technological channels to expand financial coverage. There should be a regulatory environment that supports the use of electronic payments and allows these same technological channels to be used a wide range of financial services. In the communication environment, there should be a telecommunications policy that fosters widespread access, privacy and data security. To avert fraud and also lower the high risks associated with microfinance operations, governments must institute national identification systems. A national identification card will allow holders easier access to financial services such as opening of bank accounts for customers, and also enable banks to identify individual borrowers, and build a payment history of their clients.

5.5   Conclusion

We have argued here and elsewhere that there are number of obstacles that hamper the integration of both the formal and informal sectors of financial markets in sub-Saharan Africa (Aryeetey, 1995). In the case of the formal financial sector, banks are often beset with problems of the maturity trans-formation of their liabilities; difficulties in loan administration through the screening and monitoring of relatively small borrowers and high transac-tion costs as a result of loan administration procedures and relatively high risks of default. The informal financial markets on the other hand, are lim-ited in the size of deposits mobilized from a distinct group or on the surplus funds of the lender accrued from the profits made in the lending business or other businesses. The management of their liabilities and assets is confined to ensuring a proper balance between the two, for reasons that sometimes transcend the bounds of profitability.

As we have indicated in this chapter, the two distinct segments of financial markets, invariably on the basis of their structure, offer services packaged to distinct socioeconomic groups with the exclusion of other groups. Thus, banks are more likely to transact business with relatively large corporate entities because they believe that it is easier and more prof-itable to deal with this segment of the market, as risk is minimal. As a consequence, potential borrowers who have not been able to establish the desired track record on cash flow have to look elsewhere. Looking else-where does not necessarily imply the use of informal finance. This form of market segmentation can be damaging to efficient functioning of the financial system. Giving the potential for both the formal and informal financial segments to feed off each other, an improvement of informal finance creates a better chance for the formal sector to reach new clients and to broaden its lending base.

Recent reports on financial inclusion recognize the role banks and other formal sector institutions have played in the promotion of the SHG move-ment, for example, in the countries that have adopted them; and the insti-tutional and operational reforms that have made for simpler and more efficient procedures. In sub-Saharan Africa, these financial linkages have only recently taken off. The process of establishing linkages can be long and arduous. Policy involving the official recognition of the informal sector and its inclusion in the regulatory framework are two key conditions to ensure the success of these linkages. The roll-out of any new policy requires mon-itoring of its effect and impact. Hence, future comparative studies will be able to determine positive and negative impacts of different kinds of linkage arrangements on financial service provision for individuals and businesses in general.

We note that many institutions in the formal financial sector have not linked up with informal finance because of considerable distrust, inadequate knowledge about the informal sector and in some cases prejudice. To over-come this, policies must be designed to protect all parties involved and also create the environment needed to sustain these relationships. There may not be a need for the establishment of new institutions; rather some of the existing regulatory institutions can be resourced adequately to do this.

Note

Institute of Statistical, Social and Economic Research, University of Ghana, Legon.

References

Aryeetey, E. 1994. "Financial integration and development in sub-Saharan Africa: A study of informal finance in Ghana." Overseas Development Institute, Working Paper 78, London.

Aryeetey, E. 1995. "Informal finance in Africa." Nairobi: AERC/East African Educational.

Aryeetey, E. and Gockel, F. 1991. "Mobilizing domestic resources for capital formation in sub-Saharan Africa: A study of informal finance in Ghana." Research Paper 3. Nairobi: African Economic Research Consortium.

Aryeetey, E. and C. Udry. 1997. "The Characteristics of informal financial markets in sub-Saharan Africa." *Journal of African Economies* 6 (1): 161–203.

Aryeetey, E. and A. Fenny. 2006. "Promoting access to low cost finance in sub-Saharan Africa." Paper presented at IMF-JAI Conference on "Realizing the potential for profitable investment in sub-Saharan Africa." Tunis: 28 February–1 March.

Armendáriz de Aghion, B. and Morduch, J. 2005. *The Economics of Microfinance.* Cambridge, MA: MIT Press.

Bell, C. 1990. "Interactions between institutional and informal credit agencies in rural India." *The World Bank Economic Review,* 4(3): 297–327.

Bell, R., Harper, A., and Mandivenga, D. 2002. "Can commercial banks do microfinance? Lessons from the Commercial Bank of Zimbabwe and the Co-operative Bank of Kenya." *Small Enterprise Development Journal* (SED), 13(4), December: 35–46.

CGAP 2005. "Commercial banks and microfinance: Evolving models of success." Focus Note No. 28.

CGAP 2006. "Using technology to build inclusive financial systems." Focus Note No. 32.

Christen, R.P. 2006. "Microfinance and sustainability: International experiences and lessons for India." In *Toward a Sustainable Microfinance Outreach in India.* New Delhi: NABARD, GTZ and SDC, 43–67.

Conning, J. and Kevane, M. 2002. 'Why isn't there more financial intermediation in developing countries?' WIDER Discussion Paper, United Nations University.

Floro, M. and D. Ray. 1997. "Vertical links between formal and informal financial institutions." *Review of Development Economics* 1(1): 34–56.

Ghate, P.B. 1990. "Interaction between the formal and informal financial sectors." Papers Presented at the United Nations' International Conference on Savings and Credit for Development, Denmark, 28–31 May.

Imboden, K. 2005. "Building inclusive financial sectors: The road to growth and poverty." *Journal of International Affairs,* 58(2): 65–86.

Isern, Jennifer, Porteous, D., Hernandez-Coss, R., and Egwuagu, C. 2005. "AML/CFT regulation: Implications for financial service providers that serve low-income people." Focus Note 29, Washington, DC Consultative Group to Assist the Poor. http:// www.cgap.org/docs/FocusNote_29.pdf.

Jones, H., Williams, M., and Thorat, Y. 2007. "Rural financial institutions and agents in India: A historical and contemporary comparative analysis. International Conference on Rural Finance Research: Moving Results into Policies and Practice," Rome, Italy 19–21 March.

Nissanke, M. and Aryeetey, E. 1998. Financial Integration and Development, Liberalization and Reform in Sub-Saharan Africa, Financial Integration and Development, Liberalization and Reform in Sub-Saharan Africa, London: ODI and Routledge.

Pagura and Kirsten 2006. "Formal-informal financial linkages: Lessons from developing countries." *Small Enterprise Development Journal*, 17 (1), March: 16–29.

Piprek, G. 2005. "A case study of CRDB Bank in Tanzania." Unpublished research prepared for the report prepared by the Food and Agricultural Organization of the United Nations for the Ford Foundation.

Sabana, B. 2005. "A study of financial linkages between K-Rep Bank and other financial intermediaries." Unpublished research prepared for the report prepared by the Food and Agricultural Organization of the United Nations for the Ford Foundation.

Seibel, H.D. 1989. "Linking formal and informal financial institutions in Africa and Asia. Processing of the International Conference on Micro enterprises" in *Developing Countries*. London: IT.

Seibel, H.D. 2006. *From Informal Microfinance to Linkage Banking: Putting Theory into Practice, and Practice into Theory.* Published in: European Dialogue no 36 (September), 49–60 ADA Luxembourg & European Microfinance Platform (ISSN 1990–9357).

Seibel, H.D. and Marx, M. Th. 1987. *Dual Financial Markets in Africa: Case Studies of Linkages between Informal and Formal Financial Institutions.* Breitenbach: Saarbrücken.

Schrader, H. 1994. "Moneylenders and Merchant Bankers in India and Indonesia." In *Financial Landscapes Reconstructed,* Bouman, F.J.A. and Hospes, O. eds., 341–56. Boulder, San Francisco and Oxford: Westview Press.

Thorat, Y.S.P. 2006. "Microfinance in India; Sectoral issues and challenges." In *Toward a Sustainable Microfinance Outreach in India. New Delhi: NABARD, GTZ and SDC,* 27–42.

Vargese, A. 2005. "Bank-moneylender linkage as an alternative to bank competition in rural credit markets." *Oxford Economic Papers,* 57(2), April.

6
African Stock Markets—Opportunities and Issues

Lemma W. Senbet and Isaac Otchere

6.1 Introduction

Africa, particularly sub-Saharan Africa, has seen rapid growth in the number of stock exchanges and a stock market capitalization boom has developed over the last 15 years. Two decades ago, there were only five stock exchanges in sub-Saharan countries and three in North Africa. There are now around 20 stock exchanges operating in Africa. The phenomenal growth was registered particularly in sub-Saharan Africa excluding the older markets in South Africa (Johannesburg Stock Exchange) and Egypt. Actually, the latter were established in the 1880s. Table 6.1 provides the current profile of African stock markets in terms of market capitalization and listing size.

The rapid increase in the number of stock exchanges is attributed, in part, to the extensive financial sector reforms undertaken by African countries. The reform package included a variety of measures, such as interest rate liberalizations, removal of credit ceilings, restructuring and privatization of state-owned enterprises, along with supervisory and regulatory schemes, promotion and development of capital markets, including money and stock markets. The reforms have been accompanied and stimulated by rapid improvements in global conditions and global technology connecting Africa with the rest of the world. In fact, this rapid development in the equity market sector points to Africa's new commitment to financial sector policy reform, and the region's economic awakening. It appears that most African governments have embraced stock markets as a vehicle for growth.

A particularly important feature of stock market development has been the emergence of a regional stock market domiciled in Abidjan—Bourse Regional des Valeurs Mobiliéres (BVRM). This happens to be the only regional stock exchange of its kind in the world. The BVRM regional market serves as an anchor for the CFA countries—Benin, Burkina Faso, Cote d'Ivoire, Guinea-Bissau, Mali, Niger, Senegal, and Togo, and it links the eight Francophone countries in West Africa. However, except for South Africa, sub-Saharan

African markets remain the smallest of any region in the world in terms of capitalization, and in addition, they display considerable illiquidity.

The emergence of stock markets provides an important opportunity for integrating Africa into the global financial market place and attracting global capital. It is encouraging that Africa has been receiving a growing attention from international investors, although international capital flows are still at a very low level. The Africa-oriented investment funds, which are now trading in New York and Europe, are currently number about 18. In this context, regionalization is a vital mechanism for consolidating African stock markets and promoting financial globalization of Africa. The Abidjan-based market is bound to serve as a positive role model for other regions of Africa. It is encouraging that already the Anglophone countries of West Africa are contemplating forming a regional stock exchange under the umbrella of the ECOWAS. Similarly, Kenya, Tanzania, and Uganda can be natural partners in forming a regional stock exchange in East Africa. Moreover, the Southern African Development Community (SADEC) stock exchanges have proposed the idea of a regional stock exchange.

Despite rapid growth, stock markets in Africa remain thin and illiquid, with the exception of the established markets in South Africa and Egypt. For the period 2000–2006, the mean market capitalization (as a percentage of GDP) of 32.72% (20.56%, excluding South Africa) pales in comparison to that of Malaysia (147.5%), but comparable to that of Mexico (25.50%). The size of the markets has, however, been growing, with the mean for Africa growing from 17.93% of GDP in 1991 to 62.74% in 2006, an annualized growth rate of 14.48% [These metrics exclude Zimbabwe and its unusual market]. On the listing front, the number of firms listed on African stock exchanges is also small compared to the markets in Malaysia and Mexico. For the period 2000–2006, the mean (median) number of firms listed on the African stock markets was 137(39) as compared to 911 (897) in Malaysia and 158 (159) in Mexico. Actually, the number of firms listed declined over that six-year period, with the well-established markets of South Africa and Egypt recording significant drops.

African stock markets face an additional challenge. In most these stock markets, trading occurs in only a few stocks, and these stocks typically represent a considerable portion of the total market capitalization. The non-active stocks face serious informational and disclosure deficiencies. Further, supervision by regulatory authorities is often inadequate.

The stock market wave in Africa raises a number of policy questions. Are there gains to those countries introducing the stock markets? Does the functioning of African stock markets conform to best global practices? What is their role in financial globalization of Africa? What concrete measures should be put into place to build capacity and efficiency of these markets? These are the questions that this policy-oriented chapter wishes to address.

Table 6.1 Listing and market capitalizations

Country	1991	1995	2000	2001	2002	2003	2004	2005	2006	Mean (2000–2006)	Median	Annualized % growth 2000–2006
						Panel A: Market capitalization of listed companies (% of GDP)						
Botswana	6.62	8.34	15.83	21.03	29.04	25.73	25.94	23.33	38.22	25.59	25.73	13.42
Cote d'Ivoire	5.16	7.87	11.37	11.04	11.57	12.01	13.46	14.5	23.7	13.95	12.01	11.06
Egypt, Arab Rep.	7.17	13.44	28.79	24.93	29.7	32.65	48.85	88.83	86.97	48.67	32.65	17.11
Ghana	1.15	25.54	10.1	9.93	12.02	18.7	29.8	12.82	13.4	15.25	12.82	4.12
Kenya	5.56	20.85	10.1	8.09	11.02	28.54	24.1	33.26	53.71	24.12	24.10	26.96
Mauritius	11.05	34.84	29.79	23.42	29.19	37.26	39.23	41.61	55.8	36.61	37.26	9.38
Morocco	5.5	18.04	32.7	26.8	23.8	30.02	50.1	52.73	86.13	43.18	32.70	14.84
Namibia	–	5.4	9.12	4.68	5.47	6.88	7.74	6.7	8.5	7.01	6.88	-1.00
Nigeria	6.88	7.23	9.21	11.26	12.29	16.29	20.01	19.95	28.62	16.80	16.29	17.58
South Africa	139.74	185.64	154.24	117.95	166.5	160.66	210.46	233.58	280.41	189.11	166.50	8.91
Swaziland	2.97	24.85	5.26	10.12	12.05	9.02	9.43	7.53	–	8.90	9.23	6.16
Tanzania	–	–	2.57	4.22	7.25	6.41	5.9	4.67	–	5.17	5.29	10.47
Tunisia	5.44	21.78	14.54	11.52	10.13	9.86	9.39	10.03	14.68	11.45	10.13	0.14
Uganda	–	–	–	0.62	0.83	0.76	1.4	1.19	–	0.96	0.83	13.93
Zambia	–	0.55	7.28	6.97	6.31	6.63	7.93	13.6	–	8.12	7.13	10.98
Africa—mean	17.93	28.80	24.35	19.51	24.48	26.76	33.58	37.62	62.74	32.72	26.76	14.48
Africa—ex S. Africa	5.75	15.73	14.36	12.47	14.33	17.20	20.95	23.63	40.97	20.56	17.20	16.16
Africa—median	5.56	18.04	10.74	11.04	12.02	16.29	20.01	14.50	38.22	17.55	14.50	19.89
Malaysia	–	–	–	136	130	162	160	139	158	147.50	148.50	2.53
Mexico	–	–	–	20	16	19	25	31	42	25.50	22.50	13.16

Panel B: Listed domestic companies

Botswana	9	12	16	16	18	18	18	18	18	18	18	1.70
Cote d'Ivoire*	25	31	41	38	38	39	39	40	39	39	39	-0.35
Egypt, Arab Rep.	627	746	1076	1110	1148	792	744	603	920	967	967	-7.94
Ghana	13	19	22	22	24	29	30	32	26	25	25	5.50
Kenya	53	56	57	57	57	47	47	51	52	51	51	-1.58
Mauritius	20	28	40	40	40	41	42	41	41	40	40	0.35
Morocco	67	44	53	55	55	52	56	65	56	55	55	2.96
Namibia	–	10	13	13	13	13	13	9	12	13	13	-5.12
Nigeria	142	181	195	194	195	207	241	202	205	200	200	0.51
South Africa	688	640	616	542	450	403	388	401	461	426	426	-5.95
Swaziland	2	4	6	5	5	6	6	–	6	5.5	5.5	0.00
Tanzania	–	–	4	5	5	6	6	–	5	6	5.5	6.99
Tunisia	15	26	44	46	47	44	46	48	46	46	46	1.25
Uganda	–	–	–	2	3	5	5	–	4	3	3	20.11
Zambia	–	2	9	9	11	11	12	–	11	11	11	4.91
Africa—mean	151	138	157	144	141	114	113	137	133	127	137	-1.86
Africa—ex S. Africa	97	97	121	115	119	94	93	111	108	106	111	-1.26
Africa—median	25	28	41	38	38	39	39	48	40	38	39	2.46
Malaysia	321	529	795	809	865	962	1020	1027	911	897	897	3.73
Mexico	209	185	179	168	166	152	151	131	158	159	159	-4.36

Notes: This table shows the market capitalization and number of firms listed on African stock exchanges and those in Malaysia and Mexico, selected comparative countries from South East Asia and Latin America. Panel A shows the market capitalization for firms listed on the stock exchange as a percentage of GDP, and Panel B shows the number of firms listed on the stock exchanges.

*The stock exchange in Cote d'Ivoire, the Bourse Regionale des Valeurs Mobilieres SA or BRVM, is a regional stock exchange that serves the French speaking West African countries of Benin, Burkina Faso, Guinea Bissau, Cote d'Ivoire, Mali, Niger, Senegal and Togo.

The chapter is organized as follows. The following section provides the economic rationale for stock market development in Africa. This is anchored by the potential impact of stock market development on economic performance based on the available evidence from other regions of the world. This is then followed by evidence from Africa itself. Section 6.3 examines the current state of African stock markets. In particular, we look at gaps in the functional and operational efficiencies of the stock markets. The functional efficiency is examined based on recent history of these markets in terms of their liquidity and depth. The operational efficiency pertains to the workings of the stock exchanges and gaps relative to best practices in terms of settlement and clearance. We also take note of trends in demutualization of the stock exchanges around the world and its implication for African stock markets. The section closes with a discussion of the risk factors that are potential challenges in the functioning of the African stock markets.

Section 6.4 takes a closer look at the role of African stock markets in integrating the region into a global financial economy. The prospects for financial globalization of Africa are discussed by way of providing evidence on the recent performance of the African stock markets on a risk-adjusted basis. Moreover, we provide a discussion of regionalization of these markets as a conduit for promotion of globalization. Section 6.5 examines the role of African stock markets in privatization of state-owned enterprises. It also examines issues in corporate governance that are pertinent to the development of African stock markets. Section 6.6 concludes with a catalogue of policy prescriptions,[1] at the core of which are measures for promotion of public confidence in the stock markets, provision of informational efficiency, provision of liquidity, cultivating synergy among regional stock markets, and global integration. The guides include measures for banking sector development, which also foster competition in the banking system and facilitate the development of African stock markets.

6.2   Why stock markets for Africa

Stock exchanges are mainly mechanisms for exchange and trading of stocks. A stock market fails if the stock exchange is not conducive to exchange of stocks. Thus, the mere establishment of *stock exchanges* is of no value. Liquidity and information production are central to the functioning and development of the stock market. Similarly, the mere existence of banks is of little value, if their primary activity is to merely purchase government securities and shun the provision of private credit. Unfortunately, the dysfunctional banking system that avoids business lending is prevalent in Africa. This is dysfunctional from the standpoint of financial intermediation, because banks no longer serve as informed agents or intermediaries on behalf of the society and build vital information capital that is crucial for efficient allocation of resources.

The value of stock markets to Africa can be appreciated by understanding the multiple functions that stock markets perform. In particular, in an environment characterized by uncertainty, stock markets provide functions beyond capital/savings mobilization. They also facilitate other functions such as risk allocation and risk sharing among market participants. Risk sharing in turn allows high risk, yet high return, projects to be undertaken; otherwise, such projects would be rationed out of the economy, leading to a destruction of value for the economy. Value destruction eventually aggregates into poor performance. Moreover, stock markets can serve a vital governance function in disciplining management in an environment with imperfect information and incentive problems. These problems are likely to prevail among various stakeholders to an organized enterprise: management, shareholders, creditors, employees, suppliers, customers, government, etc.

The bottom line is that the benefits of the stock markets to Africa are linked to economic performance. The available empirical evidence is that well-functioning stock markets, along with well-designed institutions and regulatory systems, foster economic growth. The evidence is particularly encouraging for African countries which have already established stock markets or to those contemplating to do so, since there is a vital link between stock market development and poverty alleviation, as well as employment creation. Below we discuss the relationship between stock market development and economic growth based on evidence from other regions; we then follow that up with corresponding evidence in the context of Africa.

6.2.1 Stock market development and economic development

There is now an abundance of scholarly literature documenting the link between the level of stock market development and economic growth of countries. This linkage is attributed in part to the role a well-functioning stock market system plays in lowering the costs of mobilizing financial resources and in ensuring that these resources are allocated efficiently in the sense of being channeled to their highly valued use. In broad terms, it appears that countries with better developed and deeper financial systems experience faster economic growth. For instance, most East Asian countries experienced high economic growth in the seventies and eighties while most Latin American countries witnessed low growth. During that same period, it was observed that stock market capitalizations were higher in East Asia than in Latin America.

The principal channel for the linkage between stock market development and economic performance is liquidity provision of the market. A liquid stock market, characterized by active trading among a large number of investors and firms, provides an exit strategy for both investors and issuing firms. Thus, liquidity is a crucial feature of stock market development. It also provides a channel for more efficient corporate governance and resource allocation, whereby resources are allocated to the most productive and innovative firms. The existing empirical evidence supports a positive linkage between stock liquidity and economic growth; countries with more liquid markets experience faster rates of capital accumulation and subsequently greater productivity (e.g., Levine, 1997; Levine and Zervos, 1998). The stylized facts in Table 6.2, which are adapted from Tadesse (2004) and Senbet and Otchere (2006), are consistent with the linkage between stock market liquidity and economic performance.

Thus, part of the answer to the question posed on the topic of this section "why stock markets for Africa" pertains to the role of the stock market in promoting economic growth. It turns out that the channels for the stock market—economic growth nexus are the multiple functions that the stock markets perform, and not just the mere establishment of the stock exchanges. The functional features of the stock markets that serve as a channel for the growth nexus include market liquidity, turnover, and efficiency of pricing of risk. This allows us to catalogue the specifics of what the stock markets can do in answering the question "why stock markets for Africa".

First, stock markets promote savings by providing an alternative financial vehicle for individuals to better meet their risk preferences and liquidity needs, potentially increasing the savings rate in the economy. *Second*, stock markets promote growth at the firm level, since the listed firms are able to mobilize capital at a lower cost of capital as risk is shared widely in the market place. This leads to value creation, as positive net present value projects that might have been rationed out in the absence of a well-functioning stock market can now be adopted. As many firms face this opportunity, the aggregate economy also benefits. *Third*, through liquidity provision, stock markets help promote the adoption of illiquid long-term projects, since investors in the firm may liquidate their stock positions through the market. Investors need not wait until the long-term project pays off to smooth out their consumption plans (Haque, Hauswald, and Senbet, 1997).

Fourth, stock markets promote efficient governance and control of listed companies by exerting external pressure and discipline on management. This role of the stock market is particularly important in an environment of uncertainty characterized by incentive conflicts between corporate decision-makers and suppliers of capital. Stock markets achieve this through the price discovery function of the stock market, whereby the market provides a signal for managerial performance. This can be illustrated through what is known as markets for corporate control. The market price and information disclosure allow investors to uncover target firms for takeover and lead to active trading for actual transfer of control. In the event that the firm is taken over by outside raiders, inefficient management may be removed and replaced by an alternative management team that responds to the interests of the suppliers of capital. Actually in most cases the takeover itself need not occur, since the very threat of such a control transfer serves as a disciplining mechanism for management.

Table 6.2   Stock market development and economic performance

Stock market liquidity measures: Selected countries by income categories; Annual averages 1980–1995

	(Turnover)	Log (Per Capita GDP)
Low income countries		
Bangladesh	0.0327	5.234
India	0.4261	5.78
Indonesia	0.1855	6.315
Pakistan	0.1413	5.794
Zimbabwe	0.0653	7.876
Average	0.17018	6.1998
Middle income countries		
Chile	0.0661	6.086
Colombia	0.0863	7.711
Egypt	0.0636	10.085
Jordan	0.1571	7.008
Malaysia	0.2392	7.73
Mexico	0.5394	7.975
Peru	0.163	7.524
Philippines	0.2161	6.566
Sri Lanka	0.0694	9.344
Turkey	0.5041	7.88
Venezuela	0.1275	9.949
Average	0.2029	7.9871
High income countries		
Australia	0.2923	9.704
Austria	0.4422	9.856
Belgium	0.1202	9.791
Canada	0.3084	9.899
Denmark	0.2086	7.096
Finland	0.2019	10.081
Germany	1.0394	9.963
Greece	0.1218	8.968
Israel	0.6492	9.287
Italy	0.2986	9.757
Japan	0.4329	9.966
Korea	0.8502	8.527
Kuwait	0.2363	9.632
Netherlands	0.3656	9.786
New Zealand	0.1854	9.444
Norway	0.3265	10.179
Portugal	0.1537	8.69
Singapore	0.3254	9.422
Spain	0.2695	6.496
Sweden	0.2984	10.123

Continued

Table 6.2   Continued

	(Turnover)	Log (Per Capita GDP
High income countries		
U.K.	0.3783	6.984
U.S.	0.5379	9.654
Average	**0.3656**	**9.2411**

Source: International financial statistics (IMF), Emerging Market Database (IFC); Table adapted from Tadesse (2004) and Senbet and Otchere (2006).

6.2.2   Stock markets and economic growth: Evidence from Africa

The foregoing discussion provides strong economic rationales for the question "why stock markets for Africa?" based on the particular functions stock markets perform and their role in economic development. Given the evidence from other regions, it would be useful to look at the extent to which the evidence holds up in the context of Africa. The very few studies on Africa (e.g., Yartey and Adjasi, 2007) provide evidence consistent with what we have learned from the experience of other regions. Here we wish to provide some evidence of our own.

Table 6.3 provides the results of our economic growth-stock market development regression. Stock market development indicators are measured by (1) stock market capitalization relative to GDP, (2) value of shares traded relative to GDP, and (3) value of shares traded relative to market capitalization. The last two indicators measure trading activity, relative to the size of the economy and the size of the stock market, respectively. The results show that the market capitalization and the value of shares traded relative to the size of the economy are the channels through which African stock markets influence economic growth. The African evidence is reassuringly consistent with the available evidence in other global contexts, although the relations are weaker, once we control for other factors. The policy implication here is that appropriate measures should be put in place to gain improvements in trading of shares and achieve greater liquidity of the stock markets. We will revisit this in the following section.

Our evidence is also consistent with a recent evidence by Yartey and Adjasi (2007) that stock markets contribute to financing of corporate investments, and hence growth of listed firms in Africa. The finding implies that corporate financing channel is another mechanism for the stock markets to impact aggregate economic performance. For instance, listed companies in Ghana obtained about 12 percent of their financing and growth through the stock market between 1995 and 2002. Similarly, the stock market contributed to a substantial component of external finance in several other countries. In fact, for listed companies the reliance on this particular form

Table 6.3 Stock market development and economic growth (Africa)

	1	2	3	4	5	6	7
Panel A: Dependent variable is Growth in GDP							
Turnover Ratio (%)	0.21	–	–	–0.07	–	–	–0.17
	(2.95)***	–	–	(–1.82)*	–	–	(–2.26)*
Value Traded/GDP	–	0.08	–	–	–0.03	–	0.17
	–	(3.05)***	–	–	(–1.24)	–	(0.80)
Market Cap	–	–	0.04	–	–	–0.01	–0.02
	–	–	(1.71)*	–	–	(–1.28)	(–0.42)
Inv in human capital	–	–	–	0.16	0.14	0.14	0.22
	–	–	–	(1.12)	(0.89)	(0.90)	(1.57)
GovCons/GDP	–	–	–	–0.02	–0.02	–0.02	0.04
	–	–	–	(–0.14)	(–0.17)	(–0.15)	(0.31)
FDI	–	–	–	0.001	0.001	0.002	0.001
	–	–	–	(0.45)	(0.18)	(0.18)	(0.75)
Exchange Rate	–	–	–	–0.0002	–0.0001	–0.002	–0.001
	–	–	–	(–0.23)	(–0.12)	(–0.15)	(–0.47)
Inflation	–	–	–	–0.02	–0.02	(–0.02)	–0.01
	–	–	–	(–0.44)	(–0.47)	(–0.48)	(–0.31)
F-stat	–	–	–	1.50	0.90	0.92	1.32
Adj R^2	–	–	–	0.18	–0.04	–0.03	0.15
Panel B: Dependent variable is Log of GDP/Capital							
Turnover Ratio (%)	0.44	–	–	0.03	–	–	–0.001
	(3.91)***	–	–	(1.52)	–	–	(–0.03)
Value Traded/GDP	–	0.23	–	–	0.03	–	–0.31
	–	(4.84)***	–	–	(4.80)***	–	(–2.13)**
Market Cap	–	–	0.08	–	–	0.01	0.10
	–	–	(2.42)**	–	–	(3.51)***	(2.51)**
Inv in human capital	–	–	–	0.15	0.04	0.04	0.03
	–	–	–	(0.48)	(1.36)	(1.33)	(0.54)
GovCons/GDP	–	–	–	0.01	0.03	0.03	0.02
	–	–	–	(0.14)	(0.41)	(0.42)	(–0.25)
FDI	–	–	–	0.001	0.002	0.0003	0.0003
	–	–	–	(0.22)	(0.45)	(0.48)	(0.61)

Continued

Table 6.3 Continued

	1	2	3	4	5	6	7
Panel B: Dependent variable is Log of GDP/Capital							
Exchange Rate	–	–	–	–0.0002	–0.0005	–0.0003	0.0003
	–	–	–	(–0.06)	(–0.12)	(–0.05)	(0.59)
Inflation	–	–	–	–0.04	–0.04	–0.04	–0.03
	–	–	–	(–1.20)	(–1.19)	(–1.23)	(–1.21)
F-stat	–	–	–	(0.85)	(0.96)	(1.17)	(1.46)
Adj R^2	–	–	–	–0.06	–0.01	0.06	0.21

Notes: The symbols ***, **, and * represent significance at 1%, 5%, and 10% respectively. This table shows the results of the regression of stock market development indictors on economic growth. The stock market variables used in this analysis are turnover, value traded as a percentage of GDP and market capitalization. The control variables are investment in human capital, foreign direct investment, government consumption as a percentage of GDP (GovCons/GDP), exchange rate and inflation. To conserve space, the intercept has been excluded.

of external finance seems higher in Africa than in the more advanced countries. However, external finance through the stock markets in Africa has a similar pattern as in other emerging countries.

6.3   The state of African stock markets

How do current stock markets in Africa hold up in terms of their functional and operational efficiencies? To answer this question, we will focus on liquidity and market depth in assessing functional efficiency and on trading mechanisms in assessing operational efficiency. Apart from the functional and operational dimensions, we need to identify various risk factors as potential challenges to stock market development in Africa, which we will also take up in this section.

6.3.1   Gaps in functional efficiency

Beyond mere capitalization, the functional efficiency of the stock markets contributes significantly to economic growth as discussed in the earlier section. African stock markets, thus, should be judged on the basis of their efficiency in carrying out these functions. Although the growth in the number of stock exchanges has been impressive, their existence alone is not consequential to economic growth. Judged on functionality as a guiding principle, these markets have been nonfunctional. Except for the South African stock market, preemerging stock markets in Africa are by far the smallest of any region, both in terms of number of listed companies and market capitalization. Moreover, trading activity is minimal. In most African stock markets, trading is concentrated in only a few stocks. These stocks themselves account for a considerable part of the total capitalization of the entire market.

We use two standard approaches to measure liquidity of African stock markets: (1) the ratio of total value of shares traded on the exchange to GDP. This indicator measures the market's trading activity relative to the size of the economy; (2) the ratio of total value of shares traded to the total capitalization of the market. This indicator known as "turnover ratio", measures the market's overall trading activity relative to the size of the market itself. These indicators do not directly measure the stock market liquidity in the sense of the ease at which investors can buy and sell securities at posted prices, but they are rough measures of the overall trading activity relative of the size of both the economy and the stock market.

Table 6.4 shows that stock markets in Africa are small, as they are characterized by low market capitalization with few listed companies (see also Table 6.1). Most stock markets are characterized by low provision of liquidity and exit strategies. While liquidity on the African markets has been improving at a very slow pace over the last decade, the mean value traded ratio of 7.84% is comparable to that of Mexico of 6.18% but significantly lower than that of Malaysia of 39.61%. The low liquidity (rather illiquidity), more than market capitalization, should be of great concern to Africa in light of the earlier evidence (see Section 6.2) from other parts of the world which suggests that market liquidity is a vital channel for linking stock market development and economic performance.

There are a number of factors that are potential impediments to the liquidity of African stock markets. Institutional investors, as well as governments which maintain minority stockholdings, are not active traders in the secondary market. Moreover, markets tend to be dominated by a few large companies. For instance, five companies account for 75% of transactions in Abidjan and the Ashanti Goldfields accounts for 90% of the total capitalization of the Ghana stock market. Fortunately, though, these dismal stories on market capitalization and liquidity do not quite capture important new developments under way in the African stock market scene. Though, African stock markets are still small and have low trading activity (see Table 6.4), they are experiencing rapid improvement both in capitalization (size) and liquidity. These improvements have been in response to improvements in regulatory and economic environments that the region has experienced over the recent past. Simultaneously, foreign participation is also growing, and Africa is gradually marching to an emerging markets club. In the next section, we will explore the role of these markets in the integration of Africa into a global financial economy.

6.3.2   Gaps in operational efficiency

African stock markets face challenges not only in their functional efficiency as discussed earlier, but also in their operational efficiency. Brokerage

Table 6.4 Liquidity of African stock markets

Country	1991	1995	2000	2001	2002	2003	2004	2005	2006	Mean (2000–2006)	Median ('00–'06)
				Panel A: Stocks traded, total value (% of GDP)							
Botswana	0.2	0.8	0.77	1.08	0.93	1.05	0.51	0.43	0.71	0.78	0.77
Cote d'Ivoire	0.07	0.13	0.32	0.08	0.14	0.18	0.3	0.19	0.64	0.26	0.19
Egypt	0.38	1.13	11.14	3.99	2.91	3.95	7.11	28.31	44.16	14.51	7.11
Ghana	–	0.34	0.2	0.25	0.18	0.6	0.74	0.42	0.41	0.40	0.41
Kenya	0.13	0.72	0.37	0.31	0.28	1.43	2.13	2.63	6.4	1.94	1.43
Mauritius	0.18	1.83	1.69	2.46	1.25	1.89	1.57	2.4	2.64	1.99	1.89
Morocco	0.18	7.35	3.28	2.87	1.63	1.58	3.35	8.03	23.56	6.33	3.28
Namibia	–	0.09	0.65	0.24	0.05	0.04	0.31	0.1	0.33	0.25	0.24
Nigeria	0.03	0.05	0.57	1.03	1.02	1.47	2.31	3	3.1	1.79	1.47
South Africa	6.7	11.28	58.32	58.51	71.09	61.69	75.23	82.92	122.53	75.76	71.09
Swaziland	–	0.03	0.02	0.79	0.02	0	0	0	–	0.14	0.01
Tanzania	–	–	0.44	0.08	0.19	0.19	0.15	0.11	–	0.19	0.17
Tunisia	0.23	3.68	3.22	1.58	1.05	0.66	0.8	1.59	1.81	1.53	1.58
Uganda	–	–	–	0	0.01	0	0	0.04	–	0.01	0.00
Zambia	–	–	0.25	1.46	0.05	0.25	0.12	0.19	–	0.39	0.22
Zimbabwe	0.89	2.11	3.77	14.91	11.35	18.18	2.88	9.7	17.9	11.24	11.35
Africa—mean	0.90	2.27	5.80	4.98	5.39	5.00	6.31	8.69	18.68	7.84	5.80
Africa—mean ex S. Africa	0.25	1.52	1.91	2.08	1.40	2.10	1.49	3.81	9.24	3.15	2.08
Africa—median	0.19	0.80	0.61	1.03	0.28	0.66	0.74	0.43	2.87	0.95	0.66
Malaysia	–	–	–	23.60	29.03	48.21	50.55	41.38	44.92	39.61	43.15
Mexico	–	–	–	6.44	4.27	3.68	6.27	6.87	9.54	6.18	6.35

Panel B: Stocks traded, turnover ratio (%)

Botswana	–	–	4.78	5.6	5.04	4.36	2.3	1.81	2.39	3.75	4.36
Cote d'Ivoire	–	2.2	2.59	0.7	0.72	1.61	2.66	1.41	3.68	1.91	1.61
Egypt	–	10.9	34.74	14.2	16.13	13.73	17.31	42.97	55.23	27.76	17.31
Ghana	–	1.3	1.48	2.6	2.47	4.12	3.24	2.24	3.42	2.80	2.60
Kenya	–	–	3.58	3.4	3.79	7.41	8.15	9.83	15.76	7.42	7.41
Mauritius	1.9	–	5.01	9.3	11.51	6.22	4.45	6.05	5.99	6.93	6.05
Morocco	–	45.9	9.22	10	10.65	6.45	9.1	15.86	32.85	13.45	10.00
Namibia	–	1.6	4.51	3	5.18	0.74	4.82	1.5	4.56	3.47	4.51
Nigeria	0.6	0.84	7.29	10.2	10.65	10.99	13.73	11.46	13.84	11.17	10.99
South Africa	–	6.51	33.9	37.4	78.86	44.8	47.37	39.32	49.52	47.31	44.80
Swaziland	–	–	–	9.8	6.68	0.03	–	0.01	–	4.13	3.36
Tanzania	–	0.1	–	2.4	1.85	–	–	2.29	–	2.18	2.29
Tunisia	–	–	23.29	12.6	13.73	7.16	9.16	16.5	15.24	13.95	13.73
Uganda	–	–	–	–	–	–	–	–	–	–	–
Zambia	4.2	–	–	20.8	22.47	–	–	1.99	–	15.09	20.80
Zimbabwe	–	7.58	10.77	29.4	19.19	26.14	9.22	15.27	7.86	16.84	15.27
Africa—mean	2.23	8.55	11.76	11.43	13.93	10.29	10.96	11.23	17.53	12.45	11.43
Africa—mean ex S. Africa	2.23	8.80	9.75	9.57	9.29	7.41	7.65	9.23	14.62	9.65	9.29
Africa—median	1.90	2.20	6.15	9.80	10.65	6.45	8.63	6.05	10.85	8.37	8.63

Notes: This table presents data on the liquidity of stock markets in Africa. Panel A shows the trend in the value of stock traded as a percentage of Gross Domestic Product, and Panel B presents information on turnover ratio. Turnover is measured as the ratio of value traded to market capitalization. The value traded/GDP ratio measures trading relative to economic activity, whereas turnover ratio measures trading activity relative to size.

services are poor, and settlement and operational procedures are slow. In some African countries, it takes months to execute a single transaction. This problem is mainly due to lack of automation and weak stock market operational infrastructure, in addition to lack of trained personnel.

6.3.2.1   Manual systems are prevalent in Africa, but automation is the global norm

Sub-Saharan African stock exchanges are gradually adapting to electronic systems, but most of them still use manual trading systems, as well manual clearing and settlement systems. Table 6.5, which presents indicators of the African stock market infrastructure, shows the prevalence of slow manual systems. So far African stock exchanges have adopted automated systems include Johannesburg Securities Exchange (JSE), Algerian Stock Exchange, Bourse Regionale des Valeurs Mobilieres (BRVM), the Cairo and Alexandria Stock exchange (CASE), Stock Exchange Mauritius, Namibia Stock Exchange, Tunis Stock Exchange, and Nigeria Stock Exchange. As Table 6.5 shows, manual systems are prevalent in Africa. The manual systems pose bottlenecks in terms of slowing down trading and information production of the stock market. The exorbitantly low turnover indicators that we documented earlier should be partly attributable to these manual systems.

Table 6.5   Infrastructural indicators of African stock exchanges

Country	Clearing & settlement	Foreign participation	Trading system	Trading days
Algeria	Electronic	Yes	Electronic	1*
Botswana	Manual	Yes	Manual	5
Cote d'Ivoire	Electronic	Yes	Electronic	5
Egypt	Electronic	Yes	Electronic	5
Ghana	Manual	Yes	Manual	5
Kenya	Manual	Yes	Electronic	5
Malawi	Manual	Yes	Manual	5
Mauritius	Electronic	Yes	Electronic	5
Morocco	Manual	Yes	Electronic	5
Namibia	Manual	Yes	Electronic	5
Nigeria	Electronic	Yes	Electronic	5
South Africa	Electronic	Yes	Electronic	5
Swaziland	Manual	Yes	Manual	5
Tanzania	Electronic	Yes	Electronic	5
Tunisia	Electronic	Yes	Electronic	5
Uganda	Manual	Yes	Manual	5
Zambia	Electronic	Yes	Manual	5
Zimbabwe	Manual	Yes	Manual	5

* Trading occurs only in the morning. No recent records are available, which is an indication of the stock market's stagnancy.

Source: http://www.undp-pogar.org/countries/finances.asp

Thus, it is important that sub-Saharan African stock exchanges adapt fast to automation and electronic systems. This adaptation will reduce the costs and inefficiencies associated with manual systems and increase trading activity and liquidity in the stock markets by speeding up operations. Of course, automation is an expensive undertaking with considerable resource implications for governments sponsoring stock exchanges. However, Africa has to be fully committed to the venture of stock market development and adopt best practices in operational efficiency. This is particularly important as African stock exchanges contemplate regional consolidation of markets, which would be difficult without automation. In fact, without such moves, the benefits of regional integration, as well as financial globalization of Africa, will be mitigated considerably.

6.3.2.2 *Mutual exchanges the norm in Africa, but demutualization is the global trend*

African stock exchanges are organized as mutual entities, but demutualization has gained popularity. Table 6.6 shows an increasing trend toward demutualization. The main reason is that mutualization breeds poor corporate governance. In a mutual exchange, stock market participants, such as traders and brokers, have monopoly power through exclusive access to trading systems. With demutualization, there are gains from competition among exchanges and improved governance due to market discipline on the insiders. These gains are being leveraged by opening up ownership of exchanges to public investors. Recently a number of stock exchanges, including the NYSE, have gone public and self-listed on the exchanges that they operate.

Demutualization transforms an exchange from a nonprofit entity into a profit entity through a change in the legal status and governance structure of the exchange. Thus, demutualization involves a change in ownership structure and a change in legal organization form. The process of demutualization assigns value per member seat by monetizing the seats. In short, members are assigned valuable shares which can be traded privately or in the public market if the exchange goes public. There are restrictions on ownership structure to mitigate concentrated ownership that would potentially destroy the benefits of good governance. Controlling shareholders and management may not act in the best interests of the minority shareholders unless such ownership restrictions are in placed. Good governance in demutualization is sustained by genuine separation of ownership and control. In the context of Africa, demutualization can also help deter undue government influence that could have occurred under mutual exchanges and help improve performance.[2] Mendiola and O'Hara (2003) and Otchere (2006) document evidence of improvement in performance and governance of demutualized exchanges. In addition, Otchere and Abou-Zied (2008) observes evidence of increased trading activity by foreign investors after Australian Stock Exchange's demutualization and self-listing and provides

Table 6.6   Stock exchange demutualization around the world

Demutualized exchanges	Demutualization date	Listing (IPO) date	Region
Panel A			
Stockholm Stock Exchange	1993	1998	Europe
Deutsche Bourse	2000	2001	Europe
Oslo Stock Exchange	2001	2001	Europe
BME Spanish Exchanges	2001	–	Europe
Borsa Italiana SpA	1997	–	Europe
London Stock Exchange	2000	2001	Europe
Euronext*	2000	2001	Europe
Athens Stock Exchange	1999	2000	Europe
Budapest Stock Exchange	2005	–	Europe
Copehagen Stock Exchange	1997	–	Europe
Swiss Exchange	2002	–	Europe
Hong Kong Stock Exchange	2000	2000	Asia
Singapore Stock Exchange	1999	2000	Asia
Philippines Stock Exchange	2001	–	Asia
National Stock Exchange of India	1993	–	Asia
Osaka Securities Exchange	2001	–	Asia
Bursa Malaysia	2004	2005	Asia
Tokyo Stock Exchange	2001	–	Asia
Australian Stock Exchange	1998	1998	Australia/ New Zealand
Sydney Futures Exchange[a]	2000	2002	Australia/ New Zealand
New Zealand Stock Exchange	2003	2003	Australia/ New Zealand
American Stock Exchange	2001	–	North America
Nasdaq	2001	2002	North America
Toronto Stock Exchange	2000	2002	North America
Chicago Mercantile Exchange (CME)[a] 2002	2002	2002	North America

Continued

Table 6.6 Continued

Demutualized exchanges	Demutualization date	Listing (IPO) date	Region
Chicago Board of Trade (CBOT)[a,b]	2005	2005	North America
New York Stock Exchange*	2006	2006	North America
New York Mercantile Exchange[a]	2000	2006	North America
Inter Continental Exchange[a]	2005	2005	North America
International Securities Exchange[a]	2002	2005	North America
Johannesburg Stock Exchange	2005	–	Africa

Region	No. of demutualized exchanges	Percent
Panel B: Geographical distribution of demutualized exchanges		
North America	9	29%
Europe	11	35%
Asia	7	23%
Australia/ New Zealand	3	10%
Africa	1	3%
South America*	None	–
Total	31	100%

* The Mexican Stock Exchange (BMV) has already started its demutualization process.
[a] These are derivative exchanges.
[b] CBOT was taken over by CME in 2007.

preliminary evidence that shows that liquidity on the stock exchange improved after the change of governance structure and the attendant conversion of the exchange to a publicly traded company.

It appears that the pressure for change is felt everywhere in the stock exchange industry, with at least one exchange in almost all the continents demutualizing. The exception is Latin America. Even so, Mexico Stock Exchange has initiated its demutualization process. Demutualization and self-listing is more popular in Europe, as over 40% of the listed exchanges are European. Perhaps the launching of the European Monetary Union may have triggered this wave demutualization as a response to the increasing competition among the exchanges brought about by the integration. As a result of the adoption of a common currency, a major factor that created national monopoly for the European stock exchanges (i.e., currency difference) is now eliminated in the EU countries except the UK, so are regulatory barriers that created the national exchanges. The demutualization movement has since spread to North America, with 29% of demutualized exchanges and Australia and New Zealand, with 10% of the world's demutualized exchanges located in that geographic region. In Africa, only the South African exchange has demutualized.

One of the catalysts for demutualization has been improvement in technology which has created both opportunities and threats for the exchange industry. On one hand, technological advancement has facilitated trading of shares on several stock exchanges. Technology has also helped exchanges to overcome national boundaries. Investors do not necessarily have to execute their trades on the local stock exchange. They can place their orders wherever and whenever they wish to do so without being limited to specific trading times. Thus, technology has expanded trading opportunities. On the other hand, the migration of order flow to other markets has affected the local franchise that the exchanges had in their respective countries (Otchere, 2006). The competitive environment is also changing. Hitherto, stock exchanges used to enjoy a monopoly in their domestic markets. The increasing globalization of financial markets has reduced barriers to access and has set national exchanges in direct competition with each other. Stock exchanges are also facing severe competition from electronic communications networks (ECNs).

6.3.3   Risk factors to worry about

African stock markets function in a volatile territory (see Figure 6.1 for the regular return volatility), albeit the volatility has been reducing overtime. It is important to have a good appreciation of the risk factors that potentially affect stock markets in Africa. As discussed earlier, one of the functions of the stock market is to provide opportunities for risk diversification and allocation and help channel risky assets to the best valued use. However, there are risk factors that are beyond the control of these markets, which largely stem from instabilities in the economic systems as well as political systems. We will catalogue below such risk factors.

6.3.3.1   *Macroeconomic and political instability*

The stability of a macro-economic environment is central to the development of the stock market. High macroeconomic and political instabilities lead to high volatility in the financial markets. The prevailing evidence is that stability, such as low and predictable rates of inflation, contributes to stock market development. Garcia and Liu (1999) find that sound macroeconomic environments and sufficiently high income levels—GDP per capita, domestic savings, and domestic investments—contribute to stock market development in emerging markets.

Other research has also shown that country risk, by implication, macroeconomic risk, is the predominant source of variation in stock returns across countries (as opposed to industry-specific shocks). Political risk is

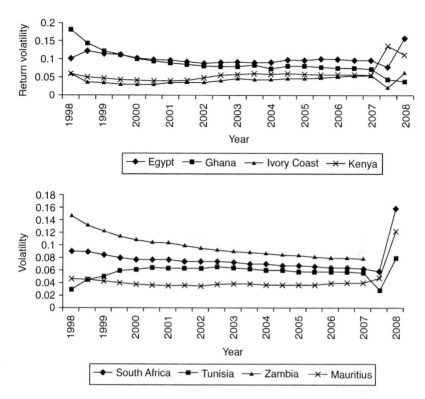

Figure 6.1   Cumulative monthly return volatility for selected African stock markets

often associated with lack of quality institutions, such as law and order and democratic accountability which lead to increased risk premium in the stock market. Further, investors would be concerned about a source of political risk stemming from the odds of adverse changes in government policies. As is often said, the best policy is no change in policy. Unfortunately, the African continent is filled with a litany of cases of abrupt changes in government policies and political climate. These abrupt changes have adverse consequences on the development of stock markets.[3]

Finally, high economic and political instability is likely to exacerbate information asymmetries in the stock market, inducing excess volatility that attracts noisy traders as well as gamblers. Converting a stock exchange into a gambling casino is destabilizing not only to the stock market but the economy at large. If that happens, African stock markets would not accurately reflect the underlying fundamentals, thus leading to an emergence of speculative bubble and irrational behavior. This irrationality would adversely affect the functioning of the stock market and the performance of the real sector of the economy.

African currency fluctuations   Depreciation and wide fluctuations in the values of African currencies can induce an important risk factor in the African stock market scene. High currency exchange volatility is endemic to African economies, creating an impediment to foreign investments. There is evidence that currency depreciation has an adverse impact on the performance of African stock markets (Senbet and Otchere, 2006). Unlike hard currencies, African currencies are readily hedged. In view of the dearth of hedging mechanisms through derivative markets (forward, futures, and options), an indirect approach would be to increase the number of export-oriented companies on the stock exchanges. In particular, those with exposure to hard currency exports should be targeted, so as to provide substantial hedging against local currency devaluation.

Crisis of international confidence   Sub-Sahara Africa still conjectures up images of war, famine, massive corruption, failed projects, grossly undisciplined governance, and gross violations of human rights in international news headlines. This is despite the extensive political, economic and financial sector reforms that have taken place in the region. This information gap has serious consequences for African stock markets and the financial systems in large. This may be conjecturing up a phenomenon called *"Afro-pessimism"*, which leads to high, and even untenable, political and investment risks as perceived by potential investors in Africa. This is, in part, captured by low ratings for creditworthiness of Sub-Sahara African countries relative to other regions (as shown in Table 6.7), although they have displayed significant improvement in the 1990s. However, these ratings are still very low, suggesting high country risk. Country risk is bad for the African stock markets as shown elsewhere (Senbet and Otchere, 2006).

This perception (of African pessimism), although it does not reflect the fundamentals, may lead to crisis of international confidence. The information gap that penalizes an entire region is not good for those countries which are genuinely reforming. The average quality of the Africa "pool" may mask the high quality of the reforming countries due to the monolithic view of Africa as a single, troubled "country" (i.e., pooling equilibrium). This information gap can be minimized through the provision of timely and reliable data required for making estimates of investment risks in Africa. Consequently, there is a need for more extensive, detailed and reliable economic and capital market data that capture the diversity of Africa.

6.4   Stock markets as a conduit for financial globalization of Africa

As Africa moves toward integration into the global economy, the development of stock market institutions and the banking sector is crucial for accessing the benefits of globalization, while controlling globalization

Table 6.7 Institutional investor credit ratings of African countries

Country	1996	1999	2003	2007
Algeria	22.8	26.5	41.6	53.9
Botswana	49.8	36.5	62.2	66.4
Cote d'Ivoire	18.5	25.5	15.7	20.1
Egypt	35.1	45.4	41.1	54.1
Ghana	29.6	30.7	25.8	37.6
Kenya	27.9	24.8	24.6	30.6
Malawi	19.7	19.5	18.8	21.5
Mauritius	50.8	53.9	53.9	56.2
Morocco	39.3	44.3	49.4	54.2
Namibia	–	38	39.8	50.2
Nigeria	15.2	17.9	20.2	40
South Africa	46.3	45.6	54.6	66.7
Swaziland	–	–	30.7	32.6
Tanzania	–	19.5	21.8	30.1
Tunisia	45.5	50.3	52.6	60.7
Uganda	16.1	21.7	20.1	29.9
Zambia	16.5	14.9	15.3	25.4
Zimbabwe	32.5	25.1	11	8
Sub-Saharan Africa	21.1	22.2	20.2	25.9
Europe and Central Asia	27.2	32.1	36.1	46.7
Middle East and North Africa	31	31.1	34.5	42.8
East Asia and Pacific	44.0	38.2	33.5	40.3
Latin America and the Caribbean	30.9	34.5	34.1	44.6
World Average	28.5	29.7	29.1	36.8

Source: Institutional Investors Credit Ratings.

risks (and the attendant financial crisis). Indeed, the surge in the number of stock markets in Africa is also part of the global trend in financial liberalization and deregulation of financial markets around the world. Well-functioning stock markets can be an important signal for Africa's commitment to private sector development and a conduit for the region's financial globalization.

6.4.1 Africa's march into an emerging markets club

There are encouraging forces in place for Africa's integration into the global financial economy. There is growing integration of world capital markets, including those in emerging economies, with increasing capital mobility. Moreover, there are rapid advances in information technology connecting Africa with the rest of the world, with the potential to facilitate capital flows. Thus, investors seeking the benefits of global diversification are now better able to access markets.

African stock markets are actually joining the wave of global integration as implied by Lamba and Otchere (2001). This evidence is indicative of African markets being increasingly integrated with the other world capital markets. Financial sector reforms have contributed to this development. As these markets become increasingly accessible and march into emerging markets club, they should provide significant diversification benefits as well as favorable risk-adjusted performance as we document below.

6.4.2   Africa's positioning in the global risk-reward tradeoffs

African stock markets continue to perform remarkably well in terms of return on investment, despite the challenges they have faced relating to low capitalization and liquidity.

6.4.2.1   Risk-adjusted performance

The stock market performance looks attractive even after adjusting for standard risk measures. Table 6.8 shows performance of African stock markets in absolute as well as risk-adjusted (Sharpe ratio). The average annual return for the period of study (1990–2006), measured in terms of local currency, was 38.35%, and the Sharpe ratio (average excess return per unit of total risk) was 0.54. These returns (both absolute and risk-adjusted) compare favorably to those realized in similar market in Latin America and Asia. For instance, the mean return on Malaysia and Mexico stock exchanges are 9.32% and 31.51%, respectively.

However, international investors would be concerned about earning returns in weak currencies. What is impressive is that, even when the results are converted into dollar returns, the performance measures remain impressive— average annual return of 21.8% and the Sharpe ratio of 0.10. When adjusted for currency effects, the U.S. dollar denominated returns from the African stock markets are comparable to the 22.97% obtained from the Malaysia, but slightly less than the 24.85% realized by Mexico. However, the sharp decline in the Sharpe ration (.54 to .10) is reflective of the weak African currency fluctuations. Given the dearth of currency hedging mechanisms in Africa, the risk stemming from currency fluctuation can be an important deterrent to investment flows into the region. Nonetheless, based on the overall data, the recent performance of African stock markets suggests that they represent largely unexploited opportunities for international investors.

6.4.2.2   Performance in the wake of global financial crisis

It is now logical to look at the extent to which African stock markets are holding up in the current global financial crisis. Has the favorable investment opportunity implied in the precrisis era evaporating? Like the other advanced and emerging stock markets of the world, African stock markets experienced sharp decline in the face of the global crisis. Table 6.9 presents the returns realized by these markets. Panel A presents the returns based on a simple buy-and-hold strategy involving buying the index at the beginning of 2007 or 2008 and liquidating the position at the end of November 2008. Panel B shows the mean monthly returns and the Sharp ratio.

Table 6.8 Risk-adjusted performance of African stock markets

Country	Mean return	Sharp measure	P/E ratio (mean)	P/BV (mean)
Panel A: Performance based on local currency (1990–2006)				
Botswana	25.93	0.50	13.50	6.73
Cote d'Ivoire	9.88	0.10	7.39	1.71
Egypt	103.07	0.39	15.02	4.02
Ghana	44.72	0.28	7.40	4.47
Kenya	18.87	0.06	17.19	2.24
Malawi	15.18	−0.64	n/a	n/a
Mauritius	15.85	0.41	8.69	1.20
Morocco	25.64	0.60	18.62	2.55
Namibia	16.69	0.08	7.11	1.74
Nigeria	33.77	0.53	15.51	3.21
South Africa	16.78	0.24	12.80	3.32
Swaziland	8.02	−0.06	n/a	n/a
Tunisia	22.00	0.45	13.16	1.33
Zambia	13.16	−0.94	n/a	n/a
Zimbabwe	164.48	0.24	10.73	3.58
Pre-1999	31.53	–	–	–
Post-1999	322.05	–	–	–
Africa	38.35	0.54	12.26	3.01
Malaysia	9.32	–	21.72	2.08
Mexico	31.51	–	18.63	3.84

Country	Mean return	Sharp ratio	P/R ratio (mean)	P/BV (mean)
Panel B: Performance based on S&P-EMDB-USD (1997–2006)				
Botswana	31.92	0.69	13.50	6.73
Cote d'Ivoire	9.20	0.19	7.39	1.71
Egypt	30.04	0.29	15.02	4.02
Ghana	0.64	−0.72	7.40	4.47
Kenya	27.82	0.25	17.19	2.24
Mauritius	9.80	0.22	8.69	1.20
Morocco	13.94	0.31	18.62	2.55
Namibia	5.57	−0.19	7.11	1.74
Nigeria	13.42	−0.03	15.51	3.21
South Africa	11.63	0.03	12.80	3.32
Tunisia	1.91	−0.14	13.16	1.33
Zimbabwe	105.67	0.05	10.73	3.58
Pre-1999	11.09	–	21.72	2.08
Post-1999	30.20	–	18.63	3.84
Africa	21.80	0.10	12.26	3.01
Malaysia	22.97	–	21.72	2.08
Mexico	24.85	–	18.63	3.84

Notes: This table shows the Sharpe measure for the African countries. The measure is based on mean stock return and mean risk free (Treasury bill) rates of return from 1990-2006. The measure is calculated for the countries for which data are available.

It would be instructive to compare these returns (both absolute and risk-adjusted) to emerging market performance. We observe, for instance, that African stock markets fare better in comparison with Malaysia and Mexico, the two countries we used as a benchmark during the precrisis period. When we focus on the crisis year (January 2008–December 2008), we observe that whilst all the markets realized negative abnormal returns, generally, the losses sustained by the African markets are less than those sustained by Malaysia and Mexico. We observe a similar pattern when we focus on the mean monthly returns and the Sharp ratio. While the Sharp ratios are

Table 6.9 Stock market performance of selected markets during the recent financial crisis

Country	Mkt.Cap/GDP* 2007	% Returns 2007	% Returns 2008
Panel A: Buy and hold returns			
Egypt	109	0.62	−0.55
Ghana	16	0.23	−0.13
Kenya	45	0.04	−0.31
Mauritius	89	1.00	−0.49
Morocco	103	0.34	−0.24
Namibia	10	0.41	−0.04
Nigeria	52	0.63	−0.59
South Africa	300	0.09	−0.33
Tunisia	15	0.09	−0.03
Malaysia	180	0.27	−0.43
Mexico	45	0.08	−0.39

Country	2007 Mean monthly returns	2007 Sharp ratio	2008 Mean monthly returns	2008 Sharp ratio
Panel B: Mean monthly returns and Sharp ratio during the financial crisis period				
Egypt	0.05	0.62	−0.06	−0.71
Ghana	0.02	0.20	−0.01	−0.09
Kenya	0.00	0.07	−0.04	−
Namibia	0.03	0.38	−0.01	−0.06
Nigeria	0.05	0.68	−0.07	−0.79
South Africa	0.01	0.10	−0.03	−0.25
Malaysia	0.02	0.32	−0.05	−0.60
Mexico	0.01	0.25	−0.04	−1.08

*Figures for 2008 are not available **The measures are calculated for countries for which data are available.

negative for all the markets, the markets in Africa seem to have performed better than the comparable markets.

The performance of the markets can perhaps be better visualized in Figures 6.2 and 6.3 which presents the cumulative returns. The cumulative returns for the stock markets in Ghana and Nigeria have been positive whether we focus on the 2007–2008 period (Figure 6.2) or just 2008 (Figure 6.3), whereas the other markets—S&P 500 Index, Malaysia, Mexico and the South African market have all experienced negative cumulative returns.

In the last 20 years, global investors have become enamored of emerging stock markets, but by comparison, Africa has received a scant portion of capital flow to emerging markets as global equity funds have maintained a low exposure to Africa. However, as noted earlier this is changing and growing, and the growth can be accelerated through putting appropriate measures to build capacity of African stock markets. This should be so even in the face of the ongoing global financial crisis and the temptation for the region not to be that integrated into the global financial economy.

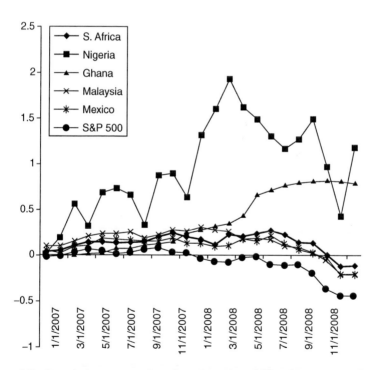

Figure 6.2 Cumulative returns in selected stock markets during the 2007–08 financial crisis

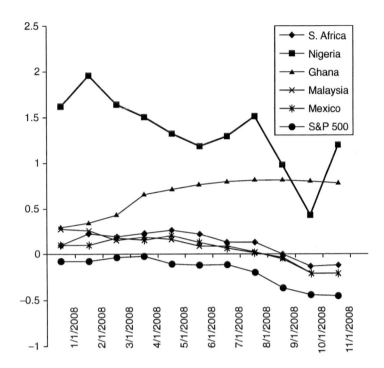

Figure 6.3   Cumulative returns in selected stock markets during the 2008 financial crisis

6.4.3   Regional cooperation and integration of Africa into the global financial economy

The thinness and illiquidity of African stock markets pose a serious hindrance against financial globalization of Africa. Regional cooperation and integration of the disparate and thin markets would be an important mechanism to overcome the barriers to global integration. Thus, regionalization of African stock markets should enhance mobilization of both domestic and global financial resources to fund regional companies, while injecting more liquidity into the markets (Senbet, 1998).

There are now growing initiatives along these dimensions. Regional stock exchanges are being contemplated along linguistic lines. The Francophone countries of West Africa formed the first regional stock exchange, the Abidjan-based BVRM in 1998. The BVRM comprises the stock markets in Benin, Burkina Faso, Cote d'Ivoire, Guinea-Bissau, Mali, Niger, Senegal and Togo. Currently, the Anglophone countries of West Africa are contemplating forming a regional stock exchange under the umbrella of the ECOWAS. Similarly, Kenya, Tanzania and Uganda are natural partners for organizing a regional stock exchange. Moreover, the Southern African Development Community (SADEC) stock exchanges are taking initiatives for the formation of a regional stock exchange.

There are certain preconditions for successful regional integration of stock exchanges. They include harmonization of legislations, such as bankruptcy and accounting laws, establishment of regional self-regulatory agencies and regulatory exchange commissions, coordinated monetary arrangements (e.g., via currency zones). In particular, the tax treatment of investments must be harmonized, since tax policy is an important incentive or disincentive for both issuers and investors. Ultimately, the regulations, accounting reporting systems, along with clearance, settlement and depository systems, should conform to international standards. Moreover, African stock markets contemplating regional integration should quickly adapt to electronic trading systems and move out of the prevailing manual systems.

6.4.4 The potential hazards of financial globalization of Africa

So far, we have emphasized the benefits of financial globalization and the role of African stock markets in promoting integration of Africa into the global financial economy. It is appropriate to close this section with some perspectives on the potential costs of financial globalization.

The other side of financial globalization is that it exposes African countries to volatility of the global financial markets and unfavorable international exchange rate fluctuations. This global risk exposure could then lead to large and suddenly unfavorable swings in capital flow to the region. The available evidence from other regions of the world is that countries that experienced large capital flows suffered commensurately large and sudden outflows. The collapse of capital inflows can be enormously costly, and it manifests itself in sudden withdrawals of deposits, leading to credit crunch in the economy. Moreover, creditors may be unwilling to supply short-term credit even for liquidity purposes.

In the wake of the Asian crisis, for instance, there were dramatic declines in the asset and currency values, with currency values for Thailand, Korea, Indonesia declining at least 50%.[4] The dramatic financial instability was accompanied by poor or declining economic performance, and for the first quarter of 1998, shrinkage in GDP was observed for Indonesia, Thailand, Korea, Malaysia, Hong Kong, and even Japan.

Similar phenomena are now being witnessed currently, except in this case the crisis is widespread and global. African economies and stock markets have not been immune and are adversely affected. It is now tempting for African countries to avoid financial globalization so as to avoid costs of potential financial crisis. However, this is a wrong lesson. The appropriate lesson is to recognize both the benefits and risks of financial globalization. This means African countries should put into place into place appropriate risk control mechanisms while integrating into the global financial economy so that the potential benefits are maximized on a risk-adjusted basis. One appropriate strategy is to develop and build capacity of a well-functioning stock market system.

6.5   Share issue privatizations in Africa and corporate governance

There has been a wide spread privatization of state-owned enterprises in sub-Saharan Africa in the wake of the extensive economic forms that have taken place in the region. This is particularly welcome, given the available evidence that privatized firms generally outperform state-owned enterprises. Consequently, the conventional wisdom for state ownership of business enterprises, particularly, banks is being challenged. A list of the top 5% privatizations ranked by size (amount raised from the sale) is presented in Appendix 6A.1.

6.5.1   Benefits of privatization through stock markets

Stock markets have been used as a mechanism for privatization of state-owned enterprises. There are now a growing number of African state-owned enterprises which are using the stock markets as vehicle for privatization (see Appendix 6A.1 which catalogues privatizations in Africa, including share issue privatizations). Share issue privatization programs contribute directly to the depth of the stock markets through increased supply of listed companies. This should be a welcome development in view of the observed thinness and illiquidity of African stock markets that we discussed earlier.

Moreover, there are less obvious benefits of privatization of state-owned enterprises through the stock market. *First,* share issue privatizations bring the privatized enterprises to the discipline of stock markets. Given the fact that the heavily subsidized state-owned enterprises in Africa generally lack effective governance mechanisms, and face little competition, bringing these firms to the discipline of the stock markets will improve efficiency and performance. *Second,* the stock market is an arena for price discovery and it makes it possible for large-scale privatization programs to take place at fair price (Senbet, 1998). This in turn depoliticizes the privatization process. *Third,* African stock markets can provide a vehicle for diversity of ownership in an economy, since they allow an opportunity for local investor participation through purchases of privatization shares. This also dispels concerns about privatization assets being grabbed by foreigners. Thus, the stock market is not just for the elite, but it actually provides an opportunity for diversity of ownership, if privatization programs are conducted through the market. *Fourth,* share issue privatizations increase public awareness about the market through a creation of first time buyers of market instruments.[5]

6.5.2   Banking privatization and stock market development

There is an accumulating evidence that countries with well-developed banks tend to have well-developed stock markets, and hence suggesting complementarity between stock market development and banking development. In particular, it is found that *there* is a significant relationship between measures of stock market development and those of bank sector development (Levine and Zervos, 1998). Part of the reason is that support services from well-functioning banking systems can contribute to the development of the stock market. This implies the prevailing weak and malfunctioning banking systems are a deterrent to the growth of African stock markets (see Senbet and Otchere, 2006). Moreover, the African banks which are state-owned lack sufficient oversight of the governance of business creditors. The African banking system also faces challenges in terms of lack of well-trained manpower that is capable of performing modern risk management and implementing an efficient credit risk policy toward enterprises.

It is encouraging that there have been extensive privatizations of state-owned banks. This is welcome, since genuine privatization of banks should lead to a well-functioning banking system that can now help foster the development of African stock markets. The traditional thinking is that state-owned banks serve underserved markets, particularly rural areas and small enterprises. However, the emerging evidence tends to contradict this conventional view. The available evidence is that state ownership is associated with less financial development, less growth, and poor bank performance, and less financial stability (Barth, Caprio and Levine, 2001).

In recent years there has been a sharp decline in the state ownership of banks in Africa, although some countries (e.g., Ethiopia) continue to resist bank privatization altogether. The performance effect of bank privatization is mixed (Senbet and Otchere, 2006). There has been a deterioration in the asset quality of the privatized banks. Indicators of performance, such as credit quality and profitability, worsened for the privatized banks. Privatized banks also experienced worse performance based on stock market data, although they were not statistically significant. This is troubling and suggestive of the possibility that there have not been gains from bank privatizations in Africa.

The evidence on the performance effects of bank privatization in Africa appears inconsistent with the overall evidence presented for other regions (Clarke, Cull, and Shirley, 2004). However, there are a couple of factors at work in the context of Africa. The first issue may be due to data generated from undeveloped and malfunctioning African stock markets. The second issue which is more likely is that poor post privatization performance of banks may be due to the prevalence of partial privatizations of banks in

Africa. Partial bank privatization leaves the banks still vulnerable to government intervention. In fact, the available evidence is that privatization performance improves with less government retention of shares (D'Souza, Megginson and Nash, 2001). This was corroborated by more recent evidence suggesting very limited privatization gains even when the government held a minority stake (Clarke, Cull, Shirley, 2004). Thus, given the evidence, the continued government ownership of privatized banks should be eliminated; this would then allow for the development of a well-functioning banking system as well as the development of the stock markets in Africa.

6.5.3   African stock markets and corporate governance

The quality of corporate governance is central to the development of African stock markets. While share issue privatizations bring the privatized companies to a disciplinary force of the stock market system, it is still the case that corporate insiders may engage in activities which are harmful to capital contributors. This problem is magnified when a few insiders have controlling shareholdings and expropriate resources away from minority shareholders. It is important that as stock markets develop in Africa, the corporate sector moves to best practices in corporate governance.

6.5.3.1   *Why good governance?*

The quality of corporate governance determines whether investors are willing to put their money into a listed company. Also, it affects the price that investors are willing to pay for the shares that they buy. Empirical studies have found that investors are willing to pay a premium for the stock of a well-governed company over a poorly governed company which is otherwise equivalent in terms of financial performance (Gompers, Ishii, and Metrick, 2003). If investors lack confidence in corporate governance, they are likely to discount the shares that they hold, and that goes in the face of the company's ability to raise funds and grow. Good corporate governance, thus, allows a company to perform efficiently and create value for the shareholders and benefit the economy at large. Good corporate governance is also an important factor in building confidence of global investors who are potentially attracted to African stock markets. Thus, accessing the benefits of financial globalization requires that corporate governance mechanisms in place are credible and transparent.

A recent Russian case illustrates the consequences of bad governance (see The Hermitage Fund case, HBS No. N2-703-010). Voucher privatizations in Russia allowed managers or the oligarchs to assemble controlling stakes through a loans-for-shares scheme. The Hermitage Fund case suggests these parties took advantage of their powerful position to enrich themselves. Controlling shareholders ignore established procedures for convening meetings of shareholders and took decisions without the knowledge of minority shareholders, and often minority shareholders' stakes were diluted without their knowledge and consent. In fact, controlling shareholders often had the votes to dominate the corporate boards and even change the corporate charters. The corporate governance crisis in Russia was in part attributable to the lack of well-functioning corporate governance institutions, such as company laws, accounting rules and regulations, securities regulators, and auditing firms and equity analysts. These institutions were slow to develop and did not function as intended in Russia.

6.5.3.2   Best corporate governance practices and the role of African Policy-makers

The internal and external monitoring mechanisms that accompany stock market development, such as structure of corporate boards and system of disclosure rules, improve transparency and boost investor confidence. The principal function of the corporate board is to maximize shareholder interests through an oversight of the risk profile of a corporation, monitoring the integrity of the company, and putting into place quality and competent management.

Best practices in corporate governance allow for a separation of the role of the government as a regulator and business operator, the appointment of independent nonexecutive directors. The growing consensus is that the board has to be independent of the chief executive officer, through appointments of directors who are outsiders with no serious business interests with the firm.

It also useful to recognize that African companies can respond to weak institutional environments by adopting voluntary measures of corporate governance. For instance, they can hire reputable external auditors. They may even list or cross/list on the large exchanges (e.g., NYSE, LSE), and hence subject themselves to global discipline (e.g., NYSE, LSE). These adaptations can create value and foster investor confidence. Moreover, the stock exchanges themselves, as part of a self-regulatory mechanism, can establish standards for listing of companies, consistent with best governance practices. However, companies themselves, as well as self-regulators, can only do so much. There is still a need for strong institutions (e.g., securities and exchange commissions) and strong laws that protect investors. Corporate governance is getting wide attention around the world, with all kinds of codes—voluntary as well as mandatory, and financial globalization of Africa calls for global integration of the region into best governance practices.

6.6   Policies for building capacity of African stock markets

This policy-oriented chapter has attempted to answer the basic question "why stock markets for Africa" (see Section 6.1) by cataloguing the various functions these markets perform and their role in promoting economic development. We have also examined their role in integrating Africa into a global financial economy by way of providing evidence of the recent performance of the African stock markets. The prospects for financial globalization are real, and the ongoing regional initiatives to consolidate these markets and to use them for large-scale privatization programs are good in this regard.

Of course, our examination of the current state of African stock markets indicates the many challenges that these markets face. It is tempting for African countries to forego the challenges of developing homesgrown stock markets, hoping that global stock markets can be accessed directly. While it is now increasingly possible for large African companies to cross-list in the foreign stock exchanges and /or issue depositary right securities traded on those exchanges, the view of avoiding the development of the local stock markets is misguided. While financial globalization can be an important complement, it cannot be an absolute substitute for domestic stock market development.

In fact, a vital source of integrating Africa into the global financial economy is the existence of well-functioning domestic stock markets. Well-functioning domestic stock markets are vital for domestic resource mobilization, since they provide incentives and profitable options for domestic capital to be retained. Retention of domestic capital is important in the light of massive financial capital flight that Africa witnessed over the years. The development of the local stock market is important both in terms of buffering the volatility of external capital flows and helping achieve the political success of privatization, as we discussed earlier. Moreover, if Africans themselves are reluctant to invest in their own local stock markets, it can be hardly interpreted abroad as vote of confidence. Consequently, domestic participation is important in building international credibility.

Thus, in cataloguing policy measures for stock market development, we should go beyond those which help attract foreign capital. Policy measures should also target mobilization of domestic resources through the cultivation of attractive investment opportunities and fostering deep and well-functioning domestic stock markets. Moreover, as in other countries, investor participation is possible directly or indirectly through such vehicles as pension plans, insurance policies, mutual funds, etc. Domestic investors are also more likely to be better informed about economic opportunities in the country than those in the other countries, and domestic stock market development is one mechanism of empowering domestic investors.

Below we list some policy measures that we regard as vital for developing and building capacity of African stock markets. The thinness and illiquidity of the current African stock markets, shortage of domestic resource mobilization, the region's marginalization in the global markets for financial capital, coupled with shrinking official aid flows, are at the heart of the challenges that these prescriptions are intended to address. The background material, as well as supporting evidence is, is contained in the previous sections of this chapter. Rather than replicating the discussions and the background material, the key policy measures are stated below in an outline form. The reader is urged to consult the rest of the chapter for more details and background material.

1. *Listing size*: Develop incentives for listing on stock exchanges (e.g., tax incentives for listed companies) as a means to achieve greater market depth and trading activity.
2. *Investor confidence*: Foster public confidence and improve informational efficiency with disclosure rules, accounting standards, and enforceability of contracts, consistent with best practices for stock market development.
3. *Stock market regulation*: Develop a well-functioning stock market regulatory scheme, including a strong securities and exchange commission capable of enforcing securities laws and developing appropriate rules, consistent with best international practices.
4. *Share issue privatization*: Privatize the state-owned enterprises through African stock markets as a mechanism for achieving market depth, diversity of ownership, fair pricing, public awareness of the stock market, and achieving better corporate governance and developing the stock market.
5. *Corporate governance*: Strengthen institutions for corporate governance and adopt best international practices in terms of measures for the effectiveness of the corporate board of directors and increased protection of shareholder rights against controlling shareholders/management.
6. *Market consolidation*: Consolidate the African stock markets and harmonize laws, regulations, capital market institutions, as monetary systems, across the integrating regions.
7. *Financial manpower*: Develop a talented financial manpower capable of managing risk both for the banking and equity market sector toward the enhancement of risk control mechanisms as markets become more sophisticated, and possibly venturing even into the derivatives arena. Support the state-of-the art finance curricula at higher education institutions.
8. *Banking development as a vehicle for stock market development*: Strengthen and build a well-functioning banking regulatory scheme with strong supervisory and monitoring role for regulators, making sure also that the regulators are not captured by the banking industry; again conform to best banking regulatory practices ala the Basle standards. Engage in full privatization of banks rather than partial privatization to avoid continuing government interference.

Appendix 6A.1   List of privatized firms (Top 5% ranked by size (transaction value)

Country	Year	Company name	Sector	Transaction Value ($m)
Egypt	1995	Eastern Tobacco*	Agriculture	163.70
South Africa	1999	South African Airways	Air Transport	235.00
Egypt	2006	CIB	Banking	2224.70
Egypt	2006	Bank of Alexandria	Banking	1610.00
Morocco	1995	BMCE*	Banking	208.62
Egypt	2006	Egyptian American Bank*	Banking	169.80
Egypt	2005	Alexandria Mineral Oils*	Energy	156.00
Egypt	2005	Sidi Kreir Petrochemicals	Energy	153.00
Morocco	1994	Societe Nationale d'Investissement*	Insurance	226.56
Morocco	2003	Regie des Tabacs	Manufacturing	1550.80
Morocco	2006	Altadis Maroc/Régie des Tabacs	Manufacturing	466.00
Nigeria	2006	Sunti Sugar Company limited	Manufacturing	427.00
Egypt	1999	Assiout Cement Company	Manufacturing	414.50
Egypt	2005	National Fertilizer Company	Manufacturing	341.00
Egypt	2005	Suez Cement*	Manufacturing	339.00
Tunisia	2000	Ciments de Jbel	Manufacturing	229.90
Tunisia	1998	Societe Les Ciments Jebel Ouest	Manufacturing	216.00
Egypt	1999	Alexandria Portland Cement	Manufacturing	178.00
Algeria	2005	Asmidal Fertilizer Company	Manufacturing	158.00
Nigeria	2005	National Fertilizer Company	Manufacturing	151.00
Egypt	1999	Beni Suef Cement	Manufacturing	150.00
Morocco	2005	Sunabel/Suta/Sura/Sucrafor	Manufacturing	146.60
Nigeria	2005	Eleme Petrochemicals Company, Ltd.	Manufacturing	145.70
Tunisia	1998	Societe Les Ciments d'Enfidha	Manufacturing	145.00
Egypt	1996	Helwan Portland Cement*	Manufacturing	144.48
Ghana	1994	Ashanti Goldfields Company(AGC)*	Mining	454.00
Zambia	1998	ZCCM - Luanshya copper and cobalt mining complex	Mining	245.00

Continued

Appendix 6A.1 Continued

Country	Year	Company name	Sector	Transaction Value ($m)
Zambia	1997	Nkana and Nchanga (part of the Zambia Consolidated Copper mines)	Mining	220.00
Nigeria	2004	West African Refinery Company, Ltd. Sierra Leone	Oil	353.00
South Africa	1984	Sasol Two	Petrochemicals	1821.95
South Africa	1991	Sasol Three	Petrochemicals	1052.12
South Africa	1980	Sasol One	Petrochemicals	514.16
Nigeria	1993	NNPC oil field	Petrochemicals	500.00
Morocco	1997	Societe Anonyme Marocaine de l'Industrie de Raffinage (Samir)	Petrochemicals	416.00
Morocco	1996	SAMIR*	Petrochemicals	172.65
Egypt	2006	Sidi Abdel Rahman Hotel and Land	Services	173.10
South Africa	1989	Iscor	Steel	1146.60
Egypt	2006	Etisalat Misr (third GSM license)*	Telecommunications	2900.00
Morocco	2004	Maroc Telecom*	Telecommunications	2530.00
Tunisia	2006	Tunisie Telecom	Telecommunications	2250.00
South Africa	1997	Telkom*	Telecommunications	1261.00
Egypt	2005	Telecom Egypt	Telecommunications	892.00
Nigeria	2006	Nigerian Telecommunications Ltd (Nitel)	Telecommunications	750.00
South Africa	2003	Telkom SA Ltd*	Telecommunications	484.80
Algeria	2004	Wataniya Telecom Algerie	Telecommunications	421.00
Algeria	2003	Djezzy GSM	Telecommunications	360.00
Nigeria	2001	MTN Nigeria	Telecommunications	285.00
Nigeria	2001	Vmobile	Telecommunications	285.00
Mauritius	2000	Mauritius Telecom	Telecommunications	261.00
Tunisia	2004	Tunisiana	Telecommunications	247.00
Tunisia	2002	Tunisiana	Telecommunications	227.00
Nigeria	2002	Globacom	Telecommunications	200.00
Côte d'Ivoire	1997	CI-Telcom (CI Telcom)	Telecommunications	193.00
Egypt	1996	Cairo Sheraton	Tourism	146.69
Nigeria	2005	APAPA Port Terminal	Transportation	1061.00
South Africa	1998	Airports Company of South Africa (ACSA)	Transportation	245.70

Source: World Bank Privatization database
* denotes "Share-issue", "public offer", "IPO" privatized fir

9. *Development of stock market institutions*: Foster the development of institutions that support and sustain African stock markets, such as pension funds, credit ratings agencies, etc.

10. *Database*: Develop a comprehensive stock market database to foster both fractioned/investment analyst research and academic research—making it possible for African stock markets to be subject to best research practices.

11. *Trading systems*: Quickly transform from manual into automated/electronic systems; the latter are now the norm in the more advanced stock markets.

12. *Stock exchange ownership*: Consider demutualizing the stock exchanges as a mechanism for improved governance stemming from separation and ownership of the exchanges and promoting investor confidence in the system. Demutualization is now a global trend, while mutualization is the norm in Africa.

13. *Promoting Financial globalization*: It is tempting to avoid financial globalization so as to avoid its adverse effects, but this is misguided for two principal reasons: (1) as witnessed from the current global financial crisis, African economies cannot run away from its effects even when they are not integrated into the global financial economy, since its adverse consequences can be transmitted through the real sector (e.g., sharp decline in trade and direct investment flows); (2) marginalization in the global financial economy loses out on the potential benefits of globalization [see Section 6.4 (c)] When promoting financial globalization, though, measures should be in place to mitigate its adverse consequences,, and developing a deep financial system, including the stock market, is one of them. Moreover, there should be enhanced capacity to manage risk.

Notes

Lemma W. Senbet is the William E. Mayer Chair Professor of Finance at the Robert H. Smith School of Business, University of Maryland, College Park. *Isaac Otchere* is Associate Professor of Finance at the Sprott School of Business, Carleton University, Ottawa, Canada. The original version of the paper was presented at the IMF/ADB Forum *"African Finance for the 21st Century"*, Tunis, March 2008. We thank the conference participants and an anonymous referee for the useful comments and suggestions.

1. This chapter has benefited from prior work: Senbet (1998) "Globalization of African Financial Markets", UNU/AERC conference (Tokyo) [also in Asia and Africa in the Global Economy, UNU Press, 2003], Senbet (1998) "Global Financial Crisis: Implications for Africa", AERC plenary conference (Nairobi) [also in Journal of African Economies, 2001], and Aryeetey and Senbet (1999) "Essential Financial Market Reforms," World Bank 21st Century project conference (Abidjan), Senbet and Otchere "Financial Sector Reforms: Issues and Policies" (ABCDE, 2006).

2. The issue of corporate governance is crucial in the context of stock market development, and we will take up the subject more fully in a later section.

3. A case in point is the dramatic price swing in the Zimbabwe stock market. The Zimbabwe market, which rose phenomenally in 1996 (89.5%), moved down by more than 50% during the final quarter of 1997 in the wake of the dramatic government farm and pension policies. The two policy changes are: (1) land reform to take over 1,500 commercial farms—mostly white-owned, and (2) a decision to pay $240 million in pensions to disgruntled veterans of the Zimbabwe independence war.
4. See Gande, John, and Senbet (2008) for the role of distorted incentives in making emerging economies more vulnerable to financial crisis and the proposed mechanisms to prevent financial crisis. See the AERC plenary synthesis by Senbet (1998) for more detailed analysis of global financial crisis and its implications for Africa.
5. Privatization should also include financial institutions so that they can perform their proper function of delegated monitoring and help achieve efficient allocation of resources.

References

Aryeetey, E. and Senbet, L.W. 1999. "Essential financial market reforms in Africa." Paper presented at the 21st Century African World Bank project. Abidjan.

Barth, J., Caprio Jr., G., and Levine, R. 2001. "Banking systems around the globe: Do regulation and ownership affect performance and stability?" In *Prudential Supervision: What Works and What Doesn't,* Mishkin, Frederic (ed.). Chicago, IL: University of Chicago Press.

Clarke, G., Cull, R., and Shirley, M. 2004. *Empirical Studies of Bank Privatization: Some Lessons.* mimeo, World Bank.

D'Souza, J., Megginson, W. and Nash, R. 2000. Determinants of performance improvements in privatized firms: The role of restructuring and corporate governance, Working paper, University of Oklahoma.

D'Souza, J., William, L., and Megginson, R. 2001. *Determinants of Performance Improvements in Privatized Firms: The Role of Restructuring and Corporate Governance.* Mimeo.

Garcia and Liu 1999. "Macroeconomic determinants of stock market development." *Journal of Applied Economics,* 29–59.

Gande, A., John, K., and Senbet, L.W. 2008. "Bank incentives, economic specialization, and financial crises in emerging economies." (with A. Gande and K. John), *Journal of International Money and Finance,* 27 (5): 707–32.

Gompers, P., Ishii, J.L., and Metrick, A. 2003. "Corporate governance and equity prices." *Quarterly Journal of Economics,* 118(1): 107–55.

Haque, N., Hauswald, R., and Senbet, L.W. 1997. "Financial market development in emerging economies: A functional approach." International Monetary Fund and the University of Maryland: Mimeo.

International Monetary Fund, *International Financial* Statistics, Yearbook.

Lamba, A. and Otchere, I. 2001. "Analysis of the linkages among the African equity markets and the world's major equity markets." *African Finance Journal* 3(2): 1–25.

Levine, R. 1997. "Financial development and economic growth: Views and agenda." *Journal of Economic Literature,* 35: 688–726.

Levine, R. and Zervos 1998. "Stock market development and long run growth." Policy Research Working Paper, The World Bank.

Mendiola A. and O'Hara, M., 2003. "Taking stock in stock markets: The Changing governance of exchanges." Working Paper, Cornell University.

Otchere, I. 2006. "Stock exchange self-listing and value effects." *Journal of Corporate Finance,* 12: 926–53.

Otchere, I. and Abou-Zied, K. 2008. "Stock exchange demutualization, self-listing and performance: The case of the Australian stock exchange." *Journal of Banking and Finance,* 32: 512–25.

Senbet, L.W. 1998. "African capital markets: Development potential and capacity building." Prepared for the United Nations Workshop "Advancing Financial Intermediation in Africa". Mauritius.

Senbet, L.W. 2001a. "Globalization of African financial markets." in *Asia and Africa in the Global Economy,* eds. E. Aryeetey, J. Court, M. Nissanke, B. Weder. UNU Press, based on a presentation at the UNU and AERC conference "Africa and Asia in the Global Economy", Tokyo, August.

Senbet, L.W. 2001b. "Global financial crisis: Implications for Africa." *Journal of African Economies,* 10, February: 104–40.

Senbet, L.W. and Otchere, I. 2006. "Financial sector reforms in Africa: Perspectives on issues and policies." in *Growth and integration,* eds., Bourguignon F. and B. Pleskovic. Annual World Bank Conference on Development Economics.

Tadesse, S. 2004. "The allocation and monitoring role of capital markets." *Journal of Financial and Quantitative Analysis,* 39(4): 701–30.

World Bank Privatization database, http://ppi.worldbank.org/

Yartey, C.A. and Adjasi, C.K. 2007. "Stock market development in sub-Saharan Africa: Critical issues and challenges." IMF Working Paper.

Part II

Finance in Africa—Policy Issues and Case Studies

7
Regulatory Frameworks in Sub-Saharan Africa: Ensuring Efficiency and Soundness

Inutu Lukonga

7.1 Introduction[1]

Sub-Saharan African (SSA) countries have been reforming their regulatory frameworks, as part of efforts to strengthen their financial systems and deepen financial intermediation. Most countries have participated in the joint IMF/World Bank Financial Sector Assessment Programs (FSAPs) to appraise the soundness of their financial systems, assess regulatory frameworks against international standards, and to develop reform agendas. Several countries have also been engaged in technical cooperation (TC) with the IMF and the World Bank in related areas. In addition, there are parallel national and regional efforts to strengthen and harmonize regulatory and supervisory frameworks.

The reforms, coupled with a supportive domestic and external environment, have contributed to greater stability, resilience, and some development of financial systems. Banking systems have been generally sound and stable, though there are some exceptions. Financial products and delivery modes are increasing in sophistication and regional banking groups are rapidly expanding across the region. Capital markets have grown rapidly and foreign investor participation increased in selected countries' debt and equity markets. As for the nonbanking sector, the microfinance has expanded rapidly in most countries while only selected countries registered growth in the pensions and insurance sectors.

The generally favorable trends notwithstanding, financial sectors in SSA countries face macroeconomic risks and balance sheet vulnerabilities. The dependence on a few export sectors, and the resulting concentrations of loan portfolios to those sectors, coupled with lax large exposure limits in some regions, render many SSA countries vulnerable to terms of trade and other exogenous shocks. Credit risk also remains high, exacerbated by the continuing weaknesses in the legal and judiciary frameworks for enforcing creditor rights, deficiencies in the infrastructure for assessing borrower creditworthiness, and shortcomings in banks' risk management capabilities.

The probability of these risks materializing has been increased by the global financial crisis and the related recession. The drop in commodity prices, export volumes, remittances, and capital flows and the slowdown in economic growth have created conditions for an adverse feedback loop between the real sector and the financial sector. Against a background of weaknesses in credit risk management by banks and the rapid growth in credit that preceded the crisis, a deterioration in corporate balance sheets could rapidly translate into increased nonperforming loans and erode bank profitability and capital. At the same time, concerns about credit risk could curtail lending volumes and accentuate the economic downturn.

This chapter reviews the regulatory and supervisory frameworks in SSA countries, evaluates their adequacy in addressing the challenges and risks facing the financial system, and discusses the policy options. To provide context to the assessment, Section 7.2 discusses selected structural features, trends and risks in SSA countries' financial systems that have important implications for financial sector regulation. This is followed, in Section 7.3, by a review of regulatory and supervisory frameworks for the financial sector and a discussion of remaining gaps and weaknesses. Section 7.4 summarizes the findings and discusses the policy options for the region.

The emerging conclusion is that regulatory and supervisory frameworks, though improved, continue to exhibit important gaps. The weaknesses are more pervasive in the frameworks for capital markets and the nonbanking sector, but the banking sector also continues to exhibit important gaps. In particular, regulatory and supervisory practices have not kept pace with developments in the financial sector, due in part to limitations in capacity, including human resources and skills, technology and systems. In capital markets, enactment of the laws and regulations sometimes has not been accompanied by actual implementation. Weaknesses in the nonbanking sector are more pervasive, covering institutional arrangements, laws, enforcement, and supervisory capacity.

Ongoing structural changes in the financial sector coupled with the deteriorating external and domestic environment place additional demands on regulatory and supervisory frameworks. The increase in the cross-sector and cross-border operations of financial institutions has increased the importance of consolidated and cross-border supervisory issues; the growth of capital markets and other nonbank institutions has increased the need for more comprehensive coverage of regulation; and financial innovations require stronger systems and controls and management of operational risk. In addition, the crisis has increased the potential for system wide stress and has therefore heightened the need for macrofinancial risk analysis and contingency crisis management.

Therefore, in addition to continuing reforms to foster the overall development of financial systems, SSA countries need to intensify financial system surveillance in order to minimize contagion from the global financial crisis; address identified gaps and institute processes to ensure that regulatory and supervisory practices are constantly aligned with emerging risks; and that there is supervisory capacity to meet the new skill requirements. Given the systemic importance of banks, strengthening bank supervision should remain a priority. However, as the global financial crisis has demonstrated, stress in unregulated segments could transmit to otherwise previously well-regulated sectors, thus it is important that there are concurrent efforts to strengthen the regulation and supervision of capital markets and nonbank institutions. Reforms of financial infrastructures also need to be accelerated.

7.2 Financial system structure, performance, and risks

7.2.1 Structure

Financial systems in SSA are bank dominated, but other financial segments have been growing rapidly. In most countries, the banking sector accounts for more than 75 percent of the financial system's assets. There are only a few countries—for example, South Africa, Botswana, Swaziland, Namibia, and Ghana—where the assets of the nonbanking sector are as large or larger than those of the banking sector (Table 7.1). At the country and subregional level, there are substantial differences in structures and level of development. In particular, three broad groupings can be discerned as follows: the first group includes South Africa an emerging market country; the second is constituted of frontier market countries; and remainder fall in the third category which are referred to as "financially developing" countries. (Box 7.1).

Most of the countries' banking systems exhibit a high degree of concentration in foreign ownership, market share, and balance sheet structure. Subsidiaries of international and regional banking groups dominate the banking systems (Table 7.2).[3] Market share, in most countries, is largely concentrated in a few banks; liabilities consist mostly of low cost deposits, with the exception of South Africa where wholesale deposits are significant. Interest income accounts for the bulk of earnings in most SSA countries. A number of countries (e.g., Malawi, South Africa, Cape Verde) also have significant cross ownership links between banks and insurance.

Capital markets also exhibit a significant degree of concentration, and most countries have underdeveloped markets that have a few listed companies, limited debt instruments, narrow investor base and few categories of issuers (Figure 7.1). For many of the countries, their capital markets consist mainly of government securities. Frontier market countries have, in addition to the government securities, developed equities while corporate bonds and Collective Investment Schemes (CIS) are in nascent stages.[4] South Africa is more advanced with deep and liquid exchange traded equities, debt and derivatives markets that is integrated with global markets and there is also a large over-the-counter (OTC) market (Box 7.1).

Table 7.1 Financial system structure

Country	Commercial banks	Other deposit taking institution	Microfinance institutions	Rural banks	Insurance companies	Pension funds	Other	Latest date
Botswana	44.0				16	17.4	6.8	2006
Central African Republic	94.0		4.0		6.0			2007
Comoros	61.0		34.0				5.0	2008
Congo. Rep of	96.0				4.0			2004
Ethiopia	85.0		6.0		2.0		6.0	2008
Gabon	87.0	4.8			7.0		10.0	2006
Gambia	73.0						27.0	2008
Ghana	50.9	6.0			2.0	15.1		2007
Guinea	98.2	1.8	1.8					
Kenya	60.4	15.0	0.5		8.2			
Lesotho	64.0		1.8		29.9		5.7	2007
Madagascar	72.0	0.6	1.6		14.0	9.0	5.0	2007
Malawi	52.0				16.0		32.0	2006

Mali	98.7							
Mauritius	94.8	4.4						
Mozambique	94.9	4.3	0.1					
Namibia	38.1				24.8			2007
Niger	61.9	1.1	1.7	0.7	7.6			
Nigeria	97.0		1.0					
Rwanda	91.0		1.0				2.0	2008
Senegal	96.0		4.0				8.0	2008
Seychelles	86.0	10.0			1.0	3.0		2008
South Africa	44.0				21.0	25.0	10.0	2008
Swaziland	41.0				2.0	56.0	1.0	2008
Tanzania	74.0				2.0	21.0	3.0	2008
Uganda	87.0	5.0			6.0		3.0	2006
Zambia	59.6	23.0	0.2		3.8	16.7		
Zimbabwe	76.6	10.2	0.1		30	2.0		

Note: Prepared by Kay Chung.

Source: Various Sources, including FSAPs, Central Bank Annual Reports.

Box 7.1   Structure of the financial system in SSA countries

South Africa has a full continuum of developed financial markets that are inter-linked with each other, and are also integrated with global markets. The bank-ing system has a broad range of institutions, though four banks dominate with conglomerate structures and substantial cross-border operations, across the sub-Saharan region and in other continents. Capital markets include a deep and liquid equities market that is very diversified in terms of issuers, sector market capitalization, a broad range of intermediaries and an active primary and sec-ondary market. The debt market comprises of a broad range of issuers, includ-ing banks, non financial corporates, municipals and central government that are active in both the domestic and international capital markets, and is supported by a diversified investor base that includes collective investment schemes, insti-tutional investors, and a hedge fund industry. Inward nonresident inflows into the equity and debt markets are substantial. The nonbanking and contractual savings sector is also large in scale, consisting of pensions and insurance com-panies with close ownership and financial links with the banking and capital markets and substantial cross-border operations. The microfinance sector is well established and some of the microfinance institutions (MFIs) have increased their cross-border operations. A number of other countries, (Nigeria, Botswana, Ghana, Kenya, Mauritius, Uganda, and Zambia) now often referred to as "frontier mar-kets" have been developing their nonbanking sectors, even though the banking sector continue to dominate.

• Nigeria embarked on a major reform program of the financial sector in 2004, covering the banking sector, insurance, pensions, capital markets and micro-finance. As a result, while the financial system continues to be bank domi-nated, the nonbanking sector has increased its share substantially. The recent bank consolidation has also led to the emergence of *mega-sized* banks that are expanding rapidly in the region and also dominate the equity market capital-ization.[2] The capital markets include a large equity market, a relatively smaller government debt market, and a declining corporate bond market, with a still relatively small, but increasing, share of foreign investor participation. The nonbanking sector includes a large pension, insurance, and microfinance sec-tor. Recent reforms in the insurance sector also forced the sector to tap local capital markets and increased the integration with local capital markets, while a few insurance companies have begun to expand their cross-border operations in the SSA region.
• In the other frontier markets, equities and local debt markets have increased in size as well as pensions though they remain relatively small in size with mod-erate liquidity. Insurance on the other hand remains small, though developing with increased penetration from South African insurance companies.
• For the remainder of the countries, the nonbanking sector remains signifi-cantly underdeveloped. Some progress has been made to develop government securities markets, in varying degrees, but other segments are either absent or nominally exist. Microfinance has expanded rapidly, but penetration ratios remain very small.

Table 7.2   Sub-urban Africa: Countries with concentrated foreign banking assets, 2008

Host country	Assets held by foreign banks (percent)	Largest foreign banks	Home countries of the largest foreign banks
Angola	68	Angolan Development Bank	Portugal
		Espiritu Santo Bank of Angola (BESA)	Portugal
		Totta Angola Bank (BTA)	Portugal
Botwana	99	Barclays Bank of Botswana	United Kingdom
		Standard Chartered Bank Botswana	United Kingdom
		First National Bank of Botswana	South Africa
Cameroon	70	BICEC	France
		Societe Generale	France
		Attijariwafa Bank	Morocco
Cape Verde	74	Banco Commercial Atlantico	Portugal
		Banco Interatlantico	Portugal
		Banco Caboverdiano de negocios	Portugal
Chad	75	Societe Generale Tchadienne de Banque (SGTB)	France
		Ecobank	Togo
		Commercial Bank Tchad	Cameroon
Comoros	92	Banque pour l'Industrie et le Commerce (BIC)	France
		EXIM Bank Tanzania	Tanzania
Congo, Dem. Rep Of	90	Banque Congolaise	United States
		Banque commerciale du Congo (BCC)	Belgium
		Rawbank	Luxemburg
Congo, Republic of	57	BGFI-Congo	Gabon
		Banque Marocaine du Commerce Exterieur (BMCE)	Morocco
		Credit Agricole	France
Cote d'Invoire	56	Societe Generale	France
		Banque Internationale pour le Commerce & l'Industrie en Cote d'J Ecobank	Belgium
		Ecobank	Togo

Continued

Table 7.2   Continued

Host country	Assets held by foreign banks (percent)	Largest foreign banks	Home countries of the largest foreign banks
Ghana	55	Barclays Bank	United Kingdom
		Standard Chartered Bank	United Kingdom
		SSB Bank	France
Lesotho	97	Standard Bank	South Africa
Madagascar	71	Mauritius Commercial Bank (MCB)	Mauritius
		Banque Malgache de L'ocean Indien (BMOI)	France
		BFV-Societe Generale (SG)	France
Mauritius	72	Barclays Bank	United Kingdom
		Hong Kong and Shanghai Banking Corporation (HSBC) Mauritius	United Kingdom
		Standard Chartered Bank	United Kingdom
Mozambique	100	Banco International de Mocambique (BIM)	Portugal
		BCI-Fomento	Portugal
		Standard Bank	South Africa
Namibia	73	Standard Bank Namibia	South Africa
		First National Bank	South Africa
Sao Tome & Principe	100	Banco Internacional de STP (BISTP)	Portugal
		Afriland First Bank	Cameroon
		Island Bank	Nigeria
Senegal	65	SGBS	France
		B.I.C.I.S.	France
		Attijariwafa Bank	Morocco
Seychelies	56	Barclays Bank	United Kingdom
		Mauritius Commercial Bank (MCB)	Mauritius
		Bank of Baroda	India
Swaziland	70	Standard Chartered Bank of Swaziland Ltd.	United Kingdom
		NedBank Swaziland Ltd.	South Africa
		First National Banak Swaziland Ltd.	South Africa
Tanzania	52	NBC Ltd.	United Kingdom
		Stanchart	United Kingdom
		Barclays Bank	United Kingdom

Note: Only those countries for which the share of banking system assets held by foreign banks that exceeds 50 percent are shown.

Source: IMF, African Department Financial Sector Survey Questionnaire.

The pension industry is at varying stages of development, with some countries having well-developed public and private pension systems and others just moving from narrow and unfunded public pensions to funded pension schemes. Major reforms are taking place in many of the countries, thus the structure is rapidly evolving. Currently, South Africa has among the largest pension funds in the world in terms of assets, and combines a means tested public pensions scheme with a highly-developed private pension and provident fund sector.[5] Other countries with significant pension fund industries, featuring public and private pension schemes include Botswana, Mauritius, Namibia, Kenya, Nigeria, and Malawi. The majority of other countries do not have meaningful publicly managed pension and social security systems, though some form of pension coverage is available in a limited number of countries.

The level of development of the insurance industry is also diverse. In some countries (Tanzania) state-owned companies dominate. Other countries

South Africa dominates sub-saharan countries capital markets, in terms of listings

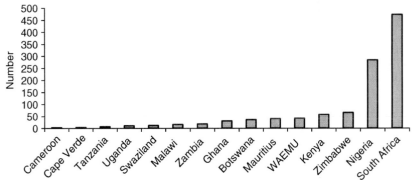

Figure 7.1a   Sub-saharan Africa stock market listings, end 2008

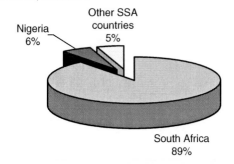

..and in terms of market capitalisation.

Figure 7.1b   Sub-saharan Africa stock market Capitalization, end 2008

Note: Data compiled by Ms. Kay Chung.

Source: Bloomberg.

(Uganda, Kenya) have numerous players, which include state and private owned insurance companies and an increasing significant presence of foreign-owned companies. South Africa's insurance industry is well developed, with substantial international operations and cross ownership links with banks. Nigeria's insurance industry recently underwent regulatory induced consolidation and some companies together with those in Kenya have commenced cross-border operations.

The microfinance sector has and continues to rapidly evolve, but currently its structure is fragmented. The range of MFIs is very broad and includes a variety of legal structures, lending methodologies, funding sources, product ranges, and target client bases. The legal forms, include commercial banks, state banks, community based institutions, credit cooperatives and unions, nonbank financial institutions, foundations, and Nongovernmental Organizations (NGOs). There is increasing convergence occurring between microfinance and main stream banking. Further, with increased popularity of microfinance, some institutions have declared themselves to be MFIs including "loan sharks", pawn brokers or nonbanks focusing on consumer loans.

7.2.2   Developments and performance

SSA financial systems have performed well on balance and the impact of the global financial crisis has so far been modest, but the resulting global recession and increased risk aversion of investors pose growing risks. The initial repercussions of the crisis have been felt primarily in the capital, foreign exchange and money markets.[6] Local financial institutions have by and large weathered the storm and have not needed liquidity assistance or official intervention, despite the predominance of foreign-owned banks, some of which have been affected by the crisis. That notwithstanding, pressures in SSA financial systems are growing due to the spill over of the financial crisis to the domestic real economy.

7.2.2.1   *The banking sector*

Banking sector performance in SSA countries has improved significantly on aggregate, although vulnerabilities remain. Most countries' banking systems are highly capitalized, liquid and profitable, though non performing loans remain high and have begun to edge up (Tables 7.3–7.5). This strong performance has been underpinned by a favorable macroeconomic environment and strong balance of payment performance that preceded the global financial crisis and contributed to excess banking system liquidity. Several countries increased the minimum capital requirements while commercial banks in many countries restructured their balance sheets and strengthened their loan collection capabilities.[7] Some countries, such as in the WAEMU, CEMAC and most of the post conflict countries, exhibit weaknesses and there have been incidences of distress.

Table 7.3 Bank regulatory capital to risk – Weighted assets (in Percent)

	2002	2003	2004	2005	2006	2007	2008	Latest
Sub-Saharan Africa								
Angola	20.1	18.1	19.6	16.5	18.5	21.9	–	December
Congo DRC	–	–3.4	6.83	7.66	10.52	–	–	December
Ethiopia	–	–	11.7	11.5	11.4	20.4	–	December
Gabon	17.2	19.9	22.3	19.8	17.8	14.3	19.6	September
Ghana	13.5	9.3	13.9	16.2	15.8	15.7	13.9	September
Kenya	–	173	16.6	16.4	16.5	18.0	18.1	November
Lesotha	–	–	22.0	25.0	19.0	14.0	15.0	September
Mozambique	14.0	17.0	18.7	16.0	12.5	14.2	14.3	June
Namibia	14.1	14.8	15.4	14.6	14.2	15.4	15.8	September
Nigeria	18.1	17.8	14.7	17.8	22.6	21.0	22.0	September
Rwanda	12.5	14.6	10.5	9.2	7.2	11.3	12.3	September
Senegal	15.5	11.7	11.9	11.1	13.1	136.0	13.7	June
Sierra Leone	15.5	27.3	36.0	35.7	36.0	38.7	46.0	September
South Africa	32.5	12.4	14.0	12.7	12.3	12.8	12.5	June
Swaziland	12.6	14.0	14.0	15.0	20.0	23.0	–	June
Tanzania	20.6	21.0	15.4	15.1	16.3	16.2	15.7	September
Uganda	22.1	17.0	20.5	18.3	18.0	19.5	20.8	June
Zambia	28.0	23.0	22.2	28.4	20.4	18.6	17.0	June
Zimbabwe	–	15.6	35.7	22.6	25.4	25.4	–	October
CEMAC	11.4	12.8	11.1	15.1	–	–	–	December
Cameroon	9.3	9.8	8.0	11.2	12.0	–	–	December
CAR	–	–	–	12.4	10.8	15.4	–	December
Chad	–	–	–	–	–	–	–	–
Congo R	–	–	4.0	12.0	14.0	16.0	–	–
Equatorial Guinea	7.2	11.0	12.4	9.2	13.0	–	–	No response
Gabon	17.2	19.9	18.1	27.5	21.6	16.1	25.0	September
WAEMU	–	10.6	11.4	11.8	8.5	6.2	–	June
Benin	–	6.2	9.5	–	1.4	3.0	–	–
Burkina Faso	–	7.9	11.0	–	10.2	13.0	13.0	June
Cote d'Ivoire	–	16.3	17.0	13.7	12.4	9.5	10.0	June
Guine-Bissau	–	53.3	38.7	–	33.6	24.8	–	–
Mali	–	7.9	7.4	9.7	9.2	7.2	7.4	December
Niger	–	15.7	13.3	17.9	13.7	12.8	–	–
Senegal	15.5	11.7	11.9	11.1	13.1	13.6	13.7	June
Togo	–	–6.6	–6.0	–0.8	–1.9	–16.0	–	–

Note: Due to differences in national accounting, taxation and supervisory regimes, FSI data are not strictly comparable across countries. The table was compiled by Ms. Kay Chung.

Sources: National authorities; and IMF staff estimates.

Table 7.4   Bank nonperforming loan to total loans (in Percent)

	2002	2003	2004	2005	2006	2007	2008	Latest
Sub-Saharan Africa								
Angola	10.4	9.0	8.1	6.7	4.8	2.9	–	December
Congo DRC	–	1.5	2.0	6.8	3.0	–	–	December
Ethiopia	–	–	27.8	20.0	14.0	10.1	6.8	December
Gabon	14.6	13.9	16.0	14.1	10.7	7.6	7.9	September
Ghana	22.7	18.3	16.3	13.0	7.9	8.7	7.6	September
Kenya	–	34.9	29.3	25.6	21.3	10.9	8.4	November
Lesotha	–	–	1.0	2.0	2.0	1.7	3.5	September
Mozambique	22.0	14.4	6.4	3.8	3.3	2.6	0.9	June
Namibia	3.5	3.9	2.4	2.3	2.6	2.8	3.2	September
Nigeria	21.4	20.5	21.6	18.1	8.8	8.4	6.1	September
Rwanda	57.0	52.0	29.9	31.1	28.0	18.5	10.6	September
Senegal	18.5	13.3	12.6	11.9	16.8	18.6	19.0	June
Sierra Leone	11.0	7.4	16.5	26.8	26.8	31.7	21.4	September
South Africa	2.9	2.4	1.8	1.5	1.1	1.4	1.0	June
Swaziland	–	2.0	3.0	2.0	3.6	6.4	8.4	June
Tanzania	8.3	4.5	3.5	4.9	6.8	6.3	6.3	September
Uganda	3.0	7.3	2.2	2.3	3.0	4.1	–	June
Zambia	11.4	5.3	7.6	8.9	11.3	8.5	–	June
Zimbabwe	–	15.6	35.7	22.6	25.4	6.4	–	October
CEMAC	13.7	14.1	14.8	13.4	–	–	–	December
Cameroon	15.2	13.7	13.5	12.1	12.4	–	–	December
CAR	–	–	–	34.2	32.9	30.4	–	December
Chad	–	–	15.5	12.9	12.4	11.6	8.6	–
Congo R	–	–	7.0	3.0	2.0	3.0	–	–
Equatorial Guinea	–	–	13.5	17.2	14.3	–	–	No response
Gabon	–	–	14.4	13.4	10.4	7.0	7.1	September
WAEMU	–	19.7	19.7	19.8	18.5	–	–	June
Benin	–	10.3	10.9	15.5	15.1	–	–	–
Burkina Faso	–	12.4	15.1	13.4	13.0	19.4	20.2	June
Cote d'Ivoire	21.3	25.1	26.2	21.0	20.0	21.5	21.5	June
Guine-Bissau	–	27.4	23.8	12.8	10.5	–	–	–
Mali	–	15.6	19.6	30.2	25.0	25.1	25.3	December
Niger	–	26.5	21.3	21.6	21.8	21.2	17.7	–
Senegal	–	14.0	12.6	11.9	16.8	18.6	19.0	June
Togo	–	41.3	34.8	33.6	29.1	–	–	–

Note: Due to differences in national accounting, taxation and supervisory regimes, FSI data are not strictly comparable across countries. The table was compiled by Ms. Kay Chung.

Sources: National authorities; and IMF staff estimates.

Table 7.5 Bank return on assets, 2002–08 (in percent)

	2002	2003	2004	2005	2006	2007	2008	Latest
Sub-Saharan Africa								
Angola	0.7	4.7	4.1	3.1	2.7	2.7	–	December
Congo, DRC	–	0.6	–1.1	1.7	2.7	–	–	December
Ethiopia	–	–	1.6	2.0	2.8	2.3	2.9	December
Gabon	2.8	0.7	2.8	2.6	2.5	2.7	–	December
Ghana	6.8	6.2	4.5	3.0	3.3	2.9	2.8	June
Kenya[a]	–8.9	2.3	2.1	2.4	2.8	3.0	2.8	November
Lesotho	–	–	3.0	2.0	2.0	2.6	2.4	September
Mozambique	1.6	1.2	1.4	1.8	3.5	3.5	2.7	September
Namibia	4.5	3.6	2.1	3.5	1.5	3.5	3.2	September
Nigeria	2.4	1.7	3.1	0.9	1.6	2.1	2.4	September
Rwanda	–5.0	1.4	0.6	0.9	1.6	1.3	1.9	September
Senegal	1.8	1.8	1.8	1.8	1.6	1.6	–	December
Sierra Leone	10.0	10.5	9.9	8.1	5.8	6.4	2.1	December
South Africa	0.4	0.8	1.3	1.2	1.4	1.4	1.8	December
Swaziland	–	4.0	2.9	3.1	5.9	2.9	3.6	June
Tanzania	1.8	2.1	3.1	3.9	3.9	4.7	3.8	September
Uganda	3.0	4.5	4.3	3.6	3.4	3.9	3.5	June
Zambia	6.5	5.4	3.1	6.5	5.1	4.7	5.0	June
Zimbabwe	–	6.3	9.7	13.4	14.6	14.6	–	Sep-06
CEMAC	1.5	–	2.5	1.0	–	–	–	December
Cameroon	1.1	1.9	2.3	2.2	1.2	–	–	December
CAR	–	2.0	–	6.8	7.0	–	–	December
Chad	–	–	0.0	2.0	1.5	18.9	2.2	September
Congo R	–	–	1.0	3.0	3.0	–	–	–
Equatorial Guinea	2.4	2.2	1.9	1.9	1.7	–	–	–
Gabon	–	–	5.9	6.0	6.3	5.2	–	–
WAEMU	–	–	0.9	0.7	1.2	1.2	–	December
Benin	–	–	0.4	–	0.2	–	–	–
Burkina Faso	–	–	1.4	–	1.2	0.6	1.0	June
Cote d'Ivoire	–	–	0.6	0.3	1.1	0.9	–	–
Guine-Bissau	–	–	2.5	–	–0.6	–	–	–
Mali	–	–	–1.8	–	1.0	–	–	–
Niger	–	–	0.6	0.7	0.5	1.5	–	–
Senegal	–	–	1.8	1.8	1.6	1.6	–	June
Togo	–	–	8.0	0.7	1.5	–	–	–

Note: The table was compiled by Ms. Kay Chung.

[a] Due to differences in national accounting, taxation, and supervisory regimes, FSI data are not strictly comparable across countries.

Sources: National authorities; and IMF staff estimates.

Credit by banks to the private sector has expanded at a very rapid pace, though intermediation levels and access to financial services remain low, due to the low starting position. Average annual growth of credit to the private sector has ranged between 30–70 percent in many countries, during 2006–2008. The credit has also increasingly gone to the retail sector and in some countries (Botswana) credit to households now accounts for the bulk of lending. Intermediation levels, on the other hand, remain low on average and are most pronounced in the CEMAC countries (Figure 7.2).

Competition has intensified in many of the countries' banking systems, due to regulatory induced consolidations and the increase in newly licensed banks. This has led to a rapid growth of credit, as banks compete for market share while also increasing financial product innovations, including credit card issuance; salary linked retail loans; pension linked mortgages. It has also increased the use of IT for delivery of financial products, most notably Automated Teller Machines (ATMs), mobile banking, and cell phone banking. On the other hand, the competition has encouraged greater risk taking among banks and the adoption of aggressive marketing strategies, resulting in predatory lending.

Dollarization in the banking system has remained moderate on average, though it is high in selected countries. The most dollarized countries include Angola, Liberia, and São Tomé and Príncipe, where the ratio of foreign currency deposits to broad money exceeds 60 percent. A few countries (Zambia, Mozambique, and Uganda) also have ratios above 30 percent; and in many other countries (Botswana, Guinea, Sierra Leone, Ghana, and the Gambia) the ratio is fairly high averaging around 20 percent.

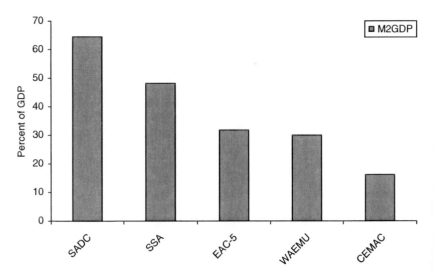

Figure 7.2   Intermediation indicators, 2008

Source: IMF and country authorities.

There is also a range of other developments that have implications for supervision. A number of banks in Nigeria, Ethiopia, Kenya and Mauritius have applied for licenses to commence Islamic banking services. Others (Ghana and Nigeria) introduced universal banking. There is also an emerging trend to have tiered capital structures for banks,[8] while some countries (Botswana, Ghana) are trying to establish financial hubs.

7.2.2.2 Capital markets

Until the recent intensification of the crisis, capital markets in the region experienced registered strong growth and returns, in marked contrast to trends in global markets. The strong performance was broad-based and cut across all product categories including equities, plain vanilla, and structured debt products and hedge funds. A number of countries began to introduce new products, most notably infrastructure bonds and structured products. Trading, clearing and settlement systems have generally functioned well and incidents of failed trades are reported to be rare, even though some countries operate in manual environments.

Equities experienced strong bull runs for several years, but tumbled in late 2008, as the financial crisis intensified, economic prospects became uncertain and nonresident investors exited the markets (Figures 7.3 and 7.4). SSA countries, whose stock market performance was previously decoupled from trends in global equity markets, began to show increased correlation, as heightened volatility in financial markets compounded domestic concerns in some countries. The precrisis strong performance of equities was underpinned by sustained high domestic economic growth and increased foreign investor participation, as global excess liquidity encouraged investors to search for higher yield and diversification (Table 7.6).

Debt markets also experienced major capital outflows and the outflows by nonresidents exerted downward pressure on yields and volumes (Figure 7.5). In South Africa, issuance of private sector debt and structured products, which had initially increased rapidly (Figure 7.6), declined sharply led by the securitized market. Investors also showed an increasing preference for short-term commercial paper, in part due to the elevated risk premiums, higher inflation, and nominal interest rates. The frontier markets (Nigeria, Ghana, Kenya, Mauritius, Uganda, Zambia), which had attracted substantial foreign investors into their local debt markets, registered huge outflows too. In addition, Ghana and Gabon which had made their first foray in international capital market with sovereign bond issues lost market access while other countries postponed their planned issues.

The financial crisis also stalled the rapid growth of securitization and hedge funds in South Africa. The securitization market grew exponentially and by the beginning of 2008 was estimated at US$6.2 billion, though this represented a very small share of banks' balance sheets (less than 3 percent of bank assets). Banks also use asset-backed commercial paper (ABCP) conduits to fund origination of corporate loans, and as is the case in other

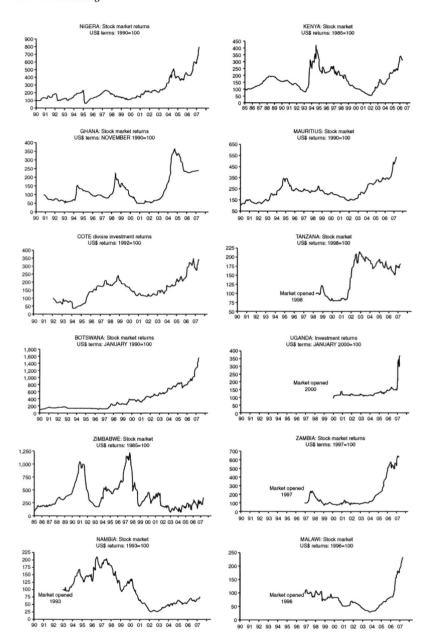

Figure 7.3   Sub-Saharan Africa: Stock price indices, 1990–2007 (US $ terms 1990=100)
Source: Bloomberg.

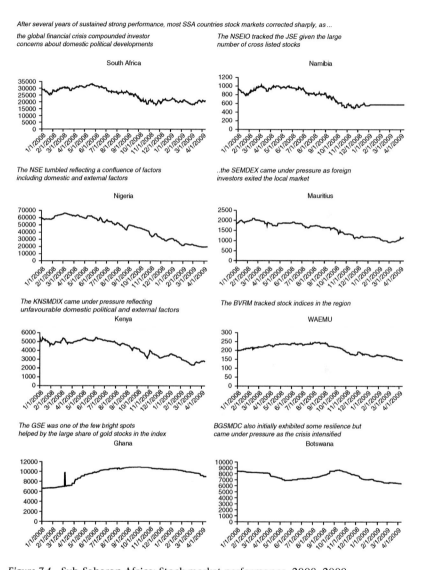

Figure 7.4 Sub-Saharan Africa: Stock market performance, 2008–2009
Source: Bloomberg.

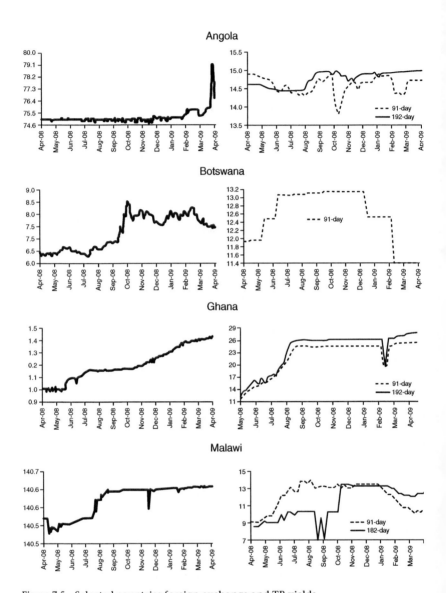

Figure 7.5   Selected countries foreign exchange and TB yields

Source: Angola: Bloomberg, Banco National de Angola & Bloomberg; Botswana: Bloomberg, Bank of Botswana & Bloomberg; Ghana: Bloomberg, Bank of Ghana & Bloomberg

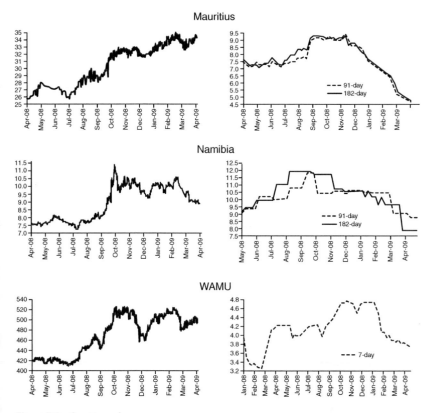

Figure 7.5   Continued

Source: Malawi: Bloomberg, Reserve Bank of Malawi, Citi & Bloomberg; Mauritius: Bloomberg, Bank of Mauritius & Bloomberg; Namibia: Bloomberg, Bank of Namibia & Bloomberg; WAMU: Bloomberg, Bank of Namibia & Bloomberg.

markets, the largest banks are the main players in securitization and ABCP markets. Hedge funds also expanded rapidly before declining sharply.

7.2.3   Nonbank financial institutions

The nonbanking sector, consisting of pensions, insurance, and microfinance, has also been growing, but financial performance has been mostly poor. The sector has not yet assumed systemic financial proportions, but has potential for widespread social ramifications. It has also been the focus of major policy initiatives.

Overall, performance of pensions has been poor with pension industries of most countries saddled with poor governance structures that lead to high operating costs and poor investment decisions. Only a few countries (South Africa, Namibia, Mauritius, Botswana, Kenya, and Nigeria) had registered strong growth, helped by reforms and strong asset price growth in

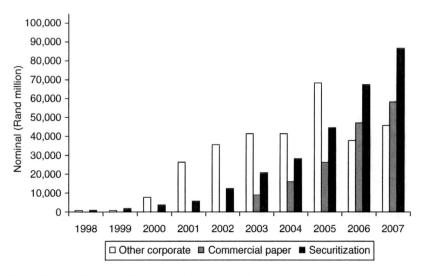

Figure 7.6   South Africa: Corporate debt outstanding by issuer class
Source: Bond Exchange of South Africa.

Table 7.6   Africa: Stock market performance

Country	Name	2005	2006	2007	2008
Botswana	Domestic	−5	51	54	−32
Ghana	DSI	−26	3	22	11
Ivory Coast (BVRM)	BVRM	15	11	122	−14
Kenya	NSE 20	44	41	7	−49
Malawi	Domestic	36	140	124	24
Mauritius	SEMDEX	5	34	77	−46
Namibia	Overall	0	21	28	−57
Nigeria	All Share	5	36	87	−55
South Africa	All Share	26	25	23	−46
Swaziland	All Share	−11	−1	17	−
Tanzania	Composite	−11	1	−	−
Uganda	All Share	64	16	25	−33
Zambia	LUSE	122	18	128	−44
Zimbabwe	Industrial	17	886	−	−

Source: Africa Market Focus, Databank.

equities, bonds, and real estate. Some countries (Botswana and Mauritius) with liberal investment policies had direct exposure to international capital markets, but even those that had more restrictive investments (South Africa) have equally been affected, as domestic assets fell in tandem with global trends. In other countries, the pension industry has been insulated by the underdevelopment nature of capital markets. The shift from defined benefits to defined contribution schemes in many countries also reduced systemic risks.

The insurance sector's penetration ratios remain very small, despite the sustained high economic growth rates in SSA. A host of factors contribute to this poor performance, including low GDP per capita, the late introduction of insurance services to the region, closed markets until recently, information asymmetry and poor claims paying records. Underdeveloped capital markets have led to significant asset liability mismatches involving reverse transformation, with long-term liabilities invested in assets of short-term tenure. The insurance sector, in many countries has begun to expand, helped by liberalization, increasing foreign ownership and in some cases (Nigeria) by regulatory induced consolidation.

The microfinance industry has a short track record and the sector is still in a transitional period, marked by institutional and regulatory challenges. While there has been a phenomenal increase in the number of institutions, substantially increased access is yet to fully materialize. Financial performance of MFIs in most countries is weak in part due to poor governance structures and weaknesses in regulation. Nevertheless, some countries (Senegal, Mali, and Burkina Faso) are beginning to witness the emergence of sound successful MFIs. In some countries, the success of the sector has led to greater competition from banks from conventional banks moving down market and placing pressure on margins and skill resources.

7.2.4 Risks, challenges, and vulnerabilities

Despite the generally favorable performance, financial systems in many SSA countries remain vulnerable to a broad range of interrelated risks. The banking sector, which is systemically important, is vulnerable to: (1) macroeconomic risks; (2) exogenous shocks such as terms of trade shocks and weather; (3) credit risks; (4) contagion from the parent banks; and (5) other selected country specific risks.[9] These risks are heightened by structural factors and deficiencies in the legal and regulatory environment and the deterioration in the external environment.

7.2.4.1 *Macroeconomic risks and exogenous shocks*

Most SSA countries have concentrations in economic activity domestically and in exports, while some are heavily dependent on aid for budgetary support. These economic structures translate into concentrations in the banks' loan portfolios and or deposits, thus shocks that weaken corporate balance sheets in these sectors quickly transmit stress to the balance sheets of banks. Therefore, macroeconomic developments can have stability implications through its effects on the asset quality, liquidity and income earning capacity (Box 7.2).

The slowdown in capital, coupled with declines in commodity prices, also poses challenges for the banking system through its impact on international reserves and banking system liquidity. The latter potentially exerts upward

Box 7.2   Transmission channels of macroeconomic risks in selected countries

Botswana: The government relies on minerals for 35–50 percent of its revenues. Thus, declines in commodity prices (diamonds, copper and nickel) affect fiscal, private sector real activity, GDP, employment and income levels and through these channels increase non performing loans. It also affects the foreign exchange reserves and the exchange rate.

Burundi: The financial system is vulnerable to shocks to the coffee sector and to developments in foreign aid. At end 2008, the trade sector accounted for over 60 percent of the banking system claims and coffee is the country's main export commodity. A deterioration in the price or volume affects the financial services to the sector and the transport industry. Over 50 percent of the budget is financed by aid and aid volumes are affected by sociopolitical stability and the quality of macroeconomic policies. Developments in both coffee and aid therefore affect banking system stability and asset quality.

CEMAC: Most of the member countries are heavily dependent on the oil and gas sector, but with very few exceptions, oil extraction firms generally have limited financial relations with banks in the subregion. Thus changes in oil prices affect the banking system through the effect on public finances, related deposits and therefore banking system liquidity. Concentration risk is also high due to weaker large Exposure (LE) limits (45 percent of capital) and weaknesses in enforcing those limits with some individual exposures averaging 80 percent of banks capital. Congo, Equatorial Guinea and Gabonese banks are heavily exposed to the forestry sector. Banks also have large foreign exchange exposures thus pressures on the exchange rate could also have adverse consequences.

Congo DRC: The sharp drop in mining output and exports is putting liquidity pressures on the banking system, which is overwhelmingly dollarized. Declines in mobile phone production at factories in coastal China's have led to closures of cobalt mines in the Democratic Republic of Congo, resulting in increased unemployment and a decline in reserves.

Nigeria is heavily dependent on the oil sector. However, like CEMAC countries, lending by domestic banks to the oil sector is limited, thus changes in oil prices affect the banking system through its impact on banking system liquidity and through the effect on public finances.

Rwanda: Risk concentration is high due to the need for crop financing and lack of sectoral diversification. Exacerbated by poor governance in some banks, prudential limits on risk concentration are frequently breached by most banks

WAEMU: The member countries exhibit significant concentrations in their loan portfolios, in part facilitated by the lax LE limits. Consequently, concentration of economic activity in the cotton sector renders banks in Burkina Faso, Mali and Togo highly vulnerable to shocks in cotton prices and demand. In Mali, government deposits account for a fifth of total deposits and withdrawals could have adverse effects of selected banks due to frequent non observance of LE limits, a default by the state-owned cotton producer and ginning company could have significant adverse effects. Ivorian banks would be affected by difficulties in coffee and cocoa sectors. Banking systems in Burkina Faso, Mali, Senegal, and Togo also exhibit significant borrower concentrations, and also hold substantial long foreign exchange positions that render them vulnerable to exchange rate changes.

Box 7.2 Continued

In Senegal exposures to Industries Chimiques due Senegal (ICS) has been a source of vulnerability.

Zambia: The financial system is vulnerable to shocks in the copper sector. The banking system has notable exposures to mining companies as well as to employees of these companies. Declines in copper prices also impact the banking system through reduced liquidity into the banking system, pressures on international reserves and the exchange rate, deterioration in credit quality and risk correlation between the corporate and retail lending books.

pressure on interest rates, which in turn constrains loan volumes as well as eroding the debt servicing capacity of borrowers. Declines in international reserves and associated pressures on the exchange rate increase exchange rate risk, though this is mitigated in most cases by low net open positions mandated in many countries. These effects are magnified by the limited depth and liquidity of money and capital markets.

7.2.4.2 Credit risk

Credit risk remains the most dominant risk in SSA countries. This is largely because of the predominance of lending in banks' balance sheet, continuing weaknesses in banks risk management capabilities and slow progress in addressing the financial infrastructure that support financial intermediation. The legal and judiciary framework for enforcing creditor rights remain weak in most countries, though some progress is being made to establish commercial courts. These deficiencies negate the protection that security is designed to provide in so far as it reduces the value of realizable collateral in the event of a borrower defaulting on the loan. Also, information infrastructure for assessing credit risk such as credit registries and accounting are just being developed in selected countries but remain absent in many.[10]

Most SSA countries also registered rapid credit growth, albeit from a low base. The need to recycle the substantial liquidity injections (from the high commodity prices and exports, capital, and remittances) against a background of few bankable projects has encouraged risk taking among banks and weakened underwriting standards. The risks in bank portfolios, previously masked by the favorable economic environment, could become evident in an economic slowdown.

7.2.4.3 Political risks

Political unrest remains a lingering risk for SSA countries. While the number of countries in political conflicts has reduced, the reemergence of political unrest (such as in Kenya or the uncertainties in political elections in South Africa) and sporadic outbreaks (such as in Madagascar and Chad) tends to fracture the still relatively fragile investor confidence in SSA financial markets and delays the speed with which the region regains access to international markets or foreign investor flows.

7.2.4.4   Contagion from parent banks

The intensification of the global financial crisis has increased the risk of contagion from parent banks as well as counterparty risks. SSA countries are host to a large number of foreign-owned banks that are not supervised on a consolidated basis. While most of these are subsidiaries and are therefore subject to local regulations, there are substantial intra-group transactions and some countries' banking systems have substantial foreign assets. The potential, therefore, exists for group risks to go undetected and for financial stress from parent banks to spread through the group. The large intra-group exposure and concentrations in placements with correspondent banks also increases counterparty risk.

7.2.4.5   Country specific risks

Finally, there are also a number of risks that are more country specific. South African banks have significant exposure to retail mortgages and are dependent on wholesale funding, thus liquidity and market risk are significant. Zimbabwean banks have been experiencing recurring liquidity crises related to the unfavorable policy and macro-environment. In a number of countries (Ghana, Burundi, Mali, and Togo), exposures to state-owed enterprises pose major risks for the banking system. In Nigeria, the practice of lending against share purchases and the heavy reliance of banks on capital markets to fund capital expansion and regulatory capital has increased the impact of the stock market decline on the banking sector.

7.3   The regulatory and supervisory frameworks

7.3.1   Institutional framework and recent trends

The institutional framework for supervision in most of SSA is fragmented along functional and sectoral lines (Box 7.3). Generally, the national central bank is the regulator for banks, other deposit-taking institutions, and money market intermediaries.[11] In selected countries though (Malawi, Eritrea, Liberia), the central bank has supervisory responsibility for all financial institutions. The WAEMU and CEMAC subregions, on the other hand, have supranational frameworks, consisting of unified regional prudential systems, a regional supervisor while national authorities retail licensing, and bank resolution powers.

For capital markets and the nonbanking sector, there are separate supervisors for capital markets, pensions and insurance. A few countries (South Africa, Namibia, and Botswana) have established a unified regulator for the nonbanking sector. Swaziland has also initiated efforts to establish a consolidated regulator for nonbank financial institutions (NBFIs). In some of the countries though, there are financial segments of the nonbanking sectors

Box 7.3 Regulatory structures (Selected SSA countries)

Regulatory structures in SSA may be classified into two broad groupings, namely countries with supranational frameworks and those with national supervisors. Within these broad groups, three categories are discernible, notably countries with a single regulator, hybrids with partial integrated regulators and multiple regulatory structures.

Countries with supranational frameworks

- CEMAC: The Central African Banking Commission (COBAC), has supervisory power over credits institutions (CI) in the CEMAC countries, including monitor their soundness and compliance with prudential rules and ethics. Laws and regulations are issued by the national authorities, the Ministerial Committee of the Central African Monetary Union (UMAC), the Bank of Central African States (BEAC), or by itself.
- WAEMU: Supervision of the commercial banks and nondeposit-taking credit institutions is the responsibility of the BC-WAEMU, but national authorities play a role in the licensing process and the resolution of problem banks. The BCEAO is responsible for accounting and prudential regulations and it shares oversight of the banking sector with the BC-WAEMU. The Regional Council for Public Savings and Financial Markets regulates the capital markets (BVRM), and is responsible for issuing authorizations and monitoring its operation. The Regional Council must authorize the issue of shares traded on the BVRM. The supervision of MFIs is the responsibility of national authorities.

Countries with national supervisors

Countries where supervisory responsibility is fragmented on functional lines

- Ghana: The institutional framework is fragmented along functional lines, with the Bank of Ghana (BOG) supervising banks; the SEC supervising capital markets; the National Insurance Commission supervising insurance.
- Kenya: the Central Bank of Kenya (CBK) supervises banks, the CMA supervises capital markets, the Insurance Regulatory Authority for insurance companies and the Retirement Benefits Authority for pensions.
- Malawi: The Reserve Bank of Malawi (RBM) is a de facto integrated financial sector supervisory agency but the MOF is the licensing authority and impacts any major enforcement action. The RBM is responsible for the regulation and supervision of banks, discount houses, insurance business, Malawi stock exchange, pension funds, and microfinance institutions. The Minister of Finance is the licensing authority for banks. Furthermore, any major enforcement action, including recapitalization and revocation of a banking license require prior consultation and/or approval of the minister.
- Nigeria: Financial system supervision is highly fragmented. The Central Bank of Nigeria (CBN) has authority to license and regulate the commercial banks; the Securities and Exchange Commission (SEC) regulates capital markets; the Corporate Affairs Commission (CAC) regulates the registration of companies; the NSE regulates its members; pension funds are regulated by the Pension Commission (PENCOM). The insurance industry is regulated by NAICOM.

Box 7.3   Continued

The DMO regulates both the primary and the secondary market for federal government debt, but does not have direct authority over the issuance of sub-national debt. While there is a coordinating body for regulators of the financial services industry—Financial Services Regulatory Coordinating Committee (FSRCC)—it is reported to be inactive.
* Zambia: The Bank of Zambia (BoZ) is responsible for the licensing and supervision of banks and nonbank financial institutions other than pensions, insurance, and other capital markets players. These are supervised by the Pensions and Insurance Authority (PIA) and the Securities Exchange Commission (SEC), respectively.

Countries with hybrid or semi integrated regulator
* Botswana: The Bank of Botswana (BoB) is responsible for the licensing and supervision of the commercial banks as well as for the supervision of collective investment funds, foreign exchange (FX) bureaus, IFSC registered banks. The BOB also examines and supervises the statutory banks but enforcement of any supervisory recommendations rests with the MFDP. SACCOs are not supervised, though they take deposits, although they also have the right to take deposits. A single regulatory authority has been established to regulate and supervise all nonbank financial institutions.
* Mauritius: The Bank of Mauritius (BOM) is responsible for the licensing, regulation and supervision of banks, money-changers and foreign exchange dealers, and deposit-taking activities of nonbank financial institutions (NBFI). The other activities of NBFI are regulated and supervised by the Financial Services Commission (FSC) In addition, the Development Bank of Mauritius (DBM) is deemed to be licensed and "shall, subject to such terms and conditions as the BOM determines."
* South Africa: The Reserve Bank of South Africa has regulatory and supervisory powers over the banks. The FSB has broad regulatory authority over the JSE Exchange (JSE) and the Bond Exchange of South Africa (BESA), financial advisors and intermediaries (FAIS), collective investment scheme operators (CIS), pension funds and insurance companies.
* Swaziland: banks and building societies are regulated and supervised by the CBS as per the FIA although the building society is not licensed by the CBS. The SACCOs, which accept deposits, are licensed, regulated and monitored by the commissioner of cooperatives in line with the Cooperatives Societies Act, even though they accept deposits, albeit from their members. Unit Trust Companies (UTCs) are licensed by the CBS but are not effectively supervised and are not governed by any legislation. There are also a number of other institutions that are neither licensed nor regulated by any authority. They have also drafted the Financial Services Regulatory Authority (FSRA) Bill to regulate and supervise all nonbank financial institutions (NBFIs), although the bill has been pending for sometime.

Countries with integrated supervisors
* Eritrea: The Bank of Eritrea (BOE) is the regulator of depository and non depository financial institutions in Eritrea, including insurance. The BOE is empowered to issue and implement regulations, directives and guidelines and to prescribe prudential ratios to be maintained by financial institutions.

Box 7.3 Continued

- Rwanda: The National Bank of Rwanda (NBR) has supervisory responsibility for banks and specialized financial institutions
- Liberia: the Central Bank of Liberia (CBL) has supervisory responsibilities for all financial institutions. But so far its supervisory activities have been limited to banks and it has not yet undertaken supervision of insurance or pensions.

---

that are expanding without a regulatory framework. For instance, private pension funds and other capital market intermediaries like asset managers, financial advisors, and micro lenders.

MFIs operate under a variety of regulatory environments, which are country specific but which also depend on the legal structure of the MFIs and their scale. Generally, large and specialized microfinance banks are subject to prudential regulations by the respective countries' bank supervisory authorities, credit cooperatives operate under a separate regulatory framework; and foundations and Nongovernmental Organizations (NGO) are not typically regulated. Another major distinction that countries are making is between deposit-taking and nondeposit-taking MFIs. The former is typically regulated.

7.3.2 Implementation overview

Financial sector reforms in most SSA countries have sought to align the regulatory and supervisory frameworks with international standards. Assessments of the frameworks have largely been undertaken through participation in FSAPs, MCM TC, and through self assessments done individually or as part of regional initiatives. There are also parallel initiatives to harmonize laws and supervisory practices in the context of regional integration initiatives such as the Southern Africa Development Cooperation (SADC), the East Africa Community (EAC), and in the context of the Committee for Insurance, Securities and Nonbank Financial Authorities (CISNA). The reforms, however, have largely focused on the banking sector, though other sectors are receiving increasing attention.[12]

7.3.2.1 Framework for banking supervision

Many SSA countries have been updating their laws, financial infrastructure, and banking supervisory practices as well as strengthening supervisory capacity. South Africa reinforced its regulatory framework for banks with the implementation of Basel II on January 1, 2008. Most countries in the region have put in place the basic elements of an appropriate legal structure and supervisory framework for banking supervision, including powers to license; issue prudential regulations; conduct ongoing supervision; collect financial supervisory information; enforce compliance as well as address safety and soundness concerns. However, weaknesses exist in the individual countries' actual practices and compliance with the Basel Core Principles (BCPs) is uneven.[13]

Initial BCPs showed widespread weaknesses in the independence of regulators, but many countries have since implemented the needed legislative reforms. Nevertheless, in several countries (Botswana, Cape Verde, Malawi, and the CEMAC and WAEMU subregions), the minister of finance continues to have powers over either licensing of banksor revocation of licenses; recapitalization or powers to make regulations. The system in the WAEMU provides for a separation between the authority to issue regulations and responsibility to implement, and supervisory resources are inadequate relative to the scope of the supervisory mandate in many countries.

The principal prudential regulations (solvency, large exposure, and provisioning) in many SSA countries follow international standards, but there are some exceptions. Although the minimum capital adequacy ratio (CAR) has been set at 8 percent or higher in most countries, several countries exercise forbearance in enforcing compliance and there are variations in the rules for risk weighting. As for credit risk management, the LE limits are mostly set at 25 percent of capital, but the WAEMU and CEMAC have higher limits of 75 and 45 percent of capital respectively and compliance with the already lax rules is poor. Loan classification and provisioning rules are also lax in some countries and the treatment of collateral varies. There is also a widespread lack of adequate guidance and supervisory review in the areas of liquidity, interest rate, country, market and operational risk.

Supervisory methods continue to evolve but generally require further strengthening. Ongoing banking supervision methods combine both onsite and offsite and there is an increasing shift towards risk-based supervision. However, inadequate resources and training of staff has, in a number of countries, led to poor coordination in the onsite and offsite functions and poor quality of risk analysis. Many countries have not yet integrated stress-testing in their analysis and supervisory tools and some of the countries (Cape Verde, Sierra Leone) still employ compliance-based supervision.

In addition, while many countries have strengthened the financial information requirements, and introduced software to improve the timeliness of the data, challenges remain. There are incidences (e.g., in WAEMU) where the centralization of accounting or prudential information submitted for offsite by banks is still insufficiently automated, and analysis of this information is a source of excessive processing delays. In many countries, the data collected are not comprehensive enough and the quality is sometimes in need of improvement. In other cases, insufficient use is made of the data received, resulting in weaknesses in the level, regularity and quality of market surveillance.

Accounting and disclosure requirements have been strengthened for banking institutions, but less progress has been made for corporations. In several countries (Zambia, Botswana, Mozambique), accounting and auditing practices are consistent with IFRS and ISA, and banks are required to publish audited financial statements annually and unaudited accounts quarterly. However, due to weaknesses in accounts for small and medium size enterprises, banks do not make use of the financial statements for lending and rely heavily on collateral. There are also some countries (the WAEMU subregion) that exhibit some notable shortcomings in financial information requirements for banks and verification of auditors.

Regulators in most countries have powers to enforce corrective and remedial measures, but implementation and the range of instruments available to countries varies. Selected countries (Kenya, the Gambia) have introduced Prompt Corrective Actions (PCA) in their legal frameworks while previous experiences with financial crises have led a number of other countries to strengthen the remedial powers. However, in some cases significant gaps remain. The Banking Commission of the WAEMU subregion does not have complete control in addressing banks' problems, particularly in light of the supranational nature of banking supervision, which in the most serious cases leads to shared authority with the finance ministers in area states.[14] Some countries (e.g., the CEMAC subregion) exhibit weaknesses in enforcing compliance and some lack guidance for application.

Consolidated supervision and regulation of financial groups—domestic and foreign—remain weak and ill defined, despite the increased scale, complexity, and significance of regional financial groups operating across the region. While many of the regulators have legal powers to conduct consolidated supervision, only a few are supervising their financial groups on a consolidated basis, and country and transfer risks are not monitored. Similarly, many countries have signed memorandum of understanding (MOUs), but there is little information-sharing in practice, and the legal effectiveness of MOUs has not been tested. Finally, there is a universal lack of formal cross-border crisis arrangements and for dealing with systemic bank crises, and in some countries, bank secrecy laws impede cooperating with foreign bank supervisors.

7.3.2.2   Capital markets[15]

Securities market regulation in SSA countries is evolving rapidly, however the regulatory systems currently exhibit significant weaknesses. Generally, most countries have been modernizing their legal frameworks, in order to align the arrangements with the state of capital market development and other contextual circumstances. The changes also reflect an increased recognition by countries of the need to long-term capital and the associated need to create an enabling environment for the development of capital markets. Progress notwithstanding, important shortcomings remain.

The nature and scope of the weaknesses differ across the countries, but there are some common themes. South Africa is one of the few countries in which regulation and supervision of capital markets is advanced. In the other SSA countries that have established capital markets, adequate laws have been enacted to govern the regulation and supervision of securities markets and the objectives and responsibilities of regulators are generally clearly stipulated. The main weakness has been with enforcement of market rules and supervision of market participants.

These weaknesses cut across a broad array of principles, but their causes appear to be interrelated. In many countries, regulators do not appear to have adequate capacity (quantity and quality of skills, technology and systems) to implement the provisions of the law and to effectively exercise authority over market operators, exchanges, self-regulatory organizations (SROs) and other intermediaries, particularly as the markets expand in size and complexity. In addition, while the trend in SSA has been towards fully independent regulators, there are many instances of political interference and vested interests by industry that either impede implementation or contribute to regulatory forbearance. Also, supporting financial infrastructures, though improved continue to exhibit important deficiencies.

SROs exist on a limited scale in the most SSA countries. South Africa is one of the very few countries where SROs are a critical component of the regulatory framework for securities. In most cases, the stock exchange is the SRO and it regulates listed companies and trading. Intermediaries and other players have not established organizations that exercise some regulatory powers over their members. Weaknesses in oversight of self-regulation are reported to be widespread, the most pervasive issue being the lack of inspection programs for SROs, which, in turn, is related to a lack of resources and capacity at the regulator. Some countries also raise concern about the governance structures at self-regulatory organizations and the handling of SRO conflicts of interest.

The extent to which regulators in SSA countries have comprehensive investigative and enforcement powers could not be ascertained in the absence of IOSCO assessments or updates. Nevertheless, available information indicates that, in many of the countries, there are weaknesses in regulators' ability to affect compliance through active regulation or to bring action against persons or entities that have violated regulations; in the standards for identifying, terminating, and correcting market manipulation in trades; and in institutions, corporate governance, and transparency. Safeguards against fraudulent treatment of investors/clients by market operators and potential failure of operators has also proved inadequate in some countries, due to lack of enforcement of rules on the separation of client accounts from dealer proprietary accounts.[16]

Significant progress has been made to improve cooperation through regional integration initiatives (SADC, EASRA and Ghana, Nigeria and UEMOA) and through establishments of committees to enable cooperation among domestic institutions. Many countries have signed MOUs with domestic and international counterparts, although the process is not yet complete. However, in many cases, greater progress appears to have been made on the international front than on the domestic front. In the latter case, the levels of cooperation, interaction, information exchange, collaboration and policy initiation and implementation between various financial markets, regulators and government agencies are inadequate to encourage the coherent formulation of policies. Weaknesses in cooperation of domestic regulators have been cited in Mauritius and Nigeria.

Disclosure standards for issuers as well as accounting and auditing, though improved, remain generally weak. Most SSA countries have disclosure requirements in place for initial offerings and thereafter, but implementation of ongoing disclosure practices and the quality of information is weak in many cases. Usually, while the criteria set out in legislation is met, the disclosure is insufficient in terms of completeness of information, frequency of release and level of detail. The contributory factors are many, and include weaknesses in enforcement, the lack of supporting infrastructure, such as rating agencies and resource limitations in accounting professions, that make it costly, especially for small and medium sized enterprises.[17]

The CIS industry, in most SSA countries, is still in the nascent stage, thus regulations are also quite new and supervisory practices are just being developed. South Africa is one of the few countries where the industry is well developed and where there is an effective regulatory framework, though legal gaps complicate the development and regulation of hedge funds. Information on the other countries (Nigeria, Mauritius, Ghana) was not adequate to enable a comprehensive evaluation of the regulatory framework, but there are reports that point to lax licensing procedures for CIS managers, weaknesses in supervisory arrangements; disclosure, valuation of fund units; and in surveillance of cross-border operations.

The regulation of market intermediaries is uneven across the region, but generally exhibits important weaknesses. In South Africa, the regulator has developed a comprehensive licensing system, sound capital adequacy standards, open position and exposure limits, though there is scope for further improvements. In many of the other countries in the region, regulation and supervisory practices are less systematized. Licensing procedures in some cases are not sufficiently rigorous, resulting in the establishment of intermediaries with inadequate systems and controls. In many cases, prudential regulations do not adequately reflect the risks that the institutions take, and ongoing monitoring of risks is inadequate. Press reports cite weak corporate governance structure, as well as inadequacies in enforcing rules on the segregation of client accounts from dealer proprietary accounts, to have contributed to recent problems of capital market intermediaries in Nigeria and Kenya.[18]

Regulatory practices for secondary markets vary across the countries, reflecting the differences in institutional structures. In South Africa, the trading of equities and listing of bonds take place on separate exchanges, the JSE and the BESA respectively, and there is also a large OTC market. Both exchanges are supervised by the FSC on an ongoing basis, with requirements for renewal of licenses yearly and staff oversight through regular meetings and reports. The OTC market is unregulated and while the FSB has the legal authority to review and approve all JSE rules, it only has consultative authority over listing.

In the other countries, trading of all securities is through the stock exchange or OTC. The intensity of supervisory oversight of the exchanges varies across the countries, but in some countries, they are virtually in existent. The factors contributing to this vary, but in an increasing number of cases the CSD or the stock exchange has just been established, thus the track record for their regulation and supervision is short. There are also indications that some of the limitations are related to the assessors knowledge and understanding of market operations and the risks they entail.

7.3.2.3   *Nonbanking sector*

Pensions, insurance and microfinance in many SSA countries lack adequate regulatory and supervisory oversight. The shortcomings cover a broad area, including both the legal framework and supervisory practices and capacity. Nevertheless, there are a number of countries in the region that have significantly strengthened their regulatory frameworks and, in some cases, the supervisory process, such as South Africa, Nigeria, Mauritius and Kenya and to a considerable degree Tanzania and Zambia.

At end 2008, very few countries had undertaken IAIS assessments, thus there is insufficient information on countries compliance with international standards or the adequacy of the regulatory frameworks in addressing the risks in insurance operations. Nevertheless, recent reviews (Stewart and Yermo, 2009) show that while most SSA countries insurance markets fall under supervisory authorities, many countries assigned the supervisory role to finance ministries or the central monetary authority, and these have so far not provided the enabling environment for supervision of the sector or monitored the industry with the necessary rigor.[19]

The reports also indicate that in many cases, the insurance regulations are outdated, restrictive and do not reflect prevailing structures. There is also inadequate expertise to undertake a full review of the legislations.[20] Regulators in some countries (Kenya) also suffer from a lack of operational independence as well as a lack of financial and human resources to perform effective supervision of insurance activities. Constraints to adequate staffing include budgetary and technical skills. Financial reporting and prudential regulation are also reported to be weak.

Pension regulation also exhibits significant weaknesses and great disparities in the quality of regulation in the few countries that have developed frameworks. As in other sectors, there are some countries (notably Kenya, Senegal, Nigeria, South Africa, Zambia, Mauritius, Botswana, and Malawi) that have initiated major regulatory reforms as part of the ongoing parametric and systemic reforms of the sector. However, even in some of these countries, there are regulatory gaps in coverage of schemes, weaknesses in licensing of pension funds, inadequacies in human and financial resources for supervision and for enforcing compliance, to disclosure requirements for funds, consumer protection. Even in South Africa, where pension regulation has been significantly strengthened, the number of pension funds makes the task of supervision difficult.

Microfinance is relatively new and the regulatory framework is still evolving, but in many countries there are MFIs that are not regulated at all and there is inadequate capacity to supervise the multitude of the institutions. Many countries (Kenya, Zambia, Rwanda, and more recently Uganda) have introduced regulations to provide for appropriate and effective supervision. In the CEMAC, the regional law that is to be enacted provides to increase the role of the Central Bank of West African States (BCEAO) in supervising and implementing a new accounting framework for MFIs. In Nigeria, the regulatory framework provided for a large number of existing community banks to convert into microfinance banks.

7.3.3 Regulatory gaps and contributory factors

Despite the progress made, important gaps and shortcomings remain in the regulatory and supervisory frameworks of SSA countries. In particular, there are still some financial segments that are unregulated; there are deficiencies in the prudential frameworks and in supervisory processes for capital markets and the nonbanking sector; some residual gaps in banking supervision; and notable limitations in the supporting financial infrastructure. Various and sometimes interrelated factors have contributed to the current state, including capacity limitations (quantity and quality of skills, technology and systems) and a related failure of regulatory frameworks to keep pace with developments in the financial landscape.

7.3.3.1 *Unregulated financial institutions and markets*

A number of institutions and markets remain unregulated in many SSA countries. In some cases, the deficiencies reflect gaps in the legal and regulatory framework while in others they are a mere product of weaknesses in supervisory practices or fraudulent practices by market players. While most of the gaps reflect a tendency for regulation to lag behind market developments, there are cases where the institutions have been in existence for a long time, such as development banks.

- In South Africa, there is little regulatory oversight of the OTC market, although a very large OTC market exists for derivatives and there is a small but growing market for interest rate swap/derivatives. Similarly, in Botswana, asset managers, pension fund administrators, financial advisors, and micro lenders were not subject to regulation.
- The regulatory framework for development banks remains unclear in many SSA countries. In some cases, the designated regulator has *neither the resources nor* the framework to undertake any supervision of the sector.
- Statutes in many countries do not prohibit "ponzi" schemes, and recent years have seen the emergence of unlicensed nonbank depository institutions

operating as a "ponzi" and "pyramid" schemes in selected countries (Lesotho, Swaziland Kenya, Namibia, Nigeria, and Seychelles) particularly as microfinance increased traction and popularity in many countries, with substantially adverse financial consequences in some cases.
- Selected countries have licensed Islamic banks, but the regulatory and supervisory framework is just developing.

7.3.3.2   Gaps in the prudential framework

Gaps in the prudential framework are most pronounced in capital markets (both equities and debt) and the nonbanking sectors, including pensions, insurances and micro finance. There are also some residual but important gaps in banking supervision that have stability implications.

The main gaps in banking supervision relate to surveillance, consolidated and cross-border supervision, and risk monitoring and management. Consumer protection is also increasing in importance and implementation of Basel II raises some supervisory challenges in some countries, there are important limitations in the provisions for bank insolvency.

- Surveillance: Effectiveness of supervision remains limited in many countries by lack of some key supervisory tools such as EWS and stress-testing. While the shift to risk-based supervision, which has continuous offsite monitoring, somewhat mitigates, not many countries implement risk-based supervision yet. In addition, while some of the countries have developed the stress-testing framework, in many cases, the risks being covered are not comprehensive and the frameworks do not include macro scenarios.
- Consolidated and cross-border supervision: Though many of the countries with conglomerate banking structures and internationally active banks have provisions in their legal framework to undertake consolidated supervision, the regulators are not yet implementing consolidated supervision in practice. In addition, despite the increase in cross-border operations and the share of foreign banks in the banking systems, country and transfer risks have not been integrated in the supervisory process. There is an accompanying and universal lack of contingent cross-border crisis management in the countries.
- Risk monitoring and management: Risk monitoring and management has largely focused on credit risk, which is most pervasive risk. The excess banking system liquidity which previously existed in many countries, reduced attention to liquidity risk. Rapid technological innovations have increased operational risk, but progress is slow in integrating IT assessments and other operational related risks in onsite supervision. Correlation risk has generally been overlooked.
- Bank insolvency frameworks: While many countries have strengthened the legal framework supporting bank insolvencies, the progress has been

uneven. Some of the countries have inadequate instruments for bank intervention, including provisions for purchase and assumption, etc.

- Basel II issues: Parent banks for some of the subsidiaries operating in SSA countries have begun to implement Basel II while supervisory capacity in the host countries to undertake supervision of such processes is limited in some of the countries.

Gaps in the regulation and supervision of capital markets are broader in scope, and cover issuers, intermediaries, and the markets. Most countries have enacted securities laws, but there are many instances where the regulators are not operationally independent and the resources and capacity to perform the statutory functions are limited. The regulations are sometimes not enforced, as inspections are not regularly undertaken, breaches are not investigated and there are still manual procedures for surveillance. There is also substantial scope to improve disclosure standards as well as segregation and protection of client assets for those countries with CIS. Often, illiquidity of some assets present challenges for pricing and valuation and governance of capital market intermediaries is also reported to be weak.

Regulatory frameworks for the nonbanking sector (pensions, insurance and microfinance exhibit more substantive gaps. Some countries do not have the regulations in place nor do they have any supervisory resources allocated for the function. Weaknesses in regulatory independence are also more pervasive as in many cases the governing body of the regulator either is a department of a government ministry or is controlled by it.

7.3.3.3   Financial infrastructure

SSA countries have made substantial progress in developing the supporting financial infrastructure and in addressing constraints to financial intermediation, but the agenda for further action is still large. Despite some improvements that include establishment of commercial courts in a number of countries, enforcing contracts in many SSA countries is still slow and the legal framework is not yet in place in some cases. Most countries do not yet have deposit insurance schemes and the LoLR has not been operationalized. There are also a number of countries with rudimentary payments systems (the CEMAC, Liberia). Moreover, while the number of countries that established credit registries has increased substantially, private registries are yet to develop and the scope of the existing registries is still limited in terms of coverage of people and the information content.

7.4   Policy issues: Ensuring efficiency and soundness

SSA countries have made significant progress in reforming and strengthening the regulation and supervision of the financial systems, but important gaps remain that warrant attention. Though the shortcomings are more pervasive in the less systemically important capital markets and nonbanking sectors, there are residual and important gaps in the oversight of banks.

Several and sometimes interrelated factors have contributed to the current state, but a major factor appear to be an inability of regulations to keep pace with the expansion in the financial system and emerging risks, due in part to capacity limitations, including quantity and quality of skills, technology and systems. Thus, there is a need for further reforms in the banking sector to align the frameworks with emerging challenges. In addition, as the financial crisis demonstrated, weaknesses in less regulated and sometimes seemingly nonsystemic sectors, could transmit stress to otherwise well-regulated sectors. Thus, the regulatory oversight should seek to be comprehensive in its coverage.

The global financial crisis also presents additional challenges that call for a reordering of priorities within the broad reform programs. There is urgent need for preventative measures to limit contagion to domestic financial systems as well as for strong liquidity management and bank resolution frameworks that can help mitigate the impact, if and when strains emerge. Such measures would involve strengthening high frequency data for risk monitoring; strengthening analytical tools for macrofinancial analysis, strengthening the skills of supervisors to undertake the analysis and ensuring adequate instruments and flexibility in the liquidity management and bank resolution frameworks.

These measures should, however, not detract from ongoing long-term efforts to develop financial systems and strengthen their resilience more generally. Given the systemic importance of the banking sector, strengthening banking supervision and regulation should remain a priority. Simultaneous efforts should also be made to foster a sound development of capital markets and other nonbank sectors, including through legislative and regulatory reforms for these sectors. These efforts will need to be underpinned by continued efforts to sustain a sound macroeconomic environment; reforms to address long-standing weaknesses; and policies to ensure financial system integrity, and supervisory vigilance to adapt regulations to emerging risks.[21]

A more detailed discussion of the policies and reforms needed is given below. The analysis is structured along sectoral lines for ease of discussion.

7.4.1   The banking sector

In line with identified gaps and deficiencies, reforms of banking system oversight should include measures to: (1) improve surveillance; (2) strengthen regulation, supervision, and enforcement of remedial actions, particularly with respect to cross-border supervision; (3) accelerate the development of preconditions for effective supervision; (4) constantly align regulation to emerging risks in the banking system; (5) bring unregulated institutions into the regulatory frameworks. These measures could also foster improved financial intermediation.

7.4.1.1 Improving surveillance of the banking systems

The financial landscape is rapidly changing and new risks are constantly emerging, thus there is a need to intensify surveillance of the financial systems so as to identify risks early and reduce potential for contagion. Measures to improve the surveillance of banking systems will require strengthening frameworks for financial risk analysis; addressing data deficiencies as well as capacity building.

A number of developments entail risks that warrant close surveillance. These include: (1) the rapid expansion of cross-border banking and the implications for LOLR facilities, contingency crisis arrangements and deposit insurance; (2) financial innovations such as mobile banking, bank-retail outlet partnerships, etc. and their implications for payment system; (3) the implications of the rapid credit growth and emerging predatory lending practices for consumer protection; and potential maturity mismatch in mortgage and other long-term lending; and (4) increasing capital flows and implications for Anti-Money Laundering and Combating the Financing of Terrorism (AML/CFT).

Improvements in data are needed in terms of the quality of the data provided to the regulator and the frequency with which the data is provided. In addition to financial soundness indicators, high frequency data will be key to early identification of emerging risks in the financial system. Such data should cover the liquidity position of banks; deposit flight; cross-border interbank loans; intra-group exposures; and off-balance sheet contingent claims.

Frameworks for financial risk analysis need to include stress-testing that is comprehensive in its coverage of risks. The risks assessed could include direct and foreign currency induced credit risk, liquidity, foreign exchange, interest rate, and correlation risk. The framework should also include macro scenarios that simulate developments that can occur simultaneously. These improved frameworks will also require that the supervisors have the appropriate training to undertake stress-testing and design EWS so that the data provided also lead to quality analysis.

7.4.1.2 Strengthening banking sector regulation and supervision

In general, countries should accelerate efforts to achieve full compliance with the BCPs. This will require that countries amend their legal frameworks in some cases; improve enforcement or develop processes that facilitate identification of emerging risks in the financial system; and also further build human technical capacity.

The granting and withdrawal of licenses is a key supervision tool, and it requires that regulators be given an adequate level of independence, legal authority and resources to carry out its functions. Thus, where licensing or de-licensing of banks and/or issuance of prudential regulations is vested in the ministry of finance (MOF) or require their authority, there is need to amend the laws or regulations. Banking laws of some countries also need amending to strengthen the framework for corrective action with a view to providing the regulators with more effective tools in dealing with problem of delinquent banks.

The expansion and increasing sophistication of financial system increase the need for regulators to develop processes to ensure that bank regulations keep pace with developments in the financial system. Within this broad effort, due to the growing complexity of ownership structures and expanding scope of banking operations, there is urgent need to ensure that consolidated supervision of both conglomerates and international active banks is enforced; home host supervisory arrangements do not stop at signing MOUs but that there is actual information-sharing and coordination; and there are ex-ante contingency mechanisms for domestic and cross-border crisis management.

Related to this is the need to integrate the monitoring and management of liquidity and market risks in the supervisory processes. As the global financial crisis has demonstrated, liquidity conditions can change very quickly, thus it is important to review liquidity management frameworks to ensure that there are adequate instruments that can be applied flexibly to provide liquidity support to solvent banks with temporal liquidity needs. Banks should also be encouraged to undertake contingency planning, including for unexpected liquidity shocks and carry out behavioral analysis as well as contractual characteristics. Similarly, in countries where capital markets are expanding rapidly, market risk should be integrated in assessments.

Capacity building should also be an integral part of the reforms in the banking sector. Countries moving towards risk-based supervisory approach will require introducing new policies and processes that would assist the supervision staff understand the risk profile of its prioritize supervisory resources and work in areas and institutions deemed banks, allowing them to as posing higher levels of risk. Supervisory staff, therefore, need to constantly upgrade their skills.

7.4.1.3   *Strengthening preconditions for effective regulation*

While significant progress has been achieved in developing the financial infrastructures, ongoing reforms need to be expedited. These include operationalizing the credit registries; (1) strengthen auditing and accounting standards for corporations; (2) addressing remaining gaps in the safety nets including aligning the deposit insurance scheme with international principles; and (3) modernizing the payments systems in those countries where rudimentary systems still exist. There is also a need to review the operation of the deposit protection scheme, including its governance structure and the share of deposits covered by the deposit insurance.

7.4.1.4   *Developing regulatory frameworks for unregulated institutions*

Interest in developing development banks has resurged, while progress has been slow in improving the financial position of state-owned banks.

Appropriate regulatory frameworks are, therefore, needed to monitor and manage risks in development and other specialized institutions. There is also a need to ensure that such institutions establish strong management structures to safeguard prudent lending policies while limiting subsidies.

7.4.2   Capital markets

Regulation of capital markets will need to go beyond the establishment of regulatory agencies and the passage of laws and regulations. There is need to strengthen oversight of issuers, market intermediaries and secondary markets as well as their governance structures. There is also need to adapt regulations to new risks, and in the case of South Africa, maintain supervisory vigilance on potential risks from securitization and hedge funds. As with other sectors, the preconditions for effective regulations need to be in place to ensure reliability of financial statements as well as ongoing disclosure.

7.4.2.1   *Strengthening regulation and surveillance of capital markets*

Regulators of stock markets in SSA need to create optimal regulations to adequately protect investors and build confidence in stock markets. Such regulations should cover issuers, intermediaries and markets including governance of stock exchanges and central depository systems. There is also a need to strengthen cross-border surveillance, in light of increasing stock market activity, increased cross-listing of stocks and regional integration of stock markets. The skill capacity of regulators should keep pace with innovations in the industry.

OTC markets need improved surveillance. Regulatory actions could focus on improving transparency and on preventing systemic risk from a substantial counterparty default; improved reporting of OTC trading and position concentrations by member firms and adoption of margin and concentration rules for member firms trading OTC.

Regional integration which is being considered raises issues of treatment of cross-listing, harmonization of take over and mergers rules, listing rules, securities regulation, accounting and auditing, trading and settlement and depository rules and matters relating to cross-border enforcement and conflict resolution.

7.4.2.2   *Oversight of hedge funds*

There is need to preserve the risk diversification properties as well as financial benefits which hedge funds bring to South Africa's financial system, while taking adequate precautions against possible systemic implications.

7.4.2.3   *Adapting regulations to new risks*

Developing private sector instruments for infrastructure finance will require clear policy and institutional frameworks for private participation in infrastructure. In light of the increasing interest on loan securitization and the use of complex products, there is need for supervisors in affected countries to ensure that associated risks are mitigated and there are clear guidelines on accounting and disclosure of these instruments. Mortgage securitization also requires a strong legal and institutional infrastructure and well-developed primary mortgage markets.

7.4.3   Nonbanking Sector

The nonbanking sector needs both liberalization and better regulation. The identified weaknesses call for efforts to establish adequate framework for supervision, enact appropriate legislation and ensure enforcement of those regulations.

7.4.3.1   *Strengthening the oversight of the microfinance sector*

The positive momentum in the microfinance sector should be supported by appropriate regulation, oversight, and proper accounting practices in order to foster a sound and sustainable expansion of the sector. There is also need for further diagnostic work on the capacity of formal and informal arrangement to supply financial services to the underserved segments of the population. Therefore, to assist policy formulation, there is a need to fill gaps in data and research. Regulation is needed to ensure soundness of the sector without stifling innovative ideas in the creation of new vehicles to expand credit.

7.4.3.2   *Reforming the pension industry and strengthening its regulation*

The growing importance of pension funds both in financial terms and with regard to their role in the provision of retirement income underscores the need to strengthen supervisory framework and enhance efficiency of surveillance over the retirement fund sector.

The reform agenda for pensions is extensive and should include several elements: (1) organizational structure of supervisory authorities; (2) the techniques and procedures used in the supervisory process; (3) basic reporting and regulatory surveillance; (4) oversight of pension fund administrators and asset managers' further review of regulations pertaining to portfolio investment regulation; and (5) investment capabilities including outsourcing of fund management to professional managers. In South Africa, where the framework has been significantly strengthened, there is scope for further development of the framework for supervision and enhancing the skills to implement a more proactive and risk-focused form of supervision.

There is also a need to reform the sector with a view to increase the coverage of pensions and improve its contribution to poverty reduction. More will need to be done to build the supporting infrastructure for a modern pension sector including custodians, private pension providers and asset managers.

7.4.3.3   *Strengthening regulation of insurance sectors*

Establish regulation and supervision of insurance sector and to develop the framework to a stage where the regulation and supervision of insurance activity could meet international standards and best practice.

Notes

The author is a Senior Economist in the Africa Regional Division, Monetary and Capital Markets Department, International Monetary Fund. The views expressed are of the author and not necessarily of the International Monetary Fund.

1. The chapter has been updated to incorporate recent trends and the initial effects of the global financial crisis.
2. Unlike most countries in SSA, Nigeria's banking system consists mainly of domestic private banks.
3. The parents of subsidiaries are mostly headquartered in South Africa, France, India, Portugal, the U.K., and the U.S. Regional banking groups with headquarters in Nigeria, Togo, and Kenya have also expanded rapidly. There are also a few countries that have cross-border operations on a limited scale from Tanzania, Cape Verde, Malawi and Mauritius.
4. Countries with relatively developed equities markets include Mauritius, Kenya, Nigeria, Ghana, Uganda, Zambia, Tanzania, Botswana, Namibia. The WAEMU has a regional stock exchange with listings mainly from Côte d'Ivoire. There are also a number that have established stock exchanges even though there are either no listings yet or very few including Swaziland, Cape Verde, Rwanda, Gabon, and the CEMAC.
5. There are also close links between pensions and insurance, through underwriting, insurance holding pension assets, and insurers selling retirement annuities.
6. For South Africa, in addition to the increase in spreads and tightening liquidity, the securitization market,of which banks are major players, also dried up.
7. Nigeria, Ghana, Zimbabwe, Burundi, Liberia, Rwanda, Zambia and member countries of the WAEMU raised the minimum capital for banks by substantial margins.
8. Off shore financial institutions in Cape Verde benefit from lighter degree of supervision and a less restrictive legal framework, including lower CAR, different risk concentration limitations, lower liquidity. In Ghana, local banks have to meet the new minimum capital at a slower pace than their foreign counterparts. Nigeria has lower requirements for community banks.
9. Due to excess liquidity and dominance of government securities in capital markets, banks in SSA were more vulnerable to credit risk than to market and liquidity risks.
10. The World Banks "Doing Business" report indicates that the cost of enforcing contracts, collecting debts and registering property is significantly higher in SSA than in comparator groups.
11. In selected cases, the central banks also supervise microfinance institutions and other intermediaries such as the foreign exchange bureaus.
12. At end 2008, FSAPs conducted on SSA countries all included assessments of compliance with the BCP. By contrast, only 11 percent included IOSCO and IAIS assessments. MCM TC programs have equally focused on bank supervision reforms. Regional initiatives exhibit a similar pattern.
13. South Africa also introduced legislation to improve consumer protection and also to limit reckless lending through the introduction of the National Credit Regulator.
14. These weaknesses were particularly evident in dealing with bank insolvencies in Togo and other member countries.
15. A quantitative analysis of weaknesses is, however, limited by the absence of formal assessments of compliance with IOSCO principles. So far only five coun-

tries have undertaken formal assessments of the standard of compliance with the IOSCO core principles, and most of the assessments are somewhat dated. The IOSCO assessments have been undertaken for Ghana (2000, 2003), Kenya (2003), Nigeria (2000), Senegal (2000), and South Africa (2000, 2009).

16. These weaknesses have been cited as some of the causes to the recent problems in Kenya and Nigerian stock markets.
17. An emerging trend in the region (Mauritius, Tanzania, Kenya) has been to introduce second tier boards that have less disclosure requirements.
18. The committee set up in Nigeria to review the recent problems in capital markets also point to these weaknesses.
19. In some countries (Eritrea, Liberia, and Rwanda) the regulators have not issued the regulations or undertaken any supervision.
20. Selected countries have autonomous and functioning regulators, most notably South Africa, Namibia, Mauritius, the Conference Intérnationale de Marchés d'Assurances (CIMA) and a few other countries. The CIMA is a regional supervisory committee that covers 14 French-speaking countries, namely Benin, Burkina Faso, Cameroon, Central Africa, the Comoros, Ivory Coast, Gabon, Equatorial Guinea, Guinea Bissau, Mali, Niger, Senegal, Chad, and Togo.
21. Developments with respect to AML/CFT were not covered in the background section, hence the absence of recommendations. Generally, though there is need to accelerate the enactment of relevant laws and regulations and establish supporting institutions.

References

African Development Bank 2007. "Fixed income guidebook." Tunisia: Tunis.
Aseffa, Yosef 2007. *Insurance Services Liberalization and Capacity-Building: The Case for Africa,*" in Trade and Development Aspects of Insurance Services and Regulatory Frameworks, United Nations New York and Geneva.
Bank of Uganda 2007. *Annual Supervision Report.* Kampala, Uganda.
Carvajal, Ana and Elliott, Jennifer 2007. "Strengths and weaknesses in securities market regulation: A global analysis." IMF Working Paper WP/07259.
Central Bank of Kenya 2007. *Banking Supervision Report.* Nairobi, Kenya.
Ghana 2008. *Annual Reports of the Securities and Exchange Commission of Ghana,* Accra.
Global Credit Rating Co. 2008. Africa Insurance Industry Bulletin. Website www.globalratings.net
IMF 2008. *Sub-Saharan Africa, Regional Economic Outlook.* Washington, DC: International Monetary Fund Publication Services.
Mauritius 2008. Financial services commission Mauritius, Annual report for the year July 1, 2007 to June 30, 2008. Republic of Mauritius. www.fscmauritius.org
Nigeria 2008. *Annual Reports of the Securities and Exchange Commission of Nigeria.* Abuja, Nigeria.
Nigeria 2008. *Annual Reports of the Central Bank of Nigeria.* Abuja, Nigeria.
Stewart, F. and Yermo, J. 2009. "Pensions in Africa." *OECD Working Papers on Insurance and Private Pensions,* No. 30, OECD publishing, © OECD.
World Bank 2009. "Doing business." Washington, DC.

8
Building Supervisory Structures in Africa—An Analytical Framework

Marc Quintyn and Michael Taylor

> Structure follows strategy and the most complex type of structure
> is the concatenation of several basic strategies.
>
> Alfred Chandler (1962)

8.1 Introduction

The world of financial sector supervision has been going through major changes in the past decade-and-half. One of the major developments has been the attention given to the reshaping of the institutional structures of supervision—sector specific regulators versus integrated (or unified) regulators, either housed inside or outside the central bank—after decades of total absence of any attention to this aspect of supervision.[1]

The structure of supervision is only a means to an end, not an end in itself—or as Mwenza (2004) puts it, "a second order discussion" in the debate about regulatory and supervisory efficiency and effectiveness. In addition, focusing too much on issues of institutional structure can often distract from the more essential, but less dramatic, business of improving the quality of supervision. Nevertheless, it needs to be recognized that an appropriate institutional structure adds to the efficiency and effectiveness of the regulatory and supervisory process. Hence, the attention devoted to it.

In this regard, the key issue for many emerging market economies is how reform of supervisory structures can be turned into an opportunity to build or strengthen supervisory capacity. This chapter analyzes this very issue in the context of sub-Saharan Africa (SSA). After decades of ups and downs and banking crises, financial sector development in SSA has been accelerating since the second half of the 1990s. Banking systems in most countries have reached a level of stability unmatched in the past 30 years. Nonbank financial institutions (NBFIs) are transgressing from the informal to the formal financial system. The quality of banking supervision, although still lagging other parts of the world, is improving, but is still coping with capacity shortages.

These developments and challenges more than justify attention for the development of financial supervisory structures in SSA that can stay in tune with these developments and are the appropriate fit for the challenges, in particular the continent's capacity-constraints. To that end, this chapter provides an analytical framework to guide the decision making process about an appropriate regulatory strategy (a strategy to define scope and intensity of regulation in an environment of an expanding financial sector) and the appropriate institutional structure to support this strategy. Thus, we first develop a regulatory strategy that takes into account the capacity-constraints that the individual countries are facing, and subsequently evaluate the pros and cons of a number of "tested" supervisory structures that would fit (mesh with) the regulatory strategy.

The structure of this chapter is as follows. Section 8.2 frames the debate about supervisory structures in Africa in the broader trends that are unfolding across the world. Section 8.3 reviews key characteristics of SSA's financial systems and supervisory structures that are important for the arguments developed in the remainder of the chapter. Section 8.4 presents an analytical framework for establishing a "regulatory strategy" in a capacity-constrained environment. Regulatory scope and intensity are used as two key tools to develop a strategy tailored to the needs of individual countries. Section 8.5 reviews the pros and cons of a number of stylized institutional models in their relation to this framework. Section 8.6 presents the conclusions.

8.2   Background

Until just over a decade ago, the institutional structure of financial regulation and supervision was not considered a topic worthy of extensive policy debate, or even one that would attract much academic attention (Goodhart, 2002). Most countries had a bank supervision agency, established either inside or outside the central bank, a regulatory agency for the securities markets—often of the self-regulatory type—and, depending on the importance of the sector, some agency that kept an eye on the insurance sector.

In the past decade, the perception that the architecture of supervision (the institutional structure) is irrelevant has changed radically, as more and more countries are reviewing, or even drastically rebuilding their supervisory structures. While the restructuring wave took off in advanced economies, it has since reached most corners of the world. Several middle- and low-income countries (MIC and LIC, respectively) have in recent years revisited their supervisory structures as well.[2]

A number of developments have pulled the debate on the architecture out of the sphere of irrelevance. First, liberalization of financial systems, accompanied by higher risk-taking by financial institutions has put a premium on corporate governance in the financial system. In this new environment, the supervisors' task has become more relevant than before as they have become "governance supervisors."[3] This fundamental redefinition of the supervisors' job content has contributed to the fact that gradually more attention is being paid to the quality of supervision and regulation, and hence to the position of the agency in charge of it within the government structure, as well as to its governance structure.

Two general examples demonstrate these trends. First many supervisors was formerly housed in a department within ministries. This was often the case with insurance regulators, and to a lesser extent with bank supervisors. Supervisors housed in ministries are now becoming rare cases. Second, while banks were typically regulated and supervised, other sector such as insurance were typically only regulated—supervision was minimal. Nowadays, all segments of the financial system have some form of supervision in response to the trends described above.

Second, it was increasingly felt that, to be effective, the supervisory structure needed to reflect the realities of the markets. Hence, given the convergence of the previously distinct banking, securities, and insurance sectors, particularly due to the development of financial conglomerates, it was increasingly argued that sector-specific supervisory agencies should be integrated (or unified) to ensure the effectiveness of regulation and supervision in this new environment (the "industry change"-argument for reform). This was the argumentation used in, for instance, the United Kingdom to establish the Financial Services Authority (FSA) in 1997, and the Australian Prudential Regulatory Agency (APRA) in Australia.[4]

Other arguments have been developed as well to justify the establishment of a unified regulator.[5] First, that it is possible to achieve economies of scale in regulation, particularly in small countries or countries with small financial systems, and, thus, to achieve regulatory goals more cost-effectively (the "economies of scale"- or "small economy" argument).[6,7]

Second, unified supervision is sometimes also adopted as a measure to build supervisory capacity. This "institutional strengthening" argument is heard most often as part of the response to a financial crisis, the intention being that institutional change can be used as a way to break down entrenched interests, cultures, and work practices that are believed to have contributed to the crisis in the first place (The Republic of Korea and Indonesia are examples in this group).

Other factors have also been at work in the trend toward restructuring the supervisory institutions. Within the euro-zone, the transfer of monetary policy functions to the European Central Bank left national central banks with an opportunity to redefine their role with respect to financial regulation. Some have done this by adding other regulatory responsibilities to their traditional banking supervision function. Finally, another factor behind some recent revisions has been that it has become fashionable to do so. Because unified regulation has been adopted in several of the most advanced financial markets, it is tempting to engage in reform merely to be seen as being part of the current trend. Thus, the decision to adopt unified regulation can be taken without considering the appropriateness of this model for the circumstances of a particular country. In some cases, the idea that regulatory reform is necessary because it is the trend in other countries can be used to provide cover for less high-minded motives for embarking on institutional reform, such as the desire by some finance ministries to obtain greater control over financial regulation by wresting it from the hands of the central bank.[8]

While initially the reform debate was cast as a choice between either separate supervisors for each of the main industry sectors, or a unified supervisory agency, the reform debate has become richer than this bipolar choice and countries have been considering a wider range of institutional forms with varying degrees of central bank involvement in regulation.[9] At the end of 2004, 29 countries had adopted the unified supervisory model, while an additional 22 countries had restructured around at least one multisector supervisor (see Courtis (2005) and Čihák and Podpiera (2007)). Moreover, even within the model of unified supervision, there is scope for some variation. The "FSA model" represents one type of arrangement (no central bank involvement), but a variety of different structures has seen the daylight— including the Irish unified regulator as a subsidiary of the central bank and the Singaporean model of locating all financial regulatory functions within the central bank.

What this diversification in the models also shows is that the restructuring debate is not conducted on purely economic grounds, but, as some of the arguments alluded to above shows, is part of a political decision making process where all stakeholders (government, supervisors, central bank, supervised entities) use their influence to ensure an outcome that serves their interests. The analysis of the determinants of restructuring in Masciandaro (2006b) and Freytag and Masciandaro (2007) demonstrates that in the reshaping of the financial supervision architectures in a sample of 89 countries, the institutional role of the central bank in the supervisory process before the reforms (the "path dependence hypothesis") is the determining factor, more than any other structural variable, such as the features of the banking and financial markets (the "convergence hypothesis"), which in some studies is only marginally significant, and seems sample sensitive.[10] In other words, the policymakers who intend to reform the supervisory structure seem primarily influenced by the actual role of the central bank in the process, and by its reputation endowment too (the South African experience discussed in footnote 10 may serve as an example here). The inverse relationship between consolidation in financial supervision and the degree of central bank involvement is confirmed by different case studies in Masciandaro (2006a).

This chapter focuses on the restructuring debate in sub-Saharan Africa (SSA). The continent is certainly not absent in the current reform debate.

Some SSA countries—in particular the MICs on the continent—have already embarked on reforms in their supervisory structures in response to changes in their financial system. Our focus seems justified by the fact that the restructuring debate in SSA introduces a number of important SSA-typical *dimensions* and *challenges* to the debate.

The major new dimension amidst the present financial deepening episode in SSA is the growing systemic significance of a number of deposit-taking NBFIs which have hitherto mainly operated in the informal sector, or at the borderline between informal and formal sectors. The second new dimension follows from the first one: since many of these operators remained in the informal sector, they are unregulated. As discussed further in the chapter, the issue in this regard is that they need to be regulated for systemic reasons, but that this regulation needs to be proportional, that is, should not choke the creative forces behind their existence which are critical from a developmental point of view.

The main challenges in SSA include (1) the persistence of severe capacity-constraints in most countries; and, (at least partially) related to this (2) the need to preserve a role of significance for the central bank in financial sector supervision of SSA. In many developing economies, only the central bank has the financial resources and budgetary independence to ensure that regulation is adequately funded. Moreover, developing economies are typically more prone to periods of financial instability than advanced countries. Hence, there is a premium in keeping the central bank involved in the regulatory process. Both factors will play a crucial role in the design of an appropriate supervisory structure. Bringing the continent's specific dimensions and challenges together boils down to saying that the supervisory debate in SSA is as much about shaping supervisory structures it is about reshaping them.

The goal of the analytical framework developed in this paper is to bring the needs of shaping supervisory structures and capacity building together. We first elaborate a strategy for building regulatory and supervisory capacity in line with the needs of the deepening and broadening financial sectors in SSA. Subsequently we review a number of possible supervisory structures and analyze how they would support the regulatory strategy (as it will be labeled henceforth). So, our analytical approach ends with the presentation of a range of policy options.

8.3 Financial sectors and supervision in SSA

This section succinctly highlights those developments in the financial systems in SSA that are of importance for the arguments developed in the remainder of the chapter in support of building strong supervisory structures.[11] We first present some salient trends in financial sector development, then proceed to an overview of the current supervisory structures and conclude with some comments on how the arguments for supervisory alignment in Africa fit into the broader picture presented in the previous section.

8.3.1   Key facts and trends in financial sector development

From the perspective of this chapter, two major developments dominate SSA's financial systems. First, since the end of the 1990s, *financial deepening* is accelerating, albeit from a low level. Second, the financial systems are becoming *more diversified*.

8.3.1.1   *Financial deepening*

SSA and, in particular, its LICs, remains home to some of the least developed financial systems in the world. The range of institutions is narrow, access to (even basic) financial services is still low, and informal systems remain a major source of credit for large parts of the productive sector. However, the past 10–12 years have signalled a number of positive developments, although their pace is still slow. Table 8.1 shows that, according to several measures, financial deepening in LICs is in progress—a process that started in earnest in the late 1990s. Interestingly enough, deepening is less visible in the MICs if we exclude South Africa.[12] While the MICs show definitely higher levels of development that the LICs, they remain by all standards

Table 8.1   SSA: Indicators of financial development by income group

	Sub-Saharan Africa						Rest of the world	
	Low income countries		Middle income countries		Middle income countries without South-Africa		Middle income countries	
	1990–1999	2000–2004	1990–1999	2000–2004	1990–1999	2000–2004	1990–1999	2000–2004
Bank deposits/ GDP	13.6	18.0	44.5	50.7	29.7	29.2	31.7	39.4
Private sector credit/ GDP	12.3	13.3	52.1	64.0	21.5	21.0	39.4	40.3
M2/GDP	21.9	26.9	49.8	55.6	35.0	32.1	77.3	94.2
Liquid Liabilities/ GDP	19.1	23.8	47.9	534	34.5	32.5	36.6	41.2

Source: Gulde et al. (2006).

still relatively less developed than their counterparts elsewhere in the world. Assuming that the current level of macroeconomic stability in SSA continues to prevail, and the emphasis on financial sector development expressed by African leaders and (bilateral and multilateral) donors continues, financial deepening is expected to continue.

8.3.1.2 Diversification

However, more is going on SSA that is not visible from the figures on financial deepening which only show developments stemming from the banking system. SSA's financial systems are also diversifying. Diversification not only adds to financial deepening, but also has implications for financial sector regulation and supervision.

Table 8.2 presents recent figures on the state of financial sector diversification in a selected number of countries. Data limitations do not allow us to compare these numbers with the past, but it is a fact that 10–15 years ago several of these subsectors were insignificant.[13] SSA is diversifying in two directions. First of all, there is diversification in what is typically called "beyond banking" such as insurance, pension funds and stock markets. However, SSA is also diversifying in what could be called "before banking" that is, those segments of the market that give poor and rural populations easier access to finance than through banks, such as to credit cooperatives and microfinance institutions. At the same time, there is a move of institutions out of the informal sector and into the formal sector, although this is, by definition hard to quantify. Both developments are critical from a regulatory and supervisory point of view.

Turning to Table 8.2, we can make the following observations. Despite the above developments, *all systems are still heavily bank-dominated.* In most countries, banks cover close to 90 percent of financial system assets. As a result of the opening up of domestic systems to foreign banks in the 1990s (for most countries), several banking systems now have a *relatively strong foreign-bank presence.* In the low-income group, their presence amounts to 40 percent of total bank assets and 60 percent in MICs (not shown in Table 8.2). Partly mirroring the above development, the *presence of state-owned banks has declined* steadily during the past decade-and-a half. In low-income SSA, they do not represent more than 20 percent total bank assets and no more than 10 percent in middle-income countries.

The sector of *NBFIs contains a wide variety of institutions* in English-speaking SSA (deposit-taking NBFIs, insurance companies, pension funds, finance and leasing companies, merchant banks, mortgage finance, and consumer credit companies). In general, these sectors are still small (with a few exceptions). However, in several countries they have started to grow and show potential to raise the level of financial services.

Among the NBFIs, *the importance of deposit-taking NBFIs is on the rise.* Microfinance is becoming a key vehicle to provide the poor and rural groups

Table 8.2 Sub-Saharan Africa: Relative importance of segments in the financial systems of selected countries (in percent of total assets of the system, latest available data)[a]

Country	Commercial banks	Other (mainly) deposit-taking institutions	Microfinance institutions	Rural banks	Insurance companies	Pension funds[b]	Other
Botswana	40	34.3	–	–	1.6	17.4	6.8[c]
Burundi	–	–	–	–	–	–	–
Central African Republic	68.5	–	2.7	–	7.6	21.1	–
Comoros	94.0	–	6.0	–	–	–	–
Congo Rep	89.8	–	7.0	–	3.2	–	–
Ethiopia	88.4	3.0	–	–	3.0	3.0	5.0[d]
Gabon	83.6	4.8	–	–	7.8	–	5.0[e]
Gambia	97.0	–	1.0	–	2.0	–	–
Ghana	50.9	6.0	–	–	2.0	15.1	–
Guinea	98.2	1.8	1.8	–	–	–	–
Kenya	60.4	15.0	0.5	–	8.2	–	–
Lesotho	91.8	–	–	–	7.8	–	–
Madagascar	97.8	0.6	1.6	–	–	–	–
Malawi	70.9	17.5	–	–	29.1	–	–
Mali	98.7	–	–	–	–	–	–
Mauritius	94.8	4.4	–	–	–	–	–
Mozambique	94.9	4.3	0.1	–	–	–	–
Namibia	38.1	–	–	–	24.8	–	–
Niger	61.9	1.1	1.7	–	7.6	–	–
Nigeria	90.5	8.1	–	0.7	2.1	0.6	–
Rwanda	53.0	2.6	4.5	–	4.3	20.6	–
Senegal	–	–	2.6	–	–	–	–
Seychelles	87.1	6.0	–	–	2.1	5.0	–
South Africa	25.3	–	–	–	14.6	–	–
Swaziland	–	–	–	–	–	–	–
Tanzania	78.0	–	–	–	4.0	13.0	–
Uganda	–	–	–	–	–	–	–
Zambia	59.6	23.0	0.2	–	3.8	16.7	–
Zimbabwe	76.6	10.2	0.1	–	3.0	2.0	–

[a] Numbers do not always add up to 100 percent.
[b] In most countries, state pension fund.
[c] Capital investment funds.
[d] Development bank.
[e] Development bank.

Source: International Monetary Fund, African Department, "Country Profiles Database" and authors' calculations.

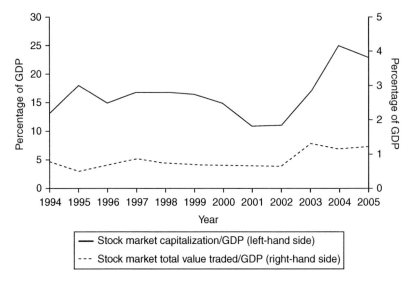

Figure 8.1 African stock exchanges: Capitalization and value traded (percentage of GDP)

Note: The figure shows the medians of the eight most active exchanges by value traded other than Johannesburg (that is, for Botswana, Côte d'Ivoire, Ghana, Mauritius, Mozambique, Namibia, Nigeria, and Zimbabwe).
Source: Honohan and Beck (2007)

access to organized finance in several countries. Governments and NGOs alike are fostering this development. Some of the microfinance groups accept deposits and provide a range of financial services. Credit cooperatives are increasing their significance as providers of (basic) financial services in a number of countries. Both sectors are increasingly attracting deposits from the informal sectors.

Figure 8.1 shows that African stock exchanges are also on the rise since the early 2000s. New stock markets have been established and stock market capitalization has been increasing in the first years of the new millennium.

8.3.2   Financial sector supervision

8.3.2.1   *Supervisory capacity*

Financial sector supervision—until recently limited to bank supervision—has been making great strides in the past decennium in SSA. Table 8.3 compares the degrees of compliance with the Basel Core Principles for Effective Banking Supervision (BCP) of the SSA countries that have thus

Table 8.3 Sub-Saharan Africa: Compliance with Basel Core Principles
(BCP) in comparison with rest of the world (percentage of compliant
and largely compliant)

Group of BCP criteria	Sub-Saharan Africa (19 countries)[a]	Rest of the world (119 countries)
Chapter 1 Objectives, autonomy, powers, and resources (CP 1)	75.8	81.4
Chapter 2 Licensing and structure (CPs 2–5)	77.7	78.6
Chapter 3 Prudential regulations and requirements (CPs 6–15)	44.4	46.7
Chapter 4 Methods of on-going supervision (CPs 16–20)	65.5	75.2
Chapter 5 Information requirements (CP 21)	57.9	76
Chapter 6 Formal powers of supervisors (CP 22)	31.6	69.5
Chapter 7 Cross-border banking (CPs 23–25)	58.4	59.33
Total	56.0	67.9

[a] Countries include: Botswana, Cameroon, Central Economic African Monetary
Union, Côte d'Ivoire, Gabon, Ghana, Guinea, Kenya, Madagascar, Mauritius,
Mozambique, Namibia, Nigeria, Rwanda, Seychelles, South Africa, Tanzania,
Uganda, and Zambia.

Source: Own calculations based on FSAP results.

far participated in the joint World Bank-IMF Financial Sector Assessment
Programs (FSAPs), with those of the rest of the world.

The table clearly shows SSA's progress and remaining weaknesses. While
compliance with the principles of Chapters 1, 2 and 3 is not very different
from the rest of the world, SSA's weaknesses come to the surface in compliance with the principles under Chapters 4, 5, and 6. In particular, Chapters 4
and 6 point at SSA's Achilles heel: several agencies are still understaffed and
lack essential skills, which leads to low compliance with those principles that
refer to actual supervision (on-site inspections and off-site monitoring), as
well as its enforcement. So while SSA's regulatory framework has caught up
with the rest of the world, it is the (crucial) supervisory part that lags because
of capacity-constraints. This is why any strategy to strengthen supervision
and its institutional framework needs to take this constraint into account.

Supervision of nonbank sectors is even weaker—or nonexistent. However,
in recent years, several countries have embarked on major reform programs
(often following FSAPs) to upgrade their regulatory frameworks and banking supervisory skills.

8.3.2.2 Supervisory structures

Partly in response to the aforementioned developments, attention for reforming supervisory structures in SSA has been growing, especially in the MICs.[14] South Africa unified NBFI supervision in the 1990s and now has a bipolar supervisory system, with banking supervision housed in the Reserve Bank of South Africa. Mauritius established a unified NBFI supervisor in 2000. Zambia regrouped supervision in three institutions—the central bank (responsible for banks, building societies, and bureaus de change); the Securities and Exchange Commission; and the Pension and Insurance Authority (established in 1997). Namibia is in an advanced stage of implementing a NBFI regulator, and Rwanda is unifying all supervisory functions in the central bank. Other countries are contemplating modifications to their supervisory structure (Botswana, Malawi, Swaziland, and Uganda). Thus far, no significant developments have taken place in central or western Africa.

A detailed overview of supervisory structures is provided in Table 8.4, with a summary overview in Table 8.5. The following are some key observations:

- Central banks are the dominant supervisors for banks in SSA. The legacy of the colonial powers is visible: countries with a British tradition typically house bank supervision in the central bank, while most former French colonies established bank supervision in a separate agency.[15]
- Central banks are also often called upon to organize supervision for deposit-taking NBFIs as a natural extension of their bank supervisory responsibility. In more than half of the countries in the sample, the central bank has some responsibility in supervising this group of institutions. As a logical consequence, the same is happening with respect to microfinance. Some countries are well advanced in supervising these institutions, while in others, central banks have been recently assigned the regulatory and supervisory responsibility over microfinance institutions, and are developing capacity in this area.[16]
- In several cases, the supervisory responsibility of the central banks goes further than banks and other deposit-taking institutions, making the central bank the dominant supervisor. For instance, in Nigeria and Uganda (recently, and meant to be temporarily) the central bank is also the pension fund supervisor; in Mozambique, the stock exchange supervisor; and in Swaziland the insurance supervisor.[17] More generally, in a number of cases the central banks seem to be the supervisor-by-default. In 10 countries, the central bank supervises each sector that is in existence, or that is considered important enough to be regulated; and
- Table 8.4 also shows that there are an impressive number of unregulated sectors. In most cases these sectors only have a marginal presence. Pension funds remain typically unregulated (among others because the pension fund is typically government-owned). Very often, regulation and supervision of specific sector remain limited to licensing by a registrar

(located in a ministry), with a light regulatory framework and without any further supervisory oversight. This is particularly true for several deposit-taking NBFIs in a large number of countries. The registrar for credit unions or credit cooperatives is in some countries housed in the ministry of agriculture, for instance.

Table 8.4 Sub-Saharan countries: Financial sector supervisory structures in selected countries[a]

Country	Banks	Microfinance institutions	Other Deposit-taking institutions	Insurance	Securities	Pension funds
Angola	CB	–	–	MOF	–	–
BCEAO-WAMU	B (regional)	–	–	I (regional)	–	–
BEAC	B (regional)	–	–	I (regional)	–	–
Botswana	CB	–	CB	M	M	M
Burundi	CB	CB	–	–	–	–
Cape Verde	CB	CB	CB	CB	–	–
Comoros	CB	–	–	–	–	–
Congo DR	CB	–	–	–	–	–
Eritrea	CB	–	–	–	–	–
Ethiopia	CB	CB	–	CB	–	–
Gambia	CB	CB	CB	CB	–	–
Ghana	CB	CB	CB	I	S	–
Kenya	CB	–	CB	–	S	–
Lesotho	CB	–	–	CB	CB	–
Madagascar	B	B	B	–	–	–
Malawi	CB	CB	CB	CB	–	–
Mauritius	CB	–	CB	M	M	–
Mozambique	CB	CB	CB	I	CB	–
Namibia	CB	M	M	M	M	–
Nigeria	CB	–	CB	–	S	CB
Rwanda	CB	CB	CB	–	–	–
Sao Tome and Principe	CB	CB	CB	CB	–	–
Seychelles	CB	–	CB	–	CB	–
Sierra Leone	CB	–	CB	CB	–	–
South Africa	CB	–	M	M	M	M
Swaziland	CB	–	O	CB	–	–
Tanzania	CB	–	CB	I	S	–
Uganda	CB	–	CB	I	S	CB
Zambia	CB	CB	CB	M	S	M
Zimbabwe	CB	CB	CB	I	S	–

Legend: CB: central bank; B: separate banking supervisor; O: separate supervisor for other financial institutions; I: separate insurance supervisor; M: multi-sector regulator (but not for all sectors, which would be U); S: separate securities supervisor; P: separate pension fund supervisor; and U: unified supervisor (i.e., supervisor of all segments).

[a] In many cases, the listed supervisor for other deposit-taking institutions, insurance companies, and pension funds is often just a registrar without supervisory functions. Blanks mean no supervisory functions.

Source: Courtis (2005) and national sources.

8.3.3   How does the emerging SSA debate fit into the broader debate?

The confrontation of the growth of financial systems in SSA with the short-comings in regulation and supervision, and in the supervisory structures in SSA, makes a strong case for reforming supervisory structures as a critical means to strengthen supervisory capacity. The need to address the short-comings is particularly pressing in light of the argument made by Goodhart (1998a) that, among all groups of countries, developing countries are most in need of effective (banking) supervision, given several specific circumstances that make them prone to financial instability, such as weak legal systems, lack of accounting standards and practices, and a lack of financial instruments and markets to hedge financial risks.

Thus, the starting point for reform of supervisory structures in SSA countries is very different from that of the advanced economies, or most other MICs. Not only do countries of SSA have comparatively weak supervisory capacity of the (dominant) banking sector, but regulation and supervision of several NBFI sectors is even weaker or absent. Some of these sectors may soon assume systemic importance, and, hence, need regulatory attention. In other words, the "institutional strengthening" and "economies of scale/small country" arguments (see background section) for reform of the supervisory architecture are the dominant ones.[18]

In this context, institutional strengthening means that institutional reform will need to be part of a broader package of measures designed to build effective regulatory and supervisory capacity. In addition, given the current trends in SSA financial sector development, any new supervisory

Table 8.5 Supervisory models in SSA—Overview

Supervisory model	Number of countries	Countries
Central bank for banks, one multisector agency for others	4	Botswana,[a] Mauritius, Namibia, South Africa
Central bank for banks (and some other sectors), one or more separate agencies for other sectors	7	Ghana, Kenya, Mozambique, Nigeria, Tanzania, Uganda,[a] Zambia[a]
Separate agency for banks, others separate or not regulated	3	BEAC, BCEAO, Madagascar
Central bank for every sector that is in existence	7	Etiopía, Gambia, Lesotho, Malawi[a], Rwanda[a], Seychelles, Sierra Leone
Central bank for banks, rest unregulated	4	Angola, Burundi, Swaziland,[a] and Zimbabwe

[a] Currently under reform.

structure needs to be built in a forward-looking manner, that is, be flexible to adapt to new needs of and developments in the sector.

8.4   An analytical framework for shaping SSA's supervisory structures

In light of the conclusion of the previous section, Chandler's statement that "structure follows strategy" is particularly applicable to the design of financial sector supervision in SSA—or LICs more generally. The first step should indeed be the development of a "regulatory strategy" that prioritizes sectors in need of a regulatory and supervisory framework and determines the intensity with which these sectors should be regulated and supervised. Supervisory structures, in turn, should be such that they allow a flexible response to future financial system developments. Any such strategy also needs to take into account two constraining factors in SSA: the ubiquitous issue of capacity constraints, which in many ways represents the crux of the regulatory problem in the SSA and the need to keep the central banks involved in the supervisory process for reasons that we will examine shortly.

8.4.1   Capacity constraints

Capacity constraints are major hurdles for any reform in SSA. As indicated above, supervisory agencies in most SSA countries are still short of skilled and trained staff, as well as the equipment and infrastructure to conduct on-site inspections and off-site supervision effectively. Salary scales are typically low, making staff retention a major challenge because, once trained and proficient, staff is easily lured away by higher paying commercial banks or other financial institutions.[19]

In addition, supervisory skills must continuously evolve in response to worldwide industry trends. In recent years, the widespread adoption of risk-based supervision, combined with a growing complexity in bank regulations and supervision (including the emerging Basel II framework) has placed a premium on the constant upgrading of supervisory skills. Thus, countries that are unable to provide the right incentives to attract and retain suitably qualified supervisory staff run the risk of falling ever further behind supervisory practices in the rest of the world.

At least for the foreseeable future, the design of supervisory structures will have to take into account the existence of these capacity constraints. Capacity constraints clearly argue against setting up (new) separate agencies for each segment of the system, as this would result in a spreading of resources too thinly across several different regulatory bodies. It also calls into question plans that would merely "upgrade" or strengthen existing separate agencies. Faced with capacity constraints it is crucial to pursue economies of scale and synergies while reforming supervisory structures.

The issue of institutional design has also implications for the ability of the agency (or agencies) to attract and retain suitably qualified staff (for example, by providing them with a career ladder) and the incentive structures faced by regulatory personnel. Finally, as we will discuss in section 8.4, capacity constraints also argue for retaining a role for the central bank in the supervisory process as one of the better-resourced institutions in most countries.

8.4.2   Regulatory strategy: Scope and intensity

A response to the capacity-constraint problem is to prioritize the need for regulation of the various segments in the financial sector. For example, if a segment is small, undeveloped, and showing little signs of growth, it may be a more efficient use of scarce resources to first regulate other segments that are more significant for financial system stability. The process of prioritization requires an analytical framework, which we refer to as a "regulatory strategy." In effect, a regulatory strategy is analogous to a risk-based approach to supervision, in which attention and resources are focused on those individual institutions considered to represent the highest risk. In the case of a regulatory strategy, the focus is on segments of the financial system rather than individual institutions, but the basic principle is the same.

Developing a regulatory strategy consists of dealing with two questions: (1) at which point in time during its development should a segment of the financial system be regulated and, thus, be brought into the supervisory net. This is the issue of **scope**; and (2) once a segment has been identified as needing supervision, what type of regulatory and supervisory regime should be imposed. This is the issue of **intensity**. Such a regulatory strategy will need to be regularly updated to stay abreast of market developments and contain, monitor, or control emerging risks, particularly in an environment where public confidence in financial systems is fragile and could be undermined easily by a crisis. The primary purpose of developing a regulatory strategy is to allow strategy and institutional structure to be considered together. The agreed-upon structure should be such that it serves the strategy by allowing for scale economies as much as possible.

8.4.2.1   *Regulatory scope*

The reference point for determining regulatory scope should be the potential social costs of institution failure. The nature of the activities of each financial institution is to make financial promises. These financial promises are typically made to dispersed debt holders, and the operations of financial institutions are known to be opaque.[20] Hence, Dewatripont and Tirole (1994) argue that the main justification for regulation and supervision is to represent the dispersed and uninformed debt holders in the governance model of financial institutions (the "representation hypothesis").

Regulators are there to make sure that financial institutions can honor their financial promises.

However, not all financial promises are these same. They differ in their level of complexity. So, financial institutions can be categorized according to the nature of the financial promises that they make, and that in turn has an impact of the systemic risk that a specific type of institution generates. Determining the regulatory scope requires a two-step process. First, following Carmichael and Pomerleano (2002), one has to rank the nature of the particular financial promises being made by given groups of financial institutions. Financial promises can be distinguished according to three characteristics, (1) the inherent difficulty of honoring the promise; (2) the difficulty faced by the consumer in assessing the creditworthiness of the promisor; and (3) the adversity caused by promissory breach. If one is to rank the types of financial institutions in order of decreasing promissory intensity, banks would typically be ranked first, followed, in this order, by other deposit-taking institutions (credit cooperatives, credit unions, or microfinance organizations that take deposits), insurance companies, defined benefit pension funds, and securities companies. Such a ranking may differ slightly for country-specific reasons, but would be fairly generally applicable.

Once such a ranking has been established, in a second step, the relative size of a particular group of institutions, and possibly other considerations[21] enter the picture as a proxy for the systemic risk that this particular segment of the system would pose. So, once a sector that has been identified as "risky" in the first step has passed a certain threshold in terms of share in the financial system, the regulatory and supervisory net should be expanded to include this sector. This step also implies that, up to a certain point of development of a segment, it might be put on a lower priority in terms of supervision.

This two-step framework can assist governments in determining whether, and at what point in time, a specific sector should fall under the supervisory umbrella. For instance, it would indicate that if two segments of the system are of the same relative size, priority should be given to that segment which, if it were to encounter problems, would give rise to the greatest loss of economic output and/or would require substantial public funds to resolve. Adopting this framework can also be of great help in avoiding regulatory gaps in the system.

Applying this framework to the SSA context, credit cooperatives, credit unions, and deposit-taking microfinance institutions should probably (already) be regulated in a number of SSA countries. In the same vein, the insurance sector and securities business should already be supervised in some other countries. In this strategy, the limited capacity issue is addressed by allowing governments to "grow into the regulatory and supervisory business" instead of having to do everything at once and at the same intensity. This analytical framework also allows countries that already have an established institutional framework for supervision but that need to revise/strengthen their regulatory and supervisory frameworks, to prioritize where to start.

Decisions as to when a financial sector segment is "ripe" for supervision require judgment as well as knowledge of the local circumstances that go beyond the sheer interpretation of numbers. For instance, the size of the microfinance sector may just be at, say, 4 percent of the total financial sector, but even at that size a possible crisis in this segment (because it is not supervised properly), could spill over into the banking system and assume systemic proportions, because in the eyes of the (not well-informed) population, the borderline between these two types of institutions could be vague.

8.4.2.2 Regulatory intensity

Once it has been decided that a sector needs to be regulated because of the (systemic) risks it poses, regulatory intensity comes into play: the authorities need to decide on the desired and desirable regulatory and supervisory intensity.

Regulatory intensity refers to (1) the nature and the number of prudential rules and regulations;[22] (2) the reporting requirements for off-site monitoring; and (3) the on-site inspection framework that should be imposed on a certain category of institutions.[23] Regulatory oversight of a particular segment of the system might begin with a basic licensing regime, be extended to requiring occasional reports to be filed with the regulator, and, at its most intensive stage, apply a specific set of prudential requirements with on-site and off-site monitoring. For example, applying an extensive set of prudential requirements to microfinance institutions might not be appropriate, but it would be appropriate to require them to be licensed and to file an annual or semiannual return with their regulator. This reporting would provide indications regarding the growth of the sector and individual companies within it. Once the reported activities pass a certain (predefined) threshold, which makes them systemically more important, the regulatory and/or supervisory regime could be intensified, either for some individual institutions or for the segment as a whole.[24]

Decisions on regulatory intensity are important because they allow scarce supervisory resources to be allocated to the areas of highest risk to the system. Low regulatory intensity requires relatively few resources, since both off-site monitoring and on-site inspections need to be less intense (or can be absent) for smaller, less-risk-prone sectors. Such "supervision-light" approach should result in less pressure on staff, and, therefore, alleviate the capacity constraints somewhat.

8.4.2.3   *The cost of regulation*

When adopting a regulatory strategy, it is important to bear in mind that regulatory scope and intensity have a direct bearing on the costs of regulation. Following Goodhart (1988), we identify direct and indirect costs.[25] The direct costs are mainly the resource costs (staff, equipment, buildings), and one purpose of supervisory restructuring is to contain them through achieving scale economies. However, in the context of SSA, the indirect costs are also extremely relevant: excessive regulation, or regulation introduced at too early a stage in the development of a particular segment, could reduce competition and stifle innovation. In Africa's fledgling financial systems, regulatory intensity should be such that it does not kill new avenues to finance.[26] The fact of being unregulated has certainly led some sectors in some countries to a certain degree of success in that it has provided access to finance for social groups that have no access to the regulated system. In bringing them under the regulatory umbrella, a balance needs to be struck between containing the risks that a sector poses and allowing it to grow and bring competition and innovation.[27] These considerations suggest that the primary focus of regulation should be on the risks to financial stability presented by a particular segment—that is, in reference to footnote 23, prudential regulations should be there, but economic regulations should be such that they do not choke innovation—and that the regulatory burden on other segments should be kept as light as possible to allow financial deepening to progress.

8.5   A typology of possible models

With the above analytical framework in mind, this section reviews the suitability of a number of supervisory models for the SSA context. However, before doing so, we argue that in the specific LIC/MIC context a role for the central bank in the regulatory process needs to be preserved.

8.5.1   The need for a role for the central bank

In the specific case of SSA, the arguments for keeping the central bank in the supervisory process seem to outweigh the often-cited drawbacks of keeping monetary policy and supervision under one roof.[28] Following Goodhart (2002),[29] we see three major arguments for keeping the central bank involved in the regulatory process.

First, it can reasonably be expected that the banking sectors will remain the dominant segment in the SSA financial systems in the foreseeable future. Moreover, as Table 8.4 shows, the central banks are currently responsible for banking supervision in a large number of countries. This role is partly the result of historical factors, but also reflects the synergies between banking supervision and monetary policy, which are particularly important in bank-dominated financial systems. There are also important informational advantages in keeping banking supervision and monetary policy in the same institution, as the information collected for the two functions overlaps to a great extent. Hence, the combination of the synergies between monetary policy and banking supervision, and the expectation that banks will remain dominant justifies a continued supervisory role for the central banks.

Second, developing economies are more prone than advanced countries to periods of financial instability or even financial crises. This places a particularly high premium on the strength and effectiveness of crisis management arrangements. The central bank is an indispensable part of these arrangements, both because of its traditional lender-of-last-resort function and also because it often possesses the greatest expertise in the financial sector. Most ministries of finance lack the skilled and experienced staff needed to take a lead role in crisis management. By contrast, there is a greater likelihood that, if these resources are to be found anywhere, they are to be found in the central bank. Thus, keeping a meaningful role for the central bank facilitates coordination at times of crises—including an easier collection and exchange of information—and increases the likelihood that high-quality staff can be hired and trained.

The third, and arguably the strongest, reason is that in many developing countries, central banks are often one of the few reputable institutions with a reasonable degree of independence from the political process and commercial interests. Several advantages come with this reputation and independence. This third argument is also a response to the capacity constraint factor discussed earlier.

- *Funding.* Typically, only the central bank has the financial resources and budgetary independence to ensure that regulation is adequately funded. The alternative is to have the regulatory agency funded by an appropriation from general government revenue, an approach that is almost universally a recipe for ensuring that the regulator lacks the resources necessary to perform its tasks with appropriate independence and professionalism. The approach used in several advanced markets in which the regulator is funded by a levy on the regulated industry remains impractical for many small, developing economies. It would risk leaving the regulator dependent on a handful of large and politically influential institutions for its main revenue source.
- *Staffing.* The central banks' status allows them to attract and retain the best staff, and pay salaries at close to market levels, which creates a virtuous cycle with higher-quality staff leading to higher credibility for the institution, which in turn strengthens its independence. The central bank is very often the only agency in a country that brings these qualities together.
- *Scale and scope benefits.* If banking supervision remains a central bank responsibility for the above reasons, the central bank can also reap some

scale-and-scope economies if some other sectors with bank-like features are also brought under its supervisory umbrella.

In sum, from a practical point of view, few developing countries can afford the creation of another agency with the same quality level and independence as the central bank, or more broadly, can afford a complex and costly regulatory system.[30] Hence, there are few realistic alternatives to providing the central bank with a role in banking supervision in many developing countries, and its role may need to be extended to cover other sectors and subsectors, if other credible regulators are difficult to create. Establishing a new agency that is properly funded, has the same quality of staff, and enjoys credibility and independence, will, in most cases, be a very challenging undertaking. Mwenda's (2004) analysis of the new supervisory agency in Zambia clearly attests to these problems. Among the main problems, he cites the fact that the Pension and Insurance Authority has no political or budgetary autonomy and that its staff has no legal immunity. These features put the agency in a weak position and will make it very hard to bring regulation and supervision to the level exercised by the central bank.

8.5.2   Review of possible models

This section identifies five possible models of supervisory structure that might be relevant to countries of SSA—four with central bank involvement and one without (Table 8.6). The pros and cons of each of the models are reviewed in the light of the regulatory strategy presented in the previous section and our arguments in favor of maintaining central bank involvement in the supervisory process. One model would be unification of all supervision within the central bank (also called the Singapore model). The second one represents a structure whereby the supervisory agency has logistical and budgetary links to the central bank, but from a governance point of view, it could operate at arm's length from the central bank. Several variations of this model exist, but we have called it the Irish model. Models three and four are bipolar with the central bank retaining or acquiring supervision over some sectors and another multisectoral agency taking the other ones. The fifth model is the "United Kingdom (UK) model" with a unified supervisor outside the central bank.

8.5.2.1   *Model 1—The Singapore model*

The unification of all supervisory functions inside the central bank has several advantages. New supervisory activities could benefit from the existing ones (scope and scale economies), there would be no regulatory gaps, regulatory scope and intensity could be built up smoothly, and contentious interagency issues could be avoided. In addition, supervision could benefit from the central bank's infrastructure, budget, and expertise, and also from its prestige and, potentially, independence. Crisis management would be facilitated as well.

On the downside, the country would be faced with an extremely powerful institution. Some scholars see this as a potential drawback, although solid accountability arrangements should be able to keep this institution "in check" (Hüpkes, Quintyn and Taylor, 2005). In addition, the commonly cited disadvantages of combining banking supervision and monetary policy (conflicts of interest, moral hazard) would apply in a particularly pronounced form. Moral hazard would be a concern if it led the customers of NBFIs to believe that they enjoy the same level of protection as bank depositors. However, in the circumstances of SSA, the advantages of this model may be sufficient to outweigh these drawbacks, especially given the relative smallness of the NBFI sector.

8.5.2.2 *Model 2—The Irish model*

The Irish model has most of the advantages of Model 1, but few of its drawbacks and therefore seems to be a model worth studying in developing countries.[31] Under this model, the supervisory function is closely linked to the central bank and yet remains at arm's length. The supervisory agency is legally separate from the central bank, is established under its own statute, and has it own governing board separate from that of the central bank (although there may be some overlap in the membership of the two boards).[32,33] However, the regulatory agency shares the infrastructure of the central bank (premises, IT systems, data collection), and its staff are employees of the central bank on the same terms and conditions as other central bank staff. This construction has the advantage that supervision can benefit from the central bank's logistical and budgetary support (scale economies with the central bank and scale economies as a unified supervisor). Since it is assimilated with the central bank, it can even benefit from the central bank's prestige and independence. On the other hand, because there is a distance with the central bank, the construction escapes the often-listed conflict of interest and moral hazard issues of supervision being too close to monetary policy.

As a unified supervisor, it can plan a strategy for regulatory scope and intensity, while avoiding any regulatory gaps. Crisis management should be easy to arrange, given the proximity of the central bank. Several variations on this model can be found, for example, in Finland and France, and (until recently) in Poland. Although South Africa provides an example of model 3, with banking supervision housed in the central bank, it also has some similarities with this model, as the governance structure for the banking supervision function within the SARB is different from the one for the monetary policy function.

Table 8.6 Overview of advantages and disadvantages of selected supervisory structures

Structure	Advantages	Disadvantages
Unified inside the central bank (Singapore model).	No regulatory gaps; not contentious (no turf battles between agencies; central bank logistical support; supervisory function benefits from central bank independence, prestige, budget, and expertise; financial stability responsibility is solely for central bank; economies of scale; crisis management unified.	Moral hazard (Lender of Last Resort (LLR), etc). All responsibility is on the central bank; central bank is very powerful; and central banks are typically small, hence, potential capacity limitations.
Separate agency sharing infrastructure of central bank (Irish model)	Agency enjoys central bank logistical and budgetary support; benefits from central bank expertise; indirectly benefits from central bank prestige; economies of scale; financial stability; close to, but not in central bank, and room for unified crisis management; compared to Singapore model, no moral hazard, no institution that is too powerful (unless perceived as such); no regulatory gaps.	Will require expansion of central bank staff/budget.
Partially unified A (only bank supervision in central bank)	Central bank responsible for banks (financial stability, monetary policy argument); central bank not too involved in all sectors (remains small and not too powerful); burden on central bank limited; no moral hazard problems (LLR); limits contentious issues (with MOF for instance).	Possibility for regulatory gaps remains; start-up problems for other agency (see above); crisis management coordination needed; transfer of responsibilities is needed when deposit-taking NBFIs become banks.

Partially unified B (all deposit-taking NB FIs supervised by central bank)	No regulatory gaps in most important segments from financial stability point of view; no moral hazard issues; banks and other deposit-taking institutions in continuum,, level playing field can be better guaranteed; limits contentious games; financial stability argument (key sectors supervised by central bank); and central bank not too powerful.	Start-up problems for new agency (capacity, prestige); possibility of regulatory gaps remains but is more limited; and crisis management coordination needed. Some moral hazard problems left for central bank (LLR) because other deposit-taking institutions are also supervised and public may not see difference between them and banks.
Unified outside central bank (UK model)	Central bank is not too powerful; no moral hazard issues;economies of scale realized by new agency and regulatory gaps can be avoided.	New agency has no tradition—has to start from scratch; capacity-building needed; coordination of crisis management with central bank will be needed. Delineation of responsibilities with central bank needed for financial stability policies. Potentially powerful institution.

8.5.2.3   *Model 3—Bipolar with banking supervision in the central bank*

The third model is a bipolar or partially unified model. It leaves banking supervision with the central bank and regroups supervision of all other segments in a separate agency—often to be newly established. The main advantages of this model are that the central bank remains involved in the key sector—banking. Crisis management (at least for banking problems) and coordination with financial stability remain guaranteed and bank supervision can benefit from the central bank's infrastructure, independence, and prestige. Moreover, being in the central bank brings guarantees of reasonable salaries and high-quality staff.

Success of this model depends largely on the way the other supervisory agency is set up and how it operates. Usually, the institution has to be built up from the ground and needs to be endowed with an appropriate governance structure and budgetary autonomy in order to be an independent and effective supervisor. In many developing countries, it has proven extremely difficult to establish new agencies without political interference and to staff them with competent people.[34]

This model has other drawbacks as well, which are (1) some deposit-taking institutions or bank-like entities will be outside the scope of the central bank's supervision, and yet they might be significant from a financial stability perspective; (2) scope economies are hard to realize because the segments with a potential for scope economies—banks and deposit-taking NBFIs—are supervised by separate agencies; and (3) when financial institutions change groupings (e.g., a microfinance institutions upgrading to bank status, or vice versa) a transfer mechanism between the new agency and the bank supervisor needs to be in place. On the positive side, the agency can gradually widen its regulatory scope and vary regulatory intensity, since it is responsible for all sectors excepting the banking sector.

8.5.2.4   *Model 4—Bipolar with supervision of all deposit-taking institutions in the central bank*

This model differs from the previous one in that all deposit-taking activities (including, for example, credit cooperatives and microfinance institutions) are supervised by the central bank and all other financial sectors by a newly established agency. In addition to the advantages listed for model 3, this model has the added advantage that the central bank supervises all those institutions that are most likely to be significant from a systemic stability perspective. It can therefore decide on the regulatory scope and intensity (and aim for a level playing field) for these sectors, and, hence, benefit from scale-and-scope economies in its operations. Transitions among deposit-taking institutions are also facilitated. Also, regulatory gaps in the deposit-taking business are eliminated in this model. In other words most of the disadvantages listed for model 3 disappear. The potential problems listed above for model 3 with respect to the establishment from scratch of a separate agency are the same in this case.

8.5.2.5 Model 5—The U.K. model

A unified regulator outside the central bank seems the least desirable for developing countries. As discussed earlier, the conglomerates-argument and the blurring-of-boundaries argument are not applicable in largely bank-dominated financial systems. Moreover, not involving the central bank in the supervisory process and instead starting a new institution from scratch will be very demanding in terms of institution- and capacity-building. In the absence of the need to supervise financial conglomerate groups, the only advantages with this model are that (1) economies of scale can be realized—although it may take some time for them to become apparent, given the extent of institution-building that is required; (2) there will be no regulatory gaps; and (3) the central bank will not be too powerful and there will be no moral hazard problems in the central bank.

8.5.2.6 Synthesis

On balance, the two models that seem to have the most to recommend them in the circumstances of SSA are models 2 and 4:

- Both models take advantage of the central bank's prestige and capacity, which makes capacity-building (and retention) easier and faster. As discussed earlier, it is easier for a central bank with an established reputation to attract new staff;
- Both keep the supervision of the systemically most significant financial activities (as defined above) within the central bank. With this, it allows the central bank to work out a supervisory strategy around regulatory scope and intensity and, at the same time, to enjoy scale-and-scope economies;
- Both allow for crisis management coordination and for coordination with financial stability policies within the central bank;
- Model 4 allows the agency responsible for nondeposit-taking institutions to build up capacity smoothly (the to-be-supervised sectors are typically still small) and establish its own supervisory culture. Transfer of personnel from the central bank to the new agency can be minimal, so the cultural adjustment will be minimal, too; and
- Regulatory gaps can be completely avoided in model 2 and are very unlikely in model 4, because there is a relatively clear boundary between the types of activities supervised by both institutions.

8.6 Conclusions

Financial sector development in SSA has entered a new stage. In the wake of numerous banking crises in the 1980s and early 1990s, renewed efforts to build more sound financial systems and to address the issues of access to financial service are beginning to bear fruit. In several countries of SSA, financial sector development is accelerating. New types of financial intermediaries are surfacing and, slowly, becoming systemically significant.

However, the success of efforts aimed to bring about financial deepening also requires the parallel development of supervision and regulation. Indeed, lack of regulation and supervision could lead to new crises that might quickly erode the achieved results of the past decade. However, as this chapter has shown, supervisory structures in SSA—perhaps with the exception of bank supervision—are underdeveloped or even nonexistent.

The past decade-and-a half has seen increased recognition of the importance of the issue of the institutional structure of regulation for the efficiency and effectiveness of regulation, leading many countries to revisit their institutional arrangements. Their experiences provide a body of knowledge on which SSA (and LICs more broadly) can draw. However, it is equally important to bear in mind that the institutional structure is only one element of an overall regulatory reform package. In particular, in the SSA case, the effort to (re)build the institutional structure needs to be accompanied by measures to strengthen regulatory frameworks and supervisory capacity.

This chapter's contribution to the debate has consisted in (1) developing an analytical framework that allows individual countries faced with severe capacity constraints to combine their thinking about how and when to regulate and supervise their emerging financial systems on the one hand, and about the institutional structure for supervision on the other hand in an evolutionary manner; and (2) reviewing a number of tested supervisory models in light of this framework.

The analytical framework involves the development of a "regulatory strategy" to be built around two types of decisions to develop regulatory capacity: (1) at which point in time during its development should a segment of the financial system be regulated and, thus, be brought into the supervisory net? This is the issue of regulatory scope; and (2) once a segment has been identified as needing supervision, what type of regulatory and supervisory regime should be imposed? This is the issue of regulatory intensity. Following Chandler's remarks on strategy and structure, we have suggested that the institutional structure of regulation should be designed in light of a country's regulatory strategy.

The chapter then proceeded by reviewing some possible supervisory models for SSA in light of this framework. Out of the five models discussed, two seem to have the most to recommend them in the circumstances of SSA. The first one has the (unified) supervisory entity linked to the central bank (in terms of infrastructure and logistics), but with a separate governance structure. The second one is a bipolar model with supervision of all deposit-taking institutions housed in the central bank and supervision of all other NBFIs in a separate agency. Both models preserve an important role in supervision for the central bank, which is deemed important under the current circumstances (capacity constraints on the one hand, and bank-dominated systems on the other hand). They also allow the supervisory agency—in varying degrees, however—to benefit from the central bank's prestige and capacity, and they would minimize the possibility of regulatory gaps.

Empirical evidence shows that the institutional structure for supervision is as much the result of economic as of political considerations. Against that background, this chapter intended to guide the debate somewhat by presenting an analytical framework that sheds light on the most critical issues in the selection process and by highlighting pros and cons of potential models that fit the strategy from an economic point of view and by taking account of the specific African circumstances.

Notes

Chief, African Division, IMF and Advisor to the Governor of the Central Bank of Bahrain. Institute. Earlier versions of this chapter were presented at the World Bank-IMF Conference "Aligning Supervisory Structures with Country Needs" Washington DC (June 5–6, 2006) and a seminar at Bocconi University, Milan (November 25, 2006). Without implication, the authors would like to thank the participants at both conferences, as well as Martin Čihák, Vishnu Padayachee and Etienne Yehoue for suggestions and comments. This chapter only expresses the authors' views and not necessarily those of the IMF or IMF policy.

1. The terms regulation and supervision are often used interchangeably in the financial system context. While both functions might be performed by one and the same person or agency, they are different tasks—respectively rule-setting and rule-implementation and enforcing—with different implications from the point of view of the topic of this chapter. Within the financial system, there are differences in emphasis. For instance, in the securities area, the term "regulator" is used more frequently than "supervisor" because the regulatory aspect dominates their tasks. The reader should bear in mind that when this chapter uses the word "regulator"s, it is only for the sake of conciseness. However, when we refer to the supervisory function specifically, we will use that term. It should also be noted that supervision has become more important in recent decades than it used to be, in response to the liberalization trends in the financial systems.
2. For up-to-date overviews, see among others, Courtis (2005) and Čihák and Podpiera (2006 and 2007).
3. For more details on this transformation of the supervisors from compliance officers to governance supervisors, see Quintyn (2007).
4. See the Commonwealth of Australia (1996). Note that Australia has subsequently moved to a type of "Twin Peaks" structure (Taylor, 1995), where responsibility for regulation is divided between agencies specializing in prudential supervision (APRA) on the one hand, and consumer protection and market regulation on the other (the Australian Securities and Investments Commission).
5. For a general discussion of arguments for and, and against unification, see, for instance, Abrams and Taylor (2000) and Llewellyn (2006).

6. This was the argument used in the Scandinavian countries who pioneered the unified model in the late 1980s and early 1990s (see Taylor and Fleming, 1999).
7. Čihák and Podpiera (2007), however, do not find evidence that the adoption of a unified supervisory model thus far has been associated with significant and systematic reductions in supervisory staff in a sample of 61 countries. They note that the results could be due to the fact that the time since restructuring has not been long enough to lead to savings, or that the new agencies took on new responsibilities not covered by any of their predecessor agencies.
8. For instance, a majority of commentators agree that the government's decision to establish a unified regulator in Poland in 2006 was mainly meant to curb the central bank's power and to regain some government influence over financial sector developments. See for instance remarks and citations in Dow Jones Commodities Service (September 14, 2006), Agence France Press (September 29, 2006), and Associated Press Newswires (October 3, 2006).
9. An example close to home for SSA is South Africa. It was argued that the industry change argument was not a valid one for the formation of a unified regulator at the time of the reforms. As a result of the deliberations, supervisory responsibilities were split between the South African Reserve Bank (SARB) who retained its bank supervision functions, and a separate, new, NBFI regulator outside the central bank (Bezuidenhout, 2004).
10. Masciandaro (2006b) finds that countries with market-dominated systems tend to favor more the integrated supervisory model. However, with a larger sample, Masciandaro and Quintyn (2008) find that the financial market structure does not matter. So far this control variable seems to be sample sensitive. Furthermore, Masciandaro and Quintyn (2008) show that there is only weak evidence that the views of the market participants are taken into account.
11. For more detailed overviews of recent financial sector developments in SSA, see among others, Gulde et al. (2006), Senbet and Otchere (2006), and Honohan and Beck (2007). This section draws on these contributions.
12. Middle-income countries include Angola, Botswana, Cape Verde, Equatorial Guinea, Gabon, Mauritius, Namibia, Seychelles, South Africa, and Swaziland. According to the World Bank rankings, low-income countries have a GNI per capita of US$825 or less and lower-income countries have a GNI per head between US$826 and US$3,255.
13. In some countries not presented in the table, such as Angola, Chad, Congo DR, Equatorial Guinea, Eritrea, Guinea Bissau, Liberia, and Sao Tome and Principe, banks cover 100 percent of the officially registered sector. This does not mean that there are no other fledgling subsectors. Official registration of, for instance, microfinance institutions is just beginning in several countries.
14. The association of several among these MICs with SADC (Southern African Development Cooperation) has been an additional driving force behind some of these reforms. SADC's goal of harmonizing cross-country financial sector legislation has prompted the individual members to focus on their supervisory structures. An important initiative in this regard is the establishment, within SADC, of the Committee for Insurance, Securities, and Nonbank Financial Authorities (CISNA), a forum for the exchange of views and experiences as well as training for the emerging supervisors in the region.
15. In the Economic and Monetary Community of Central Africa (CEMAC) and the West African Monetary Union (WAMU), banking, securities and insurance supervision is established at the regional level in separate agencies.

16. Developing capacity includes taking stock of the sector (most institutions are not registered), defining the institutions that should be supervised and establishing a regulatory and supervisory framework.

17. The solution in Swaziland is also supposed to be temporary until capacity has been built to establish a separate NBFI regulator.

18. By contrast, the "industry structure"-argument does not apply under the current circumstances in any of the SSA countries. Financial systems in SSA are likely to remain bank-dominated for the foreseeable future. In addition, as Llewellyn (2006) points out, in most sub-sectors the core business is expected to dominate the institutions' activities for a long time, and these lines of business are expected to continue to differ sufficiently, so that the "blurring boundaries"-argument in favor of a unified supervisor remains weak.

19. See also Senbet and Otchere (2006) on this point.

20. On the opaqueness of the operations of financial institutions as a justification for having a governance model that differs from nonfinancial institutions, see Caprio and Levine (2002), Harm (2002), and Quintyn (2007).

21. For instance, if in a country insurance companies typically belong to the same group as a bank, there are reasons to extend the "prudential regulatory net" to insurance companies, perhaps before any other segment.

22. The literature makes a distinction between three types of regulations: economic regulations encompassing rules regarding pricing, profits, entry and exit; information regulations governing information that needs to be provided to the supervisors and the public at large; and prudential regulations, which govern the stability of the business and its activities.

23. For instance, by now there is a broad consensus that deposit-taking institutions, other than banks, should have a lighter regulatory regime than banks (e.g., lower minimum capital, perhaps lower capital requirements), should have lower-frequency reporting requirements and longer cycles of on-site inspections (if at all necessary). On the regulation of credit cooperatives, see for instance, Cuevas and Fischer (2005). On microfinance institutions, see Hardy et al. (2002), Christen et al. (2003), Arun (2005), and Gulde et al. (2005).

24. This strategy should, of course, ensure that there is a level playing field for groups of institutions with similar activities.

25. On the costs of regulation, see also Goodhart (1998b) and, in the context of institutional restructuring, Llewellyn (2006).

26. On this topic, see also Porteous (2006) and Honohan and Beck (2007).

27. Llewellyn (2006) notes that these indirect costs—which are difficult to measure—could rise even if the direct costs are reduced. Admittedly, this can happen in any supervisory structure, that is, with or without separate regulators.

28. Even in advanced economies, the arguments for and against separation are finely balanced (see, among others, Goodhart and Schoenmaker (1995) for a summary of the main arguments for and against), but the additional factors in the SSA are sufficient to tip the balance in favor of the central bank taking on responsibility not only for banking supervision, but perhaps for (at least) a number of other (deposit-taking) segments as well.

29. See also Llewellyn (2006, 128–32) for a review of these arguments.

30. This argument has been used for small economies more generally.

31. Implementation of this model may require legal changes, which are not always easy to make. In Swaziland, for instance, this model was considered seriously, but the legal framework prevents the central bank from establishing subsidiaries,

and changing the legal framework was considered too difficult (FIRST Initiative (2004)).
32. For example, the governor or deputy governor of the central bank might serve on the board of the regulator in an ex-officio capacity.
33. Quintyn, Ramirez, and Taylor (2007) point out that in the Irish case, lines of accountability exist from the supervisory agency to the central bank governor, making, in fact, the supervisory function subordinate to the central bank. For countries studying this model, such lines of accountability can be modified as necessary, because they are not inherent to the model presented here.
34. As indicated above, Mwenda (2004) observes that the Pension and Insurance Authority in Zambia lacks many features that could make it an independent and, therefore, effective supervisor, such as the fact that the registrar is nominated by the minister of finance, has reporting lines to the permanent secretary—who also has budgetary control—and that staff has no judicial immunity.

References

Abrams, Richard and Taylor, M. 2000. "Issues in the unification of financial sector supervision." IMF Working Paper WP/00/213.

Arun, Thankom 2005. "Regulating for development: The case of microfinance." *The Quarterly Review of Economics and Finance,* 45: 346–57.

Bezuidenhout, Andre 2004. "The South African case." In *Aligning Financial Supervisory Structures with Country Needs,* eds. J. Carmichael, A. Fleming and D. Llewellyn, 115–28. Washington, DC: The World Bank Institute.

Caprio and Levine 2002. "Corporate governance in Finance: Concepts and International Observations," in Robert Litan, Michael Pomerleano and V. Sundararajan (eds.), *Financial Sector Governance: The Roles of the Public and Private Sectors,* 17–50. Washington: Brookings Institution Press.

Carmichael, Jeffrey and Pomerleano, M. 2002. *The Development and Regulation of Non-Bank Financial Institutions.* Washington, DC: The World Bank, 230.

Christen, Robert, Lyman, T., and Rosenberg, R. 2003. "Microfinance consensus guidelines. Guiding principles on regulation and supervision of Microfinance." CGAP. Washington DC: The World Bank Group.

Čihák, Martin, and Podpiera, R. 2006. "Is one watchdog Better than three? International experience with integrated financial sector supervision." IMF Working Paper, WP/06/57. Washington: International Monetary Fund.

Čihák, Martin and Podpiera, R. 2007. "Experience with integrated supervisors: Governance and quality of supervision." Chapter 8. In *Designing Financial Supervision Institutions: Independence, Accountability, and Governance,* eds. Donato Masciandaro and Marc Quintyn, 309–41. Cheltenham, U.K.: Edward Elgar.

Commonwealth of Australia 1996. "Financial system inquiry interim report." Wallis Commission. Camberra: Australian Government Publishing Service.

Courtis, Neil, ed. 2005. *How Countries Supervise their Banks, Insurers, and Securities Markets 2002.* London: Central Banking, 266.

Cuevas, Carlos and Fischer, K. 2005. "Governance, regulation and supervision of cooperative financial institutions." Notes from Lecture at IMF, November 17, 2005.

Dewatripont, Mathias and Tirole, Jean 1994. *The Prudential Regulation of Banks.* Cambridge, MA: MIT Press).

FIRST Initiative 2004. Swaziland: Supervision of nonbank financial institutions—An initial assessment and proposed strategy. Carmichael Consulting Pty Limited.

Freytag, Andreas and Masciandaro, Donato 2007. "Financial supervision architecture and Central Bank independence" chapter 6. In *Designing Financial Supervision Institutions: Independence, Accountability, and Governance,* eds. Donato Masciandaro and Marc Quintyn, 211–61. Cheltenham, U.K.: Edward Elgar.

Goodhart, Charles 1988. "Financial Regulation—Or Over-Regulation?" In *The cost of regulation,* eds. Arthur Seldon, 17–31. London: Institute of Economic Affairs.

Goodhart, Charles 1998a. *Regulation in Developing Countries* pp. 98–115 in Goodhart, C. et al., (London and New York: Routledge).

Goodhart, Charles ed. 1998b. "Financial regulation—Why, how and where now?" *The Emerging Framework of Financial Regulation,* a collection of papers compiled by the Financial Markets Group of the London School of Economics. London: Central Banking Publications Ltd.

Goodhart, Charles 2002. "The organization structure of banking supervision." *Economic Notes by Banca Monte dei Paschi di Siena,* 31(1): 1–32.

Goodhart, Charles and Schoenmaker, D. 1995. "Should the functions of monetary policy and banking supervision be separated?" *Oxford Economic Papers,* 47: 539– 60.

Gulde, Anne-Marie, Patillo, C., Christensen, J. with Carey, K. and Wagh, S. 2006. "Sub-Saharan Africa. Financial sector challenges." Washington, DC: International Monetary Fund, World Economic and Financial Surveys.

Gulde, Anne-Marie, Wajid, Kal, and Vasquez, Francisco et al., IMF 2005. "Microfinance: A view from the fund." SM/05/30, January 26, 2006, 25.

Hardy, Daniel, Holden, P., and Prokopenko, V. 2002. "Microfinance institutions and public policy." IMF Working Papers, WP/02/159.

Harm, Christian 2002. *Bank Management Between Shareholders and Regulators,* SUERF Studies, No. 21 (Vienna), 123.

Honohan, Patrick and Beck, Thorsten 2007. "Making finance work for Africa." Washington, DC: the World Bank.

Hüpkes, Eva H.G., Quintyn, M. and Taylor, M. 2005. "The accountability of financial sector supervisors: Theory and practice." *European Business Law Review,* 1575–1620.

IMF 2006. "Regional economic outlook—Sub-Saharan Africa." Washington, DC: International Monetary Fund, World Economic and Financial Surveys, May.

Llewellyn, David 2006. "Handbook of central banking and financial authorities in Europe." In *Integrated Agencies and the Role of Central Banks,* ed. D. Masciandaro, 566. Edward Elgar: U.K. and USA.

Masciandaro, Donato 2006a. "Handbook of central banking and financial authorities in Europe." In *Central Banks and Single Financial Authorities: Economics, Politics and Law,* ed. D. Masciandaro, 67–105. Edward Elgar: U.K. and USA.

Masciandaro, Donato 2006b. "Divide et Impera: Financial supervision unification and Central Bank fragmentation effect." *European Journal of Political Economy,* 285–315.

Masciandaro, Donato and Quintyn, M. 2008. "Helping hand or grabbing hand? Politicians, supervision regimes, financial structure and market view." *North American Journal of Economics and Finance,* 19: 153–73.

Mwenda, Kenneth, K. 2004. "Unified financial services supervision in Zambia: The legal and institutional frameworks." *Zambia Law Journal,* 36: 67–109.

Porteous, David 2006. "The enabling environment for mobile banking in Africa." U.K. Department for International Development, London, http://www.bankablefrontier.com/assets/ee.mobil.banking.report.v3.1.pdf

Quintyn, Marc 2007. "Governance of Financial Supervisors and Its Effects—A Stocktaking Exercise," SUERF Studies 4: 64.

Quintyn, Marc, Ramirez, S., and Taylor, M. 2007. "Fear of Freedom. Politicians and Independence and Accountability for Financial Supervisors." chapter 3. In *Designing Financial Supervision Institutions: Independence, Accountability, and Governance,* eds. Donato Masciandaro and Marc Quintyn, 63–116. Cheltenham, U.K.: Edward Elgar.

Senbet, Lemma and Otchere, Isaac 2006. "Financial sector reforms in Africa: Perspectives on issues and policies." Annual World Bank Conference on Development Economics. Washington, DC: The World Bank, 81–119.

Taylor, Michael 1995. *Twin Peaks: A Regulatory Structure for the New Century.* London: Centre for the Study of Financial Innovation.

Taylor, Michael and Fleming, Alex 1999. "Integrated financial supervision. Lessons from Northern European experience." Policy Research Working Paper, 2223. The World Bank.

9
Regional Financial Integration as a Potential Engine for Financial Development in sub-Saharan Africa

John Wakeman-Linn and Smita Wagh

9.1 Introduction

The growth-critical, poverty–reducing role of well-developed domestic financial markets can hardly be overstated.[1] Unfortunately, except for a few middle-income countries, the financial sectors in most African countries lag on most indicators of development, even when compared to low-income countries in other parts of the world (Gulde et al., 2006).

Regional financial integration could potentially address several of the issues associated with the small, fragmented financial markets in Africa. Consolidated financial markets can yield many benefits: bring together scarce savings, viable investment projects and financial infrastructure; boost the numbers and types of financial institutions and instruments; increase competition and innovation; reduce inefficiencies in lending; expand opportunities for risk diversification; help improve regulatory and supervisory bodies; insulate central banks from domestic fiscal excesses; harmonize regional laws and institutions; and create additional opportunities for learning by doing.

However, the long, uneven history of attempts to integrate markets in sub-Saharan Africa (SSA) casts doubt on the potential gains from regional integration, while the current configuration of multiple and overlapping regional arrangements in Africa may well be a significant hindrance to the realization of these gains.[2] Despite a proliferation of regional policy initiatives and institutions, actual market integration has been constrained by several factors: limited intra-regional trade, lack of political will in some quarters, underdeveloped economic and financial infrastructure, and limited regulatory and supervisory capacities. Moreover, regional integration may not solve all the problems that plague African financial markets. For example, it does not directly address low savings and productivity, market inefficiencies, barriers to access, or scarcity of assets that can serve as collateral.

220 John Wakeman-Linn and Smita Wagh

This chapter examines how regional financial integration can help address some of the obstacles that have caused financial sector development in Africa to trail behind that in most developing countries. The purpose is to assess the potential role for regional financial integration in Africa, in light of theory and past experience, both in SSA and elsewhere. To do so, we analyze in detail how regional financial integration could in theory address these problems (Section 9.2); what role regional integration has actually played thus far in African financial sector development (Section 9.3); and what lessons can be learned from instances of regional financial integration in other parts of the world (Section 9.4).

Our analysis indicates that financial integration can contribute significantly to strengthening and developing SSA's financial markets, provided (1) policymakers are firmly committed to integration, including to allowing regulators to be independent of national government interference, and (2) there is an equally firm commitment to broader economic integration and building on existing networks, reinforced by a financial commitment to building the necessary infrastructure. However, even if these factors are present, financial integration will not solve one major problem—access to financial services for economically and geographically excluded people—and may even make it worse. So, at the same time as pursuing regional financial integration, policy makers should be addressing domestic financial development aggressively through separate channels.

9.2 How could regional financial integration address Africa's financial sector challenges?

9.2.1 Regional financial integration in theory

Regional financial integration refers to a process, market driven and/or institutionalized, that broadens and deepens financial links within a region. At the very least, this process involves eliminating barriers to cross-border investments and differential treatment of foreign investors. Further deepening of financial links can take the form of harmonizing national policies, laws, and institutions. Over time, cohesion of regulatory frameworks, operational structures, and information systems, and convergence of prices and risk assessments mean that national financial markets within the region effectively function as one. Taking this concept further, a group of countries may set up a regional bond or stock market, distinct from and potentially coexisting with national markets, with the specific intent of pooling resources, risks, and returns. Whatever form they take, functioning regional financial markets have a certain minimum set of prerequisites (Addo, 2007): currency convertibility and payment systems to reduce settlement delays; information and communication infrastructure; and the removal of legal and regulatory barriers.

Regional financial integration can help small financial markets take advantage of the "systemic scale economies" that accrue to larger systems.[3] Regionalism can offer significant opportunities for allocating capital to its most productive use, propel financial development within the region, and bring additional benefits on the institutional side (Garcia-Herrero and Wooldridge, 2007).

- Regional markets expand the scale of and opportunities for financial intermediation. Pooling national savings can facilitate the financing of large, lumpy investment projects, where funding for such projects might be scarce or unavailable at the national level.
- Larger markets can make it more cost effective to improve aspects of the financial infrastructure, such as payments systems, regulation and supervisory regimes, all of which have high initial fixed costs.
- Regionalization can introduce efficiencies in financial markets. By raising the number and diversifying the types of financial institutions that operate in a particular local market, integration fosters competition and lowers the prices of financial products and services.
- Small financial systems are more likely to be incomplete. Smaller markets are typically skewed in terms of the available institutions (banks rather than non-bank institutions) and instruments (debt rather than equity). Information markets are also likely to be incomplete as high-cost credit rating services are usually absent.
- Regional markets are better able to cope with risk. They allow for greater diversification of assets and markets for individual investors. And they allow individual financial systems to tap into a collective pool of reserves in the event of an idiosyncratic shock or speculative attack.
- Regional reporting requirements can compel greater accountability and transparency on the part of national monetary authorities. Regional institutions can also inure central banks against pressures from national fiscal authorities.
- Finally, regional financial integration can lead to a harmonization of business practices, laws and institutions, closer to those prevailing in the most developed member state.

The process of regional integration does not necessarily preclude integrating globally, via an overall capital account liberalization. But the two are quite different. Low-income countries lacking in sound policies and strong institutions might be especially vulnerable to macroeconomic volatility from exposure to global financial markets (Demirguc-Kunt and Detragiache, 1999; Alfaro et al., 2005). Regional rather than global, liberalization of trade in financial services may be a more advisable first step for these countries and put less of a strain on the regulatory authorities.

But regional financial integration also raises the likelihood of cross-border spillovers of financial distress and contagion risks.[4] Where financial systems are small and underdeveloped, a few large financial institutions with complex balance sheet linkages and exposures across markets, beyond the monitoring ability of the local monetary authorities, may make it difficult for the supervisory and regulatory authorities to do their job effectively, with concomitant risks.

Moreover, there are limits to the benefits that can accrue from regional financial integration, depending on the commonalities and dissimilarities of member profiles. When the members of a regional sub-grouping have very similar structures and challenges, regionalization may pool rather than solve national problems. For instance, where all member financial systems are characterized by excess liquidity and high interest rate spreads, that might indicate a region-wide paucity of viable investment projects and long-standing structural problems. Regionalization, without national efforts to address the core problems, will not be effective here. The gains from harmonizing of practices and laws might also be limited in a regional grouping with similar low initial conditions. And even after some form of regional integration, several small country groupings may still not reach the threshold needed to benefit from scale economies (Honohan and Beck, 2007). Thus, some combination of regional and multilateral liberalization may be what works best for low-income countries (Jansen and Vennes, 2006).

In addition, while advanced members can serve as effective benchmarks for other members, a regional grouping with asymmetric partners raises the risk that financial resources will flow primarily towards the member country with the most viable investment options, stunting the development of credit markets in smaller countries—though the smaller markets may still benefit from improved payments and regulatory regimes, and possibly from improved financial services for savers. On the other hand, banks that might have sought increased market share by expanding to unserved customers and areas may instead seek to compete for the business of already-served customers in the regional markets now open to them.

9.2.2   The status of financial markets in Africa

There is a great deal of disparity in the development of financial markets among the countries in sub-Saharan Africa. At one extreme, some countries are in the process of setting up rudimentary payments systems and other support infrastructure in the aftermath of a period of political and economic disruption. And at the other extreme are those grappling with policies to promote offshore banking and effective integration into global capital markets.

In general, however, the region has shallow, underdeveloped financial markets (Figure 9.1). Their development has been hampered by a multitude of factors. Common problems include poverty, political and economic

M2 (percent of GDP)

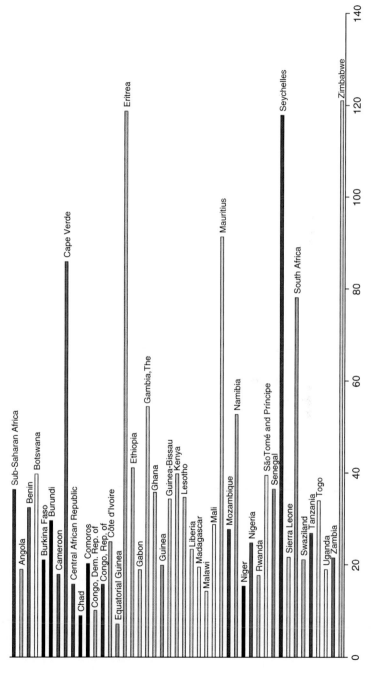

Figure 9.1 Sub-Saharan Africa: Financial indicators, 2006

Source: IMF, African Department Database, 2007

Private credit (percent of GDP)

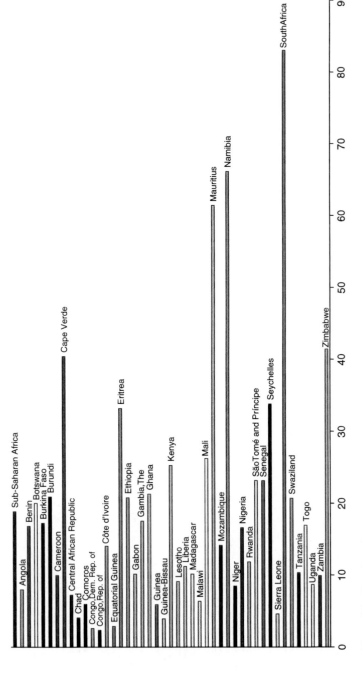

Figure 9.1 Continued

uncertainty, fiscal dominance, lack of effective collateral and information systems, weak judicial institutions, limited investment opportunities in the private sector, exposure to significant external shocks, technological constraints, and the shortage of skilled personnel with expertise in banking and finance. Theory would tell us that many, but not all, of these problems could be eased through regional financial integration.

Most financial sectors in SSA can be characterized as small, regardless of how "small" is defined: in terms of the number of financial institutions and their market capitalization; the range of financial institutions, products and services; the availability of investment opportunities; the proportion of the population with access to formal financial services; the size of the support infrastructure; or the resources of the regulatory authorities. Small market size means that most African financial systems cannot take advantage of many of the "systemic scale economies" already discussed. For instance, Table 9.1 indicates how small stock markets in sub-Saharan Africa are, even relative to low-income countries as a group.

Table 9.1   Sub-Saharan Africa: Stock market development indicators

	Number of listed companies (total)	Market capitalization (percent of GDP)	Stocks traded, turnover ratio (percent)
Botswana	18	38.2	24
Côte d'Ivoire	40	23.8	3.7
Ghana	32	13.4	3.4
Kenya	51	53.7	15.8
Mauritius	41	55.8	6.0
Namibia	9	8.5	4.6
Nigeria	202	28.6	13.8
South Africa	401	280.4	49.5
Swaziland	6	7.5	0.0
Tanzania	6	4.7	2.3
Uganda	5	1.2	3.1
Zambia	12	13.6	2.0
Zimbabwe	80	–	7.9
Low-income countries	6122	74.5	97.6

Note: Data are for the most recently available year, 2005 or 2006. Low-income countries areas defined by the World Bank.
Source: World Development Indicators, 2007.

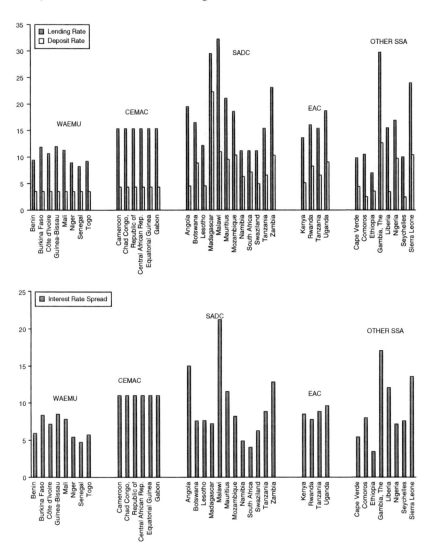

Figure 9.2 Interest rates, 2006

Note: Interest spreads are calculated as the difference between the lending and deposit rates for 2006, where data are available. For CEMAC countries the data are the interest rates set by the central bank, the effective rates may vary by country depending on charges, fees, and type of clients. For WAEMU the lending rates are the prime lending rates in July 2007.

Source: International Financial Statistics Database, 2007; BCEAO.

The banking sector dominates the financial systems in most African countries. Most banks are fairly sound but not particularly efficient, with high overhead costs. Most banking systems are characterized by excess liquidity and high real lending rates and interest rate spreads (Figure 9.2). Nonbank financial institutions and capital markets have a limited presence in only a few countries. Financial institutions in general are held back by poor governance and a non-transparent operating environment.

The public sector has long had a strong presence in African financial markets, both as owner and borrower. Although this role has been declining in recent years, the scarcity of private sector investment opportunities and the limited autonomy of monetary authorities mean that government securities still feature prominently in the portfolios of most financial institutions.

9.2.3 The theory applied to Sub-Saharan Africa

Given the small, fragmented structure of African financial markets, the most obvious advantage of regional integration is that it increases market size. Small financial systems that come together stand to exploit economies of scale in such areas as banking supervision, information sharing systems and other market infrastructure with high fixed costs. Pooling resources to finance large investment projects at the regional level can also be useful where financial markets are shallow. In fact, as the proliferation of cross-border banks in Africa indicates, given the advantages of wider markets, financial institutions find ways to operate with multiple sets of rules even without formal attempts at standardization (World Bank, 2007). But they would be more efficient and effective if national regulatory and other differences were removed.

Regionalization would promote this institutional cohesion—the upgrading and harmonization of local practices. Financial laws and frameworks in the relatively advanced financial markets in Africa could serve as benchmarks for other members in their regional groupings.[5] And the adjustment and regulatory burden of this harmonization process might be lower than that of integrating into advanced global financial centers.

Regional institutions can also serve to both attract international capital flows and act as the first line of defense against sudden reversals of such flows. African countries are only now beginning to feel the impact of the steady expansion of cross-border private capital flows that has taken place over the last decade or so. While the number of SSA countries rated by international credit rating agencies has grown in recent years, the median rating, excluding South Africa, is B—well below investment grade (IMF, 2007, Box 2.3). The pooling of reserves increases the likelihood that national financial systems will be able to withstand shocks. Thus, a group of countries could inspire more confidence in international capital markets than an individual country.

Regional integration can function as an external agency of restraint and enhance the credibility of the monetary authorities where the government has a long history of bank financing of the fiscal deficit. Supranational monetary authorities are more likely to be immune to pressures from national authorities to finance fiscal deficits. In addition, supranational supervisory authorities can more easily resist national political interference in supervisory matters. This is one way to ensure that the recent downsizing of the role of the government in the region is not reversed.

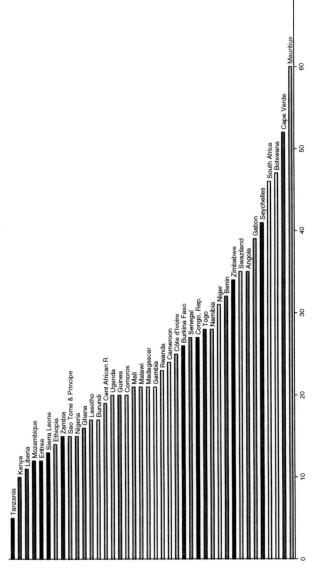

Figure 9.3 Access to financial services (percent of adult population)

Note: For details on the underlying methodoly please consult Honohan (2006).

Source: Honohan (2006).

However, regional integration may have limited success in addressing one of the main financial sector issues in SSA—access to formal financial services and products (Figure 9.3). Fewer than 20% of African adults have an account with a formal or semiformal financial institution (Honohan and Beck, 2007). Even though microfinance institutions do serve some of the financial needs of low-income households and small and medium enterprises, what might be more effective are domestic financial sector strategies with innovative savings and credit products and effective methods of reaching all segments of the population (for instance, via mobile phone banking). Regional integration, by replicating existing lending patterns on a larger scale, may in fact worsen the problem of financial exclusion.

9.3 Actual African experience with regional financial integration

Africa has a long, albeit uneven, history of attempts at regional cooperation. Established in 1910, and subsequently updated and relaunched in 1969, the Southern African Customs Union (SACU) between South Africa, Botswana, Lesotho, Namibia, and Swaziland, is the oldest customs union in the world. Monetary cooperation along historical colonial lines is more common among African countries than in other parts of the developing world. The CFA zone countries constitute one such long-standing monetary union.

Recent years have seen a renewed interest in new forms of regional cooperation and the revitalization of those already in existence. Part of the inspiration has come from the recent successes of the larger markets in the developing world, China and India. Political will, advances in information and communication technology, and a desire to consolidate markets, are all driving the discussion on how regional integration can address some of the problems that hinder financial sector development in Africa.

In what follows we look at a select sample of regional arrangements, those where the trend is toward financial market integration. We seek, in light of the previous theoretical discussion, to assess both what they have done to enhance regional financial integration, and the impact of those measures.

9.3.1 CFA franc zone

The CFA franc zone has survived decolonization, a significant devaluation, and a transformation of its peg currency. The two regions that comprise the CFA franc zone, the West African Economic and Monetary Union (WAEMU), and the Central African Economic and Monetary Community (CEMAC,) each have its own regional central bank and distinct versions of the CFA franc. While these regions represent two of the more advanced examples of institutionalized financial cooperation (WAEMU more so than CEMAC) they do not have well-integrated financial markets (Masson and

Pattillo, 2005). For instance, while it is true that banks need to obtain only a single permit (*agrément unique*) to operate within WAEMU or CEMAC, they are additionally required to get permission from national finance ministries before they can operate in individual member countries. Hence, banks typically stay within national borders and the region does not have an effective interbank market.

Both regions have shown some progress in harmonizing of structural policies via a common business law. But the most important area of cooperation thus far has been regional surveillance. Recognizing that the 1994 devaluation was precipitated in some part by the fiscal excesses of some member states, the two regions have since adopted fairly conservative macroeconomic convergence criteria.

9.3.2   WAEMU

Fostered by regional institutional arrangements and the abolition of all capital controls, integration of financial markets in WAEMU is further along than in other parts of Africa, especially when it comes to harmonization of rules.[6] A single banking commission was created in 1990 to reinforce regional banking supervision (*Commission Bancaire de l'UMOA*). However, despite the presence of the commission and the BCEAO (*Banque Centrale des Etats de l'Afrique de l'Ouest*), the regional central bank, some national banking systems are still fragile and the interbank market is underdeveloped. Given the gaps in risk assessment and the lack of collateral, activity in the regional interbank market is largely restricted to in-group subsidiaries. Excess liquidity in some banking systems continues to coexist with liquidity shortages in others. Differential reserve requirements by country, ranging from 3% in Guinea-Bissau and Togo to 15% in Benin, further distort cross-border competition.

Since 1998, the *Bourse Régionale des Valeurs Mobilières* (BRVM) has served as a regional exchange for trades in stocks and bonds. The growth of this exchange has been curtailed by the political disruptions in Côte d'Ivoire and is concentrated in the bond markets. In 2006, total market capitalization was just under 24% of regional GDP, and the bourse lists 40 companies, compared to a market capitalization of 280% of GDP and 401 listed companies at the Johannesburg Stock Exchange.[7] Prospects for further growth of the market are constrained by both supply-side factors (a dearth of large listable companies in the WAEMU region), and demand-side factors (a dearth of institutional investors).

Progress on other fronts of market integration has been achieved largely though supranational regulatory laws and bodies. Since 1995, the regulatory framework for cooperative financial institutions has been based on the PARMEC law (Projet d'Appui à la Réglementation sur le Mutuelles d'Epargne et de Crédit). In the rapidly proliferating area of microfinance, a regional institution—Banque Régionale de Solidarité (BRS), with regional institutional shareholders—has been created. The BRS tends to concentrate largely on refinancing microfinance institutions rather than provide direct loans (Bred Gestion, 2006).

One encouraging development is the rapid growth of the regional market in local currency debt, especially public debt. Spurred by the cessation of central bank financing of fiscal deficits, the market in treasury bills and government bonds has been expanding since 2000. In the absence of restrictions, regional investors within WAEMU, mostly banks, have in recent years taken up roughly half the treasury bills issued. In fact, the rapid growth of the treasury bill market in WAEMU, the excess liquidity in most banking systems, and the continuing lag in private sector investment opportunities has meant that governments in these countries have been able to raise funds at low costs largely unrelated to their credit ratings (Sy, 2007).

Despite these institutional measures, further regional integration in the WAEMU is made difficult by continuing challenges. Intraregional trade, at just over 10% of total trade, is a poor motivator for further integration. And while substantial progress has been made on the harmonization front, there are still differences across borders. For example, bankruptcy proceedings and rules on the realization of collateral vary across countries. Despite the *agrément unique,* national authorities continue to use discretion in licensing and de-licensing of banks.

The deeper structural problems that have plagued member countries also make it harder to build regional financial markets. The lack of diversification in economic activity across the region means that investor portfolios are limited to a few assets and there is very little cross-border competition in lending. One clear sign of the lack of effective integration of financial markets in WAEMU member countries is the simultaneous co-existence of liquidity shortages in some countries with substantial excess liquidity in other countries and region-wide.

9.3.3 CEMAC

Financial integration in the CEMAC remains limited and significant impediments continue to exist, despite a common currency area and a comprehensive regional institutional setup. In fact, financial integration lags behind that achieved by WAEMU despite a similar institutional setup. Some of the structural problems that hinder WAEMU financial integration are exaggerated in the CEMAC region. Because CEMAC countries are predominantly oil-producers, diversification of economic activity and investment opportunities is a bigger problem here. Institutional initiatives have also lagged behind WAEMU. Reform of the regional payments system that was launched in 2003 has been slow. This contrasts with WAEMU, where a modernized payments system (STAR-UEMOA) is in the final stages of implementation. Moreover, political will for regional integration is low among CEMAC members.

Not unlike the rest of Africa, financial markets in CEMAC countries are dominated by banks. The regional banking commission, the Commission Bancaire de L'Afrique Centrale (COBAC) is charged with overseeing bank compliance with prudential norms and granting or withdrawing licenses. Despite the harmonization of banking laws on paper, differences in operational efficiencies, reserve requirements and taxation regimes for banks mean that banking sector integration is still incomplete (Saab and Vacher, 2007). So CEMAC financial systems have not been able to realize the efficiency gains that accrue from greater competition. The interbank market is highly underdeveloped and there is no mechanism or incentives for the flow of funds from banking systems with excess liquidity to those with demand for liquidity.

A regional stock exchange (BVMAC) was established in 2003, independently of the Douala Stock Exchange (DSX) established by Cameroon; trading has not commenced in either market. Given the small base of large companies and investors it seems unlikely that both exchanges will be viable. Moreover, the simultaneous development of two securities exchange creates the potential for conflict between national and regional rules and unnecessary duplication of costs.

9.3.4   Southern Africa

In the southern part of the continent, integration is driven predominantly by the presence of the region's economic giant, South Africa. This does not mean that formalized institutional arrangements are absent. Regional integration has taken place formally between the overlapping memberships of the Southern African Customs Union (SACU) and Southern African Development Community (SADC).

The regional dominance of South African financial institutions is especially strong in the subgroup that makes up the Common Monetary Area (South Africa, Lesotho, Namibia and Swaziland). However, the incomplete convergence of interest rates within this subgroup implies that institutional differences and the limited investment opportunities outside South Africa hamper market integration (Aziakpono, 2005). Nevertheless, in 2003 South African banks accounted for more than 70% of banking assets in Namibia, Lesotho, and Swaziland, and they have been making significant inroads in other SADC markets (Jansen and Vennes, 2006).[8] The market-driven character of this process poses its own set of challenges for the host regulatory authorities, who may not have the resources or the experience to monitor the sophisticated cross-border financial institutions. Moreover, despite this regional integration, the disparity in the levels of financial development among CMA members still persists (Aziakpono, 2004).

Since 1997 the Committee of SADC Stock Exchanges (COSSE) has been promoting the harmonization of listing standards for SADC members that have stock exchanges to the listing standards of the Johannesburg Stock Exchange (JSE). The medium-term goal is to set up a system of automated trading of nationally-listed securities at the regional level.

9.3.5 East African community

Kenya, Tanzania and Uganda—the three original members of the EAC have a long—sometimes contentious history of regional cooperation based on a common legal tradition and long-standing trade ties.[9] In 2001, the EAC was relaunched, with the goal of creating a common market, common currency and ultimately a political union. Thus far, the most concrete development has been the implementation of the customs union in 2005, presumably in an effort to increase the very modest levels of intra-regional trade (Table 9.2).

While the EAC is generally not considered ready for a monetary union and common currency, it has made some progress in integrating its financial markets. The banking sector exhibits a high degree of integration, as subsidiaries of multinational banks operate in all three countries. Lack of a single currency is not seen as a barrier to further progress. The region does not have a single central bank, but regulators have shown a strong commitment to staying on top of regional developments, although there is much scope for harmonizing the rules.

In 1997, the original members of the EAC set up the East African Member States Securities Regulatory Authorities (EASRA) to harmonize and regulate capital market policies, encourage cross-border listings and develop a regional rating system for listed companies. National exchanges have also undertaken several initiatives to promote regional integration and market growth. A number of steps have been taken to ensure that EAC investors face minimal barriers to entry in member stock exchanges. The issuance of medium-to-long-term government bonds has helped market development by setting a benchmark. EAC members have harmonized trading rules around the standards set by Kenya's Capital Market Authority.

Before financial integration in the EAC can go much further, there is an urgent need to upgrade, standardize, and institutionalize at the regional level several aspects of the financial infrastructure, including regulation, payments systems, legal frameworks, accounting practices, and credit information. This process has been further complicated with the entry of Burundi and Rwanda, whose financial sector development and structures are quite different from those of the original membership.

9.3.5.1 *Why has Africa not seen the benefits from financial integration that theory promises?*

Many of the hypothesized gains from regional integration have not been manifested in the actual experience of regional organizations in Africa.

Table 9.2 EAC Countries: Bilateral trade flows (Averages for 1995–1999 and 2000–2006)

Country 1	1995–1999 Country 2					2000–2006 Country 2				
	Burundi	Kenya	Rwanda	Tanzania	Uganda	Burundi	Kenya	Rwanda	Tanzani	Uganda
Exports from Country 1 to Country 2 (percent of Country 1's total exports)										
Burundi	0.00	1.86	2.81	2.97	0.23	0.00	5.46	5.75	0.11	1.47
Kenya	0.29	0.00	2.24	10.44	14.96	1.19	0.00	2.70	8.16	17.42
Rwanda	1.02	0.53	0.00	0.15	0.00	0.52	0.07	0.00	0.05	0.45
Tanzania	0.47	3.71	2.62	0.00	1.32	1.50	3.05	0.50	0.00	1.28
Uganda	0.00	0.46	0.29	0.68	0.00	1.70	9.01	3.41	1.34	0.00
Imports from Country 2 to Country 1 (percent of Country 1's total exports)										
Burundi	0.00	4.59	0.75	2.93	0.00	0.00	13.24	0.48	9.99	3.26
Kenya	0.04	0.00	0.02	0.62	0.09	0.00	0.00	0.00	0.40	0.25
Rwanda	0.53	16.26	0.00	6.75	0.52	0.84	20.03	0.00	1.53	5.01
Tanzania	0.10	9.24	0.01	0.00	0.22	0.00	7.02	0.00	0.00	0.32
Uganda	0.03	38.15	0.00	1.14	0.00	0.00	31.09	0.06	0.85	0.00

Source: Direction of Trade, 2007.

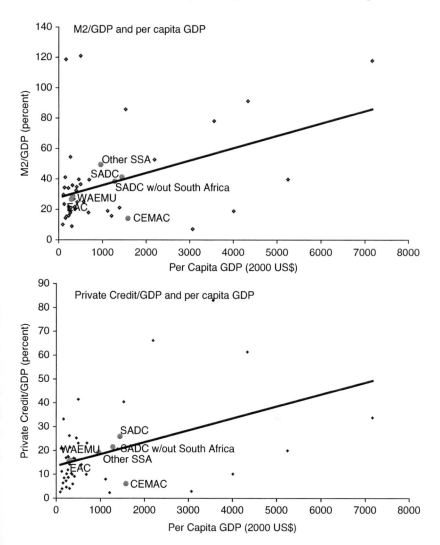

Figure 9.4 Broad money, private credit and per capita GDP

Note: The plots are based on data for 2006. Regional aggregates are calculated as simple averages of their memberships. Other SSA includes countries that are not members of the regional groupings indicated here.

Source: IMF, African Department Database, 2007.

Money/GDP ratios in all these regions remaining below the very low average of other SSA countries (Figure 9.4). The disappointing progress is attributable to a number of factors:

A large part of the problem is the current "spaghetti bowl" configuration of regional arrangements in Africa right. The pattern of multiple, overlapping, and often contradictory regional memberships and commitments endangers political cooperation and increases the likelihood of conflicts of interest and confusion regarding the priorities of individual members.

Even within the more advanced examples of financial cooperation, there have been problems with the sequencing and prioritization of the steps towards integration. The general tendency has been to concentrate on the creation of regional financial institutions while paying less attention to pre-existing financial links between multinational financial institutions that operate in more than one market. Encouraging and regulating the looser links between cross-country financial institutions might in some cases be more effective than creating a centralized regional body. *De facto* integration among banks in the SACU region has been more effective in harmonizing real borrowing costs than the *de jure* integration in the CEMAC or EAC regions (Figure 9.5).

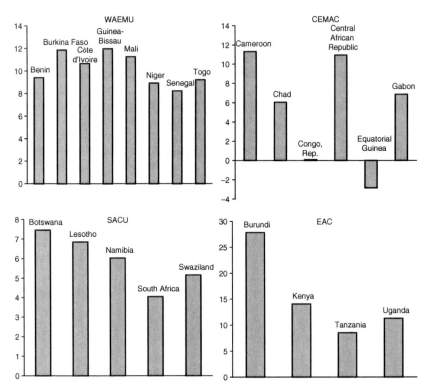

Figure 9.5   Real cost of borrowing

Note: Real cost of borrowing is the lending rate adjusted for inflation for 2006. For WAEMU countries the real cost is calculated as the prime lending rate in July 2007 adjusted for inflation in that month.

Source: World Development Indicators, 2007; BCEAO; IMF, Information Notice System, 2007.

Underdeveloped domestic financial markets have also been a stumbling block for regional integration. The functioning and growth of regional markets is easier when domestic markets provide the basic underpinnings. In a classic chicken and egg dilemma, regional pooling of resources cannot develop domestic financial markets unless the domestic markets have already reached a minimal degree of development.

While it seems clear that "systemic scale economies" await regional markets in Africa, it is not as clear what the most suitable scale actually is, or how to achieve it. Regional groupings comprised of similar members generally lack benchmarks and seem to pool their problems as well as well their resources (e.g., CEMAC). Less developed members in asymmetric groupings seem unable to bridge the development gap with the more advanced members (SACU).

But perhaps the most important reason SSA countries have not seen the benefits from regional financial integration that theory promises is that, even in the most integrated region (WAEMU), true financial sector integration does not exist. Effective regional financial integration requires the subordination of short-term national interests to the goal of regional financial market development. The continuation of national government intervention in regulatory and supervisory decisions, and in many cases of different national regulations, as well as efforts to protect national interests, undermines efforts to create true regional financial markets.

9.4 Lessons from other parts of the world

Perhaps experiences with regional financial integration in other parts of the world can offer African policymakers with some insights regarding how to pursue more effective financial integration.

9.4.1 The European Union

As the most advanced example of regional financial integration, the European Union (EU) seems like the most obvious place to begin this exercise. However, given the stark differences between European and African economies, great care must be taken in trying to apply lessons from the EU to Africa. The "European model" of financial market integration has evolved and adapted over decades, and functions in an institutional and economic environment that is in many respects quite different from that found in most African countries.

The European Commission's 1985 White Paper lays down two, seemingly irreconcilable, principles for integration—mutual recognition and harmonization (Steil, 1999). Mutual recognition or "competition among rules," as the concept is also known, ensures the continued existence of separate and distinct national legal and regulatory systems. Harmonization of minimum standards calls for member states conform to certain EU specified requirements, and thus limits the scope for "competition among rules". This tension is inevitable in any process of merging national markets. What did help the reconciliation process in the EU is that the volumes of cross-border trade and investments on the ground were quite large—quite unlike the situation in SSA. So the institutional process was actually reflecting, and may even have been lagging behind, the market. In Africa by contrast, some of the more advanced examples of regional integration are based on a pre-existing currency arrangement, based on the region's colonial history. Intra-African trade and investment, outside of certain concentrated pockets, is relatively limited. Moreover, given the similar structure of most African economies, it is not clear that there is a vast untapped potential to increase the scale of such trade (Honohan and Lane, 2000). While regional integration could address some of the barriers to regional transactions, a process driven more by theory than existing economic ties is likely to be quite challenging.

Even with the requisite political will and a long history of cross-border economic transactions, the resource requirements for creating and sustaining integrated financial markets within the EU have been considerable. Since the beginning, grants by the Structural Funds, loans by the European Investment Bank, and more recently guarantees by the European Investment Fund have played a role in making the overall process of integration effective and equitable (Griffith-Jones, Steinherr, and Fuzzo De Lima, 2006). These mechanisms have allocated substantial funds to building the necessary infrastructure, including communication and transport networks, to facilitate regional transactions. At the same time, resources have also been allocated to mitigating the income differentials between member states, including those created by the emerging pattern of regional trade and investment.

The initial institutional environment faced by the EIB was not dissimilar to that found in several Africa countries today—capital controls, small, segmented capital markets, discrepancies in banking sector development, incomplete information markets. This market-developing role of financially sound, effective regional institutions, especially the European Investment Bank (EIB), should be of particular interest to African countries. It highlights the need for an overarching regional body to play a promotional role in setting up the financial infrastructure needed to support the development and operation of regional markets. It also highlights the vast resource requirements necessary for such a body to play its role effectively. One reason for the EIB's continued financial soundness has been prudent lending policies, as it will not lend to weaker members without credible third party guarantees. This approach is likely to be severely limiting for a regional organization with several poorly rated members, and illustrates the difficulties in setting up a similar well-funded organization in the African region.

9.4.2 Developing countries

The experience of other developing countries might be more relevant to African policy-makers—except that the path of regional financial integration in other parts of the developing world has been similarly problematic.

Chronic capital shortages at the regional level has meant that countries in **Latin America and the Caribbean** have been more interested in getting access to global financial markets—regional and global financial integration have served as complements rather than substitutes. For instance, among small country groupings, such as the **Caribbean Community (CARICOM)**, common regional standards can be just as effective as a means to attract foreign capital from global markets as they are to foster regional markets. In fact, most of the *de facto* regional integration here is the result of the subsidiaries of foreign banks that operate in more than one local market (IDB, 2002).

The experience of the **Central American Common Market (CACM)** illustrates that even one of the more successful trading blocs in the developing world will not necessarily evolve into common financial markets (Cooper, 2007).[10] In principle, policy-makers recognized the relationship between trade in goods and that in financial services. Preliminary attempts at integrating financial markets were made via the establishment of the Central American Central Bank System with the Monetary Council at its apex. But the institutional initiative never really got off the ground. A marked reluctance on the part of national interest groups and authorities, including the central banks, to align their interests has meant that financial cooperation in the region remains limited. Even with thriving intra-regional trade, political will plays a significant role in integrating financial markets.

In recent years, banking integration in Central America has taken place via subsidiaries of global financial institutions.[11] But the equity and private debt markets remain underdeveloped due to problems that are quite similar to those found in SSA—small, family owned business structures, economic and political factors, weak regulation and limited institutional investor base. And while the creation of a regional capital market seems more feasible than the development of many small national markets, the task is challenging. Regional initiatives to integrate capital markets, such as the Memorandum of Understanding on building a common trading platform signed by Costa Rica, El Salvador, and Panama in September 2006, have stalled due to technical difficulties (Shah et al., 2007). African countries wanting to embark on a similar path would do well to the weigh the benefits of pooling against the considerable initial set-up costs of a regional capital market.

On the institutional front, regional development banks created in the 1960s have since evolved to provide support to new national, sub regional and regional financial instruments, and improving the terms and cost at which members access global financial markets (Titelman, 2006).[12] Having done better than national financial institutions through the crises of the 1980s and with reserves in excess of the Basel Core reserve requirements these development banks have a better credit rating than their members and hence they are able to access global markets on better terms than their members—a role that could be especially important to some smaller African economies with poor ratings.

The vulnerability of national financial systems remains a major source of macroeconomic instability in the region. Raising and harmonizing regulatory standards among members remains on the agenda, an issue that must be addressed with some urgency and separately from that of regional integration (Machinea and Rozenwurcel, 2006).

In the aftermath of the Asian Crisis of 1997–98 policy-makers in **East Asia**, not surprisingly, launched a number of regional policy dialogues to institutionalize the close linkages among their financial systems that the crisis had revealed. While the crisis had been precipitated by lack of investor confidence, it also indicated that, among the economies of East Asia, geographical proximity and structural similarities warranted the creation of some sort of a regional body charged with liquidity assistance, surveillance, and exchange rate coordination (Park, 2006). After attempts to create an Asian monetary fund were unsuccessful, the **Chiang Mai Initiative** (2000) has been the main forum to strengthen existing cooperation among the members of the Association of Southeast Asian Nations (ASEAN), plus China, Japan, and the Republic of Korea.

As East Asian economies acknowledge the need for regional coordination even when the only links between financial systems may be in the way that investors form expectations, they are also moving forward with the development of local bond markets to complement their bank-dominated national financial systems (Park et al., 2006). To this end, regional governments have created two **Asian Bond Funds (ABF)**, pooling a portion reserves from central banks.[13] ABF1 channels investment to dollar-denominated bonds issued by sovereign and quasi-sovereign Asian borrowers, ABF2 does the same for local-currency bonds. ABF2 might be of particular interest to African sovereigns trying to develop local currency debt markets, even though central bank reserves are significantly lower than those in Asia.[14] The collaborative effort has yielded many benefits from "learning by doing" for Asian central banks. More significantly, they have also learned from each other's experiences with market impediments (Ma and Remolona, 2005).

The "Asian model" of financial integration is based on cooperation rather than institutional integration. It might be especially relevant to African governments concerned about the impact of regional integration on national sovereignty.

9.5 Conclusion

Regional financial integration can play a significant role in developing domestic financial markets in Africa. But at the very least it requires that policymakers devise a coherent strategy based on the recognition that national interests can best be served by achieving regional goals.

Any strategy intending to realize the benefits of regional financial integration would be well-served by incorporating the lessons from Africa's own experiences with regional arrangement thus far, as well as those from other parts of the world.

- Regional financial integration works best when it builds on pre-existing economic relationships between member states. The progress made by the EU can be attributed in large parts to existing trade ties between member states. Given the low levels of intra-regional trade in Africa, this calls for greatly strengthened efforts to enhance regional economic integration.
- Economic ties are necessary but not sufficient for successful regional financial integration. Merging financial markets is at least as much a political process as it is an economic one. Creating and sustaining regional institutions that can oversee and regulate the process requires a considerable amount of political will, particularly the will to let regional interests overrule temporary national interests, and the willingness to back it up with ongoing resource commitments.
- Well-functioning, autonomous regional institutions can play a significant role in market development. They can catalyze the harmonization of national policies and laws and present the common face of the regional grouping to the rest of the world. But policy makers need to see the advantages of harmonized policies, and commit to supporting them.
- Most importantly, regional markets do not instantaneously fix everything that is wrong with domestic financial markets. In fact, underdeveloped domestic markets can be additional encumbrance to regional integration. Specific national problems warrant national financial sector development strategies.

Thus, for SSA countries to achieve successful regional financial integration, with all the resulting benefits in terms of larger, more efficient, more dynamic, and more stable financial systems, national governments must be firmly committed to both financial and economic integration, even to the extent of allowing short-term national concerns to be outweighed by the benefits of long-term regional cooperation. The alternative may well be the continuation of small, inefficient financial sectors, which are unable to contribute effectively to economic growth and poverty reduction.

Appendix 9A.1 Spaghetti bowl of regional trade arrangements in Africa

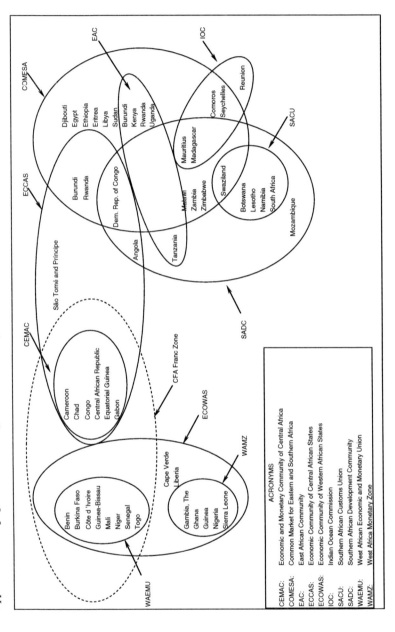

ACRONYMS

CEMAC: Economic and Monetary Community of Central Africa
COMESA: Common Market for Eastern and Southern Africa
EAC: East African Community
ECCAS: Economic Community of Central African States
ECOWAS: Economic Community of Western African States
IOC: Indian Ocean Commission
SACU: Southern African Customs Union
SADC: Southern African Development Community
WAEMU: West African Economic and Monetary Union
WAMZ: West Africa Monetary Zone

Source: Tsangarides, Ewenczyk and Hulej, 2006 (chart updated).

Notes

The authors thank, without implicating, Robert J. Corker and colleagues in the IMF's Money and Capital Markets Department for their comments.

1. For a detailed exposition on the growth-critical role of financial markets in the mobilization of savings, channeling investible resources, information dissemination, diversification and risk management, lowering transaction costs, etc. please refer to Levine (1997, 2004). Financial development also aids in poverty-reduction by alleviating credit constraints on low-income households and insuring against shocks (Galor and Zeira, 1993)
2. For a list of the regional groupings and their membership please see Appendix 9A.1.
3. The following discussion on "systemic scale economies" draws on Bossone, Honohan and Long (2001), and Bossone and Lee (2004).
4. For details on fundamental cross-border effects and contagion see Faruquee (2007).
5. In the absence of viable domestic investment opportunities, less developed members in asymmetric regional groupings do run the risk of losing their scarce savings to the more advanced members. But this risk is lower at the regional rather than the global level.
6. However, WAEMU countries have retained a number of capital controls vis-à-vis investors from outside the region and residents wanting to invest abroad.
7. Based on data from the World Development Indicators.
8. The current membership of SADC includes Angola, Botswana, Democratic Republic of Congo, Lesotho, Madagascar, Malawi, Mauritius, Mozambique, Namibia, South Africa, Swaziland, Tanzania, Zambia and Zimbabwe.
9. Burundi and Rwanda joined the organization in June 2007.
10. Since its inception intra-regional trade in the CACM, comprising Costa Rica, El Salvador, Guatemala, Honduras, and Nicaragua, has increased from 6.5% in 1960 to between 15–20% in recent years (Cooper, 2007).
11. Several regional financial conglomerates (and their subsidiaries), that dominated the banking system in Central America, have recently been acquired by global financial institutions (Shah et al., 2007).
12. The Andean Development Corporation (1968), the Central American Bank for Economic Integration (1961), and the Caribbean Development Bank (1969) were all created as subregional development banks to mobilize medium to long term resources for productive investments.
13. The central banks of China, Hong Kong, Indonesia, Korea, Malaysia, Philippines, Singapore and Thailand contribute to ABF.
14. For details on the recent activity in local-currency debt markets in sub-Saharan Africa please refer to IMF (2007, Chapter V).

References

Addo, Elsie. 2007. "Policies and strategies for enhancing the regional integration of capital markets in Africa," presented at the UNECA Meeting on Capital Flows and the Development of African Economies: Towards an Action Plan for Financing Investment in Africa. Zanzibar, Tanzania, April 24–25.

Alfaro, Laura, Kalemli-Ozcan, S. and Volosovych, V. 2005. "Capital flows in a globalised world: The role of policies and institutions." NBER Working Paper No. 11696. Cambridge, MA: National Bureau of Economic Research.

Aziakpono, Meshach J. 2004. "Financial intermediation and economic growth in economic integration: The case of SACU." draft National University of Lesotho.

Aziakpono, Meshach J. 2005. "Financial integration in the SACU countries: Evidence from interest rate pass-through analysis." Presented at the Tenth Annual Conference on Econometric Modelling in Africa of the African Econometric Society. Nairobi, Kenya, July 6–8.

Bossone, Biagio, and Lee, Jong-Kun 2004. "In finance, size matters: The 'systemic scale economies' Hypothesis." *IMF Staff Papers*, Vol. 51 (1): 19–46.

Bossone, Biagio, Honohan, Patrick and Long, Millard 2001. "Policy for small financial systems." World Bank Financial Sector Discussion Paper No. 6. Washington: World Bank.

BRED Gestion 2006. *Rethinking the Role of Banks and of Sub-Regional Banks and National Development Finance in Africa*. Paris: BRED Gestion.

Cooper, Scott 2007. "Why doesn't regional monetary cooperation follow trade cooperation?" *Review of International Political Economy*, 14 (4): 626–52.

Demirgüç-Kunt, Asli and Detragiache, Enrica 1999. "Financial liberalisation and financial fragility." In *Annual World Bank Conference on Development Economics 1998*, eds. Pleskovic, B and Stiglitz, J.E., 303–31. Washington: World Bank.

Faruqee, Hamid 2007. "Financial integration: Key concepts, benefits, and risks." In *Integrating Europe's Financial Markets*, eds. Decressin, Jorg, Faruqee, Hamid and Fonteyne, Wim, 19–40. Washington: International Monetary Fund.

Galor, Oded and Zeira, Joseph 1993. "Income distribution and macroeconomics." *Review of Economic Studies*, 60 (January): 35–52.

Garcia-Herrero, Alicia and Wooldrige, Philip 2007. "Global and regional financial integration: Progress in emerging markets." *BIS Quarterly Review,* September: 57–70.

Griffith-Jones, Stephany, Alfred Steinherr, and Ana Teresa Fuzzo de Lima 2006. "European financial institutions: A useful inspiration for developing countries?" In *Regional Financial Cooperation*, ed. Jose Antonio Ocampo, 136–63. Washington: Brookings Institution Press.

Gulde, Anne-Marie, Pattillo, Catherine, Christensen, Jakob Carey, Kevin and Wagh, Smita 2006. *Sub-Saharan Africa: Financial Sector Challenges*. Washington: International Monetary Fund.

Honohan, Patrick 2006. "Household financial assets in the process of development." World Bank Policy Research Paper 3965. Washington: World Bank.

Honohan, Patrick, and Lane, Philip R. 2000. "Will the euro trigger more monetary unions in Africa?" World Bank Policy Research Paper 2393. Washington: World Bank.

Honohan, Patrick, and Beck, Thorsten 2007. *Making Finance Work for Africa*. Washington: World Bank.

Inter-American Development Bank 2002. *Beyond Borders: The New Regionalism in Latin America*. Washington: IADB.

International Monetary Fund 2007. *Regional Economic Outlook: Sub-Saharan Africa*. Washington, April.

Jansen, Marion, and Vennes, Yannick 2006. "Liberalizing financial services trade in Africa: Going regional and multilateral." WTO Staff Working Apper ERSD-2006–03.

Levine, Ross 1997. "Financial development and economic growth: Views and agenda." *Journal of Economic Literature,* 35 (June): 688–726.

Levine, Ross 2004. "Finance and growth: Theory and evidence." NBER Working Paper No. 10766. Cambridge, MA: National Bureau of Economic Research.

Ma, Guonan and Remolona, Eli M. 2005. "Opening markets through a regional bond fund: Lessons from ABF2." *BIS Quarterly Review,* June: 81–92.

Machinea, Jose Luis and Rozenwurcel, Guillermo 2006. "Macroeconomic coordination in Latin America: Does it have a future." In *Regional Financial Cooperation,* ed. Jose Antonio Ocampo, 164–99. Washington: Brookings Institution Press.

Masson, Paul and Pattillo, Catherine 2005. *The Monetary Geography of Africa.* Washington, DC: Brookings Institution Press.

Park, Yung Chul 2006. "Regional financial integration in East Asia: Challenges and prospects." In *Regional Financial Cooperation,* ed. Jose Antonio Ocampo, 227–63. Washington: Brookings Institution Press.

Park, Yung Chul, Park, Jae Ha, Leung, Julia and Sangsubhan, Kanit 2006. "Asian bond market development: Rationale and strategies." In *Regional Financial Cooperation,* ed. Jose Antonio Ocampo, 264–90. Washington: Brookings Institution Press.

Saab, Samer Y. and Vacher, Jerome 2007. "Banking sector integration and competition in CEMAC." IMF Working Paper 07/3.

Shah, Hemant, Carvajal, Ana, Bannister, Geoffrey, Chan-Lau, Jorge and Guerra, Ivan 2007. "Equity and private debt markets in Central America, Panama, and the Dominican Republic." IMF Working Paper 07/288. Washington: International Monetary Fund.

Steil, Benn 1999. "Regional financial market integration: Learning from the European Experience." *Tokyo Club Papers,* 12: 99–125.

Sy, Amadou N.R. 2007. "Local currency debt markets in the West African economic and monetary union." IMF Working Paper 07/256. Washington: International Monetary Fund.

Titelman, Daniel 2006. "Subregional financial cooperation: The experiences of Latin America and the Caribbean." In *Regional Financial Cooperation,* ed. Jose Antonio Ocampo, 200–26. Washington: Brookings Institution Press.

Tsangarides, Charalambos, Ewenczyk, Pierre and Hulej, Michal 2006. "Stylized facts on bilateral trade and currency unions: Implications for Africa." IMF Working Paper No. 06/31. Washington: International Monetary Fund.

World Bank 2007. "Financial sector integration in two regions of sub-Saharan Africa: How creating scale in financial markets can support growth and development." draft January. Washington: World Bank.

10
Access to Finance in Africa— Consolidating the Positive Trends

Jennifer Isern, Estelle Lahaye, and Audrey Linthorst

10.1 Introduction

Microfinance offers low-income people access to basic financial services such as loans, savings, money transfer services, and microinsurance. People living in poverty, like everyone else, need a diverse range of financial services to run their businesses, build assets, smooth consumption, and manage risks.

Low-income people often manage their household finances through a variety of financial relationships, including informal money lenders, savings clubs, and village banks that have thrived in Africa for decades. Traditionally, banks have not considered these clients to be a viable market.

In response, starting in the 1970s, different types of financial services providers emerged as microfinance institutions (MFIs). Covering a range of institutions, MFIs could be nongovernment organizations (NGOs), financial cooperatives, community-based development institutions like self-help groups and village banks, commercial and state banks, insurance and credit card companies, new mobile-phone based services, post offices, and other points of sale. Especially in Africa where only one in five people have access to finance, this diversity of MFIs is a definite strength, as it could foster more competition and better services for clients.

10.2 Chapter overview[1]

In 2007, Sub-Saharan Africa experienced encouraging economic growth of 6.7 percent and continued to accelerate progress in human development, improve infrastructure, and strengthen the policy environment. Africa also received renewed attention from the private sector, domestic and international investors, and development agencies. Microfinance has capitalized on these positive developments, experiencing strong growth in 2007.

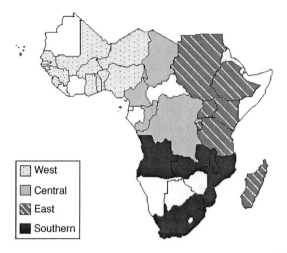

Figure 10.1 Subregional breakout

Given the diversity of experience in the Africa region, this chapter reviews overall developments throughout Africa and separate breakdowns for each of the four subregions: Central, East, Southern, and West Africa (see Figure 10.1). This chapter analyzes the development of the microfinance field, focusing on key growth trends, national and regional regulatory environments, funding flows and structure, and performance of MFIs.

10.2.1 General growth trends[2]

In 2007, 160 MFIs in Africa,[3] more than ever before, contributed to the benchmark data used for this chapter. These MFIs reached 5.2 million borrowers and 9 million depositors in 2007 alone. The total outstanding loan portfolio of these MFIs was just over 2.5 billion USD, while deposits exceeded 2.1 billion USD.

To provide further insights into growth and productivity changes, this chapter also utilizes trend data capturing information from 111 MFIs over the last two years.[4] As shown in Table 10.1, these trend data indicate a growth in borrowers of 25 percent (reaching 4.7 million borrowers in 2007), 5 percent higher than the global average growth in borrowers of 20 percent, and an even larger growth in depositors at 31 percent (reaching 7.2 million depositors in 2007). Loan portfolio grew 69 percent, exhibiting an increase of nearly 1 billion USD—a 47 percent loan portfolio growth of the median MFI when calculated in local currency. Deposits also experienced significant growth at 60 percent, reaching 1.8 million borrowers in 2007—the median MFI increasing its deposits by 17 percent when calculated in local currency (31 percent when looking only at MFIs with full financial intermediation).

Table 10.1   Volume figure trend data, by subregion

		Borrowers (Thousands)	Depositors (Thousands)	Loan Portfolio (USD Mil)	Deposits (USD Mil)
Africa	2006	3,785	5,473	1,320	1,148
	2007	4,731	7,177	2,236	1,839
	% Increase	25	31	69	60
Central region	2006	219	350	97	135
	2007	213	455	142	232
	% Increase	−3	30	46	72
Eastern region	2006	2,061	2,241	554	472
	2007	2,628	3,172	1,025	799
	% Increase	28	42	85	69
Southern region	2006	519	694	188	144
	2007	767	993	417	254
	% Increase	48	43	121	76
Western region	2006	986	2,189	481	396
	2007	1,123	2,557	652	553
	% Increase	14	17	36	40

While the general growth picture across Africa shows strong uptake in both lending and deposit taking, differences persist among the central, eastern, southern, and western subregions. Despite the larger growth in number of depositors than in number of borrowers, loan portfolio grew at a more rapid pace than deposits. The eastern and southern regions experienced the greatest growth in both borrowers and depositors, while the central region was the only one to actually decrease in number of borrowers. West Africa experienced growth, but on a much smaller scale, likely due to the much higher penetration rates in this region. Table 10.2 lists the top 10 countries by penetration rates of borrowers as well as depositors. Incidentally, these 10 countries had the greatest penetration rates for both groups. Five of them are from West Africa, indicating that microfinance is likely already meeting more of the demand here than in the other regions.

Despite having three countries in this list, East Africa continues to exhibit rapid growth; the market here is not yet saturated. The central region was the only region to experience a decrease in number of borrowers, exhibiting a drop of 3 percent. Cameroon witnessed the greatest decrease in total number of borrowers (in terms of both absolute number and percentage) of all of Africa, as MFIs worked to clean up their books, clearing them of loans with long-term delinquency. The central region represents the smallest microfinance market in Africa, with the lowest penetration rate of borrowers. Only 7.5 percent of reporting MFIs from Africa are based in this central region.

Table 10.2 Top 10 Countries in borrowers and depositors, by penetration rates

Country	Subregion	Population (Thousands)	Borrowers (Thousands)	Penetration Rate (%)	Depositors (Thousands)	Penetration Rate (%)
Kenya	Eastern	34,000	877	3	3,172	9
Togo	Western	6,000	90	2	344	6
Senegal	Western	12,000	221	2	654	5
Mali	Western	14,000	216	2	409	3
Ghana	Western	22,000	315	1	902	4
Burkina Faso	Western	13,000	129	1	523	4
Cameroon	Central	16,000	135	1	400	3
South Africa	Southern	47,000	632	1	783	2
Uganda	Eastern	29,000	216	1	482	2
Ethiopia	Eastern	71,000	1,427	2	732	1

The eastern region continued to exhibit the highest numbers across all volume figures. The total loan portfolio and amount of deposits, each demonstrating the largest absolute growth of all African regions in 2007, correspond to the significantly higher numbers of borrowers and depositors.

East Africa is the home of large-scale lenders: of the nine MFIs in this sample with over 100,000 borrowers, six are from East Africa. Despite their size, these large-scale MFIs still managed to meet Africa-wide growth rates of 25 percent, adding over half a million borrowers.

The southern region demonstrated the largest percentage growth in borrowers with nearly a 48 percent increase over the previous year (see Figure 10.2). This region also exhibited the greatest increase in average loan size as well as loan balance over GNI per capita, which grew by 27 percent from 2006 to 2007. The total loan portfolio for this region increased by 119 percent in local currency over the previous year. The market is highly segmented by types of institutions. Banks served most clients in the southern region, with 81 percent of the borrowers. NGOs served 13 percent, and nonbank financial intermediaries made up the remaining 6 percent. In addition, each institutional type served different products. Banks tended to have larger loan sizes; their median average loan balance over GNI per capita was 161.4 percent. NGO and nonbank financial intermediary median loan sizes over GNI per capita were much smaller, at 39.7 percent and 60.3 percent, respectively.

Deposit-taking institutions, such as cooperatives, banks, and rural banks, had the broadest outreach in West Africa. As a result, the region serviced twice as many depositors as borrowers. Six of the 10 MFIs reporting the highest total voluntary savings are from this subregion; five of these MFIs are cooperatives, which represent over 40 percent of the borrowers in West Africa, concentrated in the West African Economic and Monetary Union (WAEMU) countries.[5] Total deposits grew by 40 percent; cooperatives

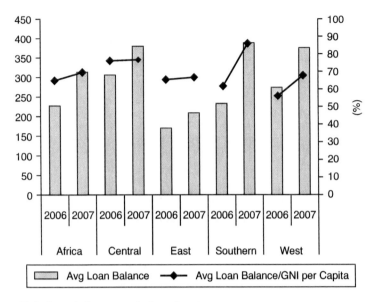

Figure 10.2   Loan balance trends, by subregion

covered 78 percent of this growth. Half of the NGOs reporting in this region also accepted deposits, and while this covers only 2 percent of the deposits, they did increase their total deposits by more than 100 percent. Lending did not grow as quickly as deposit taking, with only 36 percent growth in loan portfolio.

10.3   Legal and regulatory environment[6]

Governments in Sub-Saharan Africa increased their focus on regulating microfinance. Many countries in the region have included microfinance in banking legislation, broader nonbanking financial institution (NBFI) legislation, and microfinance-specific laws or regulations. Since 2002, 31 countries passed new or revised microfinance legislation, while 24 countries have adopted national microfinance strategies.[7]

Microfinance is becoming more integrated into formal financial systems, as a growing number of countries place the supervision of MFIs under the same body that supervises banks and other financial institutions. There are also a number of countries that are taking a more pragmatic proportionate approach to prudential/nonprudential regulations for financial institutions. Less encouragingly for improving the access of poor people to financial services, consumer protection measures, and particularly those for clients of financial services, are rare across the continent. Only one country has made allowances for small-value transactions in its anti-money laundering/combating the funding of terrorism (AML/CFT) regulations.

10.3.1 Microfinance laws and regulations

Countries have taken diverse approaches to microfinance laws and regulation, ranging from working within existing financial sector laws and regulations to developing specific new microfinance regulation (see Figure 10.3). A significant number of Sub-Saharan African countries (26)[8] have chosen to address regulating microfinance by implementing specialized microfinance laws or regulations. An additional four (Sudan, Zimbabwe, Cape Verde, and Guinea Bissau) drafted or have begun the process of drafting microfinance-specific legislation. In 15 countries, MFIs implicitly or explicitly fall under the broader banking or NBFI legislation. Only a handful of countries have no legislation in place to cover the microfinance sector.

10.3.1.1 Proportionate regulation

Sixteen countries have existing or draft legislation that provide for the categorization of MFIs by scope of activities or by size, and generally adjusts the type and level of regulation accordingly (see Figure 10.4). For example, under the CEMAC[9] microfinance law put into effect in 2002, MFIs are divided into three tiers: credit-only institutions, institutions that take savings from members only, and institutions that take deposits from the general public. Credit-only institutions and small institutions are not subject to the same prudential regulatory requirements as deposit-taking institutions. Mozambique divides institutions into two categories: those that are

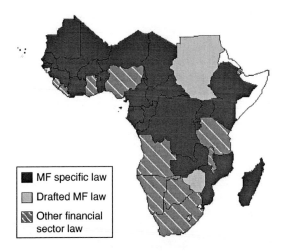

Figure 10.3 Microfinance regulation, by country

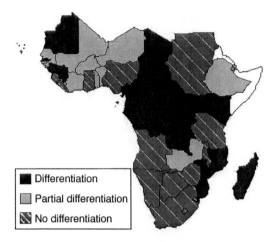

Figure 10.4   Proportionate regulation, by country

licensed and are prudentially regulated ("microbanks" and credit cooperatives) and those that are registered and are monitored by the Central Bank
(credit programs and savings and loans associations). In Uganda, legislation stipulates four different categories of financial institutions (commercial
banks, credit-only institutions, microfinance deposit-taking institutions,
and cooperatives), and it imposes different regulation for each "tier."

Ten countries partially differentiate among institutions. In Zambia, for
example, deposit-taking MFIs are subject to different consumer protection
disclosure requirements, such as posting their income statement and balance sheet in a conspicuous place on their premises.

10.3.1.2   Supervisory authority

The overall trend in Sub-Saharan Africa is to place the supervision of the
microfinance sector under the banking supervisory authority—indicating
that microfinance is becoming more integrated into the formal financial
system. The Central Bank is the regulator and supervisor in 31 countries.
Kenya, Mauritius, Namibia, and Uganda placed only deposit-taking MFIs
under the supervision of the Central Bank, while other MFIs are supervised
by the Ministry of Finance or another government authority.

In 29 Sub-Saharan African countries, the regulation and supervision of
financial cooperatives falls under the specialized microfinance or NBFI law
or even under the banking/financial institutions law.[10]

In 16 countries, cooperatives are regulated under a separate law or act
for cooperatives. In 27 countries, financial cooperatives are regulated
and supervised by the banking supervisory authority. In addition, in the

26 countries that have passed (or are about to pass) microfinance or NBFI laws since 2002, cooperatives are regulated and supervised by the banking supervisory authority in 21 of them.[11]

This indicates greater recognition of the role of cooperatives in the financial system and a trend toward more thorough supervision. In the remaining countries, where there is no specific legislation for financial cooperatives, financial cooperatives are regulated and supervised by the applicable cooperative regulatory authority (such as the Registrar of Cooperatives).

10.3.2 Broader financial sector laws and regulations

10.3.2.1 AML/CFT

As part of global efforts to ensure integrity and security of financial flows, the international community promotes compliance against a set of standards to address money laundering and terrorism financing risks. Financial institutions have a key role in undertaking AML/CFT measures. Implementation of these measures could be seen as conflicting with socioeconomic objectives of promoting financial inclusion as a means to improve income levels and address poverty. However, when implemented thoughtfully, the pursuit of financial inclusion and an effective AML/CFT regime are complementary to financial sector and national security policy objectives.

With the exception of Mozambique and Mauritius, all Sub-Saharan African countries have passed laws or regulations addressing AML/CFT since the Financial Action Task Force (FATF) issued its 40 recommendations on AML in 2003 and eight recommendations on CFT in 2001 (amended to 9 in 2004).

The key challenge, however, is implementation of such laws and regulations, especially in the context of low balance and low transaction value as seen in most MFIs. Only seven countries have a financial intelligence unit (FIU) in place (South Africa, Mauritius, Gabon, Cameroon, Niger, Nigeria, and Senegal), although at least four others have issued regulations to set up an FIU (see Figure 10.5). South Africa is the only country that seems to have adapted know-your-customer (KYC) requirements and provided appropriate exemptions on low-value transactions in recognition of the difficulties low-income people face in providing proof of residence.

10.3.2.2 Consumer Protection

In general, very little information is available about general consumer protection measures in Sub-Saharan Africa and even less on consumer protection measures for financial services. Only two countries (South Africa and Mauritius) have consumer protection measures for clients of financial institutions and three others have a consumer protection law or are considering

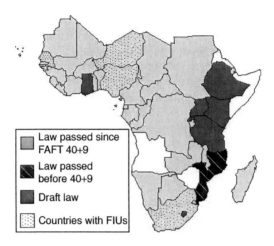

Figure 10.5 AML/CFT regulation, by country

such a law (Malawi, Kenya, and Uganda) (see Table 10.3).[12] Mauritius, for example, includes a measure in its 2004 Banking Act that provides for the appointment of an ombudsman for dealing with complaints against financial institutions by their customers. Twenty countries have included in their regulation some kind of disclosure requirement by financial institutions or specifically MFIs to their customers.

10.3.2.3 *Interest Rate Caps*

Sixteen countries have no interest rate ceilings, including countries such as Liberia and Lesotho that have lifted interest rate ceilings in recent years (see Figure 10.6). Eleven countries[13] have some type of interest rate ceilings:

- WAEMU (eight countries): Currently fixed at 27 percent for MFIs and 18 percent for banks.
- Namibia: Approximately 27 percent (linked to the prime rate).
- South Africa: For microloans [(RR x 2.2) + 20%] per year where RR is the South African Reserve Bank Repurchase Rate.
- Guinea: Legislation specifies that the interest rate cannot increase by more than 33 percent over the previous year's rate.

The CEMAC countries and Ethiopia have a minimum interest rate on deposits (3.25 and 2 percent, respectively). In other countries, interest rate restrictions are tied to certain types of loans (agricultural loans in Nigeria), to type of lending (10 percent maximum profit margin for Islamic lending in Sudan), to a targeted government lending program (Uganda, Benin), or to a particular institutional type (cooperatives in Ghana).

Table 10.3 Consumer protection regulation, by country

Consumer protection law or regulation	Countries		
Have consumer protection law	Kenya Malawi	South Africa Uganda	Mauritius
Disclosure norms	Botswana CEMAC Countries (6) Liberia	Mozambique Namibia Tanzania	WAEMU Countries (8) Zambia
No disclosure requirements	Angola Ethiopia	Lesotho Madagascar	Nigeria

IR caps for banks
IR caps for MFIs
Restrictions on some products
No IR caps

Figure 10.6 Interest ceiling, by country

10.4 Funding microfinance[14]

Funders had total commitments of 1.76 billion USD, covering 716 projects in all 48 countries in Sub-Saharan Africa. Despite a 12 percent decrease in external funding in 2007, funders continued to be strongly interested in supporting access to finance as the total number of projects increased by 61 percent. This number includes funding from a wide variety of funders, though most are noncommercial, using public monies. In contrast, a CGAP survey that focuses on microfinance investment vehicles (MIVs)—private funds that typically have more of a commercial orientation—reports that MIVs had invested only 69 million USD in Sub-Saharan Africa.[15] This decrease in external funding has meant that MFIs that use deposits mobilization as

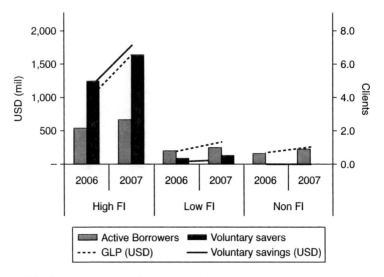

Figure 10.7 Financial intermediation trend data

a main funding source have continued to experience rapid growth, while those with low or no financial intermediation have remained relatively on par with their 2006 volume figures (see Figure 10.7).

10.4.1 Geographic concentration of funding

Funding is heavily concentrated in East Africa and certain countries in West Africa, with Uganda having the largest number (62) of financial access programs (see Figure 10.8). Funding is least concentrated in Central and South Africa. Funders are also investing in regional projects that do not focus on specific countries. However, only 12 percent of funding (210 million USD) goes to regional initiatives. Seven countries (Ghana, Uganda, Kenya, Tanzania, Ethiopia, Mali, and Mozambique) account for nearly 50 percent of total committed funding, while the 20 least funded countries account for only 3 percent.

10.4.2 Funders' activities at different levels of the financial system

Funders' activities can be distributed among three categories of the financial system: (1) projects supporting retail institutions, (2) projects supporting financial infrastructure, and (3) projects supporting policy environments. In 2007, funders favored retail institutions projects, with 59 percent of their projects supporting a wide range of financial and nonfinancial institutions. They mostly invested in projects that provided funding (64 percent) through grants and loans to MFIs and projects that provided technical assistance (31 percent) through grants (see Figure 10.9).

Funders also invested in financial infrastructure. Usually, funders look to invest in projects that will support locally available market infrastructure and services, including auditors, rating agencies, networks and associations, credit bureaus, transfer and payment systems, information technology, and technical service providers. In 2007, those projects represented 25 percent of their projects. Projects at this level are divided among (1) capacity-building activities (55 percent), such as training of trainer courses, audits, management information systems, and MFI ratings; (2) infrastructure (22 percent) in the form of support toward payments systems and credit bureaus and

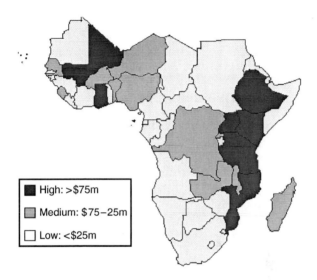

Figure 10.8 Funding amount per country (in USD)

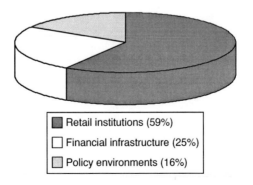

Figure 10.9 Projects, by activity level (percent based on the number of projects)

accounting standards; and (3) refinancing through apexes or banks to MFIs (14 percent).

Funders supported government policies and systems, including laws and regulations and enforcement bodies, such as banking supervision. In 2007, 16 percent of funders' projects focused on policy environments, and they were equally divided into regulation/supervision (46 percent) and broader policy issues (44 percent), such as interest rate regime, tax issues, and national strategies. There is a strong trend of funder collaboration at the policy level as these projects tended to be large, allowing funders to pool resources, provide specialized expertise, and achieve economies of scale. In 2007, 70 percent of all policy projects were supported by two or more funders, mostly multilateral and bilateral donors.

10.4.3   Funding instruments

Funders use a variety of instruments depending on activities, overall project objective, comparative advantage, country context, other stakeholders, etc. In 2007 they favored grants (34 percent) and loans (32 percent). Bilateral funders and international NGOs were the main providers of grants, while loans were funded primarily by development finance institutions (DFIs), MIVs, private foundations, multilateral funders, and international NGOs. In-kind funding (9 percent) was typically coupled with either a loan or a grant. Equity funding (5 percent) and guarantees (3 percent) came largely from DFIs (see Figure 10.10).

External funding for microfinance is heavily focused on the eastern and western regions. The central region experienced the largest percentage growth in external funding; however, this remains much smaller than in

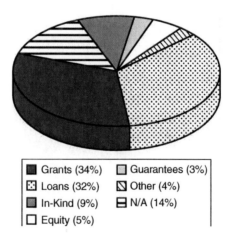

Figure 10.10   Funding instruments (percent based on the number of projects)

Table 10.4 Funding structure trend data, by subregion (USD mil)

		Deposits	Commercial borrowings	Other debt	Equity
Africa	2006	1,148	243	376	557
	2007	1,839	343	680	912
	% Increase	60	41	81	64
Central	2006	135	5	21	19
	2007	232	9	23	38
	% Increase	72	81	12	103
East	2006	472	116	196	183
	2007	799	183	413	436
	% Increase	69	58	111	138
Southern	2006	144	30	35	198
	2007	254	36	54	228
	% Increase	76	20	54	15
West	2006	196	93	124	557
	2007	553	114	190	912
	% Increase	40	24	53	64

any other region (see Table 10.4). The funding structure of MFIs in Africa differs significantly by both region and charter type. Certain regions and charter types witnessed considerable change in their funding structure over the last year, while others remained relatively constant (see Figures 10.11 and 10.12).

By far, the central region places the most weight on mobilizing deposits as a source of funding (see Figure 10.12). At the same time, it was the only region to experience a decrease in its leveraging, from 2.7 in 2006 to 2.2 in 2007. Although deposits, commercial borrowings, and other debt all increased, equity increased more rapidly. An infusion of capital in the banks in this region, which increased their equity by 309 percent over the last year, accounted for 85 percent of this total increase.

The eastern region witnessed a slight increase in its debt-to-equity ratio, from 2.3 to 2.6. Overall, commercial debt increased by 57 percent: commercial borrowings grew by 41 percent as deposits increased a significant 69 percent. This growth in deposits, the largest of all regions throughout Africa, indicates the increased importance of deposits as a funding source for MFIs in East Africa. While the southern region has increased its leverage a little bit, it remains by far the least leveraged region in Africa. Forty percent of this region's financing came from its equity, more than any other region. This is due to the combination of large banks and NGOs in the region. Banks observed a significant drop in their debt-to-equity ratio while experiencing growth, indicating an infusion of capital. They have also

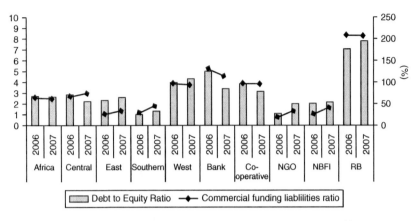

Figure 10.11 Funding structure trends, by subregion and charter type[16]

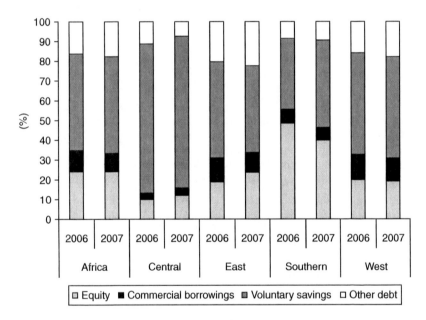

Figure 10.12 Funding structure trends, by subregion

witnessed a significant decrease in commercial funding liabilities ratio due to this increased emphasis on paid-in capital. NGOs, despite having doubled their leverage in 2007, continued to exhibit the lowest debt-to-equity ratio of all charter types. With little recourse for external funding, they rely primarily on donations and retained earnings for new capital. The increased leverage that they experienced in 2007 was due both to increased borrowings, as well as the fact that the small percent of NGOs that are allowed to accept deposits more than doubled their amount of deposits over the last year, as represented by the increasing commercial funding liabilities ratio.

Despite the decreased leverage of cooperatives, whose debt-to-equity ratio dropped from 3.8 to 3.2 over the last year, West Africa witnessed an increased leverage, with the debt-to-equity ratio growing from 3.8 to 4.3. The increasing leverage of the rural banks (from 7.1 to 7.8) plays a role in this change, as does the 72 percent increase in commercial debt. These rural banks exhibited both a debt-to-equity ratio more than double that of any other charter type, as well as a significantly higher commercial funding liabilities ratio. This is due to their emphasis on deposits, which continued to be the largest source of funding within this region. Commercial borrowings also experienced an increase of 41 percent since 2006.

10.5   Performance trend analysis

The financial performance of African MFIs varies widely, although MFIs in each African region managed to meet ongoing expenses from operating revenues, on average, before adjustments for subsidy, standardized loan provisioning, and inflation. Institutions in Africa face significantly higher operational costs than other global regions. As seen in Figure 10.13, only MFIs in the southern region achieved profitability (positive return on assets).

10.5.1   Central Africa

The central region, the only region that had not yet reached a point where MFIs were covering all operational costs, achieved sustainability. Financial

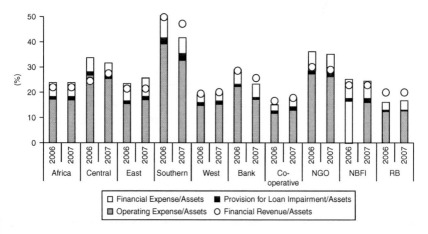

Figure 10.13   Deconstruction of return on assets, by subregion and charter type

expenses decreased by 1 percent. As cost recovery increased in the region, so did the outreach of profitable MFIs. By the end of 2007, profitable MFIs served 44 percent of borrowers, up from 24 percent a year earlier. MFIs in the central region continued to experience difficulties with their portfolio quality: PAR > 30 days remained stable at 7 percent over the last two years, and PAR > 90 remained above 4 percent. Just over 31 percent of MFIs reported PAR > 90 days greater than 10 percent (see Figure 10.14). Persistent portfolio quality problems remain a major obstacle to MFI profitability, despite the decreasing operational and financial expenses.

10.5.2   West Africa

In 2007, the West was the only region where the median MFI actually reached profitability. MFIs saw decreased operating expense ratios, predominately due to decreased personnel expenses. Staff productivity increased, with the ratio of borrowers per loan officer climbing from 209 in 2006 to 251 in 2007. Slightly increased revenues helped the western region's median MFI reach profitability for the first time in that year. Despite all of these advances, portfolio quality in West Africa remained poor. Twenty-two percent of MFIs reported PAR > 30 days at over 10 percent, while three MFIs had PAR > 30 over 20 percent, and one large-scale MFI reported PAR > 30 at over 50 percent. A majority of these MFIs with such substandard portfolio quality are cooperatives and rural banks—institutions that may have the greatest exposure to agricultural downturns. The IMCEC law that legislates the microfinance sector in WAEMU countries mandates that MFIs cover PAR starting at 90 days, without demanding any risk coverage before this point.

Rural banks overcame high portfolio risk to become the most profitable charter type in all of Africa with low expense ratios and relatively high

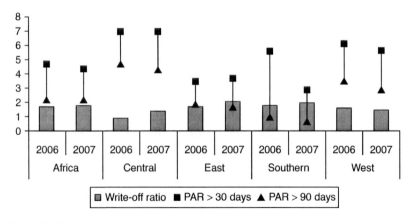

Figure 10.14   Portfolio quality trend, by subregion

revenues (their nominal yield is the highest of any charter type in Africa at 46 percent). They achieved a return on assets of 2 percent and a profit margin of 1 percent. Their overall profitability was greater than that of all other charter types, with the median MFI reporting a profit margin of 15 percent. Cooperatives, which captured the largest number of clients in the western region, experienced the lowest total expense ratio, helping maintain the positive overall financial performance of MFIs in the region.

10.5.3   Southern Africa

Moderate decreases in revenue combined with much lower expenses due to largely increased loan sizes brought the southern region's profitability up 6 percent. At the end of 2007, the region was 5 percent away from breaking even. This region continued to experience significantly higher expenses than other regions due to higher average operational costs. However, there were significant drops in financial and operational expenses (from 8 percent to 6 percent, and 39 percent to 33 percent, respectively), which led to an overall 4 percent decrease in the total expense ratio. This helped compensate for a 7 percent drop in nominal yield.

Improved portfolio quality also helped to increase sustainability in this region: PAR > 30 days decreased from 5.6 percent in 2006 to 3 percent in 2007, while PAR > 90 days exhibited less of a decrease. These trends coincide with the changes in profitability for banks, indicating the prevalence of formal financial systems in the region.

Banks accounted for nearly 78 percent of all borrowers in the southern region and tended to focus on higher balance loans. Throughout Africa, banks experienced a profit margin growth of 8 percent over the previous year. These increased revenues, along with a decreasing operating expense ratio (down from 22 percent to 17 percent) created significant improvements on overall financial performance; while return on assets and return on equity were both at 0 percent in 2006, in 2007 they rose to 3 percent and 14 percent, respectively. In the southern region, the number of borrowers participating with nonprofitable MFIs remained relatively stable, while the number of clients participating with profitable MFIs increased substantially.

NGOs also played a key role in microfinance in the southern region, particularly in Malawi and Mozambique. Despite remaining the least profitable charter type, NGOs throughout Africa had improved their performance, experiencing a growth in profit margin from –21 percent in 2006 to –14 percent in 2007. Slightly decreased expenses, along with increasing efficiency, were key elements of this change.

10.5.4   East Africa

The eastern region was the only region to witness a decrease in profitability. Revenues remained on par with the previous year's, but the total expense

Box 10.1   Start up growth

African microfinance remains a dynamic marketplace. Start-ups in Africa have experienced extraordinary growth in both borrowers and depositors over the last year. A total of 17 MFIs (all four years old or younger) spanning all regions and charter types, added nearly 130,000 new borrowers and just under 100,000 depositors in 2007. The most significant growth in borrowers was in the East at 584 percent. These start-ups in the East are in Tanzania, Uganda, Ethiopia, and Kenya; some are affiliated with international organizations, others are stand-alone MFIs. A 156 percent increase in number of depositors brought the central region start-ups to nearly 45,000, while deposits grew by 224 percent, the largest growth of all regions. The greatest growth in number of depositors, as well as amount of total deposits, was in the central region. In general, throughout Africa, among these start-ups, deposits have grown more rapidly than loan portfolio, highlighting the prominence of deposits as a commercial funding source.

NGOs gained the largest number of clients, with an absolute growth of nearly 100,000 borrowers, an increase of 200 percent. They also experienced the largest growth in loan portfolio, jumping up 245 percent to nearly 19 million USD. Banks witnessed the largest growth in depositors and deposits at 132 percent and 223 percent, respectively, ending up with over 57,000 depositors and over 50 million USD in deposits. NBFIs reached even more depositors, at over 82,000, but the deposits were much smaller, with the total amount of deposits in 2007 at just over 9 million USD. The rural banks actually witnessed a 15 percent decrease in number of borrowers, along with a 30 percent decrease in number of depositors. Their loan portfolio and total deposits, however, exhibited increases of 18 percent and 11 percent, respectively. Cooperatives cover the smallest portion of these start-ups, with fewer than 1,000 borrowers and 6,500 depositors. They have been experiencing positive growth, but it has had little impact on these overall numbers.

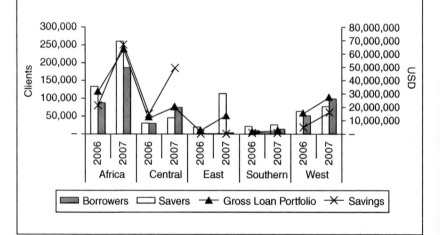

ratio increased from 24 percent to 29 percent, lowering the region's profit margin by 2 percent to reach –15 percent. While the number of borrowers reached by profitable MFIs remained constant, the number of borrowers reached by nonprofitable MFIs almost doubled in that year.

Portfolio quality in the eastern region continued to be one of the strongest in Africa, with a consistent PAR > 30 days increasing only slightly from 3.5 percent to 3.7 percent and PAR > 90 days dropping from 1.9 percent to 1.7 percent.

NBFIs accounted for just over 64 percent of the MFIs in this region, reaching almost 40 percent of borrowers. They experienced increases in overall financial performance over the last year. Profitability grew by 7 percent, leaving the median MFI just 2 percent short of breaking even. Productivity improved, with the ratio of borrowers per loan officers increasing from 294 to 306 in that year, and the ratio of depositors per staff member increasing from 21 to 47—still significantly lower than all other charter types that promote deposits, but an increase nevertheless.

10.6   Conclusion

The year 2007 witnessed encouraging trends in regulation, funding, growth, and performance of the microfinance sector in Sub-Saharan Africa. Microfinance was increasingly integrated into the formal financial systems across the region, enabling the field to grow substantially in number of borrowers and depositors, loan portfolio, and deposits. External funding decreased by 12 percent, while total number of projects increased by 61 percent.

Given the economic downturn starting in 2008 it is likely that external funding will continue to decrease; however, the effects may be mitigated since many African MFIs are strong in deposit mobilization. Microfinance in Africa continues to face challenges with low penetration rates and high operational costs. But with the increasingly integrated financial systems, emphasis on deposit mobilization, and the promising growth of start-up MFIs (see Box 10.1), Africa is striving toward increased outreach and sustainability.

Notes

Housed at the World Bank, CGAP is a global resource center for microfinance standards, operational tools, training, and advisory services. Its members—including bilateral, multilateral, and private funders of microfinance programs—are committed to building more inclusive financial systems for the poor. For more information, visit www.cgap.org.

The Microfinance Information Exchange (MIX) is the leading provider of business information and data services for the microfinance industry. Dedicated to strengthening the microfinance sector by promoting transparency, MIX provides detailed performance and financial information on microfinance institutions, investors, networks and services providers associated with the industry. MIX does this through a variety of publicly available platforms, including MIX Market (www. mixmarket.org) and the *MicroBanking Bulletin*. MIX is an independent, nonprofit company founded by CGAP, and sponsored by CGAP, the Citi Foundation, Deutsche Bank Americas Foundation, Omidyar Network, Open Society Institute and the Soros Economic Development Fund, Rockdale Foundation, IFAD, and others. For more information about MIX, visit www.themix.org.

1. This chapter is based on the joint publication by CGAP and MIX, "Africa Microfinance Analysis and Benchmarking Report." 2008.
2. For benchmarking purposes, MIX collects and prepares MFI financial and outreach data according to international microfinance reporting standards as applied in MicroBanking Bulletin. Raw data are collected from the MFI, inputted into standard reporting formats and cross-checked with audited financial statements, rating and other third-party due diligence reports, as available. Performance results are then adjusted, using industry standard adjustments, to eliminate subsidy, guarantee minimal provisioning for risk, and reflect the impact of inflation on institutional performance. This process increases comparability of performance results across institutions.
3. Data source: 2007 MIX MicroBanking Bulletin Benchmark Data. In 2007, MIX collected benchmarking data for 160 MFIs throughout Sub-Saharan Africa. These institutions were selected based on their leadership in overall outreach and their ability to provide transparent, detailed reporting. This chapter analyzes this sample to review MFI financial and operating performance.
4. Data source: 2006–2007 MIX MicroBanking Bulletin Trend Data. A balanced data panel of 111 Sub-Saharan African MFIs that reported to MIX in both 2006 and 2007 creates trend data for these years.
5. WAEMU countries include Benin, Burkina Faso, Côte d'Ivoire, Mali, Niger, Senegal, and Togo. For more information, see MIX report *UEMOA Benchmarking Report* (published in French).
6. Data source: 2007 CGAP Policy Mapping. In 2007, CGAP completed a survey of the regulatory policies for financial services in sub-Saharan Africa. The survey is based on an analysis of documents mostly found through French and English language Internet research, with limited follow-up to resolve ambiguities or confirm accuracy. Given these limitations, the survey may not be fully complete for the countries covered.
7. Typically, national microfinance strategies are publicly approved documents, developed through a consultative process, and include an overview of microfinance in the country, a vision for the sector, strategic objectives, and an action plan for implementation.
8. The number would be 27, but Guinea Bissau, though part of WAEMU, has not yet passed the first PARMEC law. PARMEC (Project d'Appui à la Réglementation sur les Mutuelles d'Epargne et de Crédit) was a project in the 1990s to support the regulation of MFIs in the eight countries of WAEMU.
9. Cameroon, Congo, Central African Republic, Equatorial Guinea, Gabon, and Chad are the members of CEMAC (Communauté Economique et Monétaire de l'Afrique Centrale).
10. This number includes six countries (South Africa, Madagascar, Rwanda, Zambia, Gambia, and Tanzania) in which cooperatives fall under both a cooperative law and a microfinance or credit law.

11. This figure includes the eight WAEMU countries and the six CEMAC countries where the Ministries of Finance also play a role in licensing and supervising MFIs.
12. Applicability to financial institutions is not explicit.
13. Additional research on interest rate ceiling in Nigeria is currently being undertaken.
14. Data source: 2007 CGAP Regional Funder Survey for Sub-Saharan Africa. In 2007, CGAP completed a survey of funder activities in the region, and 40 respondents provided self-reported information on their general projects, specific activities in each country, and funding instruments.
15. Does not include Oikocredit, Triodos Fair Share Fund, Triodos DOEN Fund, and Hivos Triodos Fund
16. Commercial funding liabilities ratio: (Voluntary and Time Deposits + Borrowings at Commercial Interest Rates)/Adjusted Average Gross Loan Portfolio

References

Note: Additional information on Africa MFI participants, indicator definitions, and Africa benchmarks 2007 can be found in the joint publication by Isern, Lahaye, CGAP and Linthorst, MIX, "Africa Microfinance Analysis and Benchmarking Report." 2008. http://www.themix.org/publications/2008-africa-microfinance-analysis-and-benchmarking-report

CGAP 2008 "2007 CGAP Regional Funder Survey: Sub-Saharan Africa." Washington, D.C.: CGAP. http://www.cgap.org/p/site/c/template.rc/1.26.3111/

CGAP 2008 "Sub-Saharan Africa Policy Mapping August 2008." Washington, D.C.: CGAP. www.cgap.org/p/site/c/template.rc/1.26.3801

CGAP "SmartAid for Microfinance Index." Retrieved November 10, 2008 from CGAP. http://www.cgap.org/p/site/c/template.rc/1.11.7956/1.26.3302

Microfinance Regulation and Supervision Resource Center. CGAP, Retrieved 2007. http://www.microfinanceregulationcenter.org/resource_centers/reg_sup

11
Developing Credit Reporting in Africa: Opportunities and Challenges

Nataliya Mylenko

11.1 Introduction

Credit information registries are essential for the well functioning credit market. They allow lenders to better assess and manage risks, help good borrowers to gain access to finance, and are believed to help reduce overindebtedness.

Until about 10 years ago, few countries outside of OECD and Latin America had operational credit bureaus. In recent years, as retail credit grew dramatically around the world and technology became more available, many countries in Eastern Europe and Asia, and now in the Middle East and North Africa, established credit bureaus. Sub-Saharan Africa, excluding South Africa, is the only region without fully functioning credit bureaus to date. Quite a few countries, including Mozambique, Nigeria and Rwanda, have registries operated by the central banks. These, however, were primarily established with the purpose of supporting banking supervision. They focus on larger loans, and due to lack of adequate technology and incentives, are not able to provide timely and accurate information. Both coverage and scope[1] of information in these registries is limited (Figures 11.1 and 11.2).

The demand for information by financial institutions on the one side and the pressure from the bank supervisors to improve risk management practices on the other, led to several initiatives in the Africa region to develop credit bureaus. Within the past five years important legal changes were made to enable private credit bureau operations in Ghana, Uganda, Tanzania and Zambia, and at least three private credit bureaus were initiated in Nigeria. Several countries, including Mozambique, Angola, Madagascar and Mauritius have initiatives to develop credit reporting to better serve needs of lenders. With these initiatives in place within a 2–3 year timeframe, fully fledged credit bureaus are expected to operate in Ghana, Kenya, Nigeria and Uganda, and other countries are likely to follow shortly thereafter.

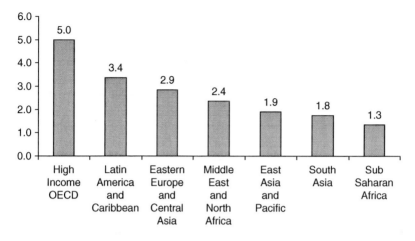

Figure 11.1   Credit information index by region
Source: Doing Business 2009.

11.2   Africa credit markets—context

African credit markets are underdeveloped, with the lowest levels of credit penetration in the world (Figure 11.2). In the region where political and macroeconomic stability is only recently established, most banks until 2–3 years ago focused on foreign exchange, trade and treasury operations. With the stabilization of macroeconomic environment, lower inflation and decreasing treasury yields, banks increasingly turn to lending to the private sector. Credit growth picked up significantly in many markets. Starting from a low base, 50–100% growth rates in terms of the number of clients are common.

But lending in Africa is challenging. Weak creditor rights and virtual inability to enforce contracts makes lending a risky business. Countries in Africa also lack infrastructure taken for granted in most countries in the world. Very few places have street addresses, multiplicity of languages complicates recording of names and often no identification documentation is available. This is on top of constant power outages and very expensive (if available) telecommunications infrastructure. It is difficult to check corporate records to make sure a company is registered. Most likely it is not possible to check if collateral is already being used for some other obligation. As a result, most lending relies on local market and community knowledge. While a perfectly acceptable practice, it significantly restricts the ability of banks to scale up lending to support economic growth. Fuzzy information about borrower creditworthiness also does not help to ensure consistent underwriting practices and makes banks vulnerable to fraud.

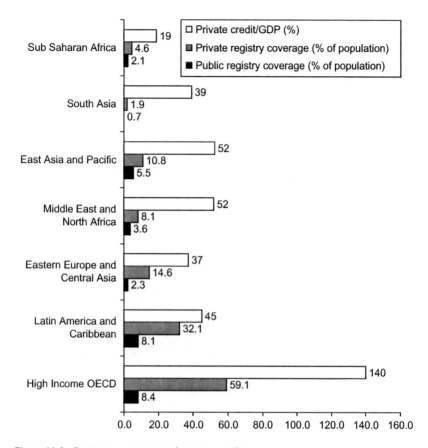

Figure 11.2   Registry coverage and private credit
Source: Doing Business 2009, World Development Indicators.

As a result, in a market with seemingly untapped potential for credit extension, credit penetration is strikingly low. Market estimates are difficult, as consistent cross country data on the numbers of credit clients does not exist. Some estimates include Mozambique, with 15 million people and 200,000 credit accounts in banks, and Tanzania, with an estimated 2–3% of the population served by the banking system.

11.3   The role of credit registries

11.3.1   Reducing defaults
Credit bureaus are not going to solve all of the problems in African credit markets. But, credit bureaus can help lenders to manage risks better. This

is particularly important as economic growth is likely to slow as the global financial crisis spreads to developing countries.

In many African countries only 1–3% of the population is exposed to credit. In this environment, the first and foremost challenge is to develop a credit culture. Borrowers know that contract enforcement is weak, so credit repayment suffers. The banks with good repayment rates are the ones with strong credit risk management and proactive approach for collections. Recent research indicates that credit bureaus are able to improve credit repayment rates by reducing information asymmetries and moral hazard problems. For example, one study[2] used data from the public credit registry in Argentina to assess the potential reduction in the default rate if a bank starts using credit registry information in addition to its own information on clients. By knowing a potential borrower's credit history with other lenders and understanding the level of that borrower's overall indebtedness, banks are able to screen better and avoid approving loans to high risk clients. Almost without exception, large banks are reluctant to join credit registries because they already have information on a large number of borrowers and are not likely to benefit from additional data available in the registry. The study confirms anecdotal evidence and estimates that small banks stand to benefit more than large ones and could reduce default rate by up to 79% from an average of 2.42% to 0.52%. But even for large banks, the study estimates a potential for 41% reduction in default rates Figure 11.3).

Another study[3] looked at the inclusion of microfinance lenders in the credit bureau and its effect on loan repayment. In this study, the fact that MFI started reporting information to a bureau and using its reports did not in itself have a major effect on repayment. However, when credit bureau

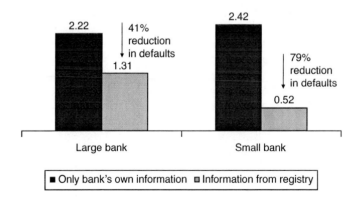

Figure 11.3 Credit registry information and potential reduction in defaults

Source: Powell, Mylenko, Miller, and Majnoni (2003). "Public Credit Information Systems: Evaluating Available Information", World Bank.

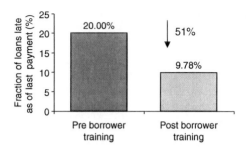

Figure 11.4   Fraction of loans late as of last payment

Source: Janvry, Alain de, Craig McIntosh, and Elisabeth Sadoulet, "The Supply and Demand Side Impacts of Credit Market Information", June 2007.

together with MFIs organized training to explain borrowers the role of the credit bureau and the importance of building a strong credit history, repayment rates improved dramatically and the number of late payments reduced by more than 50%. (Figure 11.4). This finding highlights the importance of borrower education and awareness in improving credit performance.

Overall, credit bureaus provide important tools and are able to assist banks to significantly improve their risk management practices and portfolio quality. This will only be possible, however, if banks both fully integrate the use of credit information in their loan approval and portfolio management processes, and educate borrowers on the impact their credit history has for the future access to credit.

11.4   Increasing access

Credit bureaus allow borrowers to build reputational collateral and use it as a basis for gaining access to credit and to better terms of financing. One recent study[4] analyzes the relationship between information sharing and credit in 129 countries and finds that existence of credit registries is positively correlated with the depth of financial market measured by private credit to GDP. The study also estimates that the private credit to GDP ratio is higher 3–5 years after the establishment of a credit registry, and the difference is statistically significant.

Another study[5] uses firm-level information to assess the correlations between the existence of credit registries, and use of finance, and perceptions of financing constraints by borrowers. Using information on 5000 firms in 51 countries the study finds that firms are less likely to report access to finance as a major problem in countries with credit bureaus. The study also finds that usage of credit is higher in countries with credit bureaus (Figure 11.5).

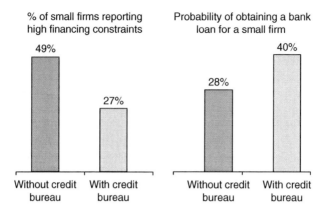

Figure 11.5 Access to finance is easier in countries with credit bureaus
Source: Love, I., and Mylenko, N. 2004. "Credit Reporting and Financing Constraints." World Bank Policy Research Working Paper 3142.

Often information sharing starts with the exchange of data on nonperforming loans or so-called negative information. While such information improves the ability of a lender to screen borrowers, it does not provide a full picture of the borrower's ability to repay. Recent studies confirm that sharing information on performing loans and overall borrower indebtedness allow creditors to estimate risks better and hence approve loans to a larger number of borrowers while maintaining low levels of defaults (Figure 11.6).

The ability of credit registries to significantly improve access to credit also critically depends on the inclusion of information from a broad set of lenders. An estimate in Figure 11.6 shows that combining information from retail stores issuing store cards with the information on credit cards from banks can potentially increase the number of approved applications by 11% while maintaining a default rate of 3%. Having only information on existing bank clients does not expand the base of served clients and has an impact only on risk management and potentially allowing good borrowers to get better terms of credit. Including information beyond the banking sector is the key, as it would allow a person paying electricity bills on time, for example, to demonstrate ability to pay even in the absence of formal income. This information can be used by lenders as a verifiable proxy of income. Combining such information with banking information would be ideal, but in reality poses a major challenge due to the legal constraints and lack of a common platform to discuss information sharing among such diverse entities as banks, utilities, telecoms and firms selling goods using deferred payment schemes. As a result, in countries where a credit bureau initiative comes from the banking industry, the initial solution is to focus

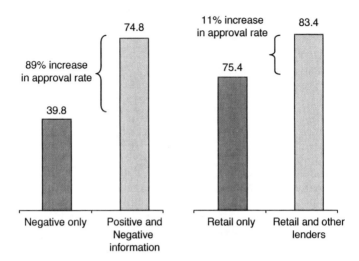

Figure 11.6   Percent of applicants who obtain a loan

Source: Barron, J. M. and Michael Staten 2003. "The Value of Comprehensive Credit Reports: Lessons from U.S. Experience", Credit Reporting Systems and the International Economy, M. Miller (ed.). MIT Press.

on the exchange of banking information only, as in Kenya for example, and expand the scope of data in the future.

11.5   Reforming the credit information system

11.5.1   Banking sector can be a catalyst for information exchange

In most developed countries where credit bureaus were set up decades ago they did not start by collecting information from banks. Originally, information came from retailers providing credit to their customers. Customer confidentiality was not restricted and (probably more importantly) these retailers did not view credit as their core business but as a means to sell more goods. Hence they did not view credit information as their key asset and a source of competitive advantage, so they were willing to exchange it. Over time, banks saw the value of the information in these credit bureaus and joined in too.

In Africa, where the estimated share of bank credit is over 90% of the total, it is a faster route to get banks on board from the start. This poses a challenge as most banks operate in a competitive environment and are not willing to share information on borrowers, especially the good ones. Part of the reason for this is probably the lack of understanding of a credit bureau operation model. Credit bureaus normally do not sell a list of all clients with all their information to anyone willing to pay for it. Only the entity supplying information can buy a report. Lenders can only obtain a report if a customer has requested a credit. Of course, a lender must trust that a bureau will actually stick to the rules and keep information confidential. Lack of such trust combined with the weak contract enforcement and governance environment can easily prevent a bureau from starting. The issue can be solved as successful examples of operating credit registries in other emerging markets demonstrate, but significant lender education work is needed.

This challenge is not unique to Africa. Eastern Europe, where no bureaus existed until 10 years ago, faced similar problems. While banks declared interest in starting a credit registry, they stopped short of initiating information exchange. The response in several countries such as Russia and Kazakhstan was to mandate information sharing by banks to a private credit registry. The result is that within 3 years of passing the laws both countries have very active credit bureaus. Several countries in Africa opted for a similar approach. The new legislation passed in Ghana, Kenya and Uganda requires banks to participate in a credit bureau.

11.6   Clear legal and regulatory framework is necessary to enable information exchange

In Africa, as in other regions, the key obstacle to information sharing is a lack of necessary legal and regulatory framework and enforcement capability. In countries with common or civil law traditions, banks are bound by strict confidentiality restrictions. In common law countries they are mostly contractual. In civil law countries these are explicitly stated in the law. Banks are generally not allowed to disclose any information relating to customer accounts. At the same time, international practice even in countries with strict bank secrecy provisions such as Switzerland, show that information can be shared if a customer agrees to it. The solution is simple: a bank has to put in a sentence in the credit agreement stating that the customer agrees that the information regarding loan performance will be disclosed to a credit bureau. It could be simple, but banks generally are not willing to share information. In the presence of a vague legal framework, where multiple interpretations as to what constitutes a sufficient authorization to share data are possible, information sharing does not occur. As a result, most countries focus on developing a legal framework which enables information sharing and provides adequate protection for data subject rights. Such laws enable sharing of positive and negative information among a broad set of creditors and provide for the mechanisms to ensure data security and resolve disputes over information inaccuracies.

Depending on the existing legal framework in a country a new law may be necessary. In some cases, where a regulator has sufficient authority a regulation issued by a bank supervisor may be sufficient to begin information sharing among banks. In the long-term, broader legislation—either specific credit information law or data protection legislation—is necessary to support a full-scale credit information exchange including bank and nonbank entities.

11.7   Private, public or a combination of a public-private solution may be optimal for a given market

Empirical evidence suggests that private bureaus may be best placed to serve the needs of lenders.[6] On the ground experience shows that private bureaus are better placed to provide new services, and in the presence of competition are able to improve the quality of information and deliver low cost solutions. However, voluntary private credit bureaus do not have information from all, and often this means the largest, credit providers. Thus they have a significant flaw—not being able to show complete picture of borrower indebtedness. Moreover, private voluntary bureaus take a very long time to establish, as many stakeholders must agree on the arrangement. An obvious solution for a bank regulator is to require information sharing. The next decision is whether to house the registry in the central bank or some other government entity, or to allow private bureau.

A variety of private, public, and private-public solutions are presently in the works in Africa. In Nigeria, the country with the largest population in Africa, two independent credit providers and a bank owned credit bureau are being set up. Nigeria is a good example of a market driven approach, where information providers and lenders have realized the opportunity (providers) and the need (lenders) to start up a credit bureau. The government is working on a legal framework in parallel.

In Kenya, for several years a private operator (CRB) struggled to initiate a credit bureau. But due to the lack of interest among banks and a vague legal framework, progress was slow. The Central Bank took the initiative and the banking law was amended in 2006 to mandate that financial institutions share information with licensed private bureaus. The Central Bank is the regulator and licensing body for private credit bureaus. The implementing regulations are expected to be published soon, and at the moment, at least four credit bureau providers are interested in operating in Kenya. In Ghana the situation was similar to Kenya's. Several operators were ready to work with banks but were not able to get the data. The government proposed, and the parliament passed, a law requiring financial institutions to participate in a credit bureau at the end of 2006.

In Uganda, the Central Bank issued a regulation for mandatory participation by financial institutions in a credit bureau and ran a tender to select a bureau operator. The selected provider will have a monopoly for credit reporting activities for a period of three years, after which the market will open up for other participants.

In Tanzania, the law establishes that that Bank of Tanzania operates a data bank and licenses credit bureaus. The Bank of Tanzania is presently working on the regulations. One possibility could be to establish a system pioneered in Ecuador and presently being implemented in Morocco, where the Central Bank operates a databank aggregating information from all lenders and then makes it available to licensed private bureaus. The central bank in this case does not provide reports directly to lenders. Such private-public solution both avoids data fragmentation by collecting all the information in one databank, and allows for a competitive market where users benefit from a better service offering and lower prices. This approach, however, may be difficult to implement in smaller markets where the market size is not sufficient to sustain multiple bureaus.

In Angola, where the credit market is booming, initiatives to set up a credit bureau did not come from the private sector. Rather, the National Bank of Angola is working on a project to establish a credit registry owned by the National Bank but implemented by a qualified provider. Mozambique, which has an operational public registry, is looking to enable a private registry operation and expand the scope of credit reporting in the country.

Each of these countries take a different approach to suit the existing market environment, but in all cases regulators had to play a strong role to facilitate the development of credit reporting in these African countries.

11.8 Ensuring long-term financial viability of the registry is fundamental

One of the major challenges with the development of credit reporting in Africa is the small size of the credit markets. As noted above, a country with a population of 15–20 million is likely to have about 200,000 credit accounts. Credit bureaus rely on economies of scale. They need to recover large up-front investment through the sale of credit reports. In developed markets, bureaus receive millions of enquiries per month and can charge low prices. In small markets where they are likely to receive 10,000–50,000 enquiries or less the price of the report has to be high. But if the report price is too high, this will further reduce demand, especially for lenders granting small size loans. A potential solution is to allow a hub and spoke system. Such a system allows for the hardware to be located in one country (hub) where all the information is processed, while other countries (spokes) have local offices for customer support which are connected to the hub. Several such systems have started operations in recent years. TransUnion Central America (TUCA) was established in 2005 and is the private credit bureau that provides services to Guatemala, Honduras, El Salvador, Costa Rica, and Nicaragua. The spokes leverage the more advanced technological system present in the hub thus allowing for economies of scale, improved efficiency, and higher profitability. In addition, the creation of a single cross-border private credit bureau enables the delivery of standardized products and services with superior information quality. TransUnion in South Africa also operates bureaus for Namibia, Botswana and Swaziland out of South Africa.

In Africa, given the small size of the markets, such an approach is the only economically viable solution which enables high quality credit bureaus for many countries. The cost of starting up a bureau may be reduced by US$500,000 or more by allowing a hub and spoke operation. Such a model also reduces operating costs as core IT personnel are located in one country and some of the maintenance costs are reduced. As a result, the price of the report may be at least US$2–5 higher in a localized bureau than in a regional one.

11.9   Going forward

The development of credit bureaus in Africa presents a significant opportunity to improve the overall credit culture and support the development of credit markets. But this process takes time. In most cases there is a need for legal change which in an optimistic scenario can take 2–3 years but in most cases actually takes five years or more. Based on the experience in other regions, it takes a minimum of 18 months from the moment "the bureau" is created to the moment it goes live, as lenders struggle to provide the data. Up to now there is no reference point in Africa for this process. None of the bureaus are fully operational in the region. Several bureaus have technological solutions deployed but the key resource of the bureau is the data, which must come from lenders. Obtaining data presents major challenges. Banks do not always have the required data. If they do, it is not necessarily in an electronic format. The difficulties are multiplied by the lack of unique identifiers. Without reliable ID numbers, no consistently recorded names and the absence of addresses it is difficult to merge records once they are loaded. In some countries, such as Uganda and Nigeria, the intent is to use biometric identification, which promises to be a major breakthrough in resolving borrower identification problems. In practice, the timeframe from the beginning of the discussion to create a credit bureau to a fully operational bureau is at least 5–7 years.

While this is a very long period compared to other projects in the financial sector, such as starting up a bank or a microfinance institution, the development of credit reporting is an infrastructure project. Once set up, the credit registry can benefit every economically active individual and firm and the operations of every lender. It has massive implications for enhancing the credit culture and changing the overall economic behavior of agents in the economy. Long term donor support which enables countries to have access to international expertise, learn from other regions and see implementation results is critical. With the radical changes financial systems in

Africa are going through, it is crucial that improvements in information infrastructure are made in parallel. Especially in the present environment of the global financial crisis which undoubtedly will affect African markets, the ability to simultaneously manage risks and continue providing access to credit for good borrowers is essential for African economies.

Notes

Financial Specialist at the International Finance Corporation (IFC).

1. Credit Information Index (Figure 11.1) ranges from 1 to 6 and measures comprehensiveness of the credit information environment including (1) coverage of firms and individuals, (2) positive and negative information, (3) availability of over two years of historical data, (4) inclusion of non-bank data such as utility payments, (5) subject of information has a right to access own information, (6) data on loans below 1% of income per capita are distributed. For methodology please see www. doingbusiness.org
2. Powell, Mylenko, Miller and Majnoni 2003. "Public Credit Information Systems: Evaluating Available Information", World Bank.
3. Janvry, Alain de, Craig McIntosh, and Elisabeth Sadoulet, The Supply and Demand Side Impacts of Credit Market Information, June 2007.
4. Djankov, Simeon, Mcliesh, Caralee and Andrei Shleifer "Private Credit in 129 Countries".
5. Love, I., and Mylenko, N. 2004. "Credit Reporting and Financing Constraints." World Bank Policy Research Working Paper 3142.
6. Djankov, Simeon, Caralee McLeish, and Andrei Shleifer 2007. "Private Credit in 129 Countries." *Journal of Financial Economics.* May; Love, Inessa and Nataliya Mylenko 2004. "Credit Reporting and Financing Constraints." World Bank Policy Research Working Paper 3142.

12
Case Study on Microfinance Institutions and Policies in Madagascar: Promoting a Viable Sector
Emma Andrianasolo

12.1   Overview and historical background

Madagascar has a population of 18.2 million inhabitants (Table 12.1). Most Malagasy people live in rural areas that are often difficult to reach, and for whom the main income sources are crop farming, livestock breeding, or fishing. Farms suffer tremendously from a shortage of financing, and this has repercussions on output. Successive governments have made a priority of looking for ways to boost production growth in the primary sector, focusing specifically on its financing. Actions mainly involve the provision of small-scale loans through private and governmental organizations. In some cases, government support has involved directly meeting financial needs or assisting them through subsidies.

In the late 1980s, following financial sector liberalization, a pilot project was set up to promote small-scale private financial services. This program helped make financial services available in rural areas by providing incentives for saving and rural credit. For that purpose, microfinance systems were set up by foreign investors, supported by technical assistants, distributed across the country's various regions. The operation of the system was inspired by current practices observed in intravillage relations, that is, the spirit of self-help and mutual cooperation. The organizations set up generally enjoyed equipment and operating subsidies. After 10 years of operation, the results are considered conclusive; public interest in microfinance services has expanded, and the funds have proliferated.

In 1995, the law on banking activities was passed, defining banking operations and establishing the Banking Commission as the sole regulatory authority for lending establishments. It also became essential to institutionalize the microfinance providers that emerged from most of the pilot

Table 12.1   Selected indicators on Madagascar

	2006	2007
Area	587,041 km²	
Population in millions	17.7	18.2
Demographic growth	2.9%	2.9%
Annual GDP growth	5.0%	6.3%
Population living below the poverty line	67.5%	66.3%
Rate of inflation	10.8%	8.2%
Exchange rate USD/MGA	2,142.3	1,873.8
Exchange rate EUR /MGA	2,686.7	2,563.2
Number of authorized lending establishments	23	25
– of which banks	7	8
– of which finance houses	7	8
– of which microfinance institutions (MFIs)	9	9

project, to establish their credibility. Accordingly, a law governing the activities of mutualist financial institutions (i.e. saving and loan associations) was published in 1996. Since 1999 such organizations, operating on a project basis, have applied for and obtained authorization from the Banking Commission, thereby regularizing their legal status. Since then, nine mutualist networks have been authorized. In contrast, nonmutualist organizations had two alternatives, either to align with one of the forms of lending establishment envisaged by the banking law, none of which specifically encompassed microfinance activity; or else to wait for a specific regulation to be adopted for nonmutualist institutions, while continuing to operate unofficially.

In the early years of the new millennium, having subscribed to the Millennium Development Goals, and in keeping with its Poverty Reduction Strategy Paper, Madagascar decided to make microfinance the key means of halving the number of people living in poverty by 2015. This policy, which aims to extend the implementation of microfinance institutions (MFIs) throughout the country, was confirmed in 2007 by the Madagascar Plan of Action (MAP), covering the period 2007–2012. Among its various commitments, the MAP provides that low-income households will have the opportunity to obtain credit under favorable conditions, thus enabling them to undertake income-generating activities; and that a wide range of financial products will be made available to a large proportion of the population.

12.2   The government's strategy to sustain microfinance

The government is committed to lifting indigent people out of their poverty situation, by facilitating access to financial services as part of a three-pronged policy, namely:

- continued implementation of large-scale projects to promote MFIs, supported by institutional partners.
- design of a regulatory framework to promote the smooth functioning of MFIs;
- establishment of an authority to supervise MFIs, adapted to their risks and, at the same time, capable of supporting the development of the institutions in question.

12.2.1 The government's commitment and support from financial partners

12.2.1.1 *Implementation of large-scale microfinance development projects*

Continuing along the guidelines that were mapped out decades ago, in 1999 Madagascar started to implement a multiyear microfinance program, with the aim of raising incomes and living standards among poor population groups, by providing a favorable environment for development of the microfinance sector. About 117,000 families were targeted, containing an average of five persons each, that is, 585,000 inhabitants altogether.

The implementation of the project was entrusted to a private nonprofit organization whose main mission was to create autonomous and permanent microfinance funds providing sustainable financial services to the poor, without having to rely on long-term external support. This organization also had to support skill development in promoting the sector.

The second component of the project, of which the central bank is the executing agency, acting through the Banking and Financial Supervision Commission (CSBF), aimed at implementing a legal and regulatory framework giving appropriate incentives for microfinance, as well as strengthening the capacities of inspectors to supervise MFIs more effectively.

Other equally important projects funded in the context of bilateral or multilateral relations have also been implemented. Some of these cover other areas, apart from the financial sector, relating to the creation of MFIs, refinancing of credit lines with banks, and technical support for senior MFI and CSBF staff.

12.2.1.2 *The National Microfinance Strategy*

During the first decade of the new millennium the government has made additional efforts to enable microfinance to fulfill its mission of providing financial services to underprivileged population groups. The National Microfinance Strategy (SNMF) was defined in 2004, with the specific aim of "engaging stakeholders around actions to strengthen and develop the sector. Its objective is to form a viable and permanent professional microfinance sector, which is diversified and innovative, ensuring satisfactory coverage of demand throughout the country and operating within an adapted and favorable legal, regulatory, fiscal, and institutional framework." The strategy also specifies the role of the various participants, the activities to be undertaken, and the corresponding budget.

To achieve that objective, the National Microfinance Coordination Unit (CNMF) was created in the Ministry of Finance. This unit was given the mission to coordinate general government policy on microfinance, promote the sector and monitor the activities of its participants. A steering committee was set up within the CNMF, to serve as a platform for observations and discussions to enhance conditions for microfinance development. The membership of the steering committee consists of MFI representatives, acting through their professional associations, the Minister for Agriculture and Livestock, the Minister for Finance, financial backers, and the CSBF.

12.2.1.3   The training and awareness-raising program

Recognition of the skill deficit among both managers and technical staff (who are often not equipped to manage an MFI—a situation that generates frequent governance crises or a high turnover rate) has led the government to launch a major training program for all microfinance operators, supported by several foreign financial partners. The program covers several areas and extends over a long period. It has various components, depending on the type of beneficiary of the training in question.

- Training programs for networks: these range from theoretical modules for technical staff lasting several days, to permanent practical training activities at the institutions, to provide board members and executives or managers with the knowledge they need to fulfill their mission;
- Training programs for the population at large: these tend to be information-training sessions, together with publicity to raise awareness of the usefulness of financial services and to provide education on managing savings and credit. More particularly, a lending culture has been inculcated among the public, who, accustomed until now to receiving nonreimbursable subsidies, did not concern themselves about honoring repayment installments;
- It has also become essential to strengthen CSBF capacities, to impose effective specific control over microfinance institutions. MFI oversight is a relatively recent activity compared to the supervision of traditional banks which inspectors have been used to;
- Training for local authorities and potential stakeholders in the creation of an MFI: dissemination programs have been implemented through publicity spots, radio and television broadcasts, and films.

12.2.1.4   Other measures

These different actions go hand in hand with other measures aimed at developing the sector, such as land reforms to provide peasant farmers with property titles, the documents needed to support their credit dossier or insure their farming operations, and tax incentives for MFIs.

12.2.2   Adequate regulation favoring sector development

In collaboration with all participants and the various stakeholders, the government defined a flexible legal and regulatory framework, whose overriding objective is to allow the sector to develop harmoniously (see Appendix 12A.1).

12.2.2.1   *Three levels of MFI, defined according to risk*

The law on microfinance activities was passed in 2005; it was the first legislation governing activities of this type, and was also applied to both mutualist and nonmutualist MFIs. The law aims to allow all microfinance initiatives, including small-scale ones, to become institutionalized and operate within a secure framework.

From the standpoint of the Malagasy legislator, providing microfinance services is a banking activity; and MFIs are lending establishments just like banks. To engage in banking activities requires prior authorization from the CSBF, the sole regulatory authority, which is also responsible for overseeing the proper functioning of lending establishments, and for sanctioning them where necessary.

The law classifies MFIs according to three levels, depending on the institution's degree of development, the risks to which it is exposed as a result of its banking operations, and its mode of operation. Its enabling regulations specify legal formats, minimum capital, and authorized operations, among other issues.

- For level-1 MFIs, which are considered low-risk given the small scale of their operations, a permit is granted, and CSBF intervention is limited to ensuring the existence of a lightweight governance structure and the regularity of banking operations.
- Level-2 and -3 MFIs must obtain authorization from the CSBF prior to engaging in the activity, and they are subject to its supervision. MFIs classified in these two levels are distinguished by the scale of their respective operations, and by their governance structure and its degree of professionalism.

12.2.2.2   *Differentiated conditions according to level*

- *The legal format is adapted to the characteristics of the institution*: nonmutualist MFIs have to be organized as commercial companies if they accept deposits from the public; otherwise they may be set up as an association. In the case of mutualist organizations, the underlying fund is established as a cooperative, irrespective of the size of its membership, since they are only authorized to accept savings from their members. In contrast, pooling structures can be set up as companies.

• *A progressive minimum capital depending on the classification level*: from the moment when the MFI becomes a company, a progressive level of minimum capital is required to exercise the activity. The required capital depends on the institution's classification level, but the amount is at least equal to that defined under common law. The amount is larger when the MFI is free to accept deposits from the public.

• *Portfolio composition*: portfolio composition is subject to conditions allowing MFIs to fulfill their social function while also helping them to achieve viability. Level-2 and -3 MFIs have to reserve 30% of their portfolio for small loans benefiting underprivileged population groups; but, in exchange, they can exceed the lending ceiling authorized for their level by up to 10% of their portfolio. The aim is to cover their costs and help them to achieve viability.

12.2.3 Supervision adapted to MFI risks

In fulfilling its legal mission of protecting small-scale savers and the integrity of the financial system, the CSBF specifically helps provide MFIs with a flexible regulatory mechanism, to facilitate their development in a secure environment. A unit has been set up within the CSBF specifically to monitor the sector's evolution, and ensure implementation of the signposts needed to enable MFIs to function effectively. In terms of its role in the surveillance of other more professional lending institutions, the CSBF-MFI relation is quite specific, in keeping with the special features of the sector. The CSBF intervenes in three specific areas: definition of the legal framework; monitoring of the networks under its supervision; and participation in the National Microfinance Strategy.

12.2.3.1 *Defining the legal framework applicable to MFIs*

It played a key role in preparing the law and its enabling decrees. It proposes regulations to the government that it considers essential for the good health of MFIs; it gave its opinion on draft laws dealing with microfinance as well as instructions for implementing the law over which it has sole jurisdiction. With a view to putting a regulatory instrument in place that is adapted to the specifics of the country setting and helps expand the sector, the CSBF adopts a participatory procedure involving all stakeholders at the different stages of the preparatory work.

12.2.3.2 *MFI monitoring and support*

The CSBF established and maintains exchanges and relations with senior MFI management, when dealing with authorization requests, with a view to improving the quality of the corresponding dossiers and creating optimal conditions for MFI viability. Experience has shown that many of the requests submitted are initially inconsistent. The CSBF Secretary-General therefore often has to hold lengthy working meetings with the promoters, before they obtain a coherent project that can be submitted for decision by commission members.

The CSBF responds flexibly to all training and assistance requests from MFIs at all times. This activity aims to provide the clarifications or explanations requested by senior executives to improve their institutions' management.

Thus, apart from MFI supervision as such, a specific type of assistance is expected from the governing authority, to allow for more effective business management. This activity, valued in particular by mutualist organizations, requires a larger number of inspectors, but the reality is that there are too few of them.

12.2.4 It is a member of the CNMF steering committee

Participation on the steering committee enables the CSBF to stay informed and contribute to the study and analysis of the challenges facing the sector. The CSBF is mostly called upon for tasks and decisions concerning the health of the institutions in question and the sector in general. Discussions in the steering committee often relate to following issues: the search for ways to deal with the threat of an MFI breaking away, thus putting the future of the network at risk; steps to be taken to overcome governance weaknesses; and protection of MFIs from attempts to exert external influence, thereby reducing opportunities for members to take control of the network.

12.3 Recent developments

12.3.1 Expansion and penetration of microfinance

The development of microfinance has been remarkable. It is now present in most regions of the country, albeit with uneven coverage—urban zones and agglomerations displaying greater density.

Since 1996 when the law on mutualist financial institutions was published, nine mutualist MFI networks have been authorized by the CSBF. These encompass 447 funds and branches. They serve the country as a whole and are located in both urban zones and, especially, in remote rural areas. The number of funds grew strongly until the start of the new millennium, at which point, having detected signs of weakness, the CSBF recommended limiting their geographic expansion to focus on consolidating achievements to date.

Thanks to promotion efforts, fund membership has been growing steadily, totaling 342,910 affiliates, and averaging 767 members each, compared to 113 ten years earlier (Table 12.2). The appeal of mutualist microfinance is remarkable compared to the bank sector, which only has eight establishments with 139 branches. A single microfinance branch nowadays provides

Table 12.2 Trend of the number of funds and members of mutualist MFIs

	1996	1997	1998	1999	2000	2001	2002	2003	2004	2005	2006	2007
Number of funds	155	204	248	271	336	363	337	370	386	399	421	447
Variation	–	31.6%	21.6%	9.3%	24.0%	8.0%	-7.2%	9.8%	4.3%	3.4%	5.5%	6.2%
Number of members	17,590	28,294	47,472	60,775	92,946	116,977	135,305	179,399	198,912	232,347	294,173	342,910
Variation	–	60.9%	67.8%	28.0%	52.9%	25.9%	15.7%	32.6%	10.9%	16.8%	26.6%	16.6%
Average number of members per fund	113	138	191	224	276	322	407	485	515	582	698	767
Variation	–	22.1%	38.4%	17.3%	23.2%	16.7%	26.4%	19.2%	6.2%	13.0%	19.9%	9.9%

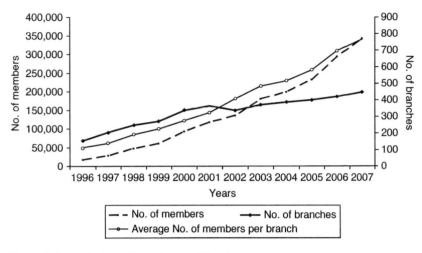

Figure 12.1   Evolutions of members and funds

services to 37,000 inhabitants, compared to one branch for three times as many people in the case of banks.

There are fewer statistics available for nonmutualist funds, which are not yet fully regulated, since the law on microfinance has not yet been applied to them. Nonmutualist MFIs have also expanded more slowly than their mutualist counterparts, in particular because of the lack of a legal framework adapted to their activities, which clearly dampens investors' interest in them. They have coexisted with mutualist MFIs in large cities, but have only begun to extend their range of implementation over the last few years. In late 2007, some ten establishments were listed among the three largest networks providing very small loans to private individuals and microentrepreneurs. These establishments are operating in several regions. In other cases, despite their relative proliferation, their banking activities are even more limited than their supply of nonfinancial services.

12.3.2   Organizations active in microfinance

The microfinance sector continues to gain ground, encompassing not only mutualist and nonmutualist MFIs, but also starting to attract banks and other types of lending establishment which previously had ignored it. Nonetheless, it is still MFIs that serve most underprivileged population groups.

12.3.2.1   *Mutualist MFIs*

Mutualist MFIs are motivated by the spirit of self-help and cooperation. Their operating surpluses are not distributed but are used to strengthen capital or finance rebates. Shareholders are the cooperative members who, in their deliberations are governed by the principle of "one person one voice" irrespective of the number of shares they hold.

The members of management bodies are elected by affiliates in the general assembly, and they fulfill their mission without payment. The management of the institution is put in the hands an executive, who, until recently, was often a former network technical assistant. Their fees are financed out of grants from foreign financial backers. Local technical staff assist the executive as coordinators, inspectors, or developers. Their low salaries in relation to their responsibilities are a source of frequent turnover.

Mutualist MFIs are generally organized in pyramid networks. At the apex of the pyramid is the top of the structure to which the underlying funds are linked. Major decisions on policy orientation are taken at the top level. The board of directors consists of persons elected from the underlying funds, some of which are represented in the villages by branches or sales points.

12.3.2.2 Nonmutualist MFIs

Nonmutualist MFIs can be classified in two groups according to their objectives:

- First, institutions that exist as associations with a social mission and extend small loans based on the funds they possess. Some networks have numerous outlets covering several regions of the country. Apart from banking activities, this category of institution provides training for the least privileged population groups, with a view to helping them set up individual microenterprises;
- Second, institutions established as commercial companies which generally operate with a profit motive based on quite substantial capital. The latter are managed more professionally. The value of the individual loans they make is higher than for MFIs with a social mission; the same is true of their portfolio volume. Following the adoption of the microfinance law, this category of MFI is now authorized to receive deposits.

12.3.2.3 Lending establishments specializing in microfinance

The 2005 adoption of a single law on microfinance activities governing all categories of institutions at the same time, whether mutualist or nonmutualist, has opened the door to foreign investors. Since 2006, three lending establishments specializing in microfinance have obtained authorization. These are highly capitalized profit-making businesses. Located in the capital and in several other large cities, they are starting to compete with already established MFIs despite unequal resources and different objectives.

12.3.2.4 Traditional banks

Lending establishments which previously reserved their operations for loans offering the best collateral, have now focused on a poorer clientele by eliminating the minimum saving threshold, either offering small-scale loans directly, or granting credit lines to MFIs, or drawing on their capital.

12.3.3 Activities

12.3.3.1 Authorized microfinance operations

To promote efficiency, and expecting MFIs to display this, the financial services they are authorized to provide are limited to extending credit and accepting deposits from their members or clients. Check administration or foreign currency operations are not allowed. Nonetheless, subject to the availability of sufficient capital and establishment as a commercial company, the microfinance law authorizes nonmutualist MFIs to accept deposits from the public to help monetize saving and increase their resources. These services in most cases are accompanied by training.

The loans granted usually finance income-generating activities, collective village granaries for storing produce while awaiting better prices; mutualist rental-sale, which is a type of leasing for equipment or draught animals; certain commercial activities and even social events such as marriage, return to school, or transport from the main residence to the native village. Loans are repaid over a short period, a few months in the case of social credits: otherwise payments can be spread out over a longer term of up to three years.

Costs sometimes seem prohibitive—over 4% per month in the case of mutualist MFIs—but that does not discourage members who previously had no other resource apart from usurers, whose rates sometimes ran as high as 250% per year. Nonmutualist MFIs, for their part, impose interest rates (2 to 2.5% per month), which are not much lower than those applied by the banks.

The funds received are mostly unremunerated demand deposits, although in the last few years the collection of longer-term, sometimes interest-bearing, deposits has developed. The constitution of proportional obligatory deposits is often necessary to obtain loans. Until the adoption of the microfinance law, only mutualist MFIs were authorized to receive voluntary deposits.

Some MFI networks also provide training sessions or workshops for their members or clients and even for third parties, or else training modules to keep their technical staff up to date. The various topics addressed in those activities aim to improve the population's living standards by addressing their financial needs. These topics raise awareness not only of the benefits of loans or making savings secure through their monetization, but also the management of household resources, small crop or livestock products, or the use of new financial products. For certain establishments that focus their efforts particularly on training, banking activities are at an experimental level.

12.3.3.2 Achievements

For the period 1996–2007, following coordination and dissemination efforts, deposits have grown very rapidly, with balances registering exponential

Table 12.3 Trends in deposit and loan balances among mutualist MFIs

(Million MGA)	1996	1997	1998	1999	2000	2001	2002	2003	2004	2005	2006	2007
Balance of deposits	184	542	1,068	3,361	7,416	11,150	10,372	18,992	21,803	25,510	31,317	42,243
Variation	–	194.6%	97.0%	214.7%	120.6%	50.4%	–7.0%	83.1%	14.8%	17.0%	22.8%	34.9%
Balance of loans	975	1,090	2,304	5,364	7,562	9,260	11,212	19,519	25,382	36,236	41,772	62,373
Variation	–	11.8%	111.4%	132.8%	41.0%	22.5%	21.1%	74.1%	30.0%	42.8%	15.3%	49.3%

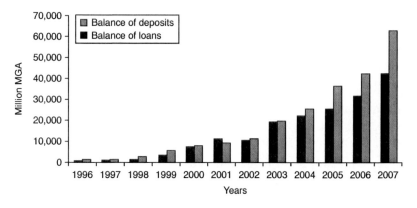

Figure 12.2   Trends in deposit and loan balances of mutualist MFIs

growth (Table 12.3 and Figure 12.2). Loans have also expanded, albeit more slowly.

At the end of 2007, the balance of loans extended by mutualist MFIs had risen from MGA 62.4 billion (i.e. US$33.3 million) compared to MGA 41.8 billion (US$19.5 million) a year earlier, that is, a net annual increase of 49%. In total, 82,307 borrowers with 114,341 loans were listed, compared to 60,447 borrowers and 72,335 loans a year earlier, that is, an increase of 36% in the number of borrowers and 58% in the number of loans. The average number of loans per individual has also increased (1.38 compared to 1.19), reflecting increasing interest among members' to make use of credit. The number of registered deposit accounts rose from 258,612 in 2006 to 311,786 in 2007, that is, growth of more than 20%. The year-end balance was up by 34.8%.

In the case of nonmutualist MFIs, although in absolute value terms the volume of loans granted by the three main networks seems small, the trend is nonetheless remarkable having tripled in relation to the previous year's figure. The year-end balance was up by 45%.

The share of microfinance in banking activities is nonetheless very small, just 2.22% in the case of traditional lending establishments, despite the increase in the number of people involved. Deposits and loans represent 1.55 and 3.43% respectively.

12.3.4   The financial situation

According to available information, the financial health of the sector has improved in recent years, at least in balance-sheet terms.

Both lending activities and deposits have been growing steadily from year to year. Despite that increase, other types of deposit still account for over 60% of the total. The loan portfolio continues to improve; the credit culture is starting to become established, even in regions where borrowers previously baulked at meeting repayment deadlines. Nonetheless, efforts are still needed to reduce the level of 30-day payment arrears, which has been around 8% throughout the mutualist sector for the last few years. Individual analysis shows, however, that some MFIs are in better shape.

MFIs abide by prudential standards that are applicable to lending establishments and, apart from a few cases, operate with more demanding ratios. In fact, specific ratios for microfinance activities are being designed to take account of the sector's special conditions.

In terms of results, net interest income, which is the main revenue generated by MFIs, has been rising in line with the volume of loans extended and interest on BTAs. When dossier study costs and other fees are taken into account, operating results are even more favorable. Nonetheless, as administrative charges, specifically the cost of technical assistance, are also quite high, operational autonomy has not yet been attained in some networks (three out of the nine authorized). The sector's net result is barely positive, but is improving. Nonetheless, certain MFIs individually can exist without financial assistance.

Overall, at least three large authorized MFI networks are in a position to bridge the gap between microfinance and the banking network, in terms of the volume of their activities and the scale of their individual operations. Trusting in the competency of network management, traditional banks are now providing them with complementary financing for their lending operations. Business relations are starting to be developed with banks. Furthermore, thanks to the efforts of certain MFIs following the growth in the volume of deposits, their internal surplus is enabling them to finance the Public Treasury budget through their participation in the Treasury bonds market. In addition, their experience and professionalism are also enabling them to enter the financial market.

12.4 The future of microfinance in Madagascar

Microfinance is on a sound course, and the target population has been easily surpassed. Nonetheless, the illusion provided by this healthy performance should not conceal risks relating to network fragility, particularly in the mutualist segment. These difficulties are not only of an internal origin but also stem from exogenous factors. Although several steps have been taken to remedy the situation, they are still insufficient to attain poverty reduction objectives.

12.4.1 Difficulties to be overcome

The development of microfinance has become difficult not only because of inherent behavior patterns in the sector, but also because of interference in decisions that do not contribute to the health of MFIs.

12.4.1.1   Difficulties of an internal origin

Governance problems   Governance problems arise regularly, relating particularly to the appropriation of the networks by nationals. Specifically,

- Elected personnel who have to give up their jobs to assume unpaid network functions, become less and less motivated;
- Overly frequent turnover of technical staff renders MFIs unable to secure the loyalty of their staff, who are tempted by more secure offers;
- Financial support is often absorbed by technical assistance fees. Given the contrast with their individual condition, affiliates do not often feel concerned for the future of their networks.

Growth crises   Growth crises are becoming an obstacle to the future of MFIs.

- Some institutions affiliated to the pooling structure, and incorrectly believing they are in a position to operate on their own, seek to disaffiliate, which causes disruption within the network;
- Difficulties arise once the network becomes more extended and internal control cannot keep pace. As a result, the self-management system, which puts decision-making power in the hands of elected but inexperienced directors, has caused a rapid deterioration of the lending portfolio, leading to the closure of several funds and subsequent institutional dysfunction. The losses thus engendered have eroded available internal funds. It has been impossible to start addressing the situation without CSBF intervention, which has had to put the network under provisional administration;
- Extending areas of implementation has sometimes been prioritized by operators to the detriment of skill transfer. This perpetuates the network's reliance on external technical support;
- The virtual nonexistence of long-term funding or stable saving restricts MFI activities. Moreover, MFIs are reluctant to lend, preferring to place their deposits in Treasury bonds, rather than turn them into loans;
- The outsourcing of certain services as a result of the spread of microfinance seems to need participation by external backers. Care must be taken, however, to deal with the risks of diluting responsibility and prevent backers from gaining control over the network.

12.4.1.2   Exogenous factors

The dilemma between social vocation and permanence   The balance between the network's social vocation and its permanence is not easy to control.

- Making financial products available to the public at concessional, subsidized, or supported rates for social purposes is clearly advantageous for the targeted population. But, this procedure does not further the development

of the institution; instead it distorts competition within the sector, particularly in areas where MFIs are already present;
- Freedom to set interest rates generates unjustified and unfair profits for institutions that are concentrated in urban zones and large agglomerations, at the expense of those operating in more remote and more risky areas, which wish to fulfill their social function;
- Uncoordinated support actions and, sometimes, inconsistencies endanger the health of MFIs: the importation of rice during the harvest period, for example, causes a drop in prices that is fatal to an establishment that has funded rice growing.

The near-total absence of competition The virtual nonexistence of competition undermines respect for microfinance ethics.

- The entry of highly capitalized profit-making institutions, in which sales volume and the confidence of their backers help lower the cost of the services supplied, compared to those of already established MFIs that do not have the same advantages, distorts competition;
- The monopolistic situation arising from the initial distribution of implementation zones slows down improvements in the quality of services and MFI management;
- The lack of local initiatives and scarcity of resources make it harder to achieve the objectives, for microfinance is in danger of becoming an industry that exploits collateral while restricting access to the poor.

12.4.2 The search for more effective mechanisms
The ideal way to underpin the government's poverty reduction strategy entails creating viable and permanent MFIs that respond to rural dwellers' financial needs. It is essential to maintain the support given to the sector; otherwise, peasant farmers will not develop trust in the corresponding institutions. Other initiatives have been taken by the CSBF and MFIs to improve the security of the sector.

12.4.2.1 *Reducing the risk of overborrowing*
With the aim of discouraging overborrowing among the clientele, given the proliferation of funds, and to enable them to choose loan beneficiaries more effectively, a microfinance risk rating agency is being set up in the central bank. This will be made accessible to lending establishments. It is expected to be provisionally managed by the CSBF and integrated into the risk-rating agency for other lending establishments also located in the central bank. It will also serve as a CSBF supervision tool.

12.4.2.2 *The establishment of a management indicators database*
Monitoring of the health of MFIs and their operations will also be reviewed more regularly by the CSBF, thanks to the establishment of a management

indicators database for individual institutions and the microfinance sector as a whole. The database will not only allow better supervision but will also be available for consultation by MFIs, to ascertain their position in relation to the sector as a whole.

12.4.2.3 Other regulatory markers

Other regulatory markers are under study or have recently been applied. For example, to encourage skill transfer, no technical assistant may support a given network for over six months and then become an executive in it. Furthermore, a CSBF instruction defines the minimal governance structures demanded for each MFI level.

12.4.2.4 Reflections on the use of technological progress

Reflections on the use of technological progress for financial service transactions are also underway, either with the aim of supplying financial services in remote areas that lack electric power, or to diversify the loan portfolio. Furthermore, computer hardware is expected to be supplied to MFIs that do not have this equipment, which is essential for more effective monitoring of their operations.

12.5 Conclusion

The microfinance sector today is expanding strongly—a situation that has been achieved with some difficulty. It is now contributing to the development of the financial market as a whole. Its health nonetheless remains precarious, but it has many positive features, including: the government's confirmed willingness to continue making it a priority tool of poverty reduction; the weak penetration rate and the population's growing needs; potentially high demand; willingness of financial backers to support the sector's development; stakeholder awareness of the need for a shared view of the actions to be undertaken; investors' interest in operating in the sector.

Conditions seem to be in place to achieve the program's goals of setting up local funds and increasing the number of people involved, unless other uncontrollable elements supervene. The goal being pursued, however, is not restricted to sector expansion, but involves ensuring permanence, so that the supply of services is sustainable and the population's vulnerability is reduced.

Following a more in-depth analysis of the results, other concerns have emerged along with related questions for which answers have not yet been found:

- Do the services supplied really meet the expectations of the targeted population, and do they effectively contribute to poverty reduction, when the cost of borrowing remains so high? How can the interest rate be lowered

Appendix 12A.1 MFI regulation

Level of institutionalization		MFI 1		MFI 2		MFI 3	
Category		Mutualist	Non mutualist	Mutualist	Non mutualist	Mutualist	Non mutualist
Legal format	Base MFI	Cooperative company	Association, NGO, SA, SARL	Cooperative company	SARL, SA SA	Cooperative company	SA
	Unions and federations	Not authorized		Cooperative company, S.A.	Not authorized	Cooperative, SA	Not authorized
	Minimum required capital	No capital required		Base MFI:$8,005 Union:$32,019 Feder°: $53,365	SARL: $32,019 S.A.: $53 365	Base MFI: $160,096 Union: $266,826 Federation: $533,652	$373,556
					$106,730		
Saving	Nomenclature	Deposits from members	No deposits	Deposits from members	No deposits	Deposits from members	Deposits from the public
	Ceiling	$267 (Individual)			Deposits from the public		
Loans	Loan maturity Individual credits	Short term $800	$1,600	Short and medium term – at least 30% of the volume of credits, individual amount < $2,668; – at most 10% of the volume of credits, individual amount > $8,005 within the limits of the risk pooling ratio		Short, medium and long term – at least 30% of the volume of credits, individual amount < $8,005 – at most 10% of the volume of credits, individual amount > $32,019 within the limits of the risk pooling ratio	
	Loans to pool	$3,202	$6,404	Not applicable			
	Related services	Consultancy and training		All related operations: internal transfer operations on behalf of clients, undertaken within a same MFI or within a MFI network, provision of advice and training; fund transfers denominated in national currencies between banks in the national territory.			

Maximum number of members of mutualist MFI 1 = 1000.

Unauthorized operations: Check issuance, operations denominated in foreign currencies or those relating to the financing of international trade.

without undermining MFI operations. How can central banks assist in financing MFIs, to enable the latter to lower the interest rates they charge and effectively contribute to improving living standards?

- Will the microfinance industry benefit only investors for whom profit maximization risks undermining efforts made thus far, if companies, which are essentially profit-making, also enjoy advantages offered by an environment created to respond to goals that also include a social mission? What solutions might be equitable? On what criteria should one judge the quality of microfinance?
- At the institutional level, should the mission of the regulatory authorities be extended to monitoring networks until their maturity? In fact, given existing operating conditions and the dilemma facing networks in terms of social mission vs. making a profit, the regulatory authorities, given their independence, are often the only agencies in a position to denounce certain practices that are harmful to the sector's integrity.

These questions all need to be reflected on, to ensure that African finance in the twenty-first century does not become a tool for further enriching the already wealthy, and does not deviate from its mission to serve the economy by lifting the poor out of poverty.

Note

Microfinance Director, Banking and Financial Supervision Commission, Madagascar.

13
Financial Sector Development Program (FSDP): The Case of Rwanda

Consolate Rusagara

13.1 Introduction

The strong relationship between financial sector development and economic growth is no longer debatable. Even if it still was, there is general consensus that a well-functioning financial system is necessary to reduce information asymmetry and transaction costs between savers and investors diversify risk and enhance efficient intermediation by allocating resources in the most efficient way. In doing so, a well-functioning financial sector will lead to rapid accumulation of physical and human capital, enhance technological innovation and therefore lead to economic growth and poverty reduction.

Despite all these well-known attributes, well-functioning financial systems still elude most of sub-Saharan Africa and past financial sector reforms have only had very limited success.

My intention is not to review the rich literature on financial sector reforms but to review Rwanda's recent experience in designing a comprehensive FSDP. The chapter briefly explains the rationale behind the FSDP in Rwanda, its scope and approach to the reform process, as well as implementation progress to date.

While there are some achievements thus far, there is need for cautious optimism because implementation has just begun and many challenges still remain.

13.2 The rationale for Financial Sector Development Program

In the last two decades, Rwanda, like most other countries in sub-Saharan Africa, embarked on broad economic reforms including: liberalization and privatization of the financial sector to reduce financial repression, encourage market determined prices of financial services, as well as entry of international players in order to enhance competition.

In 1999, the National Bank of Rwanda Act (i.e. The Rwanda Central Bank Act) was revised to grant more independence, to formulate and implement

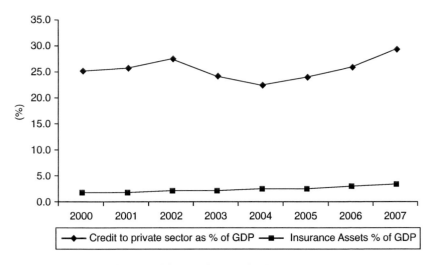

Figure 13.1   Some indicators of financial sector depth

monetary policy, and ensure financial sector stability. The Central Bank's supervisory capacity was strengthened to reduce regulatory forbearance, ensure market discipline and enhance compliance with the Basel Core Principles of effective supervision.

However, despite all the reforms, the Rwandan authorities recognized that the financial sector's ability to play its role of mobilization and effective intermediation of savings to finance its ambitious economic reform agenda was still far from achievable. The financial sector remained weak, undiversified and offered only basic financial products and services to a very limited section of the potentially bankable population.

Authorities invited the joint World Bank/IMF Financial Sector Assessment Program (FSAP) mission to carry out a diagnostic of the sector and make recommendations for further reforms. While recognizing that significant progress had been made, the 2005 FSAP report, not surprisingly, describes the Rwandan financial sector as "narrow, shallow with an oligopolistic banking sector characterized by high lending rates and very low penetration of insurance services as well as undiversified financial products". The FSAP further recognized wide interest rate spreads, poor savings rate, scarcity of long-term capital, small and unregulated pension and insurance sectors and a malfunctioning payment system.

In the context of attempting to address the weaknesses raised in the FSAP, and in line with Rwanda's Vision 2020, the long-term vision for development, Government launched the Financial Sector Development Program, FSDP in 2006.

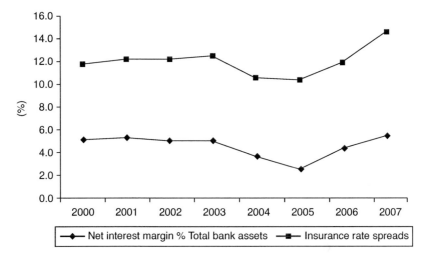

Figure 13.2 Indicators of efficiency of the financial sector
Source: BNR Bank Supervision Dept.

The overarching vision of the FSDP is "To develop a stable and sound financial sector that is sufficiently deep and broad, capable of efficiently mobilising and allocating resources to address the development needs of the economy and reduce poverty".

The Government of Rwanda recognizes the importance of the financial sector and has made the FSDP one of the key components of the Growth flagship in its Economic Development and Poverty Reduction Strategy, EDPRS, the socialeconomic development agenda for 2008–12.

The FSDP was intended to achieve four specific objectives:

First, the FSDP intended to enhance access and affordability of banking and other financial services; by developing a strong, efficient, and competitive banking sector offering a diversified array of financial products and services. This included support for the development and broad outreach of a healthy, well-regulated and professionally managed microfinance sector as a tool to extend financial services to the un-banked and contribute to poverty reduction.

Second, FSDP intended to enhance savings mobilization by creating an appropriate environment, developing institutions and fostering market incentives for the development of long-term financial instruments and an efficient capital market.

Third, FSDP aimed at developing an appropriate policy, legal and institutional framework for effective regulation of nonbank financial institutions.

Fourth, FSDP intended to organize and modernize the National Payment System.

13.3   The scope of the Financial Sector Development Program

To achieve the objectives mentioned above, FSDP needed to address weaknesses in four areas: access to finance, capital market development, regulation of nonbank financial Institutions (NBFI), and Payment systems.

Access to banking and other financial services outside Kigali and other major towns was and is still very limited. Moreover, there was very little understanding and no baseline data on the demand and uses of financial services to inform policy makers in designing appropriate policies to enhance access. What was available is supply side data on institutions that are licensed and supervised by the Central Bank. It was estimated that about 75% of the Rwandan bankable population was either being served by the informal sector or not being served at all. The FSDP recommended that a household survey be launched to obtain baseline data on the needs and usage of financial services which will inform the design of access to finance policies. A FinScope survey was subsequently launched, and results showed that Rwanda's level of access to the formal financial sector was much lower than Kenya and Uganda. However, the relative size of the population completely excluded is quite comparable to other EAC countries except Kenya which is smaller.

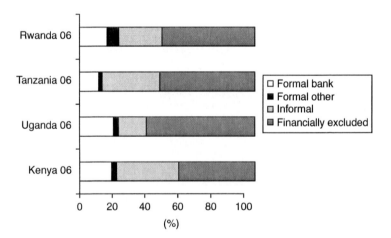

Figure 13.3 Access to financial services in Rwanda in comparison with EAC countries[*]

[*] To the extent that the survey was carried out at different times, the comparison is not very robust and it does not capture rapid expansion in financial access in 2007 as a result of MFI growth in Uganda and branchless banking in Kenya. Data on Burundi was not available. I am grateful to Mark Napier for allowing me to use the data.

Source: FinScope Survey.

Microfinance institutions which should normally play a significant role in bridging the financial access gap were still financially weak, lacked adequate financial management systems, and had poor internal controls and governance structures. Clearly, these problems needed to be addressed. The strategy recommended enactment of the Microfinance law and finalizing and adopting the draft Microfinance Policy, among other measures. The Microfinance law provided for a framework for a tiered system where the NBR would regulate the large and systemically important entities while the smaller ones were subject to a less stringent reporting system. The sector was dominated by too many small players, most of whom lacked technical and financial capacity to ensure long-term viability. It was recommended that they be organized under one umbrella organization in which support to the industry should be channeled instead of supporting individual organizations, which most NGOs in that sector were doing.

In 2005, the combined branch network of the seven commercial banks was only 38 (it has since grown to 40). In terms of business, commercial banks accounted for about 75% of total deposits and loans, but only about 10% in terms of its customers. As indicated in the FSAP report, Rwanda's banking sector was oligopolistic with three banks accounting for 69% of the total banking assets. A network of cooperative and credit union, Union de Banque Populaire du Rwanda, UBPR, with a nationwide outreach of 145 savings and credit outlets (it has since consolidated to 133), as well as other microfinance institutions, accounted for 90% of customers but only 15% of total deposits and loans. Moreover, UBPR mainly invested in government treasury bills and deposits with commercial banks instead of lending to its clients. The bank is a significant player because of its size and outreach (its

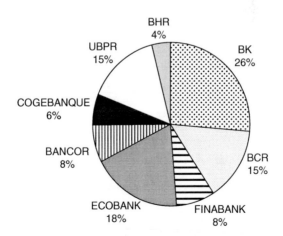

Figure 13.4 Relative market share of deposit taking banks as at 31/12/2004

deposit base makes it the third largest bank in the country), but it was classified as a microfinance institution and therefore subject to less stringent prudential requirements.

In order to improve competition in the banking sector and provide sounder regulation of this extremely important institution, the FSDP recommended that UBPR be treated as a de facto commercial bank and be subjected to relevant prudential requirements and become part of the national payment system while maintaining cooperative governance principles. This would force it to improve its credit underwriting process, internal controls, accounting and IT processes on one hand, while enabling it to maintain its customer base, which would otherwise graduate to commercial banks when they became "too sophisticated and too big to serve".

Rwanda lacked long-term capital and market-based debt or equity products essential for its economic development strategy. While the banking sector was excessively liquid, the funds were short-tem in nature. As a result, mortgages and investment projects were financed on very short maturity terms of around 5years. This weakness was exacerbated by lack of efficient mechanisms for banks to transform the long-term assets on their books into liquid funds. Moreover, the market lacked an interest rate yield curve to be able to price long-term instrument.

The strategy recommended various reforms to foster development of the long-term debt market which included:

- Establishment of Rwanda Capital Markets Advisory Council to set guidelines and oversee the operations of the Over the Counter Debt and Equity Market.
- Recommendation to the Treasury and NBR to reissue a significant portion of maturing short-term treasury bills at longer maturities in order to catalyze the Secondary Market for Securities. All new issues would be longer than 12 months.
- Securitization of existing long-term debt owed by government to Social Security Fund.
- Issuance of Commercial Paper by some of the well-performing domestic companies.

Nonbank financial institutions, NBFIs, that are key players in deepening and broadening capital markets needed to be reformed and sufficiently regulated to encourage competition, innovation and market discipline. The pension sector is dominated by one unregulated public institution with poor investment standards, imprudent investment policies and staff that lack appropriate skills. Although some companies have initiated private pension schemes, this sector remains insignificant and still lacks the appropriate legal and regulatory framework. Rwanda's insurance sector is small and undeveloped and still lacks effective regulation in spite of the existence of an

Insurance Law and the National Insurance Commission, a regulating body that was established three years ago. The size of the sector made it impossible for the National Insurance Commission to fund its operations from fees levied on the regulated companies making it turn to the Treasury for funding. As a consequence, its effectiveness as a regulator was heavily constrained by its inability to attract, build and retain the required professional skills.

The strategy recommended consolidating the regulatory function of the pension and insurance sector with the banking sector within the Central Bank. The proposal not only mitigates the economies of scale constraints but ensures that the synergy involved in supervising all the sectors is effectively leveraged. Moreover, the Central Bank has more experience and credibility within the market and is in a stronger position to pay competitive salaries to maintain capable staff.

The Rwanda Development Bank has been relatively successful in providing long-term loans to productive sectors, particularly agriculture. However, it faces a major challenge in its ability to raise adequate long-term funds for continued lending. First, the bank is largely exposed to agriculture; in addition, the government of Rwanda holds majority shares in the bank. The FSDP recommended that the government of Rwanda reduce its shareholding to less than 40% by incorporating new equity, provided the same development objectives are maintained. It also recommended that Rwanda Development Bank should develop new long-term debt instruments like Asset Based Bonds and start syndicating with commercial banks where the latter would provide working capital and loan monitoring. By attracting new private equity and consequently reducing government shareholding, the bank would be eligible to raise substantial debt capital from international financial institutions like AfDB, IFC, PTA bank and others.

The Rwandan authorities recognized that an efficient payment system is an essential component of the financial sector infrastructure. The FSDP included recommendations to develop an efficient, secure and technology-based payment system to facilitate other growing economic sectors like trade and tourism. In addition, Rwandan authorities believed that an appropriate payment system infrastructure is an essential tool for enhancing financial access in the most cost effective way. The strategy recommended a roadmap and mechanism for establishing and implementing a National Payments Strategy that would include an Automatic Clearing House and a Real Time Gross Settlement Systems.

13.3.1 Our approach to the process of designing the program

The following six elements of our approach contributed significantly to the realization of the process, particularly to the "buy-in" of key stakeholders.

1. Setting the stage for the financial sector reform process
2. Assigning responsibilities clearly

3. Ensuring widespread ownership and participation
4. Basing a comprehensive set of reforms and action plans on an integrated strategy
5. Seeking high-level endorsement of the entire strategy
6. Effective implementation

13.3.2   Setting the stage for the financial sector reform process

Probably the most important element that contributed to this reform process was having a very clear overriding national objective which was, and still is, shared by virtually all high-level government officials and the vast majority of financial sector stakeholders from the private sector.

This overriding objective, as articulated in the "Rwanda Vision 2020" statement, is to transform Rwanda into a middle-income country as well as an economic trade and communications hub by the year 2020. This common vision underpinned the positioning of the FSDP as one of the key priorities for the country's medium term Economic Development and Poverty Reduction Strategy, EDPRS.

In addition, the diagnosis by the joint World Bank/IMF FSAP mission of 2005 provided a comprehensive and independent evaluation of the sector and recommended areas for reform.

13.3.3   Assigning responsibilities clearly

The Government designated the National Bank of Rwanda to lead the process since the central bank was deemed to have a deeper understanding of financial sector issues, is more technical in orientation, less bureaucratic and with better skilled staff. With the support of FIRST Initiative, the central bank recruited a team of independent expatriate technical experts whose responsibility was to assist in designing a financial sector reform program that would effectively assist Rwanda in achieving its 2020 objective.

A team was selected whose leader had broad experience in most financial sector arenas of developing countries. The team also comprised of individual experts in each of the four identified priority areas that is, banking and access to credit, capital markets, pensions and insurance, and payments systems. The team was able to adhere to the original schedule which was to design a financial sector reform program by November 2006. It was strengthened by periodic assistance from two staff members from the World Bank and IMF who were already working on Rwanda's financial sector and had participated in the FSAP study. Their knowledge of financial sector issues and the Rwanda financial sector in particular was an invaluable input to the process.

13.3.4   Ensuring widespread ownership and participation

In retrospect, the approach followed for ensuring widespread ownership and participation in the financial sector reform process was the second most important contributing element. The Steering Committee, which I chaired, was representative of all major stakeholders in key financial reform arenas and, inter alia, included the Secretary General of the Ministry of Finance, the Economic Advisor to the President, and CEOs from financial and non-financial private sector institutions. The eight member Steering Committee consulted widely with the sector players and reviewed the consultants' reports on a regular basis.All members shared the overriding objective and they reacted according to the dual concern of ensuring the proposed reforms would achieve the overriding objective as well as considering how the proposed reforms would affect their own institutions.

The Steering Committee was supported by four subcommittees, whose responsibilities were to interact and guide the experts in their respective areas. The subcommittees were composed of mid-level officials from most of the important institutions in each arena. All proposed reforms and actions were debated in subcommittee meetings which were chaired by one of the Steering Committee members, and attended by at least one of the consultants. The subcommittees created a two-way communication mechanism: First, they provided the consultants with deeper insights and understanding of the various issues and how proposed reforms would affect the stakeholder institutions.

Second, they informed key stakeholder institutions as to what reforms were being considered and ensuring an early "buy-in" of the reforms by higher executives.

The participation of mid-level managers removed any misconception that the reforms were externally imposed to the implementing institutions. This increased "buy-in" by all levels of staff.

After the overall design was in place, the program was presented and debated in a one-day workshop consisting of about 150 key stakeholders, most of them from the private sector. It was interesting to note that during that question and answer session several members of the national steering committee made references to "our strategy" rather than to "the consultants' proposed strategy".

Presumably, this "buy-in" was a result of their participation throughout the design stage. This is particularly important because it signified a commitment to implement the actions proposed in the FSDP specific to their organizations.

13.3.5 Basing a comprehensive set of reforms and action program on a broad integrated strategy

Rwanda needed a comprehensive and integrated financial sector strategy, designed to further its stated objective, not a shopping list of specific reforms in specified financial sector sub-arenas.

Many elements in the program are interlinked and interdependent; as a result, the attention and dialogue was focused on the "forest" (i.e. the overall program and its impact,) than on the "trees", that is, the individual actions needed to implement the policy reform.

This has helped to create a stronger and more unified constituency in support of the overall financial sector reform package and its objectives, than if its focus had been on the individual elements.

A number of the individual policies within the reform program could have attracted formidable opposition but, for the most part, did not, for example, some of the sensitive issues included:

(i) Transforming the huge Union de Banque Populaire du Rwanda (UBPR) bank network into a de facto commercial bank;
(ii) Increasing private ownership in a development bank;
(iii) Consolidating supervision of the insurance and pension sector into the NBR.

Any potential opposition to these reforms was dissipated by the key stakeholders who shared a common view that the financial sector reform program would further their overall objective.

13.3.6   Seeking high-level endorsement of the entire strategy

The Governor and I provided several briefings on the key issues and recommended reforms to the President of the Republic during our periodic economic briefing sessions with him. As a result, he became fairly familiar with the key reform recommendations and the reasons for them, well before they were formally presented.

The Minister of Finance, who was represented on the National Steering Committee by his Secretary General, was on board from the onset. The Steering Committee presented all elements of the program for a Cabinet approval since it had policy implications.

This Cabinet approval and its endorsement of the entire program, together with the participative process and broad agreement among the key stakeholders on the reform agenda, created a powerful mandate and launching pad for implementing the FSDP.

13.3.7   Effective implementation

Once all the stakeholders were in agreement on the "what," the next huddle was on "how". No reform program can be truly successful if its implementation is not accomplished in an efficient, timely and high quality manner. Most of the actions in the program required skilled personnel, capable institutions and substantial funding to ensure successful implementation. It was therefore important to get our development partners on board from the onset.

To maintain the momentum for implementation, the mandate of the National Steering Committee was extended to include implementation oversight. A project management unit was set up within the Ministry of Finance to coordinate the process, monitor compliance by each of the 13 implementing institutions with the agreed milestones, and periodically report to the Steering Committee. Each of the 13 institutions assigned an individual with clear responsibility to act as a focal point for coordination with the project management unit. In addition, one of the consultants who participated in our financial sector reform strategy was to stay involved as an advisor on a regular basis over the next two years. This would provide quality assurance of the implementation process and give technical support to the project management unit.

Adopting FSDP in its entirety in the Growth flagship of the 5-year Economic Development and Poverty Reduction Strategy signaled government commitment to its implementation.

Under the auspices of the World Bank Resident Representative in Kigali, a mini donors' round table was held where the funding needs of the FSDP was presented. Development partners committed to offer both technical assistance and financial support to the program.

13.3.8 Progress so far

We immediately embarked on the components where external technical or financial assistance could be mobilized. These components included:

- Preparation of the legal and regulatory framework, as well as creating the new institutions that will be needed to implement many of the actions.
- The Central Bank Act was immediately amended to extend its mandate to include supervision of Nonbank Financial Institutions. Consequently, a new Insurance Law has been submitted to Parliament and new supervisory instructions are being prepared by the BNR.
- Minimum capital of banks was raised from $3million to $10million and all the 7 commercial banks were in compliance by the December 31, 2007, deadline except one whose negotiations with an external investor was completed by February 15, 2008.
- UBPR has been transformed and issued a full commercial bank license.
- The Capital Market Advisory Council was put in place to prepare the legal, regulatory and institutional framework for a Securities Over-The-Counter Market that will eventually trade in shares. At the same time, harmonization of rules and regulation is being done in preparation for an East African integrated regional stock market.
- A FinScope survey to get baseline data on financial access, particularly on the demand side was launched.
- A microfinance policy and strategy was launched as a sector-wide framework to provide government, MFI's, development partners, the private sector and civil society with the appropriate tools and roadmap for realization of the Government's vision of extending financial services to the rural poor.

- SIMTEL, an interbank company managing a card system has been revamped with entry into its shareholding of a strategic partner to drive the business.

13.4 Conclusion

There are a number of reasons to believe the FSDP will achieve its intended objective and change the Rwandan financial landscape:

- First, the program was designed within the broader framework of Rwanda's socio-economic reform agenda following an in-depth analysis of the sector by the joint World Bank/IMF FSAP mission.
- Second, it is more comprehensive and forward-looking as opposed to earlier piecemeal reforms.
- Third, the participative nature of the design process ensured an overwhelming "buy-in" by all stakeholders as shown by the implementation progress, as well as support from development partners who are providing the necessary funds.
- Fourth, there is political will on the part of the Rwandan government to do what it takes to implement it successfully.

While there has been some remarkable progress in implementation, much remains undone and FSDP is "living document" that will be progressively evaluated and continually adopted to the changing environment.

Note

Deputy Governor, National Bank of Rwanda.

Index

.